LETTERS *to* Christian *about* GOD

The sovereignty of God in the Salvation of your soul

DOUGLAS A. WEIGENT

WestBow Press books may be ordered through booksellers or by contacting:

WestBow Press
A Division of Thomas Nelson & Zondervan
1663 Liberty Drive
Bloomington, IN 47403
www.westbowpress.com
844-714-3454

ISBN: 979-8-3850-2337-0 (sc)
ISBN: 979-8-3850-2338-7 (e)

Library of Congress Control Number: 2024907877

Print information available on the last page.

WestBow Press rev. date: 4/25/2024

Contents

Acknowledgements

I acknowledge the help of previous Christian authors, whose writings on occasion have provided hints and guided my thoughts. They confirm my spiritual journey. Helpful authors included Thomas Brooks, Watchman Nee, Stephen Charnock, Arthur Pink, and Charles Spurgeon. The most helpful to me has been The Whole Bible Commentary by Matthew Henry. Some books have been consulted and these are listed in the back as selected references for additional reading. Most scripture citations in this book are from The New American Standard Bible (The Open Bible, 1977). A few citations are from the King James version of the Bible. I have written from my memory and previous lessons taught in Sunday School and in the Jails. I share my understanding and experience in the Lord over the past 63 years. I acknowledge the generous support of my wife Diane, my daughter Rachel, and my grandson Christian. I gratefully acknowledge many friends, that over the years have been important pieces of my life. I gratefully acknowledge my wife for editorial assistance, and the publisher for help in the preparation of this book. The most important acknowledgement I have is for the lovingkindness of God. I believe I have been led and blessed by the Lord. To God be all the glory. Amen.

Introduction

Dear Reader,

When I retired from work, I had no specific or detailed plan about how I was going to spend most of my time. But God did. By the grace of God, I started to write some letters to my only grandson, named Christian. I wanted to do something for him which I thought would help him understand the most important thing in life. I wanted him to know and have an abundant life in Jesus. I was encouraged by his mother. The original idea of writing a couple of letters ballooned into four books with fifty-five total letters over the past ten years. As it turned out, once I started writing letters to Christian, I could not stop. Inside a deeper study of the Bible and being with the Lord Jesus, I found more life and a conviction of things not seen. I found the assurance of things hoped for and a superb relationship with Jesus by faith. "Faith comes from hearing, and hearing the word of Christ" (Rom. 10:17). I experienced the power in the grace of faith from God by reading and writing about what was in the Bible. How in the world could I walk away from such a great blessing. "It is the Spirit who gives life" (John 6:63). God has magnified His word according to all His name (Ps.138:2). God sent me deeper into His word, knowing I would grow in faith (Heb. 11:1), and have the greatest blessing of more of His life in me. Spending more time with the Lord, Christian, will not leave you the same. You will learn the truth, and the love and goodness of God; this knowledge of truth about God, by the grace of God, will begin to set you free (John 8:32). You will grow to love the Lord. You will know a peace released into your soul from the victory over your sin. You will know the power of God's truth that results in holiness, and your obedience by faith in Jesus (Rom. 1:5). You will grow in spiritual maturity and be glad that the joy of the Lord is indeed your strength (Neh.8:10). He fulfills the promise to love you and disclose more of Himself to you (John 14:21). Jesus Christ, and the sanctifying work of the Spirit of God become a glorious reality. I wanted this experience for my grandson, as much as I know I needed it for myself. I pray that God will be merciful to you Christian, give you tokens of His love every day, and manifest with joy to your heart the kingdom of God and all His glory to come.

In the World, we begin our life by what the Bible describes as a natural man. This means we live under the direction of our own ideas and passions. We are destitute of the Spirit of God. Although man has some intellectual ability in gaining knowledge, he is unwilling and unable, on his own, to enter the mind of God (1 Cor. 2:14). Even though a man may have some spiritual leanings, he is still considered to be spiritually dead by God. God's way to be made spiritually alive is to have Jesus in your heart. Some folks are strongly set in their minds against Jesus, and never wake up to a spiritual life with Him. While other folks wake up to the fact that Jesus is the truth, the way to righteousness with God, spiritual life, and life after death. The Bible clearly states that no one can come to Jesus, unless the Father draws him (John 6:44, 65). Sometime in our lives, we must be drawn by the Father, born of the Spirit (John 3:6), and filled with the Spirit (Eph. 5:18) to understand the Bible is a gift from God. The spiritual teachings in the Bible tell us that "All have sinned and fall short of the glory of God" (Rom. 3:23). "The wages of sin is death, but the free gift of God is eternal life in Christ Jesus our Lord" (John 6:23). Spiritually dead men are in sin and cannot wake themselves up, they need supernatural help. They cannot know God, understand they are sinners, or be forgiven of sin and saved by the blood of Jesus Christ as their Savior. The hurdle is too high, or the pill too big to swallow, and because of their pride, they do not believe and trust what the Bible says about Jesus. God's way to be saved is by His mercy and love and grace in action, apart from your works (Eph. 2:8). God's plan is for people to be born again from above, and live with the Holy Spirit on earth to learn the profound nature of a spiritual relationship with Himself. Jesus said, "Unless you eat the flesh of the Son of Man and drink His blood, you have no life in yourself" (John 6:53). Eating the flesh and drinking the blood of Jesus, spiritually speaking, means believing in Christ. True spiritual life is produced by the Spirit working in and through the believer (Gal. 5:22-25). The extent of spiritual life in a believer is determined by one's willingness to be led by the Holy Spirit, and most importantly, by the pleasure and grace of God (1 Cor. 15:10). The gifts of the Holy Spirit may vary and be different in degree for each person. We all need to receive Jesus to know God. Amen.

The Bible tells us that, "God spoke long ago to the fathers in the prophets in many portions and many ways, in these last days has spoken to us in His Son" (Heb. 1:1-2). The Old Testament prophets were inspired by God to communicate God's will and disclose the future to the people (Deut. 18:18). God spoke by types and symbols, promises, warnings and predictions. God's truth was presented to the people over time and in a progressive fashion, to prepare them for the coming of His Son. In the New Testament, John the Baptist was a voice crying out for Jesus in the wilderness (John 1:23). Jesus Christ is the final word of God. Hear ye Him (Matt. 17:5). God created the world (Rom. 1:20) and He created us (Ps.139:14). God made the choice to reveal "the riches of His glory upon vessels of mercy" (Rom. 9:23). He chose us before the foundation of the world and predestined us to adoption as sons (Eph.1:4-5). He always knew everything about us, and "while we were yet sinners, Christ died for us" (Rom. 5:8). "God is greater than our heart, and knows all things" (1 John 3:20).

How do we get to know Him? Some people think that this is impossible because they believe we arrived into life by chance, and there is no God to know. Some people think that human beings do not have the ability to know God, and we learn our eternal fate after we die. Some people believe they know God from their religious life and it is different than Christianity. Some people might act like they do not care or think about God, or have the time to figure out the answer to the question of how to know God. The truth is, God is all powerful and reveals what He wants us to know about Himself by His grace. In this life, most Christians learn about God progressively as they grow in grace and knowledge. The Bible tells us that God opens our hearts (Acts 16:14) and our understanding (Luke 24:45). God draws us by His own love and power and grace to be born again (John 3:1-8, 6:44, 65). The Bible tells us, "That the path of the righteous is like the light of dawn, that shines brighter until the full day" (Prov. 4:18). The thought that Jesus Christ is the Son of the living God has not been revealed to you by your flesh and blood, but by the Father in heaven (Matt.16:17). You are a child of God, "Born not of blood, nor of the will of the flesh, nor of the will of man, but of God" (John 1:13). You are born again not by your parents, your will or the will of friends or pastors, but by God's choice (Eph. 1:4). It is not of your works, which removes your pride from the equation. It is a gift from God alone which humbles your soul (Eph. 2:8). Without God, you would never wake up to spiritual life, be forgiven of sin and saved for eternity. Many people murmur against the Divine operation of God, not understanding the nature and grace of God. They think they do not need help to be saved. They think they are not bad enough to go to Hades after they die. The consequences of eternity are not fully considered and the plan of God and the Bible are set aside. For the true Christian, God puts forth His grace and loving power, strongly obliging the elect soul that He has seized upon, to respond sincerely to the call to receive Jesus into their heart. We are convicted through our circumstances that we have offended God and are lost. Our self-righteousness is not enough. The will and the call of God is effectual, and His word does not return to Him void (Isa. 55:11). He especially sends us into the word of God (1 Pet.1:23) and good Bible commentaries. He allows relationships with family and friends that have a testimony for Jesus, to encourage us in the faith. We are being taught by God, and in His righteousness, we shall be established (Isa. 54:13-14). The kingdom of God, through the Gospel and glory of Christ, is setting up peace, love, and holiness in your soul for eternal life. Amen.

The book you are holding is the fourth book I have written since I retired. The first book, entitled "Letters to Christian," was about the grace of God in the battle for the future of your soul. It described how to equip and protect your soul against temptation and sin with His armor of truth. The second book, entitled "More Letters to Christian," described the gifts that God provides for our souls to establish us in Jesus, help us grow in grace and delight in our Christian experience. We are His workmanship (Eph. 2:10). The third book, entitled "Last letters to Christian," described our being transformed into the image of Jesus in our new creation. The discussion of God's attributes in these letters, allows the comparison to be made between the transfiguration of our hearts and the reflection of God's image. God provides the spiritual fountain we drink from to be like Christ. In the present book, I have chosen to focus primarily on the power, nature, and ways of God alone. God has given us a mind that is able to learn some great truths about Himself through His word (Ps. 138:2). Man's ability is clearly limited to know everything about God. By the grace of God, we can learn the Gospel plan, be forgiven of sin and saved by Jesus Christ. We can learn the truth that sets us free (John 8:32). We can learn to worship God in spirit and in truth (John 4:24). We can know Jesus and the power of His resurrection (Phil. 3:10). The study of God will change your life. The study of God on earth and knowing Jesus has eternal consequences (John 17:3). Jesus is the only way to the Father (John 14:6). Times are coming when your soul will be very troubled about the sin that lurks there, and you will pour your soul out to God for help. God is holy and sin must be pardoned. God's grace has already acted for man with good news in the Gospel of Jesus Christ. We must be born again (John 3:5). God's plans are not for calamity, but for a future and a hope. The promise is, that if you will seek Him with all your heart, you will find Him (Jer. 29:11-13). Amen.

The approach I have taken for this book is to first include letters on the fear, dominion, foreknowledge, and the glory of God. Many men do not truthfully, or seriously consider the awesome nature and the power of God. They will not be sitting around a table after they die, having a discussion with God about their eternal resting place. The righteousness of God will be on display, and God's perfect decisions made known to them. God's grace was always His own to give. God will finally get everyone's full attention. Next, I have included letters on the personality of God, the blood of Jesus, and the choices He makes according to His good pleasure. God reveals He is love and good, holy, and faithful, and a great Savior. Our salvation is personal with God. The blood of His only begotten Son was shed to secure our holiness, freedom, and eternal life. I follow this with letters on the plan of salvation, our being born of God, and the responsibility of man in salvation. Inside the sovereignty of God for our salvation, it is our responsibility to discover a fear and trembling before Him (Phil. 2:12). Finally, I have included letters on the Bible, the gift of faith from God, and the Old Testament types of our Savior. The Bible is a book of prophecy in which faith comes by reading it (Rom. 10:17). God has revealed a great deal about Himself and His Son in the gift of the Bible, especially the work He has done to bring forth our salvation. Though each letter is different, they can stand by themselves. The way to discover that God is alive and good, is to seek Him. "Seek first His kingdom and His righteousness; and all these things shall be added unto you" (Matt. 6:33). "Ask, and it shall be given to you; seek, and you shall find; knock, and it shall be opened to you" (Luke 11:9). "You will seek Me and find Me, when you search for Me with all your heart" (Jer. 20:13). In God's time and way, He brings us to places in our lives where we experience and better understand who He is. The work of His grace in our soul is the greatest evidence of His presence and blessing. I thank the Lord for giving me a heart to read His Word. To God be the glory. "Let the words of my mouth and the meditation of my heart be acceptable in Thy sight, O Lord, my rock and my Redeemer" (Ps. 19:14). Amen.

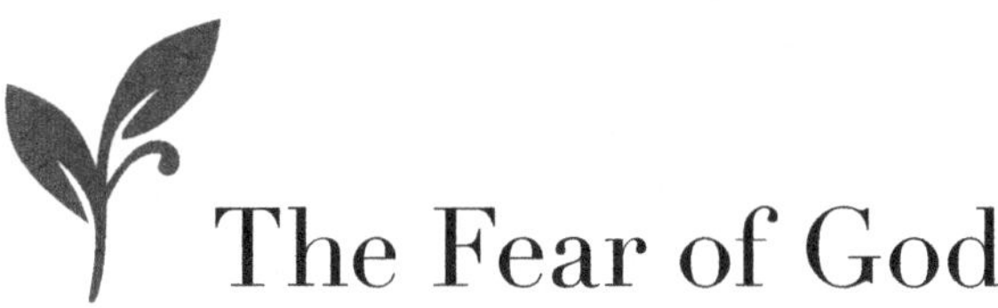

The Fear of God

"The fear of the Lord is the beginning of wisdom, and the knowledge of the Holy One is understanding" (Prov. 9:10).

Dear Christian,

"The Lord has established His throne in the heavens, and His sovereignty rules over all" (Ps. 103:19). His throne is forever fixed and immovable. The glorious sovereignty exercised from this throne is the pillar upon which our eternal security and safety rest. Our future, dear Christian, is in His hands. Our confidence in Him stems from the grace that will forever flow to us from His merciful heart. The Bible tells us that God created an "expanse in the midst of the waters" that He called heaven (Gen. 1:6-8). "By the word of the Lord the heavens were made and by the breath of His mouth all their host" (Ps. 33:6). It is God who is enthroned above the circle of the earth, and its inhabitants are like grasshoppers (Isa. 40:22). God is seated upon a throne and upholds and governs His creation. He reduces rulers to nothing, blows on them and they wither and the storm carries them away like stubble (Isa. 40:22). Man was made erect to look up and contemplate the heavens. When we look up, we are met with God's handiwork.

A clear view of God's glorious creation and supreme providence is one of the most comforting and delightful of spiritual gifts. It is an amazing wonder that the character of God, and His ways, in part, can become known. It is a great act of grace and love, beyond our understanding, that the Lord would reveal Himself to anyone and especially ourselves. The Lord's way of covenant grace with us and our experience of His mercy makes us sensible of our sin and aware of the deep precious nature of His pardon. By the grace of God, we learn to cry out "Bless the Lord, O my soul; and all that is within me, bless His holy name" (Ps. 103:1). God is love (1 John 4:8), God is good (Ps. 100:5) and God is holy (Ps. 99:5). God forgives our iniquities, heals all our diseases, and redeems us from destruction (Ps. 103:3-4). Forgiveness is a choice gift of mercy from God, and an early and great spiritual experience of grace in our soul. God removes guilt for any, and all sins, and is available to hear and help the Christian his whole life. Forgiveness as a gift of God, has immeasurable value to us, and will be experienced as our most important healing throughout eternity. The power of sin is weakened and God's grace is present to sanctify our soul for the remainder of our earthly lives. A peace arises in our soul that passes our understanding; it is greater than the guilt, sorrow and regret that arose because of our sin. A pardon for sin means a great deal. Our lives have been redeemed and saved from destruction and filled with better things. We come to know that "The Lord is compassionate and gracious, slow to anger and abounding in lovingkindness" (Ps. 103:8). His mercy pardons our sin and His grace bestows favor. The soul moves into a satisfying place it did not even know existed before it had the forgiveness of sin. As a new-born child of God, we will sing and praise the Lord for His goodness.

When we begin to know the Lord, He sets us on a journey to want to hear and know more about Him, and see Him in His glory. In the desire to know more of the Lord, He turns you into studying the Bible for more knowledge, truth, and faith (Rom. 10:17). The Bible tells us that, "There is forgiveness with Thee, that Thou mayest be feared" (Ps. 130:4). A free, full, and sovereign pardon is in the merciful nature of a great King. The fruitful root of a loving pardon of sin produces more gratitude, an awesome fear, and reverence, rather than the dread inspired by punishment. We become more fearful to offend God. We fear God for His justice and we fear God for His mercy. The purpose of God's forgiveness is to lead us to fear Him. We are not careless, but amazed. The main thing that made the prodigal son return home was that he remembered he had a loving father (Luke 15:17-22). The ransom which God found for us was Jesus Christ. The ransom encourages faith, prayer, and obedience as opposed to terror and despair. The desire and nature of God to forgive us our sins, is clear to us, by the gift of His only begotten Son to make it possible (John 3:16). This awesome act of mercy deserves our utmost reverence, fear, worship, and service. Amen.

From the Bible, we learn the Lord's ways of covenant grace and everlasting mercy for us in Jesus (Eph. 1:4-6). We learn to fear and worship God because of His sovereignty and loving providence in our lives. We are His workmanship (Eph. 2:10). From the Bible, we learn that "It is God who is at work in us, both to will and to work for His good pleasure" (Phil. 2:13). By the grace of God and the work of the Holy Spirit, we develop a holy awe and reverence of God's pardoning mercy in Jesus. We come trembling in fear to the Lord, and to His goodness (Hos. 3:5). We hope that God will be gracious to us, because He accomplishes all things for us (Ps. 57:2). He accomplishes what concerns us, and we pray that He will not forsake the work of His hands for us (Ps. 138:8). We pray that His will be done in our lives, because His love for us far outshines whatever we could do for ourselves. "He who began a good work in you will perfect it until the day of Christ Jesus" (Phil. 1:6). The beginning of God's grace for you, Christian, is the earnest of the completion. "Thine eyes have seen my unformed substance; and in Thy book they were all written down the days that were ordained for me, when as yet there was not one of them" (Ps. 139:16). "How precious also are Thy thoughts to me, O God" (Ps. 139:17). The Lord knows those individuals that belong to Jesus Christ. The bride of Christ are all believers being fashioned for the wedding day (Rev. 19:7). Being born the first time is a mystery, as well as being born again (John 3:8). The second time reveals the love of God and His saving mercy in Jesus. God has infinite knowledge of us and is fully aware of all our infirmities. "God has not dealt with us according to our sins, nor rewarded us according to our iniquities. For as high as the heavens are above the earth, so great is His lovingkindness toward those who fear Him" (Ps. 103:10-11). "The Lord has compassion on those who fear Him, He is mindful that we are but dust" (Ps. 103:13-14). God draws us up into His heart and showers us with fruits of the victory of Christ, including a heart that fears the Lord. We learn that our defects lie too deep in our nature to overcome without the love of God. Because of God's forgiveness and goodness, we do not live with a slavish fear, but with a reverence of God's majesty. We may first have a fear of torment about God, but the love of true religion casts out any torment. In eternity, it is a fear that will be revealed as evidence for our true salvation, and wrapped up into a glorious spectacle of God's future glory. In the fear of God, there is a humble, hearty reverence of God's authority, that for us is the beginning of wisdom. Amen. A Christian will tremble at this acceptance with God. The lost person will presume upon the infinite mercy of God, without knowing the true fear for a righteous God.

"The grass withers and the flower fades, but the word of our God stands forever" (Isa. 40:8). "Heaven and earth will pass away, but My words will not pass away" (Matt. 24:35). "The world is passing away, and also its lusts; but the one who does the will of God abides forever" (1 John 2:17). The history of man, who is short-lived, and his hopes, goals and vanities will disappear but the word of God will stand forever. The word of His purpose, promises and the gospel will stand forever. Your inner spiritual life with Jesus will stand forever. You have been drawn and quickened by an incorruptible seed (1 Pet. 1:23). Inside of you, Christian, flow rivers of living water (John 7:38) that will never disappear or die (John 11:25-26). God will never cease to love you, and according to His purpose, will warmly receive you into glory. "The lovingkindness of the Lord is from everlasting to everlasting on those who fear Him" (Ps. 103:17). Eternal election requires God's light to see it and God's love to believe and accept it. The gaze of His love upon us originates in His choice and grace, and will always stand because of His righteousness. Amen. The incorruptible seed, flowing with living water keeps the gaze of our filial fear on God's truth, love, and immutable promises. "Do you not know that your body is a temple of the Holy Spirit who is in you, whom you have from God, and that you are not your own? For you have been bought with a price, therefore glorify God in your body" (1 Cor. 6:19-20). Our sins are gone, the penalty was paid, Jesus has borne them away. God as a father continues to correct us in this life, and takes the erring child into His glory. The truly saved, though imperfect, will be careful and thoughtful and with reverent fear to observe and know the will of the Lord. The truly saved will regard the ways of the Lord. The truly saved will keep the covenant of faith by only looking to Jesus for the forgiveness of their sin. The truly saved will live with an earnest obedience by the grace of God, remembering to do the Lord's commandments (Ps. 103:18). We are dependent on God for salvation by His grace, and it is wise and best to follow His direction in seeking to be saved. Do not presume upon the mercy of God and choose to stay in your sin. We are called to be holy (Lev.20:7, 1 Thess. 4:3). Also, do not fear or be discouraged by your past sins, God will be glorified in your salvation.

"The mercy of the Lord is from everlasting to everlasting upon them that fear Him" (Ps. 103:17). The mercy and grace of God is a great mystery. The Bible tells us we were chosen by God to become partakers of His grace and mercy before the foundations of the world (Eph. 1:3-6, 2:10; 2 Tim. 1:9). During our time on earth, we are promised eternal life after receiving Jesus into our hearts (John 3:16; Eph. 2:8-9; 1 John 5:11-13). God does not change, Christian, He has mercy without a beginning and without an end; that is, from everlasting to everlasting. By the grace of God, the Christian wakes up and understands that there is mercy with the Lord, our God and Father. He wakes up to the richest comfort imaginable, that is, eternal life. He wakes up to know and trust Jesus. He was born spiritually dead. He is but dust, frail and short-lived. He is a great sinner and helpless to save himself, and an enemy of God (Rom. 5:6-10). In this lost state, God draws a man by the Spirit and performs an impossible feat in his heart attracting him to

Jesus. By the grace of God, we develop a searching, trusting, and believing heart with an interest in Jesus. By the grace of God, we are humbled and recognize we are in trouble about holiness and need help. When man first fell in the Garden of Eden, Christian, every part of his being was affected. That is, his understanding was darkened and his will was enslaved to sin. Man, at this point, had no power to accept Christ and was considered totally depraved. Man was alone and lost and needed help, and our God stepped in with grace to save us. The Bible says that "No one can come to Me, unless the Father who sent Me draws him" (John 6:44). The word used for "drawing" signifies some strength was used to oblige the sinner to respond to God's invitation. It means far more force than to just attract. It means to impel the sinner to respond to God's call. The love of God enters the heart with a different kind of power and strength. It brings along with it a sense of awe and reverence, which is the true meaning of the fear of God that saves. Amen. We are becoming sons of God and slaves to His righteousness. It is not the fear of God's wrath and the slavery of bondage to sin. It is a call to freedom and holiness. The power of the Holy Spirit has been engaged to wake us up, overcome our self-righteousness and produce a change in our heart and mind to come to Jesus. God is providing the answer we need through the work of the Holy Spirit to be forgiven and saved. The birth of new life is awesome and outside of our own strength to obtain. The consequences of new life are awe, respect, and worship with reverence for an Almighty God. The truth of forgiveness can be realized in our heart by our new-found understanding of the fear of God. Amen.

In the eternal counsel and sovereign pleasure of God, He chose to overcome the depravity of certain individuals. Does the potter have a right over the clay to make a vessel of honorable use and another for common use? (Rom. 9:21). To demonstrate His wrath and to make His power known, God was willing to endure with much patience vessels of wrath prepared for destruction (Rom. 9:22). "He did so in order that He might make known the riches of His glory upon vessels of mercy, which He prepared beforehand for glory" (Rom. 9:23). God does not prepare vessels of wrath for destruction, but He does prepare vessels of mercy for glory (Eph.1:9). God does not create men to destroy them. All men were prepared beforehand for glory. God could justifiably destroy sinners the first time they sin. We become ripe and fit, or prepare ourselves for destruction when we refuse to come to Christ for salvation. God endured sinners, giving them time to repent. The doctrine of election is difficult for some men to accept. That some, and not all individuals are chosen or drawn effectually to Jesus is not acceptable to some men and they walked away, even in the time of Jesus (John 6:66). Human nature does not like the sovereignty of God in salvation, and misunderstands the responsibility of man. We are born again, "not of blood, nor of the will of the flesh, nor of the will of man, but of God" (John 1:13). Jesus said, "Everyone who has heard and learned from the Father, comes to Me" (John 6:45). God makes an effectual call with power to those He has given an ear to hear and a heart to perceive (Prov. 20:12). The God of all grace gives the ear to hear His voice and the eye to see His beauty. It is our responsibility to acknowledge we are helpless and cry for help. It is our responsibility to keep applying ourselves to Christ and discover what He has put into us. Amen. We learn a lot about the Father through His written word.

God shines the truths of forgiveness and election in a man's heart, and by His grace, also provides the comfort and confidence to believe and accept them. They are difficult to understand sometimes, but God has the right to do what He wants in a man's life. God cannot do anything that would violate His perfectly glorious attributes. God is always good, faithful, and righteous. "Our God is in the heavens; He does whatever He pleases" (Ps. 115:3). God makes us differ from others by His sovereign grace alone (1 Cor. 1:29-31). We work out our salvation in this life by living before Him in fear and trembling (Phil. 2:12). We must be born again (John 3:3). "The wind blows where it wishes and you hear the sound of it, but you do not know where it comes from and where it is going; so is everyone who is born of the Spirit" (John 3:8). The movement of the Spirit is mysterious, like the wind. You cannot see the Spirit, but you can see the results of His work in your life. How do you know that you have been born again? My answer is, I have a new life with new desires and power, new hope, and a new direction. Man's salvation is in the Spirits persuasion and power. The important part of my change came from outside of me, and was fed by the word of God. God is awesome to save us, and worthy to be worshipped. God is awesome to allow us to worship and reverence Him from a forgiven and holy and fearful nature. Amen.

"He will bless those who fear the Lord, the small together with the great" (Ps. 115:13). The blessing of trust in God is common among all sorts of believers that fear the Lord. God blesses the rich and the poor, the strong and the weak, and both sexes and any race. God blesses those who have small or great abilities. God blesses those who are small or great in faith. The fear of the Lord is a great blessing. "The fear of the Lord is the beginning of wisdom, and the knowledge of the Holy One is understanding" (Prov. 9:10). "A good understanding, have all those who do His commandments" (Ps. 111:10). The starting place of wisdom begins with a right relationship with God. The real fear of the Lord is in the sense of awe and reverence that honors God as holy and just, Creator and Savior. Our hearts must be convicted with a new nature that has the fear of God. In the beginning of knowing God, the fear of God may have torments in it, "but perfect love casts out fear" (1 John 4:18). When we belong to Jesus, we do not receive a spirit of fear, but a spirit of adoption (Rom. 8:15). The Spirit Himself bears witness with our spirit that we are children of God (Rom. 8:16). The Spirit of adoption works in us a love, dependence, and delight to God as a Father. The Spirit of God is also a sanctifier and a comforter who speaks peace to our soul in Jesus' name. By the grace of God, we grow out of being "afraid" of God and only seeing His wrath as a natural man. We fall in love with Him as adopted children, and see God as our loving Father. The heart is filled with the true fear of God, and the head is filled with understanding the holy knowledge of God. The more we immerse ourselves in the word of God, the more we discover about ourselves, understand our sanctification, and seek the Lord's will for our lives. Amen.

The Bible tells us that by God's grace and work, "Christ becomes to us wisdom from God, and righteousness and sanctification, and redemption" (1 Cor. 1:30). The scriptures are inspired by God (2 Tim. 3:16) and when we read them, God uses them to grow our faith (Rom. 10:17). The scriptures are the place we learn the glorious attributes of God's power, wisdom, love, mercy and much more (Ps. 138:2). The scriptures are the place we learn that God quickens, sustains, enlightens, and comforts us in the Person of Christ by the Holy Spirit (1 Pet. 1:23). The spiritual understanding and life we receive during the study of the scriptures, Christian, leads us to praise God. Afflictions, tribulation, sickness, and old age in this life shall not suspend the praise of our God. The higher and clearer manifestations of God are learned from God. The awesome nature of God to forgive, pardon and save us from sin, is the basis of our respect, love, and reverence that define the true meaning of the fear of God. The awesome nature of God to forgive all sins, even the most egregious, leaves us with a gratitude worthy of fear and worship. God reveals the truth to our soul and gives us faith to anchor our soul on His promises in Jesus. You know God's power can save you, and you will tremble at His word (Isa. 66:2). You will know an awe of God's majesty, purity, and a dread of His justice. Your heart has become a living temple for God (1 Cor. 6:19) and by His own grace, He abides there.

The fear of God is filial not servile. Servile fear is what a slave has for his master. Servile fear arises from a conviction of judgment and separation from God. Filial fear arises from an and acceptance and love to God. We turn to God because He hates sin and we fear to offend Him. Servile fear is an expectation of eternal condemnation, while filial fear is the certainty of salvation. Filial fear is a work of God's grace in our hearts. The pardoned sinner realizes his adoption into the household of faith and the family of God. The true sense of forgiveness in our hearts, releases an acceptance with the Father and we adore Him. We realize His amazing mercy, and without question, praise the Lord. "The dead do not praise the Lord, nor do any who go down into silence; but as for us, we will bless the Lord from this time forth and forever" (Ps. 115:17-18). The Lord is mindful of you, Christian, and He will bless them that fear the Lord (Ps. 115: 12-13). God's blessings include spiritual blessings. He will bless you with grace, knowledge, wisdom, holiness, and joy fit for His presence. A reconciled Father is adored. God blesses us with a fear that loves, and a love that fears. Amen. This reminds me of the second verse of the song "Amazing Grace" which says, "It was grace that taught my heart to fear, and grace my fears relieved" (John Newton). God is always blessing us with love and grace.

We are living in a time when it is especially important to make Christ and the scripture the foundations for our soul to grow upon. Focus your interest and your work in a way that binds your heart to Jesus. Only God can separate between your doubting and believing in Christ. "For no man can lay a foundation other than the one which was laid, which is Jesus Christ" (1 Cor. 3:11). The Bible tells us that God has laid a tried stone, a corner stone, a precious stone, and a sure foundation that whoever believes in Him shall not be disappointed (Isa. 28:16; 1 Pet. 2:6). You are a chosen race, a royal priesthood, and a people of God's own possession (1 Pet. 2:9). You are a part of the people of God that has received mercy (1 Pet. 2:10). You are God's workmanship (Eph. 2:10) and a part of the house for which Christ is the cornerstone. Therefore, I say to you, "Worship the Lord with fear, and rejoice with trembling" (Ps. 2:11). Be grateful and rejoice in the riches of God's grace, and the gospel that promises the forgiveness of your sin. Let your filial fear mingle with your obedience to the great God of eternity. The more you live in the obedience of faith, the more you will live with an assurance and trust in Christ as your greatest blessing in life.

"Blessed is the man who fears always" (Prov. 28:14). Blest by God is the man who keeps in his mind a holy awe and reverence of God. Blest by God is the man who seeks God's glory and remains mindful of His goodness. Blest by God is the man that keeps a tender conscience, avoids evil, and is afraid of offending God. Blest by God is the man who lives a life of faith and fears presumption and self-sufficiency. Blest by God is the man who knows that "God has granted to him everything pertaining to life and godliness, through the true knowledge of Him who called us by His own glory and excellence" (2 Pet. 1:3). Faith is a gift of God for us, wrought by the Holy Spirit in us, who raised up Jesus from the dead. It is the glory of God's power to convert sinners through fear in Jesus' name. We are "called out of darkness into His marvelous light" (1 Pet. 2:9). It is beyond our abilities to fully understand the extent and depth of God's goodness and love for our souls. It is amazing and awesome that He cared enough to wake us up and provide the necessary grace to become His children by adoption. "He chose us from the beginning for salvation through sanctification by the Spirit and faith in the truth" (2 Thess. 2:13). We give thanks to God, and live in fear. This knowledge and new life, blesses a man with awe and reverence toward God, and according to God, is the beginning of wisdom (Prov. 9:10).

There can be a servile fear of God in the heart of the weak Christian. Be mindful, sin is rebellion and reveals a rejection of God. Any sin is wrong, but presumptuous sins are one of the worst kinds of sin. Presumptuous sins are committed willfully with light and knowledge. A sin committed after deliberation is a presumptuous sin. The light of conscience will have warned you of the danger, but you dared to do it anyway. You were checked in your conscience but you strayed against God and your faith in Jesus. You usually know better, but are spoiled by your desire and passion, even after you thought about the potential consequences. You may develop such a strength in your mind for sin, that you practice the sin as a habit. You might prepare ahead of time, and look forward to sin. You put your life in jeopardy of being ruined. There is a difference between deliberate sin compared to ignorant or weakness for sin. An attitude dictated by probability is in the definition of presumption. When it appears about lust, which is a strong sexual desire, it is called evil concupiscence (Col. 3:5). We are to possess our own vessel in sanctification and honor and not in lustful passion (1 Thess. 4:5). We are "to be wise in what is good and innocent in what is evil (Rom. 16:19). We are to "be shrewd as serpents and innocent as doves" (Matt. 10:16). The lusts of the flesh, which can become strong habits in the mind and hinder our growth in grace, are to be mortified. The love of the world is a mistake and highly provoking to God. By nature, we are children of disobedience, but by the grace of God, we "Put on the new man, which is renewed in knowledge after the image of Him that created us" (Col. 3:10). "For God has not called us for the purpose of impurity, but in sanctification (1 Thess. 4:7). Temptation can be very strong, and everyone at one time has probably sinned in a presumptuous manner. The true Christian will confess his sin and seek the Lord for the mercy. The fear of the Lord by the Christian will bring out confession and hope in the promise of God's faithfulness and righteousness (1 John 1:9). The lost person does not look to Jesus or confess His sins to God, and sadly, will not know the promises of forgiveness and cleansing of his sin. There is no fear of God before the eyes of a hypocrite. We are kept by the grace of God. Lord, have mercy and lead us not into temptation but deliver us from evil (Matt. 6:13). Have no confidence in the strength of your flesh. We have a lot to learn about the world, ourselves, and sin. We have a lot to learn about Jesus, the Holy Spirit, and the Father. Our spiritual maturity as a Christian is a gift from God. Our responsibility is to study the Bible for faith to believe, come humbly before God, and pray that His will be done in our lives.

When we presume something, we are taking it for granted and assuming a reality that does not exist. We call this self-deception. Sin distorts reality. Our corrupt hearts will take us to a place where we will try to serve two masters, ourselves, and God. When we allow this to happen, we have a conflict between the spiritual man, and the natural man (Rom. 7). The spiritual man will look to God and try to live by faith. The natural man will look to his feelings and live with his perceptions and presumptions. Presumption is the thing we wished for and is dangerous. It will be exposed when we stand before the Lord. The doing of things by presumption is shallow thinking. It is a weakness and a way we can keep our sin. Self-deception will be exposed and may result eventually in the Lord declaring "He never knew you" (Matt. 7:21-23). We need God's help to hear the true fear of God standing against presumptuous behaviors. True salvation is growing in grace and knowledge and holiness. We will not be perfect in our lives, but by the grace of God, we will know the difference between God's way through the narrow gate and our way through the wide gate (Matt. 7:13-14). You will know the difference in yourself and others by the fruit you bear (Matt. 7:15-20). Your words and actions, and the way you live is your fruit. God's good fruit in you will be humble and holy and filled with love and charity. The bad fruit will be proud and worldly, careless in living without love and uncharitable. You must build your life upon Jesus, and not your opinions, hopes and desires with presumption mixed in to deceive yourself. We must strive against our desires to sin, and in due time, God's grace will have the victory (Heb. 12:4,14; Matt. 24:13; Luke 13:24; Col. 1:29). We get the testimony of Jesus and blessing in our hearts that God's grace is greater than our sin (Rom. 5:20). "The law of the Lord is perfect restoring the soul, the fear of the Lord is clean, enduring forever" (Ps. 19:7,9). David prayed for God's grace and power to prevent him from presumptuous sins (Ps. 19:13). David was a man after God's heart (Acts 13:22) and a great servant of God who wrote the book of Psalms. He was humble before God and confessed that He needed the Lord to be obedient. Sin may first, rather easily, enter our natural lives out of selfish desires and ignorance. The nature of sin is to hang around, try to grow into a delight and then into a habit with presumption. We are spiritually weak, and sin becomes a bully and a tough taskmaster and a serious hindrance on our way to heaven. Ignorance and presumption explain our servile of fear of God, and are uncertain lights to live your life by. By the grace of God, Christian, a time comes when we wake up, and discover the error of our ways and turn to Jesus. An important step is when God helps us to know the true fear of the Lord.

Sin is defined as missing the mark. Sin is disobedience to God's law and can show up in our conscience as a witness (Rom. 2:15) and an accuser (John 8:9). The testimony in the conscience can also be a source of confidence that you have conducted yourself in a godly manner by the grace of God (2 Cor. 1:12). The Bible tells us, that "All have sinned and fallen short of the glory of God" (Rom. 3:23). It also says that the "wages of sin are death" (Rom. 6:23). Sin, as a transgression of God's law, places us in a state of guilt and fear, with a troubled conscience and liable to God's judgment (Gen. 3:10). The Bible tells us that only the "blood of Christ" can cleanse your conscience from dead works to serve the living God (Heb. 9:14). We need our hearts sprinkled clean from an evil conscience to gain a sincere heart in full assurance of faith (Heb. 10:22). We need forgiveness of sin and deliverance from the domain of darkness and fear, to be transferred to the kingdom of a loving God (Col. 1:13-14). The Bible tells us that God "will be merciful to their iniquities and I will remember their sins no more" (Heb. 8:12). We are pardoned of all sins by the mercy of God. The scriptures tell us that the experiential truth from the gift of forgiveness lies the peace and comfort of being right with God. Forgiveness becomes true to the believer because the conscience is cleared of guilt. We still remember we committed the sin, but we do not bear the guilt with condemnation (Rom. 8:1). If we sin after we are saved, God promises us that if we confess our sins, He will cleanse us of all unrighteousness (1 John 1:9). This is not a license to continue in sin. Penitent confession proves God is faithful to the covenant He has made with us in Jesus. The true penitent fears to sin against God, who provided a sacrifice for him in His only begotten Son (John 3:16). Our forgiveness is on the account of Jesus. We are also cleansed from guilt and fear by God's justice, Christian, and in due time will be delivered from the power of sin. I know that God works this miracle in a Christian's life, because He has worked on it in me. Amen. The greater the mercy with God, the greater the fear of God (Ps. 130:4). The fire of God's love does not invite carelessness. The fire of God's love invites us home like the prodigal son (Luke 15). The fear a Christian may have with God is that he may be carried away from His grace and love and not pleasing Him. We fear we may lose some of God's presence and assurance of faith in Jesus. The promise of God's forgiveness is awesome. It is the proper foundation for faith, repentance, love, obedience, prayer, and the godly fear of the Lord. "The wages of sin are death, but the free gift of God is eternal life in Christ Jesus our Lord" (Rom. 6:23). His love cast out the fear.

The forgiveness of sin and our pardon in Jesus covers all kinds of sin except blasphemy against the Spirit (Matt. 12:31). Some folks categorize types of sin into sins of attitude (ex. Pride), sins of action (ex. Stealing), sins of neglect (ex. Church), and sins of intent (ex. adultery). Some folks describe three grades of sin; secret, presumptuous and unpardonable. Other folks distribute types of sins into ignorant, infirmity and presumption. I think the later one can be more useful because it allows a clearer distinction about what is going on in the soul when we sin. The Bible has three clear examples. The first one I would suggest is about Paul and his persecution of the church as a sin of ignorance. He says "I was formally a blasphemer and a persecutor and a violent aggressor, and yet I was shown mercy, because I acted ignorantly in unbelief" (1 Tim. 1:13). In Paul's case, his understanding was most at fault for the sin. The second one is about Peter and his denial of Jesus as a sin of weakness or infirmity (Matt. 26:69-75). He denied Jesus with his tongue, but not in his heart. He was grieved over it and wept bitterly. His main fault appeared in the affections of fear and anger, which corrupted his judgment. He knew who Jesus was and had been with Him for a while. David's sin is considered a sin of presumption because he resolved to do it from his own will regardless of the outcome. There may have been some weakness in David also, but the murder of Uriah was a planned crime. The sin with Bathsheba was done in the heat of lust and therefore a weakness in the affections. Willful murder of an innocent man in cold blood was clearly a presumptuous sin. The thing "David had done was evil in the sight of the Lord" (2 Sam. 11:27). The sin was committed deliberately with design and against conscience and was rebellion against God.

We are to watch our hearts diligently against all sin (Prov. 4:23). Take heed of sinning willfully against the conviction showing up in your heart. Take heed of sinning willfully against the light and knowledge God has generously and mercifully given you. My life has included a journey about sin and the fear of displeasing God. I have been guilty of the sins of ignorance, weakness, and presumption. In the Christian dispensation, believers who have been found guilty of sin, are made clean by the blood of Jesus. At times it seems I acted in weakness that had presumption and a hope in Jesus all at the same time. I tried hard to be right with God but struggled to have the victory. As it turned out, I needed to know more of the truth from the Bible and have more of God's help from the Holy Spirit, so that He indeed would get all the glory. I have learned the great value and complete necessity of God's grace and patience and mercy for me in the battle against sin. I needed to fear God for the glory of God. God gave me the victory for the sake of Jesus, and He deserves all the glory. Amen. The scripture says, "Sin shall not be master over you, for you are not under law, but under grace" (Rom. 6:14). "The older will serve the younger" (Rom. 9:12). By the grace of God, I have lived long enough to experience the older man, that is sin, serve the younger, that is the new man. We are to perfect holiness in the fear of God (2 Cor. 7:1). Keep looking to the Lord for grace and help to strive against your sin (2 Cor. 5:21).

What is the answer to all the fears and doubts that arise in our souls about eternal life? The answer is that the righteousness of Christ presents us perfectly righteous in the sight of God. Our being right with God is made to us (imputed) in Christ. Christ is made to us wisdom, righteousness, sanctification, and redemption (1 Cor. 1:30). Christ takes away all your unrighteousness and servile fear (Isa. 53:5-7; Col. 2:12-15). The blood of Jesus cleanses you from all your sins (1 John 1:7). When I think about my sin, guilt, and the punishment I deserve, Christian, I fear and tremble, but I also remember how good God really is for us. I recall that the righteousness of God is ours through faith in Christ (Phil. 3:9; Rom. 3:22). It is a gift from God (Eph. 2:8). It is God's plan for the way we can be reconciled back to Himself. It is God's choice and power that puts me in a state of righteousness, where once I was lost. God's way for forgiveness is love, and it takes away servile fear. The love of God is declared in the Bible (John 3:16). God cannot lie (Heb. 16:18), and therefore He cannot be doubted. Amen. God Himself in Christ is our surety. God accepts His own grace as legal justification in His own sight. We were sinners with a curse on us, God's wrath against us, and deserving of eternal death in Hades. We become His blest children with love and peace from God Himself, and chosen for eternal life in heaven. No servile fear can stand before the fear and righteousness of God in Christ imputed to His children. Look to God in all your fears and doubts with the Lord's truth, mercy and justice and receive His victory. Being made the righteousness of God in Jesus (2 Cor. 5:21) is an everlasting righteousness. "He Himself has said, I will never desert you, nor will I ever forsake you, so that we confidently say, the Lord is my helper, I will not be afraid. What shall man do to me?" (Heb. 13:5-6). "If God is for us, who is against us?" (Rom. 8:31). God is our God and we are His people (Jer. 30:22). To be God's people means we are God's inheritance (Eph. 1:11, 14, 18).

Godly fear is satisfying (Prov. 14:27), sanctifying (Ps. 19:9), and the beginning of wisdom (Prov. 1:7). Natural fear is guilt, uncertainty, judgment, poor health, and death. Natural fear is worry and godly fear is peace. "The hand of the Lord is mighty so that you may fear the Lord your God forever" (Josh.4:24). We are to "fear God and give Him glory, because the hour of His judgment has come" (Rev. 14:7). We are to "only fear the Lord and serve Him in truth with all your heart; for consider what great things He has done for you" (1 Sam. 12:24). It is not just because of all the good things He has done for us that we fear the Lord, Christian, it is more about who He is. Our lives are filled with good and difficult times and God is not just a "sugar daddy" to get our good times and gifts from. We were dead and lost, and He woke us up to forgive us of our sin to walk with Jesus in this life and forever. The idea that God would bless us with this decision before we were born is a mighty fearsome thought. God proves He is good and we are grateful. Our will becomes His will and this also is a mighty fearsome thought. "He who has found his life will lose it, and he who has lost his life for My sake shall find it"

(Matt. 10:39). Again, a fearsome thought, that only occurs and is understood in a born again, spiritually alive Christian. "We are fearfully and wonderfully made; wonderful are Thy works, and my soul knows it very well" (Ps. 139:14). Our anatomy and physiology are awesome. God is building up our spiritual lives to make us more perfect as the bride of Christ. We are beneficiaries of God's grace of kindness, to be seen in the glory of Christ for ages to come (Eph. 2:7). It is not so much about what we get, as it will be the great and all-consuming revelation of God's kindness. He will be worthy of worship. Amen.

We have a cloud of witnesses that have gone before us from our own families, church's we have attended, as well as the examples of believers in the Bible (Heb. 11,12). "By faith Noah, being warned by God about things not yet seen, in reverence prepared an ark for the salvation of his household" (Heb. 11:7). Abraham feared God by showing that he did not withhold his only son from God (Gen. 22:12). Reverence for God was shown in the life of Jacob (Gen28: 16-17), Joseph (Gen. 42:18) and David (Ps. 5:7). The Lord tells us that Job was "a blameless and upright man, fearing God and turning away from evil" (Job 1:8). Nehemiah's life reflected the fear of God (Neh. 5:15). In the New Testament, "The church was built up and going on in the fear of the Lord and in the comfort of the Holy Spirit" (Acts 9:31). Paul was fearless (Acts 21:10-14). Peter and John, under threat by the rulers, elders, and scribes, showed confidence and were recognized as having been with Jesus (Acts 4:13). The examples cited above show that God was with His people and the Holy Spirit was in the church. God is love (1 John 4:8), and perfect love casts out fear (1 John 4:8). By the grace of God, God's love nourishes and cherishes a godly fear which becomes a strength in us. Amen.

"The secret of the Lord is for those who fear Him, and He will make them know His covenant" (Ps. 25:14). God makes the answer to a secret available to those who are His possession by grace through faith in Christ. God makes Christ intelligible to our hearts and we enter the Door. "I am the door, if anyone enters through Me, he shall be saved, and he shall go in and out, and find pasture"

(John 10:9). In a mysterious and miraculous way, Christian, we respond to the call of the Lord. We hear the call and are enabled by the Spirit of God to fear the Lord. The Bible can be a difficult book to understand spiritual events in our lives sometimes, because it is from God. We need to grow in grace and learn to trust a loving and faithful God. When we fear the Lord, He gives us directions. The Bible says, "There is none who understands, there is no one who seeks for God" and "There is no fear of God before their eyes" (Rom. 3:11, 18). "The fear of the Lord is the beginning of knowledge; fools despise wisdom and instruction" (Prov. 1:7). The warning for despising wisdom is clear. God has poured out his spirit on them and made his words known to them and called them, but they refused (Prov. 1:23-24). When anguish comes, they will call on me, but they shall not find me (Prov. 1:27-28). "Because they hated knowledge, and did not choose the fear of the Lord" (Prov. 1:29). The fool will not accept the counsel of the Lord, and they shall eat of the fruit of their way (Prov. 1:30-31).

The rewards of wisdom are clear. Trust in the Lord with all your heart, and acknowledge Him and He will make your paths straight (Prov. 3:5-6). "The fear of the Lord leads to life" (Prov. 3: 19-23). The Lord "will fulfill the desire of those who fear Him; He will also hear their cry and save them" (Ps. 145:19). "By the fear of the Lord, one keeps away from evil" (Prov. 16:6). The fear of God is the soul of godliness (John Murray). To make us know the covenant (Ps. 25:14), God helps us to understand it and want to do it. We are made to see the true meaning of the cross of Jesus Christ; the forgiveness of our sin and gain His righteousness for our security. To know the covenant is to have the truth sealed up in your soul by the power and witness of the Holy Spirit. Walking with God is the best way to know the mind of God. Studying the inspired scriptures that He has given to us, will make you attentive to God's wisdom, and incline your heart to understanding His truth and the live in the true fear of the Lord (Prov. 2).

I want you to know and believe for your comfort, dear Christian, that it is only in the imputed righteousness of Christ (Rom. 3:22) that God answers all your fears, doubts, and the objections in your soul. In Jesus, you will find acceptance with God. You will find peace about death and judgment because of the righteousness of Christ. To whomever God gives the pardon of sins, and imputes the righteousness of Christ, is a man that is justified and blessed before God (Rom. 4:6-7; 1 Cor. 1:30). His perfect love has cast out the fear of being afraid of God (1 John 4:18). The righteousness of justification is called; the righteousness of the Law (Rom. 7:18), the righteousness of Christ (1 Cor. 1:30), the righteousness of God (Rom. 3:22), and the righteousness of faith (Phil. 3:9). We will be saved and secure, and His name will be called, "The Lord our righteousness" (Jer. 23:6). In the new covenant of grace, Christian, God accepts our standing as perfectly righteous, in the righteousness of Christ. The assurance of God's love is the substance and triumph over fear in the Christian religion. I want you to live in the power of this glorious truth. Amen.

Humbly pray to God. "Search me, O God, and know my ways; try me and know my anxious thoughts; and see if there be any hurtful way in me, and lead me in the everlasting way" (Ps. 139:23-24). Do not try to hide from God or ignore His teachings because you are afraid of Him or prefer your sin. You cannot hide or ignore God and get away with it safely. This would not be in your best interest. God already knows everything about you, and knows how much you need Jesus. Choose the fear of the Lord, and seek His knowledge, instruction, and wisdom to learn His love and goodness and eternal life. Salvation lies in intimacy and the fear of the Lord in your heart. God will always be God, and to be with Him will be your best present time, and a great and glorious future. God is graciously inclined to you, Christian, by His love, mercy and providence, and this promise is forever. God has been with you before the beginning of you days, and in your present days (Ps. 139:16). Wonderful are all His works in your soul from your new birth (Ps. 139:14). Let whatever comes out of your life be gratitude and honor and glory to God Almighty. Thank you, Lord in Jesus name. Amen.

The Dominion of God

> "Thine O Lord is the greatness and the power and the glory and the victory and the majesty, indeed everything that is in the heavens and the earth; Thine is the dominion, O Lord, and Thou dost exalt Thyself as head over all" (1 Chron. 29:11).

Dear Christian,

The dominion of God is exercised in perfection for His glory and His creatures good (1 Chron. 29:11). God has the perfect wisdom and goodness in the application of His complete authority. He has the power and the will to bring about whatever He has decreed. God has woven the truth of His sovereignty in our soul and placed in our conscience the fact of His authority to rule us as our Creator. God has written His law in a man's heart, and given the conscience as a witness that He will be the perfect judge showing no partiality (Rom. 2:11-16). The true notion of God is inseparable from His complete sovereignty and dominion, justice, power, and lovingkindness. A true understanding of God attracts reverence because He possesses infinitely and perfectly all the wisdom and virtue in His nature. The dominion of God is founded upon the work of His creation (Job 38). "The God who made the world and all things in it is Lord of heaven and earth and gives to all life and breath and all things" (Acts 17: 24-25). God has had the right of dominion in His nature from eternity. He holds everything in His hand and everything is maintained and preserved in His hand. "For from Him and through Him and to Him are all things. To Him be the glory forever. Amen." (Rom. 11:36).

"Let us kneel before the Lord our maker. For He is our God, and we are the people of His pasture, and the sheep of His hand" (Ps. 95: 6-7). The reason for worship is given; He is our God. He has chosen us to be His elect. He belongs to us and we belong to Him. He feeds and protects us, and His hand guides us. We hear His voice (John 10:27). God forbid that our nation would close its ears to the voice of God. All things resolve into the sovereignty of God. The grace we need to thrive and survive physically, mentally, and spiritually is in His hand. Our time is in His hand (Ps, 31:15). Our joys and benefits are in His hand. He is a rewarder of those who seek Him (Heb. 11:6). We belong to God by the nature of our creation. We had nothing to do with what time and where we would show up for life in the world. Our skin color, gender, and physical and mental faculties were designed and given to us by God. We belong to God by the great benefit of redemption. When, where and how we come to Jesus is according to God's gracious plan. "You have been bought with a price: therefore, glorify God in your body" (1 Cor. 6:20). Our redemption by God reveals His dominion over us in a most spectacular fashion with the gift of the Holy Spirit and eternal life. We come under the Lordship of Jesus Christ, and by His love and dominion, reap the privilege of serving in this life for the glory of Jesus to come. It is a glory that extends even to ourselves (Rom. 8:17; 2 Thess. 2:14). God's dominion of grace overrules our natural creation and the guilt of sin when we are born again and receive the gifts of faith and forgiveness. "Behold, God is my salvation, I will trust and not be afraid; for the Lord God is my strength and song, and He has become my salvation. Therefore, you will draw water from the springs of salvation" (Isa. 12:2-3). Salvation is a wonder provided by God. The possession of God is salvation (Isa. 12). The devil traffics in fear while God deals with us in love and faith. The water we draw from salvation in Jesus, is living and refreshing.

He is "Lord of lords and King of kings, and those who are

with Him are the called and chosen and faithful" (Rev. 12:14). God depends on no one or anything for the foundation of His government. He does not become a Lord by our votes, in fact, as natural men, we would not have elected Him. We were drawn to Jesus by the Father (John 6:44, 65). If a vote were held today, we would only vote for Jesus. The government is only upon His shoulder (Isa. 9:6). The government of Jesus Christ depends only upon God's dominion and commission. The Bible tells us God "has put all things in subjection under His feet" (1 Cor. 15:27), that is, the feet of Christ. Jesus said, "All authority has been given to Me in heaven and earth" (Matt. 28:18). As God, all power was originally His; but as Mediator, all power was given to Him. He has power to forgive sins and give eternal life. He has the power over angels and intercession with the Father. All souls are His, and every tongue will confess Him to be Lord (Phil. 2:11). "Worthy art Thou our Lord and our God, to receive glory and honor and power; for Thou didst create all things, and because of Thy will they existed, and were created" (Rev. 4:11). "The Lord has made everything for its own purpose, even the wicked for the day of evil" (Prov. 16:4). He gave the wicked the power to fight against Himself, and employed them as instruments of His wrath. They would not let Him rule over them, so He could not save them.

The Lord our God created us, chose us, called us, and enabled us to be faithful to Jesus. The Lamb of God is Jesus Christ who has supreme power over all things. By the grace of God, we wake up and find ourselves as soldiers in a war. We are marching home in the victory of Jesus. Although all the saints are always with Christ spiritually, the Bible does describe a time when many of the called and chosen and faithful will be with Him when the beast wages war against the Lamb (Rev. 17:14). These may be believers baptized by the Holy Spirit into the church since the Day of Pentecost (Acts 2). This group may also include the believers from the Rapture of the church (1 Thess. 4:13-18). The angels will come with Him (Matt. 16:27). The kings of the earth and the folks influenced by Satan will fight a war against God they cannot win. The followers of the Lamb will be hated. The natural men of the world do not understand being chosen out of the world, and called to be with Jesus. The natural man does not know faith in Jesus. The natural man will not surrender the dominion of the world he believes he owns without God. The call to receive and trust Christ for forgiveness of sin has God's saving dominion and power inside it. That is, the Holy Spirit lives within the believer to provide the power to overcome sin and the tribulations of life in this world. "Whatever is born of God overcomes the world; and this is the victory that has overcome the world---our faith" (1 John 5:4). The Christian has the testimony of the Holy Spirit in his heart, shows love to others and overcomes worldly sins and temptations. A Christian has become a new man (2 Cor. 5:17). A Christian has been saved by grace through faith (Eph, 2:8-10). A Christian knows that nothing is impossible with God (Luke 1:37). A Christian knows that God has dominion. Amen.

God alone is the creator of all things, including life, which is dependent upon His will for existence (Rev. 4:11). He has supreme authority, dominion, and sovereignty, and He alone is worthy. "God in these last days has spoken to us through His Son, whom He appointed heir of all things, through whom He also made the world" (Heb. 1:2). Jesus said, "I am the first and the last, and the living One; and I was dead, and behold, I am alive forevermore, and I have the keys of death and Hades" (Rev. 1:17-18). Death holds the bodies of men, and Hades holds their souls. In His resurrection, Jesus demonstrated dominion over death. He is "Lord both of the dead and the living" (Rom. 14:9). Jesus is the, "First fruits of those who have fallen asleep" (1 Cor. 15:20). The resurrection of Jesus and the promise of eternal life liberates us from the bondage and fear of death (Heb. 2:15). The power of Hades and death was overcome when the resurrection of Jesus freed those souls from the curse (Gen. 3:19). Hades is thought to be an unbridgeable chasm separating the wicked and righteous dead (Luke 16:19-31). The wicked rich man is in torment, while the righteous dead are experiencing joy. The wicked are held in punishment and waiting for judgment. The righteous dead are at home with the Lord (2 Cor. 5:8). The New Testament tells us that, after the resurrection of Jesus, "He ascended on high, and led captive a host of captives, and He gave gifts to men" (Eph. 4:8). Some folks believe that this means that Jesus took the righteous souls to heaven, and when we die today, we go straight to be with Jesus. He conquered and led captive our spiritual enemies of sin, the devil and death that had held us captive. The triumph of Jesus was complete at His ascension when He became Lord of all and took the keys of death and Hades. He gave the gift of the Holy Spirit to men, and equipped the saints for the work of service, to the building up of the body of Christ (Eph. 4:11-12).

"He delivered us from the domain of darkness, and transferred us to the kingdom of His beloved Son, in whom we have redemption, the forgiveness of sins. He is the image of the invisible God, the first-born of all creation" (Col. 1:13-15). "He is before all things, and in Him all things hold together, He is also the head of the body, the church" (Col.1:17-18). The church is a living organism, with Christ as the living head. Each member of the church is made alive with the life of Christ by the work of the Holy Spirit of God. Amen. Creation was absolutely the work of God's sovereignty. What God wills is absolute and managed by the perfections of His nature. God's sovereignty is ruled by His perfections, including infinite wisdom, righteousness, and goodness. There is greatness in God's goodness. God will always have the glory of His dominion. The depths of God's ways are beyond our reach. "Oh, the depth of the riches both of the wisdom and knowledge of God! How unsearchable are His judgments and unfathomable His ways!" (Rom. 11:33). God brings about His own purpose for His own glory. The path of providence may be different every day and seem to take some time, yet there is no unrighteousness with Him. God allows the discovery of His grace, justice, patience, and mercy by us, revealing the vast scope of His love. The gift of knowing more of the truth, dominion and nature of God is truly humbling, and a reason for great joy. God made us rational human beings with a purpose, a future, and a hope. He made us able to call upon Him in prayer and He would listen. He made us able to search for Him with all our heart, with a promise that we would find Him (Jer.

29:11-13). In God's wisdom, while we were yet sinners, He made us able to praise Him instead of destroying us for sin. God sits on a throne of holiness (Ps. 47:8). "The Lord is righteous in all His ways, and kind in all His deeds" (Ps. 145:17). God has chosen to not leave us foolish and sinful because of His infinite wisdom, love, and holiness.

God's sovereignty is managed according to the rule of goodness. Much of the world however, seems to be ruled by the survival of the fittest and dog eat dog mentalities. Do it to others before they do it to you. There is more fear than love. A lot of people rest their hearts on what they think God is like, rather than what He really is by His good nature. If things are bad, they blame God because He must have allowed it. What kind of God is He, if He allows such tragedies to happen to innocent people. He gets blamed for wars. They hear a demand for holiness, and do not want to hear that. What they like to do is a sin. They feel they are being judged unfairly, and the idea of going to Hades when they die, is annoying when they think they are not that bad. All the things they do not like about God leaves them with the idea He is a tough taskmaster. The idea of Jesus being God and that you might need Him for eternal life is questionable, given their belief in evolution which includes no life after death. They do not understand the fear of God and His dominion over their life. The truth is, God's dominion is ruled from a throne of grace (Heb. 4:16). The Lord is generous and has made a way to be saved. The truth is, God's presence is a strength that comes with joy and holiness. A Christian will recognize God's dominion and power over creation, for sure, but it is His true goodness that draws out the most gratitude in worship. A throne of grace for believing sinners is the place God calls us to for forgiveness, encouragement, and cleansing. We come to the throne of grace with godly fear and faith in Jesus as the ground for our confidence. We come humbly with a spirit of adoption in the hands of our Mediator, the Lord Jesus. We come confessing our sins, and we experience the faithfulness and justice of God confirming the covenant of grace in Jesus (1 John 1:9).

The dominion of God's goodness extends into the soul of man.

When we are born again, God gives a new heart and a new spirit, and His own Spirit within us to cause us to walk in His statutes (Ezek. 36:26-27). God is sovereign in His dominion at work in the hearts of His people (Phil. 2:13). The king's heart is like channels of water in the hand of the Lord (Pro. 21:1). The Jews attempted to disgrace Christ by crucifying Him between two thieves, but in doing so, fulfilled the prophecy that He would be numbered among transgressors (Isa. 53:12). On the road to Damascus the Lord turned the heart of Saul from persecuting Christians to following Jesus (Acts 9). Our heart becomes God's throne on the earth, when He fills it with convictions and comforts and calls us into His service. In His goodness, He can wound us and we do not bleed to death. In His goodness, we take up our cross and follow Jesus (Luke 14:27).

The dominion and sovereignty of God is manifested in the choice of some people to be the elect of God from eternity past. God made laws, and all judgment is committed to Him. He has power to reward obedience and punish disobedience. The best of God's children need discipline (Heb. 12:7). Discipline yields the peaceful fruit of righteousness to those who have been trained by it (Heb. 12:11). "There is only one Lawgiver and Judge, the One who is able to save and destroy" (Jam. 4:12). He has the power to save the soul for heaven and ruin it in Hades. He chose to reveal the efficacy of His grace in preparing certain people for glory. The One who has all the dominion, "chose us in Him before the foundation of the world that we should be holy. He predestined us to adoption as sons through Jesus Christ to Himself, according to the kind intention of His will" (Eph. 1:4-5).

Holiness is very important and you will sense this strongly in your soul from God. Pursue sanctification without which you will not see the Lord (Heb. 12:14). Why did God choose some to receive grace through faith and the work of His Spirit, and not others? The Bible says that God, as a sovereign, acted by His own will and pleasure, and not something He saw He liked in some of the people. (Rom. 9:13-15). "So, then it does not depend on the man who wills or the man who runs, but on God who has mercy"

(Rom. 9:16). The natural man has a big problem with the idea of election in the will of God. The merit is in Christ and not the man. The merit is in Christs work and not the man's work. We must be humbled and understand we cannot earn it. It is our responsibility to be diligent and study the word of God to find out the truth, and discover what God is doing inside of us. We were chosen in Him, before we were born and the world was made, to be holy and blameless (Eph. 1:4). God saw nothing good in man that deserved the gift of faith (Eph. 2:8). "He called us according to His own purpose and grace which was granted us in Christ Jesus from all eternity" (2 Tim. 1:9). We believe because we were chosen, and we have faith by the virtue of being God's elect. This is the dominion and absolute sovereignty of God. He could have chosen all. He could have chosen none. "All have sinned and fallen short of the glory of God" (Rom. 3:23). The reasoning behind God's choosing us is inscrutable or not readily comprehensible to us. God chose to have vessels of mercy and vessels of wrath to make known the riches of His glory (Rom. 9:22-23). It is within the dominion of God and we cannot fully understand God. God always had complete dominion, sovereignty, and authority in creation. It is our responsibility to let God be God. We have the responsibility to cast ourselves before Him, with "fear and trembling" (Phil. 2:12). God's pleasure was not to make everyone new again, but "both to will and to work for His good pleasure" (Phil. 2:13). "In the exercise of His will He brought us forth by the word of truth, so that we might be, as it were, the first fruits among His creatures" (James 1:18). Christ Himself "is the image of the invisible God, the first born of all creation" (Col.1:15; Rom. 8:29; Heb. 12:23). Jesus was the first, or prototype of "the dead" to be resurrected. He was also referred to as a first fruit, which means the start of the harvest (1 Cor. 15:20,23).

The sovereignty of God appears in the various influences of God's grace. God has the dominion to distribute His grace by any, every and all options where ever it pleases Him. "The wind blows where it wishes and you hear the sound of it, but do not know where it comes from and where it is going; so is everyone who is born of the Spirit" (John 3:8). Both the wind and the Spirit are sovereign in their operations. The Spirit, when He comes into your life, can convict a man concerning sin, righteousness, and judgment (John 16:8). The Spirit can break down a man's prejudices, subdue His rebellious ways, and get him thinking about life after death. The Holy Spirit can work gently and patiently and with power in a man's soul. The wind and the Spirit can both be invisible and refreshing. We know we are alive and that we have been changed or born again, but how the Spirit operates in our soul is a mystery. God commanded light to shine out of darkness (2 Cor. 4:6). Sometimes, the clearest promises and strongest arguments have no effect on us, but later, by the grace and mercy of God, the truth can appear or be revealed to be rich in virtue, knowledge and wisdom. We desire to know more of the truth, and live inside it, so to help ourselves but especially honor Jesus who made forgiveness a reality. "To own God as a sovereign in a way of dependence, is the way to be owned by Him as subjects in a way of favor" (Stephen Charnock). Sometimes God gives a greater measure of knowledge to some people than others. There are varieties of gifts, ministries, and effects but the same God who works all things in all persons. There can be words of wisdom, knowledge and faith, gifts of healing, miracles, prophecy and distinguishing of spirits and tongues (1 Cor. 12:4-10). "The same Spirit works all these things, distributing to each one individually just as He wills" (1 Cor. 12:11). Some folks are called to a special service in their generation, according to God's pleasure. God's sovereignty is manifest in bestowing more honor and gifts to some than others, independent of how hard they may have worked. The dominion of God is manifested in raising up men to act such as Moses (Ex. 2), or restrain the passions of men like Abimelech (Gen. 20:6) or Nimrod (Gen 10:8-10).

"But now, O Lord, Thou art our Father, we are the clay, and Thou our potter; and all of us are the work of Thy hand" (Isa. 64:8). God has dominion over us. By creation, God formed us into a human being, and shaped us as He pleased. He says, "There is no god besides Me; It is I who put to death and give life. I have wounded and it is I who heal; and there is no one who can deliver you from My hand" (Deut. 32:39). God has sole supremacy and absolute authority. He gives the light of your life, the darkness of death and the purpose of our existence. By the exercise of His authority, "He determined their appointed times, and the boundaries of their habitation" (Acts 17:26). He prescribes the nature of our work. He separated Paul to preach the Gospel (Rom. 1:1), called Moses to free His people from Egypt (Ex. 3:10), and chose Adam to tend the garden of Eden (Gen.2:15) and name the animals (Gen 2:19). The dominion of God is evident in your calling to come to Jesus, and your station and type of work you do to make a living in this world. The wisdom, work, and the events in the providence of God were appointed and fixed for you in an eternal counsel (Eph. 1:4). Job himself proclaimed that God performed what was appointed for him and said, "Many such decrees are with Him" (Job 23:14). "In Him we live and move and exist" (Acts 17:28). The places and the times of our living in the world have been appointed by God. The people that cross our path are in the purpose of God for us and them also. The providence of God was at work in the means and occasion of our conversion to Christ. Amen. Sometimes, a particular word or song, a certain friend or minister, and affliction or special event touches our conscience about God, and we wake up with more determination to follow Jesus. The influence of these things can turn out to be a great blessing by the providence of God. You may not see it at the time, but you will see it later in life. Our times are always in His hands. God will send you into His word to grow in grace and knowledge and faith. Sometimes, we may not know what God is doing, but the light to understand His presence and work will someday shine more brightly in your heart, and the brightest in God's glory.

The dominion of God was manifest in Jesus being our redeemer. The Gospel is a declaration of God's sovereign pleasure concerning His Son Jesus Christ, and a revealing of His riches for us in Him. "God made known to us the mystery of His will, according to His kind intention which He purposed in Him" (Jesus) (Eph.1:9). The whole work of the Messiah, as well as the His death and resurrection, was appointed by God. God required a payment in the form of the shedding of blood for the sin of man. "Jesus gave Himself for our sins, that He might deliver us out of this present evil age, according to the will of our God and Father to whom be the glory forevermore" (Gal. 1:4-5). "I delight to do Thy will, O my God; Thy law is within my heart" (Ps. 40:8). Jesus was the Mediator by Divine will. The dominion of God was clearly seen when He transferred our sins onto Christ. "He made Him who knew no sin to be sin on our behalf, that we might become the righteousness of God in Him" (2 Cor. 5:21). The dominion of God was violated in the disobedience of Adam, but the dominion of God was vindicated by the obedience of Christ. All sin is a contempt of Divine dominion. The victory we have in Christ Jesus becomes ours because of His surrender and willingness to take our penalty onto Himself. Christ satisfied the justice of God in the dominion of God. In this sense, Christ is considered a sinner by imputation. The amazing love of God is revealed, in that we are declared righteous by the imputation of the righteousness of Jesus, who knew no sin, to us. The transfer of the righteousness of Jesus to us is an act of the sovereignty of God in the dominion of God. More than this, we have also been reconciled to God (Rom. 5:10). By the grace of God, we have become a new creature that God has reconciled to Himself (2 Cor. 5:17-18). We have entered God's dominion and been brought near to God by the blood of Christ (Eph. 2:13). When the penalty for sin had been fully paid, God could have just moved on to something else. Instead, He chose to exalt Christ as our Redeemer, and draw us closer to Himself in reconciliation as the bride of Christ. Christ was a gift of God's sovereign will to us, and the redeemed believers are a gift of God's sovereign will to Christ. In the dominion of God, He gave Christ all authority in heaven and earth (Matt. 28:18), gave Him a name above every name (Phil. 2:9), and made Him "Head over all things to the church" (Eph. 1:22). The natural man abhors the sovereignty of God, mostly because of his pride. The natural man wants to earn salvation and get some credit for making a good decision. In God's dominion, Christian, God will get all the glory. The natural man needs a miracle of grace to be born again to believe that Jesus is the Christ, the Son of the living God.

The sovereignty of God is clearly taught in the Bible, and is a great source of comfort. It reveals God's love and goodness for our peace and security about the future. The Bible reveals God has the dominion to chose the vessels of mercy based on His own gift of grace (Rom. 9:23). The pardon for sin is fully secure because it is God's pleasure in God's word. He wipes away the guilt and promises to not remember our sin (Heb. 8:12). The consummation of redemptive history will be in a New Jerusalem with Christ as a husband and the people of God in the church as His bride. "He will tread our iniquities under foot. Yes, Thou, wilt cast all their sins into the depths of the sea" (Micah 7:19). The dominion of God is a comfort in affliction and encouragement for prayer. "You shall be My people and I will be your God" (Jer. 30:22). Upon His sovereign dominion I build my trust, and He is worthy of all my worship. All my stuff belongs to Him and He makes me want to be charitable. I am attentive to God when I feel affliction. I fight to arm myself against temptation. I am not my own, I have been bought with a price (1 Cor. 6:20). I am not perfect in holiness, Christian, but I have experienced God's grace against temptation. The sovereignty and dominion of God have taught me humility and patience and that nothing is impossible with God (Luke 1:37). I would rather see His work in my life, then I would see mine by rushing ahead of Him. I am grateful to God for everything, and I am in awe of His actions on behalf of His children. I want to live the Christian life to be a true testimony for Jesus and I need His grace to accomplish this goal. Knowing the truth about creation, God's sovereignty, and His goodness, inspires me to want to be a new man in Jesus. I want to give to the Lord the reverence and live in obedience to such a great King. I want to live with His will for my life and His glory as the end. "The Lord has given and the Lord has taken away, blessed be the name of the Lord" (Job 1:21).

The dominion and supreme authority of Christ to govern was predicted (Isa. 11:1-10) and announced (Luke 1:32-34). "For a child will be born to us, a son will be given to us; and the government will rest on His shoulders; and His name will be called wonderful Counselor, Mighty God, Eternal Father, Prince of Peace" (Isa. 9:6). Christ being given to us is the great foundation of our hopes and joys. He has a name above every other name. As a King, He has the power and wisdom to provide grace and peace in the Gospel. The kingdom of Christ will grow to perfection and be ruled by love. The more we follow Jesus and the closer to Him we get, the safer we are. The glory of the Redeemer and the redeemed will last forever. "Righteousness will be the belt about His loins, and faithfulness the belt about His waist" (Isa. 11:5). Righteousness and faithfulness are His dominion and the belt is figurative of His readiness for conflict. The dominion of the Lord was confirmed by His resurrection (Acts 2:32-33). All authority has been given to Him in heaven and on earth (Matt. 28:18), and He has the keys of death and Hades (Rev. 1:18) over the invisible world. Because He humbled Himself, God exalted Him and gave Him all power in heaven and earth. He is Lord of all (Acts 10:36). He has the power of intercession (John 17:1-26) and to receive for Himself a kingdom (Luke 19:12). "When all things are subjected to Him, then the Son Himself will also be subjected to the One who subjected all things to Him, that God may be all in all" (1 Cor. 15:28). The Son will put Himself under God's authority, so that God, who gave the Son authority, will be supreme over everything everywhere (NLT). When all is conquered, Christ will return the entire kingdom to the Father. After this, God will be "all in all" and His glory will reign supreme. The government of heaven will be the perfect government of God; Father, Son, and Holy Spirit over the saints to all eternity. The glory of all will be ascribed to God; all the Father has done in election, all that the Son has done for salvation of His people, and all that the Holy Spirit has wrought in the saints. All the glory of the grace and the praise will be given to our triune God. God has dominion. Amen.

God created the male and the female and blessed them to be fruitful and multiply, fill and subdue the earth, and rule over every living thing on the earth (Gen. 1:26-28). Man had dominion that was delegated to him by God. Though man did not create living things, God gave power over them to man to honor the man. The dominion of man was diminished by the fall in the garden of Eden. Because Israel did not obey God's words, they lost the power to have dominion over their own land, and were taken into captivity (Jer. 25:7-11). The Bible describes a time when a man called Belshazzar misused his power and lost his kingdom to the Medes (Dan. 5:18-23). The Bible describes an earlier time when Satan challenged God's dominion by rebellion because of pride, and was thrust down to Hades (Isa. 14:12-16). Our own nation has cast God out, and can expect judgment and trouble in learning that it is God who has the dominion.

The chief opponent of God and the man that God created has been Satan (Luke 10:18). He has numerous other titles and names. These include: serpent (Gen. 3:4), accuser (Rev. 12:10), adversary (1 Pet. 5:8), the god of this world (2 Cor. 4:4), ruler of demons (Matt. 12:24), ruler of this world (John 14:30), prince of the power of the air (Eph. 2:2), among others. Satan was an angel created by God, who because of his pride turned against God's dominion (Isa. 14:13-14). He fell from heaven like a bolt of lightening (Luke 10:18). He became the head of a kingdom of evil spirits called demons and his angels (Matt. 25:41). He is a created and limited being that does not know everything. He depends upon God for the nature of his existence. Satan has a kingdom (Matt. 12:26) and a throne (Rev. 2:13). He has the power to manifest evil in the world by influencing people and commanding demons. Over the wicked; he blinds (2 Cor. 4:4), deceives (Rev. 20: 7-8), ensnares (1 Tim. 3:7), and secures men's worship (2 Thess. 2:4). He attempts to destroy God's work and make men turn away from God (Job 2:4-5). His power is manifest against God's people by affliction (Job 2:7), temptation (1 Chr. 21:1), accusation (Zech. 3:1), sift (Luke 22:31), deceive and disguise (2 Cor. 11:3, 14-15). He is crafty (2 Cor. 11:3), fierce (Luke 8:29), and evil (1 John 2:13). He misuses scripture (Matt. 4:6) and uses schemes against men (2 Cor. 2:11). He fights for sin to reign in you, and gain dominion over you. He wants you to defend it, delight in it, and make provision for it. As our adversary, he prowls about like a lion, seeking someone to devour (1 Pet. 5:8). The Lord knows our thoughts (Ps. 94:11; Matt. 9:4) but not Satan. The Lord knows the future (Isa. 46:9-10) but not Satan. All authority and power belong to God, not Satan. Satan is the father of lies (John 8:44). It is likely that Satan lied to Jesus, when he promised Him all the kingdoms of the world and its glory, if Jesus would bow down and worship him (Luke 4:6). While Satan and his forces are formidable enemies to us of darkness (Eph. 6:12) in this world (Eph. 2:2), they have been judged (John 16:11), crushed (Rom. 16:20), and assigned to eternal fire (Matt. 25:41). The triumph of Christ was predicted (Gen. 3:15), portrayed (Matt. 4:11), and Satan destroyed (1 John 3:8; Rev. 3:20). "Greater is He who is in you than he who is in the world" (1 John 4:4).

"Who is like Thee among the god's O Lord? Who is like Thee, majestic in holiness, awesome in praises, working wonders? (Ex. 15:11). The only true God is eternal, self-existent, immutable, and holy. "I am who I am" (Ex. 3:14). He always will be what He always has been. A saving knowledge of God is the greatest need of every human being, because it has eternal consequences. It must be, by the grace of God, that His truth is applied to your conscience and heart, so that your life will be transformed and you prepared for His glory. "Let not a wise man boast of his wisdom, and let not the mighty man boast of his might, let not a rich man boast of his riches; but let him who boasts boast of this, that he understands and knows Me, that I am the Lord who exercises loving kindness, justice and righteousness on earth; for I delight in these things" declares the Lord (Jer. 9:23-24). The unsanctified heart may not be receptive to the character of holiness, but to the soul that has been enlightened from above, the Lord God brought us Jesus, and holiness will be a crowning glory of the Godhead. Amen.

In the beginning, God was perfectly complete and in need of nothing. He chose to create a universe and man (Gen. 1). He knew the man would sin, and chose to reveal the riches of His grace in Christ Jesus to save him (Eph. 2:7). He knew the man would need to be born again (John 3:3) to see and begin to understand some things about God, or remain as a natural man (1 Cor. 2:14). God cannot be dishonored because He is perfectly righteous. He chose us to be holy, and predestined us to adoption as sons in Jesus Christ, according to the kind intention of His will (Eph. 1:4-5). We have obtained an inheritance, having been predestined according to His purpose who works all things after the counsel of His will (Eph. 1:11). God is glorified by creation, providence, and redemption, which is a manifest glory. He chose to reveal this to us by His own will. Sadly, the manifest glory of God is dishonored by some men. They do not like God or consider His power to save them. God is the One who has shone in our hearts the light of the glory of God in the face of Christ. We have this treasure in our hearts by the will and work of God and not from ourselves (2 Cor. 4:6-7). To God be the glory. The gospel shines in our heart. Amen. The powerful light of God convicts the conscience, and establishes a new man in the soul that rejoices from a new heart. We are only instruments, and we gladly and completely desire that God receive all the glory. The truth about Jesus comes to us in the precious gift of faith from God (Eph. 2:8). The testimony of Jesus comes with a spirit of prophecy (Rev. 19:10). Jesus is coming again. Pray to be "filled with the knowledge of His will with all spiritual wisdom and understanding, so that you may walk in a manner that is pleasing to the Lord" (Col. 1:9-10). Give thanks to the Ones who have qualified us to share in the inheritance of the saints in light (Col. 1:12). The grace in your heart, Christian, is the power of God. The power of God in your heart, Christian, proves the dominion and kind intention of His will for you.

"Known unto God are all His works, from the beginning of the world" (Acts 15:18). Whatever takes place in time was foreordained, before time began. Some folks use the word "decree" to describe the course of action of God. God's purpose is concerned with everything in our lives. When, where and how we are born and die, what happens in time and our eternal state has been decided by God. Scriptures tell us that believers were chosen in Christ before the foundation of the world (Eph. 1:4). The scriptures tell us that He called us and saved us according to His own purpose and grace granted us in Christ Jesus from all eternity (2 Tim. 1:9). This means that God had all supreme authority, dominion, and ability to bring you forth and save you for eternity. "He made known to us the mystery of His will according to His kind intention which He purposed in Him (Eph. 1:9). The affair of our redemption was God being faithful to His eternal decree. The promises of the forgiveness of sin and eternal life in the righteousness of Jesus was God's dominion in action, and not a result of our desire and effort. God calls us to holiness and "fits us" by the almighty power and love of the Father, Son, and the Holy Spirit (John 14: 26, 15:26;2 Cor. 13:14; Eph. 1:13).

By God's dominion, He sets us on a journey to discover inside us the unsearchable riches of Christ. Inside the great treasury of Christ is the grace, mercy, power, and love of God. Inside our heart and soul is the dwelling of Christ for eternity. "I will surely tell of the decree of the Lord: He said to Me, "Thou art My Son, today I have begotten Thee" (Ps. 2:7; see also Heb. 1:5, 5:5). The words in this Psalm were divinely inspired by the Holy Spirit about Christ, probably to David as an antitype and forerunner of Christ. The Son of God has the same nature as God. The kingdom of the Messiah is founded upon a decree. A decree from God is the result of divine wisdom and will. The decrees of God include election and providence and here the Sonship of Jesus. God has fulfilled the promise of redemption by the resurrection of Jesus (Acts 13:33). He was declared the Son of God with power by the resurrection from the dead, according to the spirit of holiness, Jesus Christ our Lord" (Rom. 1:4). God has made a covenant with His chosen people in the decrees of election and redemption. Lovingkindness will be built up forever, the heavens will establish Thy faithfulness, and it will include all generations (Ps. 89:1-4). Jesus Christ will deliver us into His kingdom, we cannot be lost. Jesus said, "My sheep hear My voice, and I know them, and they follow Me; and I give eternal life to them, and they shall never perish; and no one shall snatch them out of My hand" (John 10:27-28). Jesus is the Son of God in whom the Father is well pleased (Luke 3:22). "The Father loves the Son and has given all things into His hands (John 3:35). We are to receive Him as King. "Since you are precious in My sight, since you are honored and I love you, I will give other men in your place and other peoples in exchange for your life" (Isa. 43:4). Everyone who is called by My name and whom I have created for My glory, whom I have formed, even whom I have made" (Isa. 43:17). Take comfort in the promises of God.

The Lord will be triumphant in your soul for eternal salvation, and the kingdom of Christ, that is the church, shall be established. Your election and the providence of God are connected to the Sonship of Jesus decreed by God that cannot fail. Jesus is the Lamb of God (John 1:36). Jesus will be the Prince of Peace and a Wonderful Counselor in your soul (Isa. 9:6). He will be the author and perfecter of your faith (Heb. 12:2). He will be your Lord (2 Thess. 2:1) and Savior (1 Tim. 4:10). He will be the light of your world (John 9:5). The decrees of God will bring you consolation to believe "all things are working together for good" (Rom. 8:28) and lead you to pray "not my will but Thine be done" (Matt. 6:10). The decrees of God will inspire humility and faith in Jesus. The dominion of God is good, and will be done in heaven and earth. The power, authority and love of Jesus will become closer than a brother in your soul. You will have the great benefit of knowing He is always close, and that nothing will ever happen to you without His approval. God's dominion covers you like a blanket. He will become all you will ever want, and all you will ever need. To God be the glory. Amen.

God's plans for you are for your welfare and not for calamity, to give you a future and a hope. When you call upon Him and pray, He hears you. By the grace of God, He has promised when we search for Him with all our heart, we will find Him (Jer. 29:11-13). It is in the dominion of God, that His purpose will be served and His will be done. He is the potter and we are the clay (Isa. 64:8). God did not just create a bunch of people and put them on the earth to live their lives the best they could. Our days are numbered (Job 14:5; Ps. 139:16). God's infinite wisdom and power have been revealed in His providential plan to care for believers that have been chosen before the world began (Eph. 1:4). Our being chosen by His grace in Jesus was a judicial decision ordained by God. "How precious also are Thy thoughts to me,

O God! (Ps. 139:17). The origin and purpose of our earthly lives were determined inside the eternal counsel of God. We are called and enabled to hear and respond by God's grace alone. We cannot earn or deserve this special attention by God. Christianity is a holy calling from God that you will labor with great diligence and desire to discover the nature of goodness in the dominion of God. You will learn about your sin, and the love of Jesus to save you. You will know that God has begun a work in your heart to save you. You will grow in grace and knowledge and gain assurance that His work is saving you. By the dominion of God, the gospel call is a holy call. You will know it is an effectual call to salvation by your sanctification. Amen. You will behold the Bible as the living word of God, and find it profitable for training in righteousness (2 Tim. 3:16). "He who began a good work in you will perfect it until the day of Christ Jesus" (Phil. 1:6). "The confidence of Christians is the great comfort of Christians" (Matthew Henry). God gives us a new heart and spirit, and His Spirit, to cause us to walk in His statutes (Ezek. 36:26-27). We surrender our will to His perfect will. "We are predestined to be conformed to the image of His Son" (Rom.8:29). God does a work, that we are responsible to strive in, that progressively transforms us into the image of His Son (2 Cor. 3:18). It can take us a while sometimes to get serious and sincere about Bible study and with God. By the grace of God, we work out our salvation with fear and trembling (Phil. 2:12). He keeps working in your heart, Christian, from His authority and faithfulness to the covenant He made with Jesus. He has His own way of showing you that He is near. He has the dominion. "The righteous man shall live by faith" (Hab. 2:4; Gal. 3:11; Heb. 10:38). Amen.

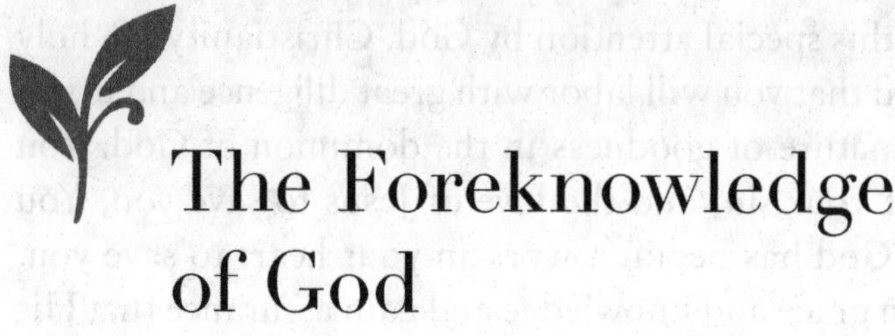

The Foreknowledge of God

> "And we know that God causes all things to work together for good to those who love God, to those who are called according to His purpose. For whom He foreknew, He also predestined to become conformed to the image of His Son, that He might be the first-born among many brethren; and whom He predestined, these He also called; and whom He called, these He also justified; and whom He justified, these He also glorified" (Rom. 8:28-30).

Dead Christian,

The topic of the foreknowledge of God is important, and at the same time has been debatable. The Bible clearly teaches the foreknowledge of God. Some folks, however do not believe the Bible was inspired by God, and they do not like the idea that God already knows everything. The fact that God is omnipotent (all-powerful) (Jer. 32:17), omnipresent (ever-present) (Ps. 139:7-12), omniscient (all-knowing) (1 John 3:20), and eternal (Isa. 57:15) is clearly taught in the Bible. God has infinite awareness, understanding, and insight. God's understanding is inscrutable (Isa. 40:28), and He proclaims things before they spring forth (Isa. 42:9). The Bible tells us that because of Israels obstinacy and their foolish idols, God declared things before they took place (Isa. 48:4-5). God admits He has foreknowledge, and God cannot lie (Num. 23:19; Heb. 6:18). He is able, to accomplish what He promises. The promises we have from God, Christian, are abundant life (John 10:10), and to be revealed with Him in glory (Col. 3:4). In this world we are hidden with Christ in God (Col. 3:3). In this world, we know by God's grace of faith, we are being strengthened and transformed by the Holy Spirit to lay hold of the promised possession of Christ (John 14:21). God providentially controls everything to His own joyous end. The Bible teaches us that all life is lived in the sustaining will of God. "For in Him we live, and move, and have our being" (Acts 17:28). The Christian has been born again spiritually and can be at peace. God is the "only Sovereign, the King of kings and Lord of lords: to Him be honor and eternal dominion" (1 Tim. 6:15-16).

When we are born into the world the first time, we are called a natural man. The natural man, because of original sin, is considered spiritually dead to God. The natural man has not been born again, and therefore cannot "accept the things of the Spirit of God; for they are foolishness to him, and he cannot understand them, because they are spiritually appraised" (1 Cor. 2:14). The natural man does not believe the Bible is the inspired word of God (2 Tim. 3:16). Since the existence of God is not subject to the world's scientific proof, the natural man misses the path for salvation that God has provided by the inspiration of faith. He does not study the Bible and remains blind to the affirmation of faith. The natural man does not have a life that develops, grows, matures and lives daily in a personal relationship with Jesus as his Savior. He does not fully realize it, but he lives with a huge problem of not letting God be God in his life. He will be exposed in the future and regret the eternal consequences. He will miss the purpose of his life, and the peace and joy of knowing God's only begotten Son (John 3:16). Some day he will know that God spoke to him by a call in his heart to follow Jesus, to be holy and be saved (Heb. 1:3). Some day he may learn God's foreknowledge about his life, and the opportunities he had to come to Jesus. Some day he may know that God was the sovereign disposer of his affairs, according to the counsel of His own will (Acts 17:26). Our times are in His hands, and He performs the things that are appointed for us (Job 23:14). God is not far from us (Acts 17:27). We owe God for life and the ways of providence that come from Him for us. Some day we may know a lot more about how we lived, and moved and existed by the grace of God. Amen.

God transcends His creation and can only be known by His self-revelation. He alone has life within Himself. God is pure spirit (John 4:24) and is called the Father of spirits (Heb. 12:9). God is an infinite spirit with no physical presence. Every element of God's nature is unlimited. Nothing is impossible with God (Luke 1:37). The infinite and spiritual nature of God completely passes out of the reach of our understanding and experience (Ps. 145:3). God can be known as personal (Isa. 43:3) and sovereign (Prov. 16:9) by His self-revelation from the scriptures. The Bible tells us that "Thou hast magnified Thy word according to all Thy name" (Ps. 138:2). God has made Himself known to us in creation and providence, but especially in His word. All scripture is inspired by God (2 Tim. 3:16). The name of God includes His perfections, His truth, and His faithfulness. God sends you into His word. God reveals truth to your soul from the scripture and gives a faith (Rom. 10:17) that anchors us into the promise of forgiveness of sin and eternal life in Jesus.

The Bible tells us, "You shall know the truth and the truth shall make you free" (John 8:32). This scripture is a gracious and powerful truth and promise by Christ to us. Justification makes us free from the guilt of sin and the fear of judgment. Sanctification makes us free from the bondage of corruption and available to serve the living God. We are set free from prejudice and false notions to experience free thinking from the God of all truth. The power of God's truth gives spiritual liberty and frees us from the prison-house of sin. Be patient, it may take a while, but God knows what He is doing to transform our souls to be safe in His presence. The Bible tells us, that He makes us to lie down in green pastures, leads us beside quite waters and restores our soul (Ps.

23:2-3). It is in God's time and way that He proves His faithfulness, and confirms the veracity of the scripture. We gain experiential knowledge, by the grace of God, when He opens our hearts to the scriptures (Acts 16:14) and we walk with Jesus. The progressive revelation of God in our soul reaches a fulness and we become believers and disciples of Jesus. In the foreknowledge of God, He knew you would be drawn (John 6:44), called (Rom. 8:28), born again (John 1:13, 3:3), and free to serve the Lord (1 Cor. 7:22). The natural man does not understand the things of the spirit of God, and is unwilling to enter the mind of God. He misses the fear of God which is the beginning of wisdom (Prov. 2:5, 9:10). He misses the truth of God and growing in grace. He does not know or love God and keep His commandments (John 14:21). If anyone loves God, he is known by Him (1 Cor. 8:3). Those that love God have been taught by God (John 6:45).

The supreme intelligence, creative power and dominion of God means He can make His own plans, and carry them out in His own time and way. God is sovereign. Theologians distinguish between an active will of God which will always be accomplished, and a passive or permissive will which He enjoins upon His creatures, which is often disobeyed. Man was created with a free will, but his will was damaged by the fall in the garden of Eden. Man cannot come to receive Jesus on his own, he needs God's grace (John 6:44). The entrance of sin into our world through Adam, is attributed to the permissive will of God. God's will to act is dominant, and man was given liberty or permission to act. An example of the divine will being resisted by human unbelief was given by Jesus. Jesus wanted to gather the children of Jerusalem the way a hen gathers her chicks under her wings, but they were unwilling (Matt. 23:37). The eternal purpose of God will not be overruled by man. "Thy will be done on earth as it is in heaven" (Matt. 6:10). The natural man is unable to reconcile God's sovereignty and man's responsibility in salvation, because he does not sufficiently understand God or himself. We live our lives in the sustaining grace and will of God. We work out our salvation with fear and trembling, to discover what God works and wills in us for His good pleasure (Phil. 2:12-13). God is immutable and sovereign, man was mutable and responsible.

God foreknew and set His heart upon certain individuals for salvation the Bible calls the elect (Eph. 1:4). Those whom He foreknew, He predestined to be made like Christ and saved (Rom. 8:29). God is completely in control, and we make choices and are accountable for the choices we make. God is not stumped or unfair by the mutual existence of His sovereignty and our will. God's election of individuals to salvation is based on the free, sovereign grace of God. All men are not predestined to be saved and therefore they are not foreknown. All men are not objects of God's affection and concern. "The Lord knows those that are His" (2 Tim.2:19), even from the womb (Jer. 1:5). It is a sovereign distinguishing love that determines our existence. Our salvation is dependent on the fulfillment of New Covenant promises purchased by the blood of Jesus. The New Covenant promise is that God will give us one heart and a new spirit and His Spirit to cause us to walk in His statutes (Ezek. 11:19-20, 36:26-27). God says, He will put a fear in our hearts that we will not turn away from Him (Jer. 31:33). God chose us and keeps us from stumbling (Jude 24). We "are chosen according to the foreknowledge of God the Father, by the sanctifying work of the Holy Spirit, that you may obey Jesus Christ and be sprinkled with His blood" (1 Pet. 1:2). We are called the elect according to the free grace of God, the Father, Son, and Holy Spirit. The end is eternal life with the Lord. On the way, God renews our mind, mortifies our sins, and produces fruit in the heart of a Christian (Rom. 8:13; Gal. 22-23). On the way is obedience. Sanctification follows our being born again and being justified by God. The gifts from God of faith and repentance take on a priority in a new Christians life, and he grows more mature in these graces by the mercy of God. The Holy Spirit spends more time getting our attention, convicts us of our sin and sends us into the word. The Holy Spirit leads us to the cross of Jesus for gratitude and worship. The Holy Spirit leads us to confess our sins for forgiveness and cleansing (1 John 1:9).

The Holy Spirit empowers us to be more like Jesus, and

when we live more like Him, we gain more evidence He has been resurrected and is alive. The grace of obedience is a game changer. When a person is obeying the gospel, he is living the truth of Jesus that has set him free. He gains greater conviction of being saved. Walking with Jesus is a kind of sprinkling of the blood of Jesus on your soul that seals the Bible as the word of God, and provides a greater assurance that you belong to Jesus. The shedding of the Saviors blood provides a daily cleansing as we walk in His light and confess our sins. We are saved sinners. When we confess our sin, the faithfulness of God is revealed to our hearts by the cleansing. I do not know why God chose to love me. I do know that He chose me in His Son. Having a relationship with Jesus is the most important part of my life. The reason He chose me is from something deep inside of God, that I cannot reach or understand. God's foreknowledge is beyond my comprehension, but I know I am very grateful to be found. What I do know is the work of the Holy Spirit. He woke me up to fear God, and follow faith and repentance in Jesus. He woke me up to the importance of holiness. He woke me up to Jesus about sin and forgiveness and the idea of eternal life. He woke me up to Bible study. I know He is the reason that I have grown in grace and knowledge and in the obedience of faith in Jesus. The journey has not been easy, and just take place overnight. It was a struggle, but my growth was progressive. I learned a lot about myself and God, and peace, love and joy that comes along with being a Christian. I still struggle with sin at times, Christian, but I know the blessings of the confession of sin, and growth in holiness with the Lord. I know the faithfulness of God to forgive and cleanse me of unrighteousness (1 John 1:9). I know the hope seeing Jesus and eternal life. Amen.

The foreknowledge of God is based upon His infinite knowledge and eternal nature. No created creature can determine future events. Only God has infallible foresight and irresistible power. "All things always were, and perpetually remain, under God's eyes, so that to His knowledge there is nothing future or past, but all things are present" (John Calvin). The foreknowledge of God is manifested by His determining the boundaries of nations (Acts

17:26), and indicating the succession of nations (Dan. 2:26-47). He announced Israels captivity (Dan. 9:2, 24) and Christs death (Eph. 1:3-4). He named the birthplace of Christ (Micah 5:2, Matt 2:6). The Bible is rich in prophecy, especially about Christ (Luke 24: 25-27). "No prophecy was ever made by an act of human will, but men moved by the Holy Spirit spoke from God" (2 Pet. 1:21). "Behold, the former things have come to pass, now I declare new things; before they spring forth, I proclaim them to you" (Isa. 42:9). The accomplishment of God's promises made to you, and the church, are proofs of the truth of His word and the kindness He bears for our souls.

God made many promises about the Messiah (Isa. 53). Jesus gave the promise of the Holy Spirit (Luke 24:49). He knew that the Holy Spirit would provide the help and comfort we would need to grow in grace (John 14:16, 26). He knew that we would need our eyes opened to see Jesus and our heart engaged to serve the living God. He knew that we would need to wear spiritual armor to fight the good fight of faith for the comforting hope of eternal life. The glory of God's grace will not be defeated and the honor of God ever impugned. The plan of salvation was designed in eternity (Eph. 1:3-12), and announced to man after the fall in the garden of Eden (Gen. 3:15). The plan of salvation was elaborated in detail (Isa. 53:1-12) and consummated in Christ's death (John 19:30). The plan of salvation was extended to Gentiles (Gal. 3:8). God cannot lie (Heb. 6:18). He chose us in Him before the foundation of the world, and predestined us to adoption as sons according to the kind intention of His will. In Him we have redemption and an inheritance (Eph. 1: 4-5,7,11). We have been sealed in Him by the Holy Spirit of promise (Eph. 1:13). We know, Christian, that the grace of God has begun for us, and the gift of holiness proves to our hearts God's loving power and faithfulness. Chapter one of the book of Ephesians is a masterpiece of scripture, to the praise and glory of God. All these blessings are ours according to the foreknowledge of God. The incredible truth was revealed by the will of God the Father (Eph. 1:3-6), the work of the Son (Eph. 1:7-12) and the witness of the Spirit (Eph. 1:13-14). The spiritual gifts from God to our soul are life's greatest blessings. By the grace of God, we understand His love and favor and the mercy in His glorious faithfulness to us. Amen.

The Bible is clear that God is all powerful and not limited or confined by time. The Bible is clear that God foreknew and chose some people and predestined them to be conformed to the image of His Son. The Bible is clear that God is sovereign and acts providentially to redeem and seal His elect people for eternal life with an inheritance in heaven. It is born out of God's love for us that we trust God, and believe and follow Jesus. "For we are His workmanship, created in Christ Jesus for good works, which God prepared beforehand, that we should walk in them" (Eph. 2:10). We are to work with fear and trembling to bring our salvation to a place it becomes a thorough work in our souls (Phil. 2:12). We are responsible to improve, employ and exercise the gifts and graces God has given us. We are to make a discovery of the work God has done within us. We are to live out the Christian life in full surrender and dependence on the Holy Spirit. We are to be serious and diligent and personal with Jesus in Bible study, prayer, and service. The incentive for us to work is that God is working in us to will and to act (Phil. 2:13). We are to "work out" and not "work for" our salvation. It is both God's sovereignty and man's responsibility that works together for salvation.

We must use all means to strengthen our spiritual life. We must guard our minds and emotions for the will of God. Your sanctification is about the direction of your life, not the perfection of your life. The seed for Jesus has been planted by God, your responsibility is to encourage the seed to grow. To be in a hurry in reading the Bible is of little benefit. Taking time to meditate on the word and comparing passages is a lot more profitable. You will behold your salvation the most clearly in holiness. The work of God for our salvation is for us and in us. Our fear and trembling (Phil. 2:12), means humility and vigilance. How we think about God, Christian, will always influence the way we act. How we act is a testimony to ourselves and the Lord about where we are spiritually. There should be a fear of the Lord, not so much of what He could do to us, but that it shows how we really feel about Jesus and His sacrifice for us. We live before the face of God. Where we go, we take Him with us. We ought to be afraid, and fear the behaviors of pride and selfishness, carnal security, sin, and presumption, and not walking in obedience. "Therefore, having these promises, beloved, let us cleanse ourselves from all defilement of flesh and spirit, perfecting holiness in the fear of God (2 Cor. 7:1). Holiness in believers is a work of God's grace that comes in His time and way. The desire and power for holiness comes from God (1 Thess. 5:3; Heb. 10:14; 1 Pet. 1:2). Holiness requires our cooperation by our working out what God has put into us (Phil. 2:12-13). Be serious and submit yourself entirely to God. We are always in the presence of God. How can we choose to offend such a good God?

"Worship the Lord with reverence and rejoice with trembling" (Ps. 2:11). The word of God was given to us to develop the filial fear of God in our hearts (Ps. 119:38). "The fear of the Lord is the beginning of wisdom: A good understanding have all those who do His commandments; His praise endures forever" (Ps. 111:10). Read the word of God carefully. The Christian life takes commitment and diligence. "Blessed is the man who fears always" (Prov. 28:14). God mingles filial fear with joy when we walk with Jesus in the comforts of the Holy Spirit. The filial fear of God promotes spiritual joy and rest in the mercy of God. True spiritual growth is mostly realized through peace and joy and an expansive frame of mind or freedom, and acceptance with God. We temper our joy with reverence, as we remember who we are, and Whom we are walking with. It is a trembling with hope and confidence in the Lord. The joy can be great because it is in the inner man and free of outside circumstances. The light of Jesus in a man's heart is the wisdom of God, and brings confidence and strength because of His real presence. We never forget that once we were blind, but now we can see; we were lost but have been found. We remain humble because we know that we needed God's grace to fear God and be saved from ourselves. Trembling is a healthy fear of offending God through disobedience, and being respectful of His majesty and holiness. Amen.

"For whom He foreknew, He also predestined to become conformed to the image of His Son, that He might be the first-born among many brethren; and whom He predestined, these He also called; and whom He called, these He also justified; and whom He justified, these He also glorified" (Rom. 8:29-30). Those people that God foreknew; He destined, called, justified, and glorified for the honor of His Son. In God's eternal counsel and prior to human history, He deliberately, and freely chose and ordained some for salvation. He planned it all ahead of time. The full meaning of this action by God is beyond our finite comprehension. That He chose us and we call upon Him of our own volition (Eph. 1:4; Rom. 10:13) is a completely righteous act of God, though we do not completely understand it. God is in control. The destiny of the believer is from God and brings comfort, encouragement, and gratitude. God is all good. Predestination applies only to the saved person; a nonbeliever refuses to trust Christ. Some people get angry at you about this piece of scripture, not realizing that God has given you the faith to believe. They really are angry and disagree with God. They cannot get at Him, so they attack you. The ear of the nonbeliever may not be hearing the Lord. Their heart may not be bleeding or pleading for help in a way of repentance for holiness. The idea of what Jesus and the church were about, was or became embarrassing to believe and or trust as the truth about life after death. In place of seeking and searching for God, they become ignorant of Him and choose evolution as the origin of life. Christ becomes unbelievable and they cannot "taste of the good word of God and the powers of the age to come" (Heb. 6:5). They remain stubborn and stiff-necked in their will against Christ and are storing up wrath for themselves at the righteous judgment of God (Rom. 2:5). Their conscience is not bearing them the witness of Jesus Christ (2 Cor. 5:11). They may think lightly of the riches of His kindness and patience that leads to repentance (Rom. 2:4). A judgment day is coming when they will be directed to give an account about their life and sin (Matt. 25:31-46; 2 Cor. 5:10-11; 2 Pet. 3:7; Rev. 20:11-15). God created man with the ability to remember the times of His life, including his sin for repentance.

We remember a lot, God whose memory is perfect, remembers it all. The Bible tells us, "God will judge the secrets of men through Jesus Christ" (Rom. 2:16). The Lord is patient, not wishing for any to perish but for all to come to repentance (2 Pet. 3:9). Amen.

Jesus was delivered up to death by the foreknowledge of God with man taking the responsibility for it (John 19:15; Acts 2:22-23). We receive by the gift of faith what we cannot fully comprehend. God's purpose was the salvation of the elect. The doctrine of election, Christian, means that salvation is the gift of God alone. We are vessels of mercy (Rom. 9:23). The doctrine of election means that God is also providentially attending to the events of our life. Praise God for His saving grace. The goal of predestination is to have the body of our humble state transformed and conformed with the body of the glory of Jesus Christ (Phil. 3:21). We are to examine ourselves to recognize whether Jesus is in us or not (2 Cor. 13:5). Are you in the faith? Our Savior, the Lord Jesus Christ has the power to subject all things to Himself (Phil. 3:21). God says of the Messiah, "I shall make Him My first-born" (Ps. 89:27). Jesus is the first-born in relation to the church. God's sovereign work from His foreknowledge involves an effectual call to the spiritually dead to come to life as a Christian. Those who are called, hear, and experience the power and wisdom of God (1 Cor. 1:24). We are called to hear about Jesus for salvation, holiness, and service with the Holy Spirit to live in the light. "For many are called, but few are chosen" (Matt. 22:14). The verse John 3:16 reveals the call is for everyone, but because of humanity's depravity, no one will turn to God without God drawing them and impressing Himself upon them (John 6:44). Those whom God has called are declared justified, and glorified (Rom. 8:30). We are declared justified and righteous by faith in Jesus which manifests the righteousness of God (Rom. 3:21-26, 5:1, 18-19). Glorification is the final removal of the power and presence of sin, and God's purpose of foreknowledge and our destination. We are "to live sensibly, righteously and godly in the present age, looking for the blessed hope and the appearing of the glory of our great God and Savior, Christ Jesus" (Titus 2:13). Now we see in a mirror dimly and know in part; in the future, we will see as we have been fully known (1 Cor. 13:12). When our Savior returns, He will transform our lowly bodies to be like His glorious body (1 John 3:2). "In all these things we overwhelmingly conquer through Him who loved us" (Rom. 8:37). The Spirit of God strengthens us, gives us assurance and comforts us along the way when we grow in grace and knowledge. To God be the glory.

After we grow in grace and knowledge, we begin to believe that nothing is impossible with God (Luke 1:37). "We know that God causes all things to work together for good to those who love God, to those who are called according to His purpose" (Rom. 8:28). God helps all our weaknesses in His time (Rom. 8:26). He searches our hearts to know what the mind of the Spirit is, and intercedes for us according to the will of God (Rom. 8:27). The providences of God, divinely sanctified, work together for the best for the people of God. God can only be perfectly good and righteous in bringing us to Christ and growing our hearts and souls for Him. We can be persuaded that all things, even in affliction, the Spirit makes intercession to the Father for His good work in us to follow Jesus. We know that God is holy and righteous and sovereign and faithful and good and has the foreknowledge and power to keep all His promises. Amen.

When you know the truth and follow Jesus, then you can be free (John 8:32). You become free to recognize your passion and purpose in life. God made you and has blest you with passions and purpose that He chose for you to use and share in this life for His glory. "I know the plans that I have for you, declares the Lord, plans for welfare and not for calamity to give you a future and a hope" (Jer. 29:11). God knows all His own thoughts and works, and He does everything according to the perfectly good counsel of His own will. We are to be patient with fear and trembling to see His perfect work. God will not give us the expectations of our fears and fancies, but will show us the expectations of our faith in Jesus. Amen. God made you in an awesome way, and from your new birth your soul knows it very well (Ps. 139:13-14). In the historical context of the passage above in Jeremiah, he was speaking to his suffering people as they were forced into exile from Jerusalem to

Babylon. This scripture speaks to us today of encouragement to hope and trust in God, even when we are suffering with sin and the ways of this world, about our good future in Jesus. We know that God's purpose, according to His choice will stand, not because of our works, but because of Him who calls (Rom. 9:11). God's purpose for us is to know the love of Christ. God's purpose for us is for Christ to dwell in our hearts, and be strengthened with power through His Spirit according to the riches of His glory (Eph. 3:16-19). The manifold wisdom of God was to be revealed, and the unfathomable riches of Christ proclaimed in the world through the church to the rulers and the authorities in heavenly places (Eph. 1:8-10). Before the world was made, Christian, God knew that Satan would fall, and that man would follow him in sin. God's plan already included the incarnation, death, resurrection, and glorification of Christ. God's plan already included the saving of ungodly Jews and Christians as holy members of the body of Christ, and honor them as the bride of the Lamb throughout eternity. This was the plan of God (Isa. 41:21-23), to be revealed by Christ (John 13:19) and the Spirit (John 16:13). God's call to salvation is an effectual call, and equates with those who are called the chosen or the elect. The gift of faith is the condition of salvation and not the works of the flesh or the law.

God makes the difference for our salvation. The Word arrives in power and assurance, and the Christian desires to be like Jesus. There is a spiritual joy, and a sense of the presence of Jesus in spiritual service. We do not fully understand election, but we know we have been "born again to a living hope" (1 Pet. 1:3). We know that we are being conformed to the image of Christ (Rom. 8:29). The Lord performed a miracle of mercy in us, we know His love and have a relationship with Jesus. We have learned obedience by the things which we have suffered (Heb. 5:8). The will of God conforms us to the image of Christ. He made us willing in the day of His power (Ps. 110:3). We are God's work (Eph. 2:10; Phil. 2:13). It is our responsibility to work with God to become like Christ (Phil. 2:12). "Lord, Thou wilt establish peace for us, since Thou hast performed for us all our works" (Isa. 26:12). The work of grace in our hearts, and the consequences in our world, is God's work for His glory. Many people in the world are ignorant and oppose the doctrines of God's election and foreknowledge. Satan tries to keep our soul from trusting in Christ by making you believe that your sins are unforgiveable, and that you are not worthy of being saved. Satan will work a man against his duty. Satan will work your soul to doubt your election and conclude you are not elected, to rob God of His glory and worship in saving you. The truth is, that all our sorrow, shame and trouble from sin is only forgiven by God, when our hope flows from faith in Christ. No one is worthy, and no one can make themselves worthy to be saved (Rom. 3:10-11). We are responsible to labor in prayer, Bible study and communion with Jesus for more wisdom, and to be filled with the Spirit. Resist Satan's motions against you. Pray to grow in God's grace to gain the hope and strength that the Lord is with you. God's promises are complete in His power, blood, and oath, and cannot be but true. The Lord will allow you to discover and know in fear and trembling (Phil. 2:12) that He is with you by His own mercy and grace.

"God has saved us, and called us with a holy calling, not according to our works, but according to His own purpose and grace which was granted us in Christ Jesus from all eternity" (2 Tim. 1:9). "God called you out of darkness into His marvelous light" (1 Pet. 2:9). God has called you to fellowship with His Son (1 Cor. 1:19), to freedom (Gal.5:13), peace (1 Cor. 7:15), holiness (1 Thess. 4:7) and glory (2 Pet. 1:3). All of this becomes ours in Christ according to the kind purpose of God (Rom. 8:28). The basic meaning of the word "called" is to be invited or welcomed. Believers have been invited by God in the Gospel to obtain eternal life in the kingdom of Christ. It is an effective summons to people for faith in Christ to be saved, otherwise no one would have come. The elect will hear the summons of God to be holy and to make a difference in the world for Christ. The Lord adds to the number being saved (Acts 2:47). "As many as had been appointed to eternal life believed" (Acts 13:48). By a secret and graceful operation, He brings people into subjection to the Gospel of Christ and makes them willing in the day of His power (Ps. 110:3). To those who hear the call, Christ becomes the power and wisdom of God (1 Cor. 1:24). "Fight the good fight of faith; take hold of eternal life to which you were called" (1 Tim. 6:12). Walk in a manner worthy of your calling (Eph. 4:1) and "press on toward the goal for the prize of the upward call of God in Christ Jesus" (Phil. 3:14).

Those called to salvation, by the grace of God, are virtually synonymous with the term "elect." The calling, election, man's free will and responsibility, and God's sovereignty are deep spiritual truths of God that cannot be completely understood or explained by man. The righteous man shall live by faith (Hab. 2:4). Many hear the call to repentance and faith, but only a few will respond because they are chosen (Matt, 22:14). The effectual call that the few hear, is the supernatural drawing of God (John 6:44, 65). The call is personal and inward, according to the purpose of God. The Bible tells us that, whom He foreknew, He predestined, called, and justified solely by His own sovereign will and purpose (R0m. 8:29-30). The effectual call of God, Christian, is heard by the sheep who have ears to hear (John 10:3-4, 27). "The hearing ear and the seeing eye, the Lord has made both of them" (Prov. 20:12). Christ is both the door and the good shepherd (John 10:9, 11). The grace of God opens the ear, the eye, and the door, and leads the sheep to holiness and heaven. Amen. The grace of God gives the ear that hears His voice, and the eye to see the beauty of His holiness. The grace of God opens our minds to understand the scripture and the meaning of Jesus for salvation. In His time, Christ, as the good shepherd, leads us through the door of darkness, sin, and death, and into the light of being forgiven, saved and into good pasture (John 10:7-11). Jesus Christ is the only way to go through the door to find rest and the peace of God.

The calling of a Christian is manifested through the Father, the Son, and the Holy Spirit to be born again by the word of God (1 Pet. 1:23). "I desire compassion, and not sacrifice, for I did not come to call the righteous, but sinners" (Matt. 9:13). God is not pleased with religious routine and practice that is not filled with a sincere love of Christ and other people. Compassion is to show mercy and kindness, and is much preferred over pretentious sacrifices. The message of the Gospel is love. The call we hear from the Lord is to repentance for holiness to come into His presence. It is a call to change our mind and way of life. The sinner becomes sensible and sick of his sin. Let the one come who hears the invitation and is thirsty, and "wishes to take the water of life without cost" (Rev. 22:17). The kingdom of God is for the spiritually poor, sick, and hungry, who want to be healed, cleansed, and made alive. The man who thinks he is already righteous is fooling himself. In his pride, he thinks he is good enough to not need Jesus. He does not know God. The Bible tells us that, "God has chosen you from the beginning for salvation through sanctification by the Spirit and faith in the truth. And it is for this He called you through our gospel, that you may gain the glory of our Lord Jesus Christ" (2 Thess. 2:13-14). God has called you for a personal relationship with His Son (1 Cor. 1:9) for the purpose of gaining the glory of His Son. The future will not be what you think it should be, it will be what God has ordained it will be. In this life, Christian, the Lord brings about a progressive sanctification, in which we experience His power, wisdom, and love revealing His grace, goodness and glory to come. We "are being transformed into the same image from glory to glory, just as from the Lord, the Spirit" (2 Cor. 3:18). The glory is faint now, but the promise is that when we see Him, we will be like Him (1 John 3:2). God's purpose in calling us is for eternal life (1 Tim. 6:12), holiness (1 Thess. 4:7), freedom (Gal. 5:13), and peace (1 Cor. 7:15). God "called us by His own glory and excellence" (2 Pet. 1:3).

We are called to be the bride of Christ (2 Cor. 11:2; Eph. 5:25-27; Rev. 19:7-9). God knew us and called us to be the bride in the marriage of the Lamb of God. The call is from heaven (Heb. 3:1). God "demonstrated His own love toward us, in that while we were yet sinners, Christ died for us" (Rom. 5:8). Our responsibility is to "press on toward the goal for the prize of the upward call of God in Christ Jesus" (Phil. 3:14). Be "diligent to make certain about His calling you and choosing you" (2 Pet. 1:10). God has called by His grace (Gal. 1:15; 2 Tim. 1:9) and His calling is irrevocable

(Rom. 11:29). "God is not a man, that He should lie, nor a son of man, that He should repent; has He said, and will He not do it? Or has He spoken and will He not make it good?" (Num. 23:19). God's perfect decisions do not require a change in His mind. He gives us grace to come to Jesus and be saved. God does not regret or recall the gift of grace He gives to us. Our election is rooted in the immutable and faithful nature of God. In our lives, the sorrow about sin that is according to the will of God produces a repentance without regret, leading to salvation (2 Cor. 7:10). God is merciful and faithful and loves us to the end. The sovereignty of God cannot be separated from His love, grace, providence, mercy, and foreknowledge. The Gospel is a declaration of the sovereign pleasure of God concerning Christ. God was called "the head of Christ" (1 Cor. 11:3). Though Christ is equal to God in character and deity (John 10:30), He offered submission to the Father (John 14:28). The fact that Christ acknowledges the prominence of the Father, does not imply inferiority. The triune nature, and the foreknowledge of God, are mysteries to man that we cannot fully understand in our present state. Perhaps in the future, we may know more, but for now we walk by the gift of faith that God has given to us.

God knows all things whether they lie in the past, present, or future. God is omniscient (Isa. 40:28). The things possible, and even before they were created were known in the power of God's mind. He did not create something and then learn about it. God knows all things past (Isa. 41:22). God knows everything as being present. "There is no creature hidden from His sight, but all things are open and laid bare to the eyes of Him with whom we have to do" (Heb. 4:13). As a great high priest, Jesus is merciful and compassionate and touched with the feelings of our infirmities. The omniscience of Christ should encourage us to persevere in faith and obedience until the time He perfects our affairs. "If we confess our sins, He is faithful and righteous to forgive us our sins and to cleanse us from all unrighteousness" (1 John 1:9). God knows everything because of His nature or essence. Though the foreknowledge of God is complete and infallible, it does not determine the decisions of men. It is not God's fault that Adam would fall, Judas would betray Jesus or that we would be sinners. God knew that His law would be disobeyed, and that His grace could have prevented Adam's choice. Adam sinned in the liberty of his own free will. Adam blamed the women for his sin and God for giving him the women (Gen. 3:2). God did not only foreknow, but determined the suffering of Christ (Acts 4:27-28). The Bible tells us that Jesus the Nazarene, attested to you by God with miracles, was delivered up by the predetermined plan and foreknowledge of God to be put to death (Acts 3:22-23). What was foretold was fulfilled (Acts 4:26; John 19). Jesus was a man marked out by God that had many witnesses to His miracles, wonders, and signs. He was permitted to be put to death for us. In infinite wisdom and the foreknowledge of God, sinners were saved and Christ glorified. In infinite wisdom and the foreknowledge of God, His justice and mercy were perfectly satisfied in Christ paying the penalty for sin, and our souls being saved for eternity. The crucifixion of Jesus and our forgiveness was based on a definite, prearranged plan in the purpose of God to reveal the riches of His grace. God foreknew the destiny of His Son. God was not just a mere onlooker seeing into the future, but had the most important part to bring about His goodness. God acted in creation, crucifixion, resurrection, and redemption (Gen.1; Acts 2:23-24; Eph. 1:7). God wrote history before time began. "The mind of man plans his way, but the Lord directs his steps" (Prov. 16:9). "The wrath of man shall praise Thee" (Ps. 76:10). The wrath of man will turn and bring honor to God and serve His purpose. We depend upon God. The truth is our lives "are just a vapor that appears for a little while and then vanishes away" (James 4:14). We live in the providence of God and do not always know what tomorrow will bring. Since our time is in God's hands (Job 14:5), our thoughts and actions ought always to be referred to God. We ought to pray that His will be done and not ours (Luke 22:42). Knowing the power, love, and goodness of God, we ought to run to the throne of grace for help in time of need (Heb. 4:16).

The foreknowledge of God is a controversial topic. To

appropriately discuss this topic, it is important to be firmly established in faith and have spent some time in the word of God. Scripture tells us that God, in His sovereignty, appointed certain people to receive the gift of faith and believe into eternal life (Rom. 8:29-30). A Christian is "chosen according to the foreknowledge of God the Father, by the sanctifying work of the Spirit, that you may obey Jesus Christ and be sprinkled with His blood" (1 Pet. 1:2). God's foreknowledge is based upon His purpose or decree (Ps. 2:7). He foreknows because He has elected out of His own pleasure (Rom. 9). Our conformity to Christ is the effect of God's foreknowledge and predestination. Our conformity to Christ is the result of God's call into our conscience. We are justified and will be glorified from the victory of Christ. Our acceptance and salvation, is by God's grace and not our works (Eph. 2:8-9). "We are His workmanship, created in Christ Jesus for good works, which God prepared beforehand, that we should walk in them" (Eph. 2:10). God's action in predestination is based solely on Himself and His own free will. We believe through grace and our election is of grace. Faith is God's gift to believe, and without it, no sinner can believe (Acts 18:27). "It is from Him that we are in Christ Jesus" (1 Cor. 1:30). "Let him who boasts, boast in the Lord" (1 Cor. 1:31). Amen.

The Glory of God

> "For from Him and through Him and to Him are all things.
> To Him be the glory forever. Amen." (Rom. 11:36).

Dear Christian,

God is an incomprehensible Being. A man's mind gets lost in wonder at His infinite power and abilities. My mind gets lost in wonder of His creative genius, and His love and goodness for the soul of man in Jesus. God created an incredible and complex body for man and chose grace, love, and forgiveness for his soul. When I think about God's spirit and eternity, and the perfections of His nature and the wealth of His attributes, my mind is overwhelmed. God is all-glorious. Amen. "Can you discover the depths of God? Its measure is longer than the earth, and broader than the sea" (Job 7:7,9). His judgments are a great deep. We may apprehend parts of the Lord, Christian, but we cannot comprehend Him. We may find out something about God by a diligent search of scripture, but we cannot find Him out to perfection. The brightness of God's glory cannot be fully described. At some time, you may be afraid of God because you cannot fully understand Him, but never forget that God is love (1 John 4:8). Remember that the fear of God is an awe and a reverence of His Being, and the beginning of wisdom (Prov. 9:10). Paul prayed "that the God of our Lord Jesus Christ, the Father of glory, may give you a spirit of wisdom and of revelation in the knowledge of Him" (Eph. 1:17). Paul prayed for you to know the love of Christ (Eph. 3:19). Paul prayed "that the eyes of your heart may be enlightened, so that you may know what is the hope of your calling, what are the riches of the glory of His inheritance in the saints, and what is the surpassing greatness of His power toward us who believe" (Eph. 1:18-19). For himself and us, Paul prayed "that I may know the power of His resurrection" (Phil. 3:10). In the ages to come, God's glory will be revealed in the surpassing riches of His grace in kindness toward us in Christ Jesus (Eph.2:7). Amen.

In the Bible, we learn that it is by God's grace we gained Christ (Eph. 2:8). In the Bible, we learn that it is by God's grace that we gain a righteousness by faith in Jesus (Phil. 3:8-9). Faith is called knowledge (Isa. 53:11). Faith comes by reading the word of God (Rom. 10:17), and God sends you into His word. "Faith is the assurance of things hoped for, the conviction of things not seen" (Heb. 11:1). The assurance and conviction in the gift of faith, by the grace of God, leads to knowing Jesus. The definition of knowing Jesus is eternal life (John 17:3). Faith in Jesus is revealed to your heart by the grace of the Father (Matt. 16:17). Faith in Jesus becomes an experiential knowledge of the power of His resurrection. Faith in Jesus becomes an experiential knowledge of the transforming efficacy and virtue of being in a fellowship with Jesus. Faith in Jesus leads you to know more of His love for you, and a desire after the power to kill sin in your life. Faith delivers assurances to the heart and convictions in your conscience that Jesus is the Christ, the Son of the living God. Throughout the Bible, the words for faith and believe are used interchangeably. The Gospel of John was "written that you may believe that Jesus is the Christ, the Son of the living God; and that believing you may have life in His name" (John 20:31). In our day, the word "belief" refers more to mental agreement, while the word "faith" refers to wholehearted commitment. True biblical faith and belief is not just giving assent to a certain set of facts, Christian, it is trust and commitment that results in a change of behavior. Demons believe in God and shudder because they do not have faith in Jesus (James

2:19). True faith includes belief, but is deeper, stronger, and more enduring than just belief. Faith stirs a person to action (James 2:17). Faith is a gift of grace from God that saves (Eph. 2:8). Examine yourself, is Jesus Christ in you? (2 Cor. 13:5). True faith arises from God's real presence within you, and the results of the gift of faith in Jesus for your life will all be to God's glory in our future. Amen.

From the gift of faith and justification with God after receiving Jesus into your heart, you will gladly choose the path of sanctification and exult in hope of the glory of God (Rom. 5:2). Having been apprehended by Christ, you will experience the joy and pleasures of a new man in you growing in more grace and knowledge. The miracle of being born again and the emerging spiritual life was God's will and work in you according to His good pleasure (Phil. 2:13). You will know that the One responsible for these supernatural events deserves all the glory. You will walk much more carefully after Jesus with fear and trembling to discover His presence, and to receive grace to be obedient. You will study the Bible, pray, listen for His voice, and serve Him through a local church. You will grow in love with Jesus, and learn to love others, especially members of your own family. You will learn to walk humbly and live by the fruit of the Holy Spirit (Gal. 5:22-25). You will know that "you have been bought with a price: therefore, glorify God in your body" (1 Cor. 6:20). God made you and God bought you, Christian, therefore use your body for His glory in the service of the Lord.

The Bible tells us, "As a result of the anguish of His soul, He will see it and be satisfied; By His knowledge the Righteous One, My Servant, will justify the many, and He will bear their iniquities. Therefore, I will allot Him a portion with the great, because He poured out Himself to death" (Isa. 53:11-12). Jesus paid the highest price in a moment of time on the cross, but the joy in His soul would be eternal. By His knowledge means He knew the Father, and knew what He was doing by His sacrifice. It was a change from suffering to triumph and satisfaction when He saw our eternal salvation in heaven. We receive His righteousness through His bearing our iniquities. Christ saw the fruit of His suffering in the building of the church and the glory it would bring the Father. God was glorified, believers justified and Christ satisfied. Christ shall have the glory of bringing in an everlasting righteousness (Dan. 9:24). Christ purchased our salvation. "But by His doing you are in Christ Jesus, who became to us wisdom from God, and righteousness and sanctification and redemption" (1 Cor. 1:30). Christ, through the gift of faith to us, gains our will and affections, and enlightens our spiritual understanding to receive divine truth. We grow in faith by reading His word (Rom. 10:17). "We love Him because He first loved us (1 John 4:19). Amen.

The incomprehensible nature of God's work has taught us humility and reverence leaving no place for our pride. "No flesh should glory in His presence" (1 Cor. 1:29). "Let him who boasts, boast in the Lord" (1 Cor. 1:31). "Let him who boasts boast of this, that he understands and knows Me, that I am the Lord who exercises lovingkindness, justice, and righteousness on earth; for I delight in these things" (Jer. 9:24). In this passage, the King James version of the Bible uses the word "glory" for the word "boast". Jesus Christ came to His glory by the vanquishing of sin and Satan, death and Hades, and the flesh, and the world. This is a great glory for Christ, and "He will divide the booty with the strong" (Isa. 53:12). The spoil which God gives to Christ, He divides with His faithful followers, by the grace of God. The Bible tells us that in "all these things we overwhelmingly conquer through Him who loved us" (Rom. 8:37). "We are children of God, and if children, heirs also, heirs of God and fellow heirs with Christ" (Rom.8:16-17). Heaven is our inheritance purely by an act of God. The Lord Himself is the best part of our inheritance. We shall partake of His glory (John 17:24). We will be where He is and behold His glory. The Lamb is the glory and light of the New Jerusalem" (Rev. 21:23). Christ says, "I desire that those Thou hast given Me, will be with Me where I am to behold My glory" (John 17:24). Our place will be established according to the grace and power of God. It is certain. It is assured. Heaven will be ours by the word and authority of the Son. "Such knowledge is too wonderful for me" (Ps. 139:6). It is a legacy He bequeaths to us as His children. The Father gave the Lord Jesus this glory because He loved Him before the foundation of the world (John 17:24). We will see Him and probably know a lot more about spiritual life. We will always be finite creatures dependent on God's grace and promises. We will be perfectly grateful to God for saving our souls. Amen.

At the time of creation, man was made a little lower than the angels and crowned with glory and honor. Man was appointed over the works of God's hands, and all things were put under in subjection under his feet (Heb. 2:7-8; Ps. 8:4-6). Man was made with noble powers and faculties of soul with a right and dominion over the inferior creatures (Gen. 1-2). God magnified man with glory and honor in the work of creation. Man sinned and fell short of the glory of God (Rom. 3:23). Man lost his glory because of sin. We lost our righteousness which was a glory before God. We failed to trust and obey God. God offers Himself to us as a great treasure in the person of Christ, and we still choose ourselves. We say to God, no thanks (Rom. 1:23). We desecrate and profane the glory of God and set ourselves up for judgment and condemnation. We committed a crime against a holy and perfect God and deserve to feel God's wrath. We were created to live for God's glory and not our glory, which disappears when we die (Ps. 49:17). The good news is that God had a plan in the Gospel of Jesus Christ to restore man back to Himself as a new creature (1 Cor. 5:17). We can be delivered from God's wrath (1 Thess. 1:10). "There is therefore no condemnation for those who are in Christ Jesus" (Rom. 8:1). We needed a Savior. It will forever be God's glory that He chose to bring forth a Savior for lost sinners.

The Bible tells us, "The Word became flesh, and dwelt among us, and we beheld His glory, glory as of the only begotten from the Father, full of grace and truth" (John 1:14). Our Divine Savior took upon Himself human nature and became a sinless man. God manifest in the flesh is a mystery of godliness (1 Tim. 3:16). The disciples clearly and directly beheld His glory. We see the glory of Jesus also. "We all with unveiled face behold as in a mirror the glory of the Lord, are being transformed into the same image from glory to glory, just as from the Lord, the Spirit" (2 Cor. 3:18). The disciples saw the perfections of Jesus on display through His doctrine, miracles, and holiness. He went about doing good. They witnessed His transfiguration (2 Pet. 1:16-18) and resurrection (John 20-21). We see the glory in the Person of Christ by faith (2 Cor. 4:18,5:7). We see Jesus, by the grace of God, through the discernment of our new man and the operation it performs in our hearts. We are fed and transformed by His gracious presence daily to see His glory. The new man in sanctification, "is renewed to a true knowledge according to the One who created him" (Col. 3:10). We were not alive to see Jesus on the earth, but we do behold His glory in our mind's eye by the gracious work of the Holy Spirit. We behold His truth, love, holiness, patience, and faithfulness. We behold Him in the word of God. He cares for us (1 Pet. 5:7). We see the glory of God in the providence of God. God provides things we do not ask for, or even know we need, to bless us (Eph. 3:20).

We see the glory of God in the Word of God. The Bible has great spiritual rewards inside the study of it. We see the truth of Jesus in the Bible and can be convicted to trust and believe the Gospel to be saved and transformed into His image (Acts 16:31). "The god of this world has blinded the minds of the unbelieving, that they might not see the light of the gospel of the glory of Christ" (2 Cor. 4:4). It is in our relationship with Jesus, expressed by diligently beholding Him in His word, that enables us to continually draw from the Holy Spirit the power for a godly life. God is glorified in our hearts when we see Him as He really is according to the scripture. Satan blinds the mind and blocks spiritual vision. The Lord gives sight to the blind (Ps. 146:8; Isa. 42:16). "The Lord is my light and my salvation" (Ps. 27:1). At the new birth, Christian, divine light is poured into the soul and we see our own darkness. After conversion, we see the light of the gospel of the glory of Christ. We see the possibility of the forgiveness of sin, justification, and the strength of salvation. Light has shone into our heart of darkness. The light is the glory of God in the face of Christ that is the great treasure of salvation (2 Cor. 4:6). This power is of God and not ourselves. The Spirit of God illuminates and convicts our soul about our sin, convinces our conscience we need the help of Jesus and rejoices the heart for forgiveness and acceptance by God. The grace of faith is the kind of medicine that God gives us to support our continuing journey into His heart. By the grace of God, we are humbled to look at things that are not seen, and not our own efforts to still be acceptable with God. If we are already a Christian, we confess our sin (1 John 1:9), and recall that light affliction is producing for us an eternal weight of glory (2 Cor. 4:17). In the world, you will experience afflictions called trials, tribulations, and suffering. Afflictions allowed by God are intended to make you better not bitter. They are for God's glory and our glory. They let you know where you are at spiritually and can strengthen you. When you walk through them by faith in Jesus, you honor God. When we see things the way that God does, they weigh a lot less. The idea that something has more weight is meant to mean that it is more valuable. The weight of the eternal reward awaiting us for leaning upon and trusting Jesus will be far greater than the momentary affliction we have here on earth (Rom. 8:18). The good news is that God is working for us an eternal weight of glory. The glory of God is the manifestation of His Being. Jesus is the revelation of God's glory, and the Spirit works to glorify Christ (John 16:14). Our glory comes from God, and the salvation we now experience will inherit an eternal glory from a generous Father in heaven.

God's glory was displayed in the creation of our world. Glory can also be thought of as an attribute of God, because He is the Father of glory (Eph. 1:17). Glory is the expression of God's holiness and character traits such as His wisdom, righteousness, and majesty. He is the King of glory (Ps. 24:8-10). The God of glory (Acts 7:2) is also the Father of mercies (2 Cor. 1:3), Father of spirits (Heb. 12:9) and Father of lights (James 1:17). Our heavenly Father is the source of every blessing. The radiance of God was displayed at the birth of Jesus (Luke 2:9). God has enlightened our hearts so that we may know the hope of His calling and the riches of the glory of His inheritance in the saints (Eph. 1:18). The Christian will behold the glory of Christ (John 17:24; 2 Cor. 3:7-4:6). Only the Lord has meaning, Christian, and we derive our meaning by knowing Him. Amen. To be where God is will be glory. To be like Christ and to do God's will, will be glory. God's glory encompasses His Being and everything He does. He is always all glorious. We are sons of the Father of glory and the King of glory.

The King of kings, that is Jesus; has defeated sin, death, and Hades. He has led captivity captive and gave gifts to men (Eph. 4:8). He opened the gates of heaven (Ps. 24:7, 9) and invited even the weakest believers to enter. I never had clean hands or a pure heart, Christian, but Jesus did, and by the gift of faith from Him, we are in Him and will be conformed to His image and enter heaven. Jesus said, "I am the door; if anyone enters through Me, he shall be saved, and shall go in and out, and find pasture" (John 10:9). Without Christ we can do nothing (John 15:5); the Father draws us (John 6:44) and Christ brings us in (John 10:16). The King of glory is the good shepherd where we find pastures. "He makes me lie down in green pastures; He leads me beside quiet waters, He restores my soul; He guides me in paths of righteousness for His name's sake (Ps. 23:2-3). The Lord is our shepherd (Ps. 23:1; John 10:11). We are the sheep of His pasture. The grace of God showing great love and care for His people is from the exalted office of Christ, a throne of glory indeed. In heaven, we will gladly and sincerely worship the Lord, the Father and King of glory. By the benefits of God's mercies, favors, patience, and faithfulness, that I have experienced, Christian, I long to see His glory. By His healing and saving my soul, I feel safe and welcome because of what He is like. He accepted me, a sinner just as I am. He can only be all-glorious. "The heavens declare the glory of God" (Ps. 119:1). Forever, His infinite beauty and manifold perfections, creation, the Gospel, and all the glory yet to be revealed, He is worthy of all our worship. "Worthy art Thou, our Lord and our God, to receive glory and honor and power; for Thou didst create all things, and because of Thy will they existed, and were created" (Rev. 4:11). We owe all our graces and the glory to come for us to God, Christian, and it is our glory to glorify God. Our gratitude and praise, however deeply and sincerely felt, falls far short of His excellencies. By the grace of God, we have the great honor and privilege to worship Him. Amen.

We were made to bring glory to God. "Everyone who is called by My name, and whom I have created for My glory, whom I have formed, even whom I have made" (Isa. 43:7). Those created by grace and called by God, Christian, will be gathered in Christ as their King into heaven as their home. "For from Him and through Him and to Him are all things. To Him be the glory forever. Amen" (Rom. 11:36). He made us alive and raised us up with Christ because of His love and mercy (Eph. 2:4-6). "In order that in the ages to come He might show the surpassing riches of His grace in kindness toward us in Christ Jesus" (Eph. 2:7). "Whether, then, you eat or drink or whatever you do, do all to the glory of God" (1 Cor. 10:31). We were dead but God quickened us in Christ and gave us spiritual and eternal life. "We are His workmanship" (Eph. 2:10). In our new creation, God has designed and prepared us for good works. God has blessed us with the assistance of the Holy Spirit and with the knowledge of His will. We are to glorify God by our perseverance in holiness. Amen. The riches in the grace of God will be demonstrated in the ages to come (Eph. 2:7). We see some of these riches in being born again in Christ in our time. We know that the next age will be the Messianic age (Heb. 6:5; Rev. 20:4), followed by another age with a new heaven and a new earth (Rev. 21). Beyond this, we do not yet know God's plans. What we do know however, is that the discovery of the beauty and glory of God's grace and holiness will never end.

God's glory is the magnificence and grandeur of His many perfections. God is all glorious in His person and in all His works. God's glory lies in the work of creation, providence, and our redemption. We glorify God when we praise God. "He who offers a sacrifice of thanksgiving honors Me; and to him who orders his way aright I shall show the salvation of God" (Ps. 50:23). To honor God is to glorify God. The song of a redeemed man delights the ears of God. Holy living is evidence of salvation and honors God. Holy living comes with the promise of some assurance to know the Lord's salvation. The mind of a man takes a special notice of the peace that accompanies walking with Jesus. The evidence of the work of God is an increase in holiness of your heart and life with gratitude and praise. We glorify God by fruitfulness. "Herein is My Father glorified, that you bear much fruit, and so prove to be My disciples" (John 15:8). The fruit is love and mercy from graces growing to be like Jesus and works of charity. Fruit is the outflow of a true union with Christ. Fruit is of the Spirit (Gal. 5:22-23) as well as works of service (1 Pet. 4:11). If anyone suffers for being a Christian, let him not feel ashamed, but in the name of Jesus, let him glorify God (1 Pet. 4:16). "Offer to God a sacrifice of thanksgiving, and pay your vows to the Most High; and call upon Me in the day of trouble; I shall rescue you, and you will honor Me" (Ps. 50:14-15). We glorify God for showing us mercy (Rom. 15:9), rescuing us and supplying the needs of the saints in obedience to the gospel of Christ (2 Cor. 9:12-13). We have been bought with a price, and are encouraged to glorify God in our bodies (1 Cor. 6:20).

The scripture communicates the presence of God as the glory of God. This was evident for the person of Christ (John 1; Col. 1-2), the Holy Spirit (John 14-16; Acts 2:1-4) and in the new heavens and earth (Rev. 21-22). The glory of the Lord has always existed. The Old Testament describes several times when the manifestation of God's glory was associated with God's presence. Although the word "Shekinah" is not used in scripture, it expresses the visible glory and presence of God. It means "One who dwells" and is associated with God's glory dwelling with man. The first instance in scripture may have been in the garden of Eden where God placed a "flaming sword" to guard the way to the tree of life after sin entered the world. The flaming sword was to be removed by Jesus Christ. The curse of sin would be broken, and a new and living way open to man by looking for the promised seed of Jesus. In another instance, "there appeared a smoking oven and a flaming torch which passed between the pieces" of the sacrifice (Gen. 15:17). On this occasion, God gave assurance and made a covenant with Abraham that his seed would be given this land. God's covenants with man are made by sacrifices (Ps. 50:5). We may know that God accepts our sacrifice, that is Christ, if He kindles in our souls a holy fire of devout affections for Himself. The Shekinah glory was displayed before Moses in the burning bush that was not consumed (Ex. 3:2-10). At this time, God gave Moses the important mission to bring the sons of Israel out of Egypt. Later, both Moses and Elijah would experience the manifestation of God's glory on Mt. Sinai. Moses prayed to see God's glory, and the Lord graciously let him see His back and proclaimed His goodness (Ex. 33:18-23). On the other hand, Elijah was called out of a cave when the Lord was passing by and a great wind broke the rocks. This was followed by an earthquake and then fire, but the Lord was not in any of these strong terrible effects. After the fire, the sound of a gentle wind blowing was heard and in it was the voice of God. God chose the way to make known His mind and will for Elijah in a whisper (1 Kings 19:9-15). The still, small voice of God is unlike anything you have heard before, and will inspire humility and reverence. Amen.

God has chosen His own specific ways and times He will speak to your heart. Hearing His voice speaks favor to you. Sometimes the voice will be clearer and with understanding than at other times, but you will know He has spoken. We cannot flee from the Spirit of God (Ps. 139:7). In the gospel of Christ, we do not come to a mountain with terrible effects and full of fear, but to Mt. Zion and Jesus, the mediator of a New Covenant (Heb. 12:18-24). God usually speaks to us in ways that have a still and small voice, but not always. The warnings of God can mean you are in trouble, and He can notice what you are thinking and doing, and set circumstances up around you that will get your attention. God can speak with power to our conscience. The gospel has a glorious kindness in it. Christ is the mediator that speaks pardon for our sin and peace and love to our souls. God is holy, and He speaks most clearly to us when our thoughts and behaviors violate the testimony of being a Christian. He cherishes for us to walk in a way that matches an obedience of faith. He can be patient, but not forever without meaningful consequences to get your attention. In Jesus, He displays a patience and a faithfulness that is a kinder justice for His children than was heard from the law on Mt. Sinai. He has not lowered the standard. A Christian is called to holiness (1 Thess. 4:7). A Christian is predestined to be conformed to the image of His Son (Rom. 8:29). We are to put on the new self, which in the likeness of God has been created in righteousness and holiness of the truth (Eph. 4:24). We need the grace of God to walk and worship the Lord acceptably. Our responsibility is to discover, with fear and trembling, what God has put into us; while His grace is present to will and to work for His good pleasure (Phil. 2:12-13). Our perseverance in Jesus is to the glory of God and not something from our good nature. It is our responsibility to work with God's gifts of faith and fear that leads to obedience and the true worship of God. Let God's glory always be in the conclusions from your mind in your life's thoughts. God will take us to a place for sincere and serious worship that is worthy of our great King Jesus.

The appearance of the glory of God also appeared in the events surrounding the exodus of God's children from Egypt. The personal manifestations of God to Moses (Ex. 3-4, 32-34), and from the glory cloud, the Tabernacle and in the Ark of the Covenant (Ex. 13-14, 20, 24-25), all confirm the truth of God's presence in the covenant that He made with the people through Moses. In the Old Testament, Moses was commanded by God to build an Ark of acacia wood to be called the Ark of the Covenant (Ex. 25:10). The Ark contained the Mosaic Law, a pot of manna and the rod of Aaron. It had a cover called the mercy seat where God would dwell inside the Holy of Holies of the tabernacle behind a curtain or veil. The symbolism of the Ark in the tabernacle for us today, is as a picture of the Person and saving work of Christ. Later, the curtain or veil in the temple was torn in two, from top to bottom, between the Holy Place and the Holy of Holies when Jesus died on the cross. It signified that the way to God was now open to man through His Sons obedience even unto death. We can now draw near to God's throne of grace with confidence because of the shed blood of Jesus (Heb. 10:19-22). The veil that was upon our hearts to know and trust Jesus for salvation has been torn and removed by the power of God. He made a new and living way for us to see and experience the glory of God. Amen. Before Jesus died on the cross, the Holy Spirit did not come into the hearts of people who believed in the Messiah. Today, we are in the presence of God continuously, and can call upon Him anytime. We have been born again (John 3:5), and have received a new heart and spirit (Ezek. 36:26). Moreover, God has put His Spirit within us (Ezek. 36:27). The Spirit of God intercedes for us with groanings too deep for words (Rom. 8:26). The miracle of spiritual life that God gives and nourishes in us reveals His strong power and authority in the spiritual realm. He is the foundation for our ability and blessing to worship God in spirit and in truth (John 4:24). It is the glory of God in us that proves our victory in Christ. Amen. The first way to the tree of life in the garden of Eden had been closed for a long time. The only way back to the tree of life today is by receiving Jesus Christ into your heart as Savior and Lord. God draws and calls souls to Jesus to be saved from the penalty of sin that was paid by Christ. The grace of God to save us, is as it should be, the glory of God in heaven.

God's glory was revealed in visions to Isaiah (Isa. 6:15), and Ezekiel (Ezek. 1:22-28, 3:12-23, 10:1-22) and, also God's people (Isa. 40:5, 43:6-7). The glory of God was revealed in the temple of God. David's son, Solomon built a beautiful temple, and when it was completed and the Ark brought into it, that the cloud of glory filled the house of the Lord (1Kings 8:10). God chose the temple where His name dwells and where His mercy may be obtained. Several hundred years later, Ezekiel was given a vision of the glory of the Lord progressively departing from the temple (Ezek. 10), and shortly after this, another vision of a new temple (Ezek. 43:2-5). The new temple was rebuilt in Jerusalem under Ezra and Nehemiah around 560 BC, partially fulfilling Ezekiel's prophecy. The promise of the Messiah was yet unfulfilled. According to the New Testament, the fulfillment of the Old Testament prophecies, are found in the person and work of Jesus Christ. "The word became flesh, and dwelt among us, and we beheld His glory, glory as of the only begotten from the Father, full of grace and truth" (John 1:14). The connection to God's dwelling and the Tabernacle and God's glory is compelling (Ex. 33-34). The new tabernacle and temple are Jesus Christ, meaning "God with us" (Isa. 7:14). The glory of God in the face of Christ is seen by true believers. We do not see the pillar of cloud and fire, but we do see the obedience of faith from our new life. We see Jesus by faith from a renewed spirit that works in our heart the truth, the life, His love, and the comforts of holiness (John 14:6).

"Christ is the radiance of God's glory and the exact representation of His nature, and upholds all things by the word of His power. When He had made purification of sins, He sat down at the right hand of the majesty on high" (Heb. 1:3). Christ is the Shekinah of God. "It was the Father's good pleasure for all the fulness to dwell in Him" (Col. 1:19, 2:9). Christ is the "Lord of glory" (1 Cor. 2:8). He made known the riches of His glory upon vessels of mercy, which He prepared beforehand for glory" (Rom. 9:23). Thus, the same Shekinah glory now dwells or rests upon those who are in Christ. Amen. Paul wants us "to know the riches of the glory of His inheritance in the saints" (Eph. 1:18), "which is Christ in you, the hope of glory" (Col. 1:27). The presence of the Holy Spirit in us is a representation of the Shekinah glory in the tabernacle. The indwelling of the Spirit makes the believers body a temple for the indwelling of the Lord Jesus Christ, the Shekinah glory (Rom. 8:9-11;1 Cor.3:16, 6:19-20). The power of Christ dwells in you (2 Cor. 12:9). Jesus has risen, and ascended to the Father, the new temple is complete. By the grace of God, we discover it is operational. Amen.

The glorification of Christ was predicted. The Father promised to glorify the Son by giving Him a people and nations that did not know God (Isa. 55:5). The glorification of Christ was prayed for. "Father, glorify Thy name. Then came a voice out of heaven, saying, I have both glorified it, and will glorify it again" (John 12:28). The name of God was glorified by the doctrine, miracles, holiness, and goodness of Christ. He can and will secure His own glory. He has overcome the world. The Father would glorify His own Son (John 8:32). The glorification of Christ was accomplished by the Father (John 13:31-32), and the Holy Spirit (John 16:13-14), as well as His own miracles (John 11:4), and resurrection (Acts

3:13). In the case of Lazarus, his death and resurrection "was not unto death, but for the glory of God, that the Son of God may be glorified by it" (John 11:4). The Holy Spirit would glorify Jesus by taking from Him and disclosing it to us. The Spirit was given to abide with us (John 14:16) and be our guide (Rom. 8:14) for our journey of spiritual life. The Holy Spirit would teach us the truth for our strength and comfort, and to honor and glorify Christ in our hearts (John 16:7-14). His presence will humble and convince us of our unspeakable blessings in following Jesus. Once we were blind, but now we can see the glory of God in Jesus, our Lord.

What God does in us and for us in this life, through His grace, will appear in the future as His glory. We have the power, providence, promises and the love of God to live upon in this life. He carries our hearts in His own heart, and fills our soul with His riches in Christ (Eph. 3:8). The Lord becomes the complete and perfect portion of our soul (Lam. 3:24). The bestowing of God's favor, good will, love, and pleasure upon His people in the Gospel covenant of grace is all great and glorious. God becomes the most precious gift, with unimaginable value, in the soul of the believing Christian. The Spirit of God grows faith in Jesus into a clear conscience, with a profound hope and assurance of a glorious union and fellowship with God. The glory of the riches of Christ, that before was only a hidden mystery with God, "is Christ in you, the hope of glory" (Col. 1:27). God gives gifts to us, that will be glory for us. He gives light (John 1:7-9; Eph. 5:14), and repentance (Rom. 2:4). Christ gives His blood (Matt. 20:28), His Spirit (Rom. 5:5), the pardon of sin (Acts 5:31) and precious promises (2 Pet. 1:4). He gives glory (John 10:28) and a crown of righteousness (2 Tim. 4:8). He gives grace (John 1:16) and peace (John 14:27). The glory that God gives us is understanding of Jesus, freedom from sin, and joyful affections for Himself (Ps. 16:11). In a serious examination of ourselves, we come to know and rejoice in Jesus. The righteousness of Christ becomes ours by the gift of faith and we love the brethren (1 John 3:14). Our hope in Jesus is a light from the work of God, disclosing to our hearts (John 14:21), that Christ is all glorious in our eternal life. Amen.

The glorious Father sent the Son to accomplish the work He gave Him to do before the world was created, and the Son glorified the Father on earth (John 17:4-5). God chose, adopted, redeemed, and sealed believers "to the praise of the glory of His grace" (Eph. 1:6, 12, 14). In saving a people for Himself, God displayed His grace and brings glory to Himself and Christ. The glory can be realized in the incarnation (John 1:14), birth (Luke 2:9,14), and miracles (John 2:11). The glory of Christ was revealed in His transfiguration (Matt. 17:1-5), in His suffering and crucifixion (John 12:23-28), in His resurrection and exaltation (Luke 24:36; 1 Tim. 3:16), and ascension (Acts 1:9-11). The glory of Christ will be seen at His return to earth (Matt. 25:31; Mark 13:26) and in heaven (Rev. 5:12, 2 Thess. 1:7; Titus 2:13; Matt. 25:31). Jesus was briefly humbled, but "because of the suffering of death crowned with glory and honor, that by the grace of God He might taste death for everyone" (Heb. 2:9). He will have the glory forever and ever. Amen. (Heb. 13:21). Because He humbled Himself to the point of death on a cross, "God highly exalted Him, and bestowed on Him the name which is above every name, that at the name of Jesus every knee should bow, of those who are in heaven, and on earth, and under the earth, and that every tongue should confess that Jesus Christ is Lord, to the glory of God the Father" (Phil. 2:9-11). He was both divine and human. He put on the rags of human nature and the form of a servant and died for us. He will be honored and empowered to the glory of God. "All judgment has been given to the Son, in order that all may honor the Son, even as they honor the Father" (John 5:22-23). Instead of the Father being the judge, the Son will be the judge, and honored and received as equal with God.

In God's eternal plan to glorify Himself, He decided to share His glory with "vessels of mercy" whom He "prepared beforehand for glory" (Rom. 9:23). The glory would not only be for Himself, but was for us also. We have peace with God "by grace through faith in which we stand; and we exult in hope of the glory of God" (Rom. 5:2). He predestined us to adoption, as through Jesus Christ to Himself, to the praise of the glory of His grace (Eph.

1:5-6). Christ pours out the Spirit for His glorious indwelling on all who believe (John 7:38-39). The Holy Spirit is the bond of our union with Christ, and He bears witness with our spirit that we are children of God (Rom. 8:14-16). Our goal, is to "be glorified with Him" (Rom. 8:17). "From our innermost being shall flow rivers of living water" (John 7:38). When you have been filled and satisfied by the Lord, Christian, His life can flow to other people. "The glory which Thou has given Me I have given to them; that they may be one, just as We are one" (John 17:22). We are to be perfected by unity. Jesus expressed the desire that we would be with Him that we may behold His glory (John 17:24). In our life in this world, Christian, this prayer has, in part, been answered. The glory mentioned here is not a glory that as God He already possessed, but rather a glory that the Father has given Him as the reward for His work as the incarnate Son. An inheritance has been given to Christ (Heb. 1:2), and we become joint-heirs with Christ Jesus (Rom. 8:17). In bearing our iniquities, He poured out His soul unto death. He received a portion with the great and will divide the spoil with the strong (Isa. 53:12). The "strong" are the believers and followers of Christ. The glory for us now is by the confidence and assurance, that is by faith, that God can do this and will keep His word. The glory for us now is the sense and enjoyment of the gift of faith of being one with Christ. The gift and presence of the Spirit of God and our unity with Christ now is a great glory, that is yet to be perfected. The best is yet to come. Amen.

We are being transformed by the Spirit from glory to glory (2 Cor. 3:18) through Christs sacrifice for us in His death (Heb. 2:9-10). God is the first cause and the end of all things. To God be the glory. We have been regenerated and adopted to enjoy the glorious privileges of grace in the gospel to be heirs of Christ. We will be among the many sons He brings into glory, by the grace of God. He is the Author, Captain, and Maker of our salvation. God thought to make us righteous through the suffering of Jesus (Heb. 2:10). Many sons will be raised to honor and brought into Christs glory as the reward for His suffering. We are brought into His glory as lost sheep. How great is our God. Any "suffering we have in the present time will not be worthy to be compared with the glory that will be revealed to us" (Rom. 8:18). The eternal weight of glory will be seen by us, and revealed in us, to be enjoyed by us forever. The suffering now is short and small compared to a future glory that will be priceless and eternal. Our hope of glory is Christ living in us (Col. 1:27). Our life is now hidden with Christ in God, to be revealed in the future with Him in glory (Col.3:3-4). We know our soul has been born again, and that the gift of faith God provides is supernatural. He nourishes us with His love and we are secure in His power. The promise to us is from God, who cannot lie (Heb. 6:18). Jesus said, "because I live, you shall live also" (John 14:19). "I have been crucified with Christ; and it is no longer I who live, but Christ lives in me: and the life which I now live in the flesh I live by faith in the Son of God, who loved me, and delivered Himself up for me" (Gal. 2:20). It will be the glory of Jesus to have His redeemed with Himself when He comes (1 Thess. 1:10); and it will be our glory to be coming with Him. Amen.

"If Christ be in you, the body is dead because of sin; but the spirit is alive because of righteousness" (Rom. 8:10). The indwelling of the Holy Spirit is the indwelling of Christ Himself. We are strengthened with power through His Spirit in the inner man so that Christ may dwell in our hearts through faith (Eph. 3:16-17). "The Spirit of Him who raised Jesus from the dead dwells in you, He will also give life to your mortal bodies through His Spirit" (Rom. 8:11). Sin destroys us, but our spirit is made alive because Christ lives in us and the righteousness of God has been imputed to us. The new nature cannot sin, because it is the divine nature of God (1 John 3:9). "So now, no longer am I the one doing it, but sin which indwells me" (Rom. 7:17). We are a saved man, wrestling against the sinful propensities. We have no excuse to sin. By the grace of God, we wake up and discover its presence. By the grace of God, we own it and then disown it. Sin dwells in the flesh and nature of the old man. The believer is a divided person, and needs God's grace to be rescued from himself. Our rescue from sin and the old man, is only by the love and power of God. That is why, God gets all the glory. Amen. We find ourselves in the conflict of two natures (Rom. 7:14-23). "It is the Spirit who gives life" (John 6:63). Our spirit is made alive by the Holy Spirit of God. God's grace in the soul is the origin of our new desires and nature. We must appear as if we have never sinned, which happens by the forgiveness of our sin. This is made possible only by Jesus. He removed the penalty for sin from us and bore the consequences of our sin in His body. It is called justification, and God gets all the glory. It is by the imputed righteousness of Jesus to our account, that we are made spiritually alive. The miracle of our justification, by the grace of God, will be a grand centerpiece inside the glory of God.

"Behold, I tell you a mystery; we shall not all sleep, but we will be changed, in a moment, in the twinkling of an eye, at the last trumpet; for the trumpet will sound, and the dead will be raised imperishable, and we shall all be changed" (1 Cor. 15:51-52). "Thanks be to God, who gives us the victory through our Lord Jesus Christ" (1 Cor. 15:57). The saints will be in glory by the power of God and we will praise the Lord forever. Death is swallowed up in victory (1 Cor. 15:54). To God be the glory. It is a mystery; our old self was crucified with Christ and we died with Him. The Christian life becomes a life where Christ is increasing and we are decreasing. It is a glorious transaction that is complete when we are citizens of heaven (Phil. 3:20). We are hidden from a world that does not understand us, from a devil that is trying to destroy us, and even at times, our own selves. The truth is, Christian, the security of our life is not realized in our own weak experience, but in His glorious power and love by faith. Let your mind and heart live in heaven with Jesus, and begin now to live and enjoy the light of your glorious inheritance.

The same Spirit that calls individuals to Christ, unites us all together as a body of believers called the church. "Do you not know that you are a temple of God, and that the Spirit of God dwells in you? (1 Cor. 3:16). "We are the temple of the living God; just as God said, I will dwell in them and walk among them; and I will be their God, and they shall be My people" (2 Cor. 6:16). Christ is the head of the body, the church (Col. 1:10). God "put all things in subjection under His feet, and gave Him as head over all things to the church, which is His body, the fulness in Him who fills all in all" (Eph. 1:22-23). Christ is the foundation or cornerstone upon which the temple or church is built (1 Cor. 3:11). "For we are God's fellow workers; you are God's field, God's building" (1 Cor. 3:9). "We are Christs body and individually members of it" (1 Cor. 12:28). The body is built up by the equipping of the saints for ministry and the building up of itself in love (Eph. 4:12,16). The mission of the church is to evangelize the world (Matt. 28:18-20), guard the truth (2 Tim. 2:1-12) and edify the saints (Eph. 4:13). The church is to function as a witness and give a testimony of praise to the glory of God in Christ. The church was formed on the day of Pentecost (Acts 2), and to God be all the glory for the church. The calling of the church is very important and is fully associated with Christ and His dominion and glory. A lot of folks today minimize the value of the church, and speak of it as being unnecessary for salvation and growth in grace and knowledge. Perhaps, some of these folks do not really know the Lord, and that He Himself is building the church (Matt. 16:18). Tragically, someday these folks may suffer eternal destruction, away from the glory of His power (2 Thess. 1:8-10). "Christ loved the church and gave Himself up for her, that He might sanctify her," and "that He might present to Himself the church in all her glory, having no spot or wrinkle" (Eph. 5:25-27). The church is described as faithful saints (Eph. 1:1), His workmanship (Eph. 2:10), children of light (Eph. 5:8), the brethren (Eph. 6:23), and a dwelling of God in the Spirit (Eph. 2:22). We grow, by the grace of God, into a holy temple in the Lord (Eph. 2:21). The glorifying of the church is intended in the sanctifying of its members, and the mission work it performs.

The church exists to magnify and make known the glory of God in Jesus Christ. Members of the church are being sanctified by the grace of God, and will know the full glory in heaven. We are "being transformed into the same image from glory to glory as we behold the glory of the Lord (2 Cor. 3:18). We will suffer (Rom. 5:3-5; 1 Pet. 5:10), but "keep on rejoicing: so that also at the revelation of His glory, you may rejoice with exultation" (1 Pet.

4:13). "If you are reviled for the name of Christ, you are blessed, because the Spirit of glory and of God rests upon you" (1 Pet. 4:14). When Jesus comes again, He will be glorified in His saints and marveled at among all who have believed (2 Thess. 1:10). The Holy Spirit will rest upon the Christian as the Shechinah glory cloud rested upon the Old Testament tabernacle and Solomons temple. God's presence strengthens and encourages believers today as the first-fruits of our future inheritance to come. The glory can rest on a believer at any time, but especially at times of great suffering and death. We will be raised in glory, being conformed to the glorious image of Christ (1 Cor. 15:43). The future will reveal the great depth of the glory of God. "I saw a new heaven and a new earth and the new Jerusalem coming down out of heaven from God. The Lord God, the Almighty, and the Lamb are its temple. The city has no need of the sun or the moon to shine upon it, for the glory of God has illumined it, and its lamp is the Lamb, and the nations shall walk by its light" (Rev. 21:1-2, 22-24). Amen.

God shall reign over everything forever, Christian, in the glory of His mercy and justice, founded in the covenant of His grace. The people of God will ultimately receive glory, honor, and eternal life. He chose "to make known the riches of His glory upon vessels of mercy, which He prepared beforehand for glory" (Rom. 9:23). The bodies of believers will be raised in glory (1 Cor. 15:43) and faithful elders will receive an unfading crown of glory (1 Pet. 5:4). God will supply every need of yours according to His riches in glory in Christ Jesus (Eph. 4:19). God is rich in mercy, He loved us, quickened us, saved us, and raised us up to sit in heavenly places in Christ Jesus (Eph. 2:4-6). He has acted in kindness toward us in Christ Jesus. Why would He do this? He did this because He chose to do this, of His own free will and it was pleasing to Him (Isa. 46:10; Ps. 115:3, 135:6; Rom. 9:15-18,23; Eph. 1:4-12, 2:10). He had the power to accomplish this great work (Luke 1:37; Rom. 8:29-30; Heb. 7:25). All things are possible with God (Mark 10:27). He did this "in order to show that in the ages to come He might show the surpassing riches of His grace in kindness toward us in Christ Jesus" (Eph. 2:7).

It is through Jesus Christ that we derive every benefit. Thus, it is only fitting that He receive all the glory. He is the only channel and mediator between God and man. We are saved by the unsearchable riches of the kindness in His grace. God sent forth (Gal. 4:4) and gave His Son (John 3:16). He did not spare Him (Rom. 8:32) and made Him to be sin for us (1 Cor. 5:21). The Lord laid on Him the iniquity of us all (Isa. 53:6). The Being and love of the Father is a great mystery. The cost, grief, and suffering for us to become His children is an unsearchable measure of grace. He is called the Father of spirits (Heb. 12:9), the Father of lights (James 1:17), eternal Father (Isa. 9:6), and the Father of glory (Eph. 1:17). God is the source and the embodiment of all glory. God is glory and what He does is always all glorious. The glorious Father glorified the Son while He was on earth, and God was glorified in Him (John 13:31). The glory that is in Him is shared with us and He will manifest His glory to us (2 Cor. 3:18; John 17:22-24). We will stand in the presence of the Father of glory. Paul prays that the eyes of our hearts may be enlightened to know the riches of His glory in the saints (Eph. 1:18), and the kind intention of His will in the Beloved, to the praise of the glory of His grace (Eph. 1:5-6). He predestined us as sons through Jesus Christ to Himself to the praise of the glory of His grace. The Son made Himself of no reputation and took unto Himself human nature (Phil. 2:6-8). In life, He was a man of sorrows (Isa. 53:3) and endured the contradiction of sinners (Heb. 12:3). For our salvation, He endured the pain and suffering of being crucified and buried in a grave (John 19). He bore the full penalty of all sin, a suffering we cannot imagine. This is the amazing grace that will show the riches of the kindness of God the Father, and God the Son, and God the Holy Spirit. Amen.

God has done what was impossible for us to do, "to the praise of the glory of His grace, which He freely bestowed on us in the beloved" (Eph. 1:6). Let me be clear, Christian, our salvation is not about our goodness in any way. The great truth is that forgiveness of sin and eternal life is a revelation of the glory of God. Amen. The Old Testament is important, especially in the passages that foretell of the coming of the Messiah, Jesus Christ the Son of God (Isa.

9:6, 11:1-5, 53). Our redemption is the glory of God. The presence of the church is the glory of God. "Glory to God in the highest" accompanied the announcement of the incarnation of Jesus to the shepherds (Luke 2:14). God commanded the light about Jesus to shine in our hearts the knowledge of the glory of God because of Jesus (2 Cor. 4:6). When we sin, we are not giving God all the glory He deserves. Our salvation is the glory of God. The heavens declare the glory of God (Ps. 19:1). The defeat of Satan and the power of death reveals the glory of God. The righteousness and holiness of God are the glory of God. The glory of God's grace is seen in His grace that made us accepted in the Beloved. We have been highly favored by the grace of God, which is the glory of God. God has fully manifested His glory in our salvation in and through Jesus Christ. Our salvation in Jesus reveals the love of God (John 3:16). He made His Beloved a sin offering for us that we might be made the righteousness of God in Him. The love of Jesus for us and our salvation was revealed in what He was willing to endure in becoming a man. He felt forsaken by God (Matt. 27:46). His relationship to the Father was one of love, and He was called the beloved Son (Mark 1:11). Because we are in Him, we are loved by God. In the High Priestly Prayer, Jesus prayed for us to be one with God and perfect in unity, and that we would be loved by the Father even as He loved the Son (John 17:23). It is the pinnacle of spiritual revelation and salvation to be in the Beloved, and know God loves the Christian as He loves the Son. This is the indescribable height of the richness of God's grace and glory that will draw forth an everlasting and adoring worship.

Glorifying God is the expected and fitting response of God's people to God. "Ascribe to the Lord the glory due His name" (Ps. 29:2). All the glory belongs to God. "For from Him and through Him and to Him are all things. To Him be the glory forever. Amen." (Rom. 11:36). God's glory, Christian, is the conclusion, for in His divine counsels and actions of creation, providential influences and salvation was by His choosing for His glory and our blessing. "To the only wise God, through Jesus Christ, be the glory forever. Amen." (Rom. 16:27). To Him who released us from our sins by His blood, be glory and dominion forever (Rev. 1:5-6). Our salvation was done in love and made personal when He gave His only begotten Son (John 3:16). The Son was a faithful witness, the first-born from the dead and a great friend of the church. He will be the judge of the world. We are saved by His grace through faith (Eph. 2:8). By the grace of God, we fix our eyes on Jesus, the author and perfector of our faith (Heb. 12:2). Jesus Christ trusted God the Father, and purchased the spirit of faith for us in His own work. He is the cause of faith and the finisher of the work of faith in power in our souls. "We are His workmanship, created in Christ Jesus for good works, which God prepared beforehand" (Eph. 2:10). He is the judge and rewarder of our faith. In time, we learn the gift of faith was indispensable and became a conquering grace. In time, by the grace of God, we learn to be personal with God. In time, we learn to confess our sins and find that "God is faithful and righteous to forgive us our sins and to cleanse us of all unrighteousness" (1 John 1:9). In time, we learn "that whatever is born of God overcomes the world; and this is the victory that has overcome the world----our faith" (1 John 5:4). Faith cleaves to Christ, and by the Spirit of grace, sanctifies the heart. Faith sees the work of Christ alone was necessary for our salvation. You will know a life of progressive holiness. To God will be the glory.

"Now to Him who is able, to keep you from stumbling, and to make you stand in the presence of His glory blameless with great joy, to the only God our Savior, through Jesus Christ our Lord, be glory, majesty, dominion, and authority, before all time and now and forever. Amen." (Jude 23-24). God is willing and able to bring you before the glory of God. Never forget; the righteousness of Jesus has been imputed to you because of the Savior. Your sins cannot ruin this privilege or your hard work earn it. The object of faith is to become the object of sense and life. We all will be given to Jesus as His reward to share in His glory, not one will be lost (John 18:9). Now, we look at this glory from a great distance, but soon it will be more visible and fill our only reality. Now, our faults and weakness fill us with doubts and sorrows, but soon we will have perfect joy. We will be in the best to come. What a great glory that God has let His ways become known for us with a great Savior. We will be like Him (1 John3;2). We will not be disappointed (Rom. 9:33). The precious value of Christ will be for those who believe (1 Pet. 2:7). "Worthy is the Lamb that was slain to receive power and riches and wisdom and might and honor and glory and blessing" (Rev. 5:12).

The main question for everyone who ever lived to answer is, whom do you believe Jesus is? Although several names were offered by other people, Peter answered, "Thou art the Christ, the Son of the living God." Jesus answered him, "Blessed are you Peter, because flesh and blood did not reveal this to you, but My Father who is in heaven" (Matt. 16:16-17). The confession of Christ as God in the Christian faith is an act of revelation by God into the heart and mind of man. God the Father, by supernatural means, revealed the truth about Jesus to the saved sinner. You cannot come to Jesus unless the Father draws you (John 6:44). The gift to know Jesus is revealed by the gift of faith; it means to have the conviction of things not seen and the assurance of things hoped for (Heb. 11:1). To know Jesus is to know spiritual joy (Luke 2:10-11), and is a token of God's favor. Amen.

It is impossible to give God the glory if you do not know that He is real, what He has done, or have a saving relationship, with understanding, what He is really like. If you have not read the Bible or studied it much, then there is a good chance you do not know about the glory of God or His goodness or fear Him in a godly manner. You may be living with your opinions given to you from the world, and you may die with those same opinions. Everybody's life is different. Too many people ignore God. It may be that the church or a salvation experience is not something you give much thought to. Life can get busy. The only suggestion or advice I can make here is to take some time to get to know Him for yourself. The conscience is the place that the Lord will speak to your heart about sin, Jesus, forgiveness, holiness, judgment, and eternal life. Your decision has eternal consequences. If you desire to know the Lord and or draw closer to Him, I suggest you take some time to be with Him. Take time to recall and understand the origin and growth of your faith in Christ. Take time to recall when you came to Jesus and were baptized. Take time to recall when you started to read the Bible, and it became the word of God to you. Take time to recall the value of the church and the testimony of fellow believers. Take time to read good commentaries and get help to understand some parts from trustworthy believers. If necessary, take time to recall why you quit going to church. Take time to recall all the times of your growth in grace and knowledge. Take time to recall your service, hopes, dreams, and beliefs in the Lord. Be diligent and not lazy about your spiritual life. Take time to recall the regrets and failures in your Christian life and the patience of God. Take time to recall whether you are sincere with God. "Greater is He that is in you than he that is in the world" (1 John 4:4). In my life, Christian, it took time for me to learn and grow in grace and knowledge. God gets all the glory.

In my past, I surrendered some things to the Lord, but not everything, and I was wrong. Be patient, God is patient. God is kind, good, gentle, and faithful. He is a source of peace and love for us because of Jesus (Gal. 5:22). Come with your all to God, and He shows up when He knows you are ready. "Draw near to God and He will draw near to you" (James 4:8). Pursue intimacy with the Lord our God. "Humble yourself in the presence of the Lord and He will exalt you" (James 4"10). Man is guilty with a sin problem and subject to the penalty of not being right with God. By the grace and power of God, we are drawn humbly and sincerely by God to the gospel to see the answer in Jesus to be forgiven. In our drawing near to God, we discover He has drawn near to us. We discover God's love, the godly fear of God, and the glory to come with following Jesus. Coming to Jesus is the first step. God sends us into His word to grow by grace in faith (Rom. 10:17), and in the knowledge of the way, the truth, and the life with God (John 14:6). You will discover Him coming to help you in every hour of your need. When you draw near to Him in faith, trust, and obedience, He draws nearer in His presence and deliverance. God comforts us, raises our hearts above the world and lifts us up to see the wisdom and glory of Christ. "He that must be knighted must kneel for it"

(Thomas Adams). We need the grace of God to see God, and when we see Him, we see more of His glory. When we see more of His glory, it leads us into a deeper worship. We must let God, be God.

The patience that God has shown me has been incredible. I will be eternally grateful. I was ignorant and weak, and He still took the time to love me, and grow me in grace, faith, and knowledge to be sincere with Him. In my life, God demonstrated perfect patience, which strongly supports His love for me. To know the love of God in Christ for us, is to begin to see the glory of God. I have learned that "God is merciful and gracious, slow to anger and abundant in lovingkindness and truth" (Ps. 86:15). To God be all the glory for showing grace in place of our unworthiness, mercy and patience against our sin, and His remaining faithful to the promises He gives us in Jesus. "Now to the King eternal, immortal, invisible, the only God, be honor and glory forever and ever. Amen." (1 Tim. 1:17). God's gracious ways with us fills us with admiration and awe of His glorious attributes. "Praise the Lord, praise the Lord, let the earth hear His voice! Praise the Lord, praise the Lord, let the people rejoice! O come to the Father, thro' Jesus the Son, and give Him the glory, great things He hath done" (F. Crosby, W. Doane;1875).

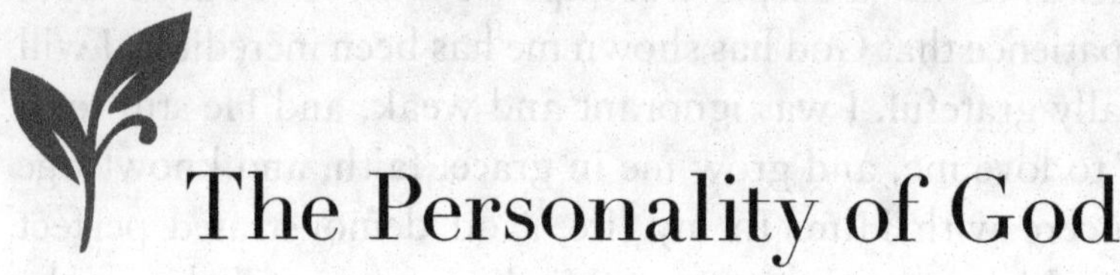

The Personality of God

> "The Lord, the Lord God, compassionate and gracious, slow to anger, and abounding in lovingkindness and truth; who keeps lovingkindness for thousands, who forgives iniquity, transgression and sin; yet He will by no means leave the guilty unpunished" (Ex. 34:6-7).

Dear Christian,

"The Lord is the true God; He is the living God and the everlasting King" (Jer. 10:10). God exists as a Trinity and is the Person who created us (Gen. 1:26). He loves us and offers salvation to us (John 3:16). He cares for us and desires to provide for us (1 Pet. 5:7). The Lord is Life, has life in Himself and is the fountain of life for man. He is the king of eternity. Amen. We cannot begin to know or understand God, or have a relationship with Him unless He reveals Himself to us. We should not form an opinion about God until we are informed about God. Fortunately for man, we have His word. We have the scripture that God has given us to study, to learn what He has said and done. He tells us that "He has magnified His word according to all His name" (Ps. 138:2). The name of God includes all the perfections of God. He tells us that "His word which goes forth from His mouth; it shall not return to Him empty without accomplishing what He desires" (Isa. 55:11). The Bible is the book of the revelations of God. There is especially the knowledge of how to be forgiven of sin and your soul saved. The Bible is the place we discover the promises of God and the faithful power of God to keep His word. In the Bible, we behold the wonders of creation and the providence of God. In the Bible, we discover the precious Person of Jesus Christ. In the Bible, we discover the mystery of godliness; that is, the incarnation, death, and resurrection of Jesus Christ (1 Tim. 3:16). The Bible tells us that He was proclaimed among the nations and believed on in the world. He is being vindicated in our hearts today by the Spirit, and is coming again (Rev. 19:11-16). How we will be judged, and the future destiny of every human established is clearly outlined in the word of God. The Christian knows the Bible is the Word of God. Amen.

It is into the Word of God that He sends man to have His truth revealed to him. "The word of God is living and active and sharper than any two-edged sword" (Heb. 4:12). "All scripture is inspired by God" (2 Tim. 3:16) and "men moved by the Holy Spirit spoke from God" (2 Pet. 1:21). David said, "The Spirit of the Lord spoke by me, and His word was on my tongue" (2 Sam. 23:2). The word of God is powerful in the heart to convince, convert, and comfort the sinner and the saint about the kingdom of Christ and the love of God. Since the word is alive, its message can seize upon our conscience and move to strengthen the gift of faith in Jesus. It carries supernatural power through the Holy Spirit to transform your life, by "beating down" the old man, and "raising up" a new creature in Christ. Some people do not believe in a faith that comes from reading the scripture (Rom. 10:17). I have been captured by the scriptures; it changed my life. I believe that God speaks to me through His word. The inspiration of God from the Holy Spirit in the scripture, influenced the writers of the Bible to communicate the truth to man from God. The Holy Spirit "breathed out" the text into the hearts of men that God chose to write it down. The men used their own gifts and personal style, but they all were moved to write by the same God. The scripture is both authoritative and profitable for training in righteousness (2 Tim. 3:16). The Bible is the inspired, inerrant, infallible Word of God. Men are saved by reading the Bible (1 Pet. 1:23). God's choice for the way to know the truth about God is to study His word, where He has revealed His character and personality. It is a wonder to think about it, but God is a Person. He is not like you and I but much greater (Isa. 55:8-9). His plan is to forgive sin, and love and save souls to demonstrate the grace in His glory (Eph. 2:7).

Some men reject God and the Bible because they do not like what it says to them. They do not fear God, repent of sin, humble themselves and cry out to God for light and help. Their hearts do not understand His word, and they do not become as little children before Him. They cannot hear and believe because they are not of His sheep, and the idea of faith remains a mystery to them. "The hearing ear and the seeing eye, the Lord has made both of them" (Prov. 20:12). Hearing, seeing, and understanding God's word is a great gift from God for your heart. Our heart must be prepared by the grace of the Lord to receive His wisdom and understanding (Prov. 16:1-22). Man is responsible to be diligent, with fear and trembling, to hear the voice of the Lord. Some men remain as natural men (1 Cor. 2:14), and do not respond to being drawn to Jesus by the Father (John 6:44). It is a mystery, we need Divine help to read the word and come to Jesus for salvation, or else we choose ourselves and the world. Perhaps some folks choose evolution over creation, unholy sinful desires, their will, and pride, or have an unjust view of the church or believers, in place of God's call. The natural man is beyond repair and needs the Lords gracious help to be spiritually minded. The Bible holds the truth about the personality of our Creator. The self-revelation of God over many generations described in the Bible, tells us what God, and true religion, are really like. "The fear of the Lord is the beginning of wisdom" (Prov. 9:10).

"God, after He spoke long ago to the fathers in the prophets in many portions and in many ways, in these last days has spoken to us in His Son, whom He appointed heir of all things, through whom He made all things, through whom also He made the world, and He is the radiance of His glory and the exact representation of His nature, and upholds all things by the word of His power"

(Heb. 1:1-3). God revealed Himself; His heart, mind and will to men in both the Old and New Testaments. God spoke to the prophets in the Old Testament concerning the Redeemer. He spoke to Adam that the Messiah should come of the seed of the women (Gen. 3:15). He spoke to Abraham that the Messiah would come through his loins (Gen. 12:3). He spoke to Jacob that the Messiah would be of the tribe of Judah (Gen. 49:10). He spoke to David that the Messiah would be from his house (Jer. 23:5). He spoke to Micah that the Messiah would be born in Bethlehem (Micah 5:2). He spoke to Isaiah that the Messiah would be born of a virgin (Isa. 7:14). The true and living God has spoken to men by dreams, visions, angelic visitations, and sometimes in an audible voice. In the case of Moses, the Lord spoke openly mouth to mouth or face to face (Num. 12:8). With Elijah, He spoke in a still small voice (1 Kings 19:12) and to Moses from a burning bush (Ex. 3:2). At the burning bush, God revealed His holiness to Moses (Ex. 3:5), and His interest to deliver His people from their misery and suffering (Ex. 3:7-8). Thus, we learned that God is holy and compassionate. When God commissioned Moses to bring His people out of Egypt, He reveals His name as I AM (EX. 3:14). "I AM that I AM" includes a self-existence and self-sufficiency for eternity. God is also declaring His involvement in human affairs by sending Moses to Egypt and telling him that He would be with him (Ex. 3:12-12). The use of "I" by God implies an individual and distinct Person. We will stand someday in the presence of God, who is a Person. He is a Person with personality and holy character. To God be all the glory. Jesus said, "Truly, truly, I say to you, before Abraham was born, I am" (John 8:58). In the Gospel of John, Jesus followed the Old Testament use of "I AM", underscoring His connection to God, and revealed great personal and spiritual meaning for our souls. For us, Jesus is the bread of life; light of the world; the door, the good shepherd; the resurrection and the life; the way, truth, life; and the true vine (John 6:35, 8:12, 10:9-11; 11:25, 14:6; 15:1). Jesus declared that "I and the Father are one" (John 10:30). The identity of Jesus as the second Person of the Trinity, reveals a lot to us about the character and personality of the Godhead. We gain a knowledge that directs and inspires our devotion, trust, and gratitude. The Person of God is all good. "God is a Person, and in the deep of His mighty nature He thinks, wills, enjoys, feels, loves, desires, and suffers as any other person may. The continuous and unembarrassed interchange of love and thought between God and the soul of the redeemed man is the throbbing heart of the New Testament religion" (A. W. Tozer).

The Lord "made known His ways to Moses, His acts to the sons of Israel" (Ps. 103:7). Knowing God's "ways" speaks about knowing the personality of God, and is more intimate than just knowing His deeds or acts in our life. Quality time in prayer and Bible study is one way to build intimacy with God. Another way is to give your time, resources, and service at the church and in sharing Christ. God has stepped into our world and into the life of every Christian. God is love (1 John 4:8). Moses gained understanding of God, when God let him know His ways, while the children saw the deeds without always understanding what motivated God. The Christian, in Jesus, sees the acts and the ways of God. Moses pleaded with God to let Him know His ways (Ex. 33:13). Moses wanted to see God's glory. God graciously granted the request of Moses, but he only saw His back and not His face (Ex. 33:18). He told Moses, "I will make all My goodness pass before you" (Ex. 33:19). God's goodness is His glory. Amen. At this time, God proclaimed "The Lord, the Lord God, compassionate and gracious, slow to anger, and abounding in lovingkindness and truth; who keeps lovingkindness for thousands, who forgives iniquity, transgression and sin; yet He will by no means leave the guilty unpunished" (Ex. 34:6-7). We have no description of what God looked like, but more importantly, we do have a description of His personality. The testimony of God for Himself is one of grace, compassion, slow to anger and abounding in love and truth. Amen.

When Moses came down from Mount Sinai, his face shined and the children of Israel saw it, and he covered his face with a veil (Ex. 34:29-33). When Moses went in to talk to the Lord, he took the veil off and put it back on when he came out (Ex. 34:34). Spending time with God, Christian, will bring a healing and a sunshine like heaven into your heart. I would note here also that the Bible tells us that, "Whenever a man turns to the Lord, the veil is taken away" (2 Cor. 3:16). The veil in the Old Testament was a curtain that hung between the Holy place and the Holy of Holies in the Tabernacle. The function of the veil was to keep the Israelites from the direct presence of God. After Jesus died on the cross, the curtain was torn from top to bottom (Matt. 27:51). The atoning death of Jesus on the cross, as a sacrifice, provided a new and living way for believers to have access to God (Heb. 10:19-20). In this passage, the veil is a picture of ignorance, unbelief, self-righteousness, prejudice, enmity, and hypocrisy. When we come to receive Jesus, the veil falls off, by the grace of God, and we see the truth of the glory of God in Jesus. When a man turns to Jesus from his heart, Divine sovereignty has taken the veil away. Amen. The best evidence we have of God's love and the pardon of our sin, is the peace we have in our conscience with God. The putting of God's laws into our minds, and the writing of these laws in our hearts (Heb. 8:10), means the veil over our hearts has been dropped by God. The Person of God is generous and abounds in kindness. His personality is rich and generous, to provide the way we come to know Jesus and be saved. The Person of God is powerful enough to bring forth the good desires He has in His heart for us, and save a wretch like me. In the New Covenant, we have the promises of acceptance, assistance, progress and perseverance in grace and holiness. We have the hope from God that He will be our God, and we will be His people (Heb. 8:10). God says, "I will be merciful to their iniquities, and I will remember their sins no more" (Heb. 8:12). In the new heart, God gives the grace to know the laws of love (Rom. 13:8-10), faith (Rom. 3:27), and liberty (James 1:25), and the grace to practice them sincerely. God will complete the work (Phil. 1:6). Thank you, Jesus. Amen.

God's final word to us is in His Son (Heb. 1:2). The times of the Gospel are the last way God will be communicating His mind, will, and Himself to men. Both the old and new dispensations are very good, but the new is much more excellent because we are more able to understand the Spirit of Christ through the work of the

Holy Spirit. The final revelation was made by His only begotten Son (John 3:16). As God, He was equal to the Father; but, as God-man and Mediator, He was appointed to be the heir of all things, including His children. He is the radiance of the Father's glory and "the exact representation of His nature" (Heb. 1:3). The Son of God is the Redeemer and the true Shechinah. The Son is in God the Father, and the Father is in the Son; and they are one (John 10:30). They are the express image of each other. The unity and the omnipotence of God, the Father, and the Son, means nothing can pluck you from God's hand. The innate merit in the death of Jesus and the intrinsic value of the blood of Jesus has made atonement for sin. The grace of God will forever be honored in His glory. The Bible tells us that the Son is the express image (KJV) and the exact representation of the nature of His Father (AM. STD Bible). In the Old Testament; through the prophets, at creation, during the flood, and at Mount Sinai, God revealed Himself as light in judging sin. Love was not completely absent, but He was insisting upon holiness. In the New Testament, through Jesus, God revealed Himself as love (John 3:16). The Son expressed the affections of God, and called us to love God and our brothers (1 John 4:7, 8, 21). In the New Testament, God promised a new heart through which God would become known (Heb. 8:10; 2 Cor. 3:3).

The heart of God was revealed when the Son was born for us. "Behold, I bring you good news of great joy, there has been born for you a Savior, who is Christ the Lord" (Luke 2:10-11). In the heart of God was great love to fill our greatest need, forgiveness of sin and reconciliation with the Father. He came as a Savior, not only as a teacher to inform us, or a judge to point out our failures, He came because He loved us. He is patient with us, as we learn to love Him in return. Amen. The true knowledge of God, Christian, has come to us because God Himself chose to give it to us. Deep in God's personality is the nature of being generous with His goodness and grace. Since the incarnate Christ is the substance of God, in nature and character, we can learn through Him the true manifestation of God. The Son explains God the Father (John 1:18). The Father declared Jesus Christ to be His beloved Son at

His baptism (Matt. 3:16-17), and at His transfiguration (Matt. 17:5). Jesus said, "he who beholds Me, beholds the One who sent Me (John 12:45). Whatever God is, Christ is, "He is the image of the invisible God" (Col. 1:15). The Son of God is equal in essence to the Father, and a distinct Person in the Godhead. When we see the nature of Jesus, we see the nature of the Father.

God is not at all what the world and the natural man thinks He is. God is not at all whatever else the devil might present to your mind. The natural man thinks God is unfair, unreasonable, angry, and too demanding about holiness. They think that He only acts with wrath and revenge as described in the Old Testament. They get confused by the message of love from the same God in the New Testament. They forget that God hates sin (Ps. 5:4-5; Prov. 6:16-19), and is not willing that any should perish but for all to come to repentance (2 Pet. 3:9). The devil hopes that he somehow killed God at Calvary, and I think he knows God will never trust him in the future. The fact is, "all have sinned and fall short of the glory of God" (Rom. 3:23). The fact is, all men deserve to die. The fact is, "the wages of sin is death, but the free gift of God is eternal life in Christ Jesus our Lord" (Rom. 6:23). The fact is, "God has shut all up in disobedience that He might show mercy to all" (Rom. 11:32). The fact is, "God so loved the world, that He gave His only begotten Son, that whoever believes in Him should not perish, but have eternal life" (John 3:16). It is amazing that God has chosen, at all, to reveal Himself to any lost and disobedient people. Through the acts of creation, salvation and providence, a great and powerful God is revealed in the Christians heart. The lost person does not feel it or sense that this is correct in their heart. It could be that they think the worlds teachings have something they can believe is true, without faith, called science. Thinking they are wise, they become fools (Rom. 1:18-22). The wonders of grace that appear in our souls when we believe, are riches beyond reason. They glorify and magnify the goodness of God. The revelation of the Gospel and the Person of Jesus Christ in our hearts is all glorious. What we find out about the personality of God is that He is gracious and forgiving. Sadly, the lost person believes that God is a difficult taskmaster and judge, and they prefer to stay happier, they think, in their sin. They do not fear God and lack wisdom. They remain dull in their mind regarding the consequences of the future and avoid His presence.

Understanding that the righteousness of God through faith in Jesus Christ can be imputed to believers, is altogether missed in a lost persons thinking. This generous idea fails to rise to a level that becomes important. How can the blood of a man, executed by crucifixion, pay the debt I owe for my sin? They say, I am not that bad of a sinner anyway. The Bible says that all have sinned and deserve death, "but God demonstrates His own love toward us, in that while we were yet sinners, Christ died for us" (Rom. 5:8). God defines what righteousness means, and proclaims it is what is necessary for you to be reconciled to God. Righteousness is required by God to be at peace with Him. The only way to be righteous with God is to accept His definition. God decided that the only way to be right with Him, was to accept to be covered by the righteousness of His only perfect Son. We regain the favor of God through His blood by faith. We are justified by a gift of His grace, through the demonstration of His righteousness. It is freely imputed to us by God's loving personality. The righteousness of Jesus has been declared by God sufficient for the remission of sins. The death of Christ was the moment in time when God gave a righteous demonstration of both His justice and holiness. We must let God be God. "He made Him who knew no sin to be sin on our behalf, that we might become the righteousness of God" (2 Cor. 5:21). The acts of grace and mercy have become an act of righteousness in God. It is a righteous act for God to accept the satisfaction that Christ made to His justice when He died to pardon the sins of penitent believers. It is safer and more glorious to wear the righteousness of Christ. Christ willed to stand in the place of the guilty. He takes our sins and we take His righteousness. The Bible tells us that "The Lord is our righteousness" (Jer. 33:16). To God be the glory for being righteous and faithful. Divine patience kept us out of Hades, gave us time to repent and prepared us for heaven. To secure this promise, God required the blood of His

Son. God Himself makes it known that in His personality are the attributes of holiness, justice, patience, mercy, and truth.

To pardon the sin of believers by faith in Jesus Christ is called justification. Some folks think of justification as just if they never sinned. The providing and accepting justification of sinners by faith in Christ alone is called the righteousness of God (Phil. 3:9). It is a righteousness that is imputed to us, we do not and cannot earn it. The righteousness of Jesus, imputed to us, is the Rock upon which our hope and faith are built. Love and reconciliation were in God's plan and personality for us all along. The law convicts us and condemns of sin, and only gives us the spiritual knowledge of sin. The merits of Christ in the Gospel reveal that God is patient and forgiving. God is righteous (John 17:25). God will "be just and justifier of the one who has faith in Jesus" (Rom. 3:26). The natural man thinks he has, or should have some personal righteousness before God. He does not. All have sinned, and need the patience and forgiveness of God. We all need the righteousness of Christ to be saved. If you do not believe this, then try this prayer. Dear God, I do not know if all this talk about righteousness is true. I need your help to believe. Help my unbelief (Mark 9:23-24). Amen. Faith is God's way, it is humbling. It does not require your work and stabs at your pride, so God gets the glory. Read the Bible. Let not a wise, mighty, and rich man, boast about himself, but let them boast that they "understand and know the Lord who exercises lovingkindness, justice, and righteousness, for He delights in these things" (Jer. 9:24). The Bible also tells us that "those who act faithfully are His delight" (Prov. 12:22). He delights in steadfast love (Micah 7:18). "The Lord delights in those who fear Him, who put their hope in His unfailing love" (Ps. 147:11). When a sinner is laid low in affliction and finds prayer, the Lord will show delight in him. God is to be feared and trusted, and when He is, He will delight in you. By the grace of God "delight yourself in the Lord and He will give you the desires of your heart" (Ps. 37:4). The delight and desires of God are the same delights and desires emerging from your new man. The delights and desires of the spirit of this new man will thrive and rest in the Spirit of God forever.

"This is eternal life, that they may know Thee, the only true God, and Jesus Christ whom Thou hast sent" (John 17:3). In this prayer, Jesus prays that the ones who have been given to Him may know the Father and the Son. This defines eternal life. By the grace of God, we can know, in part, the generous gift of eternal life. We come to eternal life by the knowledge of God imparted by grace in Jesus Christ. The Bible tells us that Jesus Christ was sent (John 17:3) and came forth from God (John 16:30). The Lord calls Himself Jesus Christ, the Messiah (John 17:3). "Whoever believes that Jesus is the Christ is born of God (1 John 5:1). The one who overcomes the world believes that Jesus is the Christ (1 John 5:5). Faith, love, and obedience, are all the natural outgrowth and evidence of being born of God. We are not perfect, but after we sin, the true light of Christ leads us to reject and hate sin, and confess it and continue to move forward with Christ. God will prove His patience and forgiveness in His soul for you, and reveal the gift of endurance, which is also evidence of eternal life. "In the world you will have tribulation, but take courage; I have overcome the world" (John 16:33). By the grace of God, we never cease believing in Jesus. We learn His love for us when we overcome sin in Jesus' name. Knowing God in Christ is to have peace and rest that your sins have been forgiven. The knowledge spoken of here is not just theoretical or intellectual, but experiential and spiritual. It consists of an intimate relationship of walking with Jesus, having communion with Him, and enjoying His word. Saving knowledge will love, trust, and serve the Lord in a manner that walks in obedience to faith in Jesus. "By this we know that we have come to know Him, if we keep His commandments" (1 John 2:3). By the grace of God, we come to know Jesus and to be known by Him, and He gives assurance of our present and future safety. God is always at work for His good pleasure (Phil. 2:13).

"Great is the Lord, and highly to be praised; and His greatness is unsearchable." "The Lord is good to all and His mercies are over all His works." (Ps. 145:3,9). "The Lord is righteous in all His ways, and kind in all His deeds. The Lord is near to all who call upon Him, to all who call upon Him in truth. He will fulfill the desire of those who fear Him" (Ps. 145:17-19). Who is God? He is the Lord and greatly to be praised forever for His goodness. He makes Himself known to us and blesses us every day. Independent of what He finds in us, the work of His grace is still His amazing choice for us. My memory gushes forth in gratitude. I understand more of the things of my past, and sense His presence to protect and provide for me in this life. I wandered away in disobedience and He never forgot me. In His mercy, He made me deal with my sin. He created a new "me" to rejoice in the holiness of God. Love and kindness are embedded in God and are laws in the creation of His universe and its inhabitants. The people that know God, know He woke them up and saved them for Himself. The people that know God will praise Him and worship Him in spirit and truth (John 4:24). God loves us to be sincere with Himself. He enlightened our mind, and was generous to give us an affectionate heart to worship Him in a manner suited to His infinite goodness. The people that know God, recognize the goodness in His Person. The collection of God's traits and ways are all perfect and good for mankind. He is love, mercy, kind and generous. He is great to us by choice. He is patient. He gives us strength in joy and gladness. A Christian glories in Christ Jesus.

"The world is passing away and also its lusts, but the one who does the will of God abides forever" (1 John 2:17). By the grace of God, "we are the true circumcision, who worship in the Spirit of God and glory in Christ Jesus and put no confidence in the flesh" (Phil. 3:3). We have been born again and changed by the power of God. "In hope we have been saved" (Rom. 8:24). We groan within ourselves, which by the love of God, is evidence of spiritual life and not death. We are helpless, but God's work is strong and mighty to save. We are rescued from the bondage of sin by the Spirit helping our weakness "with groanings too deep for words" (Rom. 8:26). The Spirit has interceded for us according to the will of God (Rom. 8:27). God is a Savior. We have been redeemed, and talk to the Lord every day. God's personal way of dealing with us, is as a child of His, with a peaceful heart and rejoicing spirit. We know "that all things are working together for good to those who love God and are called according to His purpose" (Rom. 8:28). True worship is a gift from God filled with gratitude because of the amazing, forgiving and saving nature in the personality that He shows us throughout our lives. He is faithful.

"For God so loved the world, that He gave His only begotten Son, that whoever believes in Him should not perish, but have eternal life" (John 3:16). "The Lord is near to all who call upon Him, to all who call upon Him in truth" (Ps. 145:18). Our call upon Jesus and the worship of Him in truth, means to be sincere. God exists as a Person who created us and loves us and instructs us how to be saved in Jesus. We call upon and look to Jesus to see the love and righteousness necessary for salvation. The Son of man is 'lifted up" in our hearts (John 3:14), and we are born again (John 3:7) to worship Him by His grace in spirit and in truth (John 4:24). God has been honest with us, and we must be honest with Him. God is close to us and invites us to receive Jesus into our hearts to save us. It is not like one and done, He works with us our whole lives to keep us leaning into Jesus. The personality of God is rich in goodness. He builds our faith up by sending us into His word. The saved sinner knows that "His word is a lamp to my feet, and a light to my path" (Ps. 119:105). The saved sinner, by the goodness of God, believes the Bible is the word of God. The saved sinner has experienced the power from Bible study to walk in newness of life. The truth is important to God, and He keeps His word. When you experience the truth about God, you will rejoice greatly, because you will be confident that, His great nature can accomplish His good will. Nothing is impossible for God (Luke 1:37). The Bible tells us that the believer has been "clothed with garments of salvation and wrapped with a robe of righteousness" (Isa. 61:10). As the Church is called the body of Christ, believers are considered the bridegroom of Christ, and He will be the eternal husband of our heart. God's grace will be a significant and magnificent experience in those who have God's image in heaven. We are the children of a King. The personality of our King will be the masterpiece of heaven. Amen.

"He is able to save forever those who draw near to God through

Him, since He always lives to make intercession for them" (Heb. 7:25). God has the inherent power to achieve His minds will. God "is able to build you up and to give you the inheritance among all those who are sanctified" (Acts 20:32). Let us draw near with confidence to the throne of grace that we may receive mercy (Heb. 4:16). Let us draw near with a sincere heart in full assurance of faith (Heb. 10:22). Without faith it is impossible to please God (Heb. 11:6). The faith we come with unto God, and draw near is in Jesus Christ. We need help, and God furnishes this to us through the intercession of Jesus (Heb. 7:25) and the Holy Spirit (Rom. 8:26). Thank you, Jesus for your lovingkindness for my soul. The Bible tells us that although God shows no partiality (Rom. 2:11), many men will not draw near to God through Jesus Christ. God is holy and will have nothing to do with sin (Hab. 1:13). The Bible tells us that God made Himself known to man, but they chose not to honor Him or give thanks (Rom. 1:21). Since the creation of the world, His invisible attributes, eternal power, and divine nature have been clearly seen (Rom. 1:20); but they have chosen selfish ambition, and do not obey the truth, but obey unrighteousness, wrath, and indignation (Rom. 2:8). They exchanged the truth of God for a lie and serve the creature rather than the Creator (Rom. 1:25). One of the lies that the natural man has been deceived by is the idea that mutations in DNA can result in the origin of novel biological traits necessary for molecules-to- man evolution. It comes down to faith in evolution or faith in God. Most folks do not read the Bible or study the science, so they really remain ignorant of both subjects. They end up basing their decision on their own feelings, or another person's opinion.

The natural man remains blind and "does not accept the things of the Spirit of God; for they are foolishness to him (1 Cor. 2:14). In a spiritual state, having been born again, a man sees with a new and different understanding about life. The spiritual man sees that he was created and born again by God, and that the Bible is the word of God. The spiritual man knows he was born again by the grace of God. The spiritual man knows that he is called to be holy and walk by faith in Jesus. The personality of God is alive, and rich in mercy and grace for salvation. The natural man cannot understand the Bible, and perhaps even scoffs at it, and fails to choose Jesus. The Gospel is not suited to a mind full of natural inclinations. A selfish man prefers his own will be done, and in sinful desires and pride rebels against the interest and invitation to be holy and come to Jesus. The world, and its way of thinking without God turns his mind away from spiritual truth. The idea of following Jesus is embarrassing to them. The natural man is in a depraved state and cannot be repaired, except by being drawn to Jesus (John 6:44). The power of God overcoming the sinner is essential for coming to Christ. All men are born naturally and deserve to be separated from God for eternity. Instead, God has chosen to be gracious, and make "known the riches of His glory upon vessels of mercy, which He prepared beforehand for glory" (Rom. 9:23). God's grace is unmerited favor. God will always be God. Our responsibility is to always let God be God.

For a long time, some folks decided that God must be fair. In their mind, if it seems He is not fair, then He is a bad God. If He is a bad God, then He is not worthy of their interest. To them, God is dead. They set themselves up as the righteous judge of God's character. Whatever their life is and or becomes, they always consider themselves as a pretty good person. They do not deserve to go to Hades after they die. They keep their life the way they want it and consider themselves as fair judges of their own life, and perhaps also, another person's life. Besides, they think God should be mostly about love and peace and less about holiness and wrath, which belongs in the Old Testament. The wrath of God is a Divine perfection like His mercy and faithfulness. There are no defects in the character or personality of God. God is holy and He hates all sin (Isa. 6:3; Ps. 5:5). Sin opposes God's nature and is the work of the devil (John 8:44). God hates sin because it blinds us to the truth (1 John 2:11), leads us to bondage (Rom. 6:16), and lessons our love for Him (1 John 2:16). It is the holiness of God that is stirred into action against sin. The natural man's understanding of sin is shallow and weak. The truth about sin is so bad, it brings forth death. The good news is, it brought forth the wrath of God. We learn that the personality of God is holy (1 Pet. 1:15-16). It really bothers me to think about what our world, and our lives would be like if God was unholy.

God is unique in power and purity and separate from us. It took His Son, Jesus, to bridge the gap between us and God and enable us to strive for holiness. God calls us to be holy. We are to "cleanse ourselves from all defilement of flesh and spirit, perfecting holiness in the fear of God" (2 Cor. 7:1). Our sincerity with God means we endeavor to be holy, as He is holy. Striving to be holy, by God's grace out of reverence, is the appropriate response to God's presence (Ps. 119:38). We are made clean by the sovereignty of God, but we are still responsible to cleanse ourselves in hope, fear, and trembling (Phil. 2:12). The inheritance we receive in heaven will be ours from the heart of God. Heaven and eternal life are attractive, no doubt, but the real, major, and meaningful event will be in seeing Jesus. The testimony of the Holy Spirit to my heart is about seeing Him and not the potential material benefits and or any new power we might come to know. It is already enough for our hearts to be forgiven of sin, and to be safe in Jesus. A real Christian, in the future, hopes to be humble, pure in heart and to serve the Lord. Whatever comes from His hand will be righteous and acceptable. Amen.

God is the enemy of sin. A Christian learns to hate sin, by the grace of God, because it grieves the Spirit of God (Eph. 4:30). "For the wrath of God is revealed from heaven against all ungodliness and unrighteousness of men" (Rom. 1:18). God's wrath is turned toward sin and sinners and does not take place on a whim. "The wages of sin is death" (Rom. 6:23). God's wrath has been described as anger (Num. 32:10-13), fury (Ps. 90:9), great (Zech. 7:12) and willing (Rom. 9:22). God's wrath is caused by a response to evil that can be provoked by sin in this world, that He will not allow to exist. God is the Lord, and His sovereign authority and holiness will rule. To God be the glory. His wrath is not malicious or vindictive, but is the reflection of His Divine nature. In a world of sin, injustice, violence, and oppression, it is righteous that God will bring forth a judgment on the wicked. The weak and the poor will know the answer of a perfect God that will bring forth a righteous judgment. God delights in love and purity and hates the impure and vile. He is the sum of wisdom and virtue and rejects folly and vice. The Christian may know persecution, but not the wrath of God. To be clear, apostasy (2 Chr. 34:25), unfaithfulness (Josh. 22:20), and fellowship with evil (2 Chr. 19:2) will not inherit the kingdom of God. They will know the wrath of God. To be clear, provocations (2 Kings 23:26), idolatry (Ps. 78:58-59), profaning the Sabbath (Neh. 13:18), and speaking against God (Ps. 78:19-21), will also know the wrath of God.

The Bible records examples of the effects of the wrath of God. God's wrath was seen in the destruction of Egypt with plagues to let the people of Israel go. "In the greatness of Thy excellence Thou dost overthrow those who rise up against Thee; Thou dost send forth Thy burning anger, and it consumes them as chaff" (Ex. 15:7). "The Lord's anger burned against Israel and He made them wander in the wilderness forty years, until the entire generation of those that had done evil in the sight of the Lord were destroyed" (Num. 32:13). The anger of the Lord burned a few times after the people left Egypt. His anger appeared when the people complained (Num. 11:33, 17:46), when Miriam and Aaron spoke against Moses (Num. 12:9), at Korah's rebellion (Num. 16) and at the making of the golden calf (Ex. 32:9-10). The Lord took the kingdom from Saul, because he did not follow God's instructions to act against the Amalekites (1 Sam. 28:18). Later in the kingdom. The unfaithfulness of the priests and the people defiled the house of the Lord, and mocked the messengers of God. They scoffed at His prophets, and finally the wrath of God appeared against His people. The temple was burned, the temple treasures and the people were taken into captivity to Babylon by King Nebuchadnezzar for seventy years (2 Chron. 36:14-21). Though the temple was rebuilt when the people returned, the second temple, which lasted over 400 years, was destroyed by the Romans in 70 AD. The destruction of this second temple was prophesied by Jesus (Luke 21:23-24). God's wrath burned against the leaders and the people for baseless hatred. They refused Jesus; they could not get along and tried to rule by the letter of the Law.

What used to be a place of worship and where God dwelt, it was replaced with commercialism (Mark 11:15-19)., and politics (Mark 12:38-41). Jesus broke with the religious leaders (Mark 11:17, 12:24). The Divine presence in their midst was removed, and it would last until the time of the Gentiles was fulfilled (Luke 21:24). The temple was burned, melting the gold that covered the east wall and it leaked down into the cracks of stones in the pavement. The Romans, to get the gold, tore the paving apart stone by stone, and the prophecy of Christ was fulfilled (Matt. 24:3). Genealogical records were destroyed, making it impossible to correctly trace the lineage of any pretending messiah that might come along. The fact is, Messiah had come, and His lineage through David was known and recorded in the New Testament.

By nature, we are children of wrath (Eph. 2:3). God's wrath is just. Because of an unrepentant heart, we store up wrath for ourselves. A day of revelation is coming of the righteous judgment of God (Rom. 2:5). The Bible tells us that God will render judgment "to every man according to his deeds (Rom. 2:6). It is the nature of God to act justly and judge sin. God can judge the secrets of men (Rom. 2:16). Those by patient continuance in well-doing seek acceptance with God will know a favorable judgment of eternal life. Those who are selfishly ambitious and do not obey the truth but do evil, will know the unfavorable judgment of the wages of sin. For a sinner, it will be "a fearful thing to fall into the hands of the living God" (Heb. 10:31). We are all sinners, falling into the hands of a powerful God who can make us quite glad or forever sad. We know now how great the joy can be in Christ, we can only imagine how deep the misery can be in the price of rejecting His goodness. "Our God is a consuming fire" (Heb. 12:29). We are to work out our salvation with fear and trembling (Phil. 2:12), and wait for the Son from heaven, "that is, Jesus, who delivers us from the wrath to come" (I Thess. 1:10). The wrath of God will be certain and terrible. Those who refuse the excellence of His love in Christ, and the pardon for sin will know His wrath. The doctrine is very important because it has eternal consequences, but it is not popular because you must surrender your life to Jesus.

God steps in and makes His people willing in the day of His power (Ps. 110:3). If we have no personal relationship with Jesus, we will not escape God's wrath. Do not hesitate to follow Jesus; seek and discover what He has put into you now for life after death. The consequences of unbelief in Hades are quite chilling; it is a place of darkness (Matt. 22:13) and eternal hopelessness (Matt. 18:8-9). It is a place "where their worm does not die, and the fire is not quenched. For everyone will be salted with fire" (Mark 9:48-49). The reflections and reproaches of the sinner's own conscience will be like the action of a gnawing worm that will not die. The guilt in the conscience will be like a fire that cannot be quenched. For eternity, the unbelieving sinner will condemn himself. There will be no grace or the merit of Christ to appease the violence going on in their conscience. Take heed of ruining your own soul. In the Christian, the living principle of grace works out the corruption of anything that offends God. Knowing this terror and fear of the Lord, let yourself be persuaded, and persuade others (2 Cor. 5:11). Be persuaded to keep coming and growing in the saving knowledge of the Lord Jesus Christ. Come to Jesus and allow His presence to let you behold your salvation in your own heart and mind. Amen.

There are several places in the Bible where God takes an oath or swears by Himself, since He could swear by no one greater. God is the truth (John 14:6) and He cannot lie (Heb. 6:16-18). When God swears by an oath, even in His wrath, it is from a Divine perfection. The first time we see an oath used in the Bible was in the story of Abraham and the sacrifice of his son, Isaac (Gen 22). "By Myself I have sworn. Because you have not withheld your only son, I will multiply your seed as the stars of the heavens" (Gen. 22:16-17). At another time, God took an oath to deprive a wicked generation its inheritance in the promised land for unbelief (Deut. 1:34). God has sworn by His holiness that He would not lie in making a covenant with David that his descendants would endure forever (Ps. 89:35). In another passage, God tells us He was angry at the people that provoked Him in the wilderness for unbelief and not knowing His ways (Heb. 3:8-10). He says, "as I swore in My wrath, they shall not enter My rest" (Heb. 3:11; Ps. 95:11). God can use an oath in showing great mercy, making judgments and covenants. There will be no rest for an unbelieving heart. It is the creature's duty to tremble (Phil. 2:12). God's word is like His nature, unchangeable (Mal. 3:6). "The grass withers, the flower fades, but the word of God stands forever" (Isa. 40:8).

In our natural state since the fall, all men desire evil and deserve to go to Hades when they die (Rom. 3:23, 6:23). God does not force men against their will to go to Hades. However, some people are passed over, while others, He has chosen in mercy and changes their desires to love Him forever (John 6:44). God's grace, and how He calls men is a mystery (Rom. 8:28-30; Eph. 1:11). As the Creator, God is just and righteous to do with His creation as He pleases, for His glory. "What if God, although willing to demonstrate His wrath and to make His power known, endured with much patience vessels of wrath prepared for destruction? And He did so in order that He might make known the riches of His glory upon vessels of mercy, which He prepared beforehand for glory" (Rom. 9:22-23). We all were dead in our transgressions, but by the mercy of God, He made us alive for the ages to come to show the surpassing riches of His grace toward us in Christ Jesus (Eph. 2:5-7). God's wrath is from righteous reason and holy law against sin. God's will, was to display His wrath, but give ample opportunity to repent. God did not create men for destruction, they fit themselves for destruction by their sin. God prepares men for glory (Rom. 9:23). The lost prepared themselves by rejection of His word and failure to believe in His Son. God patiently endured their antagonism while they prepared themselves for condemnation. The Bible tells us that "because of your stubbornness and unrepentant heart you are storing up wrath for yourself in the day of wrath and revelation of the righteous judgment of God" (Rom. 2:5). Every sin we do or harbor in our mind, public and private, every day, is contempt of the goodness of God. It can be stored up as wrath against ourselves. The heart of a lost sinner may not be aware of this, but a believer very much regrets the choice to sin. We know that we will not be perfect (1 John 1:8), but we quickly confess our sin and seek cleansing. That God hates sin is clear. It is because of sin that God exhibits wrath. It is because of sin, that God's only begotten died. It is because of sin that some people will go to Hades and suffer for eternity. "He who believes in the Son has eternal life; but he who does not obey the Son shall not see life, but the wrath of God abides on him" (John 3:36). Vessels of wrath are fitted to destruction compared to vessels of mercy prepared for glory (Rom. 9:22-23). God never created a man to destroy him, but a man's nature is revealed as fit for punitive justice, or prepared for glory. Vessels of mercy are receptacles of God's mercy, kindness, grace, and forgiveness. To be where God is and to do what God has intended for us to do, will be glory (Eph. 1:4). Amen.

The good news is that God has revealed His love and grace for sinners in the Gospel of Jesus Christ. "Christ Jesus came into the world to save sinners" (1 Tim. 1:15). God's wrath is set at ease in the Christian by the merits of Jesus Christ. "For God has not destined us to wrath, but for obtaining salvation through our Lord Jesus Christ" (1 Thess. 5:9). "By His doing you are in Christ Jesus, who became to us wisdom from God, and righteousness and sanctification and redemption" (1 Cor. 1:30). We will live humbly by faith, hope, and love, in Jesus Christ because His purpose, according to election, will stand. We are justified and forgiven of our sins as a gift by His grace. We regain the favor of God through the shed blood of Jesus. He made the payment for our sins at Calvary. "This was to demonstrate His righteousness, because in the forbearance of God He passed over the sins previously committed" (Rom. 3:25). "We shall be saved from the wrath of God through Him" (Rom. 5:9). "He delivered us from the domain of darkness and transferred us to the kingdom of His beloved Son" (Col. 1:13). We could have been taken in the very act of sin, but Divine patience gave us time to repent. I am grateful today for the riches of His kindness and forbearance and patience, knowing that the kindness of God led me to repentance (Rom. 2:4). I believe that God stored up the righteous wrath that I deserved and unleashed it upon Jesus at the cross. I believe that God also put a stop to the wrath that I was storing up for myself. I believe my sins are forgiven, but the punishment was not forgotten. The penalty for my sin was not paid until Jesus died. I was not destined for wrath, but for obtaining salvation (1 Thess. 5:9). Praise the Lord, oh my soul. My salvation was appointed by God before the foundation of the world (Eph. 1:4), and given a purpose from an infinitely merciful, faithful, and gracious God. God acted in His own good pleasure (Eph. 1:11). The believer has been transferred from darkness, slavery, guilt, and the power of Satan, into light, freedom, and forgiveness, by the power of God. I was needy and He found me. I was transferred from my sinful self to the kingdom of Jesus with a heart of obedience. The kingdom of God, for me, has a present reality of "righteousness and peace and joy in the Holy Spirit" (Rom. 14:17). I have been called to turn from sin and myself and "serve a living and true God, and to wait for His Son from heaven, whom He raised from the dead, that is, Jesus, who delivers us from the wrath to come" (1 Thess. 1:9-10).

A time is coming when God will have His day of righteous wrath. God knows both the people with genuine faith and those who never knew Him. He knows that some will be waiting sincerely for Him, while others will be terrified when He arrives. The terrified people will be hiding and pleading for rocks to fall upon them to avoid the wrath of God on the throne and the Lamb they rejected (Rev. 6:16). Men will experience great fear, and mighty sorrows will take hold of them. They will not be able to stand. It will be clear to all that our Creator God was always alive. The universe will be coming apart. It is my opinion that believers may pass through some of this tribulation, but not the great day of wrath (Rev. 6:17). The timing of the rapture (1 Cor. 15:51-52; 1 Thess 4:16-17) is unclear, but the ideas exist that have God's people may be translated from the earth at either pre, mid, or post-tribulation. I think the church will endure some persecution for their testimony of Jesus, and Satan's wrath, but not God's wrath. Some folks, like me, think the rapture occurs before the book with the seven seals is opened, at the beginning of Revelation chapter four. Other folks see the rapture in Revelation chapter 6, sometime early in the opening of the seals. Christians are being persecuted today, and some folks want to criminalize Christianity. "Behold, the day of the Lord is coming; cruel with fury and burning anger, to make the land a desolation; and He will exterminate its sinners from it" (Isa. 13:9). The proud will be at their wits end. There will be no hope and comfort. There will be confusion, consternation, and horror. No one will escape justice. The God of infinite mercy will make the sinners infinitely miserable. Judgment is coming. The wrath of God abides on the man who does not obey the Son (John 3:35). There are only two choices; two roads (Matt. 7:13-14) and two foundations (Matt. 7:24-27). These will be the most important choices of your life. Indecision is a fatal decision. The Gospel is both a Person we receive, and a life that we live (Eph. 2:8-10). Obedience to God is an essential element of saving faith. The wrath of God cannot be softened away. The citizenship in Hades is a result of the wages of sin that you bear without coming to Jesus. It will abide on a man, which means he will have no hope of escape. Please God, have mercy on our loved ones, for Jesus' sake.

"The thief comes only to steal, kill, and destroy; I came that they might have life, and might have it abundantly" (John 10:10). We are born as natural men and must be born again to know Jesus Christ. We must grow in grace and knowledge and follow Jesus to develop the assurance that we indeed belong to Him. He brings the peace, mercy, comfort, and gratitude, that we have life and believe on the Son. We abide in Jesus, and by His grace, we will not know His wrath. At some point in our life, we are brought into a consciousness of our oneness of life with Jesus. We can know the Holy Spirit abides with us (John 14:16-17). "In that day you shall know that I am in My Father, and you in Me, and I in you" (John 14:20). How good and great is the personality of God to comfort us with His grace and love. God is generous to give the spiritual manifestation of Christ to our hearts. God spends time with us to be comforted by a living Christ. He is alive. Jesus has made the promise to us that if we keep His commandments and love Him, the Father will love us and Christ will love us and manifest Himself to us. The Father, and Son will come and make an abode with us (John 14:21, 23). In these verses, the "commandments of God" (V. 21) becomes "His word" (v. 23), and "disclose Himself" (v. 21) becomes "make our abode with him" (v. 23). This change, reveals a deeper love and fellowship with God. God brings the truth into your heart, and proves the competency of scripture in our daily life. "All scripture is inspired by God and profitable for teaching, for reproof, for correction, for training in righteousness" (2 Tim. 3:16). God equips us for His good work.

God writes the commandments in the Bible on our heart, by the finger of the Spirit of God. We are a letter of Christ, written by the Spirit of God on the tablet of our human heart (2 Cor. 3:3). The writing by God enables us to enjoy and remain influenced by the grace He gives us. There is an obedience of faith in the gift of God's love. We learn to love Jesus and He makes Himself known to us. Daily, He becomes more spiritually manifest to us, and we see more of His glory to come. We see Christ being formed in our hearts, and His presence brings a clearer understanding of the nature of God's love. The spiritual revelation of Christ becomes our most precious reality. He is with us always, whatever we do and wherever we go. The Lord Jesus is faithful to "guide us into paths of righteousness for His name's sake" (Ps. 23:3). We deeply value obedience, by the grace of God, and submission to His will. The blessing we have from God's generous heart is both to give us the desire, and then the power to do His will (Phil. 2:13). Our success lies in the grace of God. Our success lies in the ways of God's personality to love, and be faithful with us. God fulfills the promise of being with us to finish the work He has begun (Jer. 31:33; Matt. 1:23; John 14:16-17; Phil. 1:6).

"Little children, let us not love with word or with tongue, but by deed and truth. We shall know by this that we are of the truth, and shall assure our heart before Him" (1 John 3:18-19). God has chosen to bless us with a great sense of love in Jesus. God has chosen to bless us to abound in love and works of love towards Christian brothers. God gives us the inward joy and peace in our own hearts, as evidence of the gift of sincerity from His own heart. The knowledge and assurance that we have passed from death to life lies in the evidence of our faith in Christ. Amen. God is love (1 John 4:9). Love is of God (1 John 4:7). "We love, because He first loved us" (1 John 4:19). "If we love one another, God dwelleth in us, and His love is perfected in us" (1 John 4:12). The greatest evidence for the invisible God is love. The love of God is revealed to our hearts by the Holy Spirit. The perfection of that love, by God's grace and knowledge, in us becomes the fruit of His love. The perfecting of God's love is the experience of Divine love in your heart. We are temples where God dwells. God's love is your personal blessing, and as a personality trait, it is intended to be shared with other believers, as well as unbelievers, as a testimony to God's goodness.

God's children are chosen to eternal life by sovereign grace. We are called to work out our salvation by fear and trembling in Bible study, prayer, and service (Phil. 2:12). When we discover, sense, and believe we are growing in grace and knowledge in Christ, we know God was moved by love to draw us up into His heart. We know that there was not anything in us, or done by us, that He saw and liked to confirm His choice. We know that we are being transformed by love and the sanctifying work of the Spirit. God is at work to will and to work for His good pleasure (Phil. 2:13). Deep down in our heart is a strong yearning to walk with Jesus and to please God. "Not my will, but Thine be done" (Luke 22:42). I am not perfect, "but I press on in order that I may lay hold of that for which also I was laid hold of by Christ Jesus" (Phil. 3:12). My hope is in the personality and perfections of our great God and Savior. God's heart, nature or personality will be best realized in your own conversion and Christian life. Make yourself familiar with the word of God. The Lord looks at your heart, which He knows better than you (1 John 3:20). The Lord sees the inward longing in your new heart and your desire to be conformed to His will. Throughout my whole life; as a child, a youth, through manhood, and as an old man, God's love has always been seeking me. I have been apprehended by God. He kept great thoughts in His heart for me, and set my feet upon His Rock. He is a great Savior. "If God is for us, who is against us? (Rom. 8:31). "We are His workmanship, created in Christ Jesus for good works, which God prepared beforehand, that we should walk in them" (Eph. 2:10). Praise God from whom all blessings flow. Amen.

The Choices of God

> "You are A CHOSEN RACE, A royal PRIESTHOOD, A HOLY NATION, A PEOPLE FOR GOD'S OWN POSSESSION, that you may proclaim the excellencies of Him who has called you out of darkness into His marvelous light" (1Pet. 2:9).

Dear Christian,

Our God is alive and makes choices. God chose Moses and told him that He was sending him to Pharaoh to bring His people, the sons of Israel, out of Egypt (Ex. 3:10). God chose Joseph, Jacob's son, to preserve many people (Gen. 50:20). God chose Abraham to be a blessing to all the families of the earth (Gen. 12:1-3). God chose David to be King over Israel (1 Sam. 16:12). Esther attained royalty to save the Jewish people from Haman (Esther 4:14). God chose Paul to bear the name of Jesus before the Gentiles, and write a large part of our New Testament (Acts 9:15). God told Moses that He would have mercy and compassion on whom He chose (Ex. 33:19; Rom. 9:15). God chose Jacob over Esau, "in order that God's purpose according to His choice might stand, not because of works, but because of Him who calls" (Rom. 9:11). "God causes all things to work together for good to those who love God, to those who are called according to His purpose" (Rom. 8:28). To those who are called, Christ becomes the power and wisdom of God (1 Cor. 1:24). God has chosen the foolish and weak things of the world to shame the wise and strong, that no man should boast before God (1 Cor. 1:26-27). God often chooses to work through unexpected people and not the mighty, wise, and noble. "But by His doing, you are in Christ Jesus, who became to us wisdom from God, and righteousness, sanctification, and redemption" (1 Cor. 1:30). By the grace of God, we turned to God from ourselves to know and serve a living and true God, "and to wait for His Son from heaven, whom He raised from the dead, that is Jesus, who delivers us from the wrath to come" (1 Thess. 1:9-10). Amen.

Believers were chosen in Christ before they became alive on the earth. The Bible tells us, "He chose us in Him before the foundation of the world" (Eph. 1:4). This truth is difficult for man to understand and believe. For a believer, the time comes when he must let God be God. The truth is that God has a loving personality and makes perfect choices according to what pleases Him (Luke 10:21; Eph. 1:4-6,11; Rom. 9:11, 22-24). The idea that we are chosen in Christ is abundant in the Bible. The truth about election gives the believer a peace and assurance about the future. The Bible tells us that "God called us according to His own purpose and grace which was granted us in Christ Jesus from all eternity" (2 Tim. 1:9). "Those who have been chosen of God, holy and beloved, are to put on a heart of compassion" (Col.3:12). You are a chosen race (1 Pet. 2:9). You are to be diligent to make certain about His calling and choosing you" (2 Pet. 1:10). Our connection to Jesus Christ is from eternity. "He predestined us to adoption as sons through Jesus Christ to Himself, according to the kind intention of His will" (Eph. 1:5). "We have obtained an inheritance, having been predestined according to His purpose who works all things after the counsel of His will" (Eph. 1:11). God chose Jesus Christ to be the Savior. God chose all those that answer to the strength in His call, from the Spirit, to become born again with a living faith in Him. The thought of being chosen by God to live eternally with spiritual blessings in Christ is overwhelming. We are predestined and effectually called, justified, and sanctified, to become conformed to the image of His Son (Rom. 8:28-30). Being chosen and elected by the sovereignty of God, Christian, is from

His decision to save us as a vessel of mercy (Rom. 9:23). It was totally God's choice, and it is all good. Only those truly saved can and will love God and keep His commandments (John 14:15). We need the work of His Spirit to desire and keep His commandments. Election is a mystery God's grace. God's grace proves He is kind and generous, patient and forgiving, and that the choices of His will, will be perfectly done. To God be the glory of His grace. God's grace is His own to give where He chooses.

God is not like what the world thinks He should be like. The devil works hard to blind and confuse you to choose the world and not God. The devil chose himself to live by, and he wants you to make the same choice, and choose yourself to live by. The devil wants you to believe that because you cannot scientifically prove God is present, then God must not be real. A lot of people do not want to go to Hades after they die, if to them, there happens to be such a place. They think they are not "bad" enough for God to choose them to go to a punishing place after they die. The idea of needing a Savior and making no contribution on their own for salvation is something their pride cannot understand. The devil knows that if you find out the truth about God, you will be attracted to His nature and goodness. The devil is a liar (John 8:44), and in this world, paints the wrong picture of God as a tough taskmaster to your heart. The devil wants you to dishonor God and share in the misery that is planned for him. He attacks you to get at God. The devil wants you to know very little about God so that you will not trust Him about your sin. The devil wants you to stay ignorant of God, and serve yourself and enjoy the passions that control your flesh. The devil wants you to be afraid of spiritual life and remain a natural man. The Bible tells us that we are born as "a natural man that does not accept the things of the Spirit of God; for they are foolishness to him, and he cannot understand them" (1 Cor. 2:14). Without God's help, we cannot choose to follow Jesus Christ. We must be born again (John 3:3). The devil removes the importance and interest in the Bible from the mind of the natural man, so he cannot learn the truth about God. The natural man ends up making the choice to avoid growing in faith, and fails to gain the sight of seeing Jesus, who forgives and saves him from the penalty of his sins. (Rom. 10:17).

"That which is born of the flesh is flesh, and that which is born of the Spirit is spirit," so "you must be born again" (John 3:6-7). Heaven is a prepared place for a prepared people. The new birth is imperative, because from it we become able to know the things of God. We must be made spiritually alive by the Holy Spirit. It is not becoming religious or reformed or quitting sin; we become partakers of the divine nature (2 Pet. 1:4). It is the creation of a new man (2 Cor. 5:17). We know we have new life, but how the Holy Spirit creates new life in us belongs to the deep things of God. We learn that our salvation was initiated by God's choice. We learn that He is the One who sought us out and enabled us to believe. He is the One who gives "the hearing ear and the seeing eye" (Prov. 20:12). The goodness of God's grace opens our understanding and turns the will with a desire to come to Jesus. "For by grace you have been saved through faith; we are His workmanship, created in Christ Jesus for good works, which God prepared beforehand that we should walk in them" (Eph. 2:8, 10). Our responsibility is to "work out our salvation with fear and trembling; for it is God who is at work in you, both to will and to work for His good pleasure" (Phil. 2:12-13). God tells us, that "as the heavens are higher than the earth, so are My ways, and My thoughts than your thoughts" (Isa. 55:9). "The mind of man plans his way, but the Lord directs His steps" (Prov. 16:9). We learn to be humble. A man can make the choice to try to save himself by his own work. God says we need the righteousness of Jesus, as a gift from the creator to be saved. Our own righteousness is like a filthy garment (Isa. 64:6). Salvation was not left to chance. God has a predetermined purpose and goal and man lost a genuine freedom. It is a mystery; but our choices will shape our history in the way of our responsibility, and the grace, election, and the sovereignty of God. He moves in us for our salvation. We are His choice.

God first moved in us before we moved closer to Him. After the fall in the garden of Eden, as a natural man, we lost the freedom to choose Jesus. The whole world, and our very life was always in His hands, for "in Him we live and move and have our being" (Acts 17:28). We have physical life because He created us (Gen. 1:27). We have spiritual life because He drew us to be born again (John 5:5). God chose to save us as a vessel of mercy (Rom. 9:23). God chose to send the Holy Spirit to take up residence in us, transforming our souls and body into a sanctified place (Heb. 10:10). We were purchased (1 Cor. 6:20) by the perfect sacrifice and the shedding of the blood of Jesus Christ. This was in the plan of salvation for us all along by God (Eph. 1:4, 2:10). God is holy, omnipotent, just, free, glorious, and good. We are weak, sinful, selfish, and deserve to perish away from God. In Jesus, God granted man justification and reconciliation. By faith and belief in Christ the elect Christian hears the Divine Word as his creator, Redeemer, Prophet, Priest, and King. Election in Jesus is the reason people respond to the Gospel and become saved. Election precedes faith, and our calling is the manifestation of God's choice and mercy. Everything occurs as God ordained it. God is in control and omniscient, and nothing can surprise Him. He governs in heaven and on the earth by His gracious providence. God regulates everything according to His own counsel. Predestination is an eternal decree of God. God is sovereign and man is responsible. The lost man does not think he should be responsible for something He has so little control over. The created man is not like the perfect God. The fact is, all men deserve to go to Hades, but God chose some to save He calls the elect. We discover and work out our salvation by fear and trembling (Phil. 2:12). He is the potter and we are the clay (Isa. 64:8). All have sinned and fallen short of the glory of God (Rom. 3:23). God knows that no natural man will choose to receive Christ. At the same time, it pleased God to choose some, according to His own purpose and grace ((2 Tim. 1:9). Only God understands Himself. The righteous man will live by faith (Hab. 2:4).

God speaks to our heart about the value of Jesus our whole life. God also speaks to us a lot about the importance of holiness. God's choice or will for our lives is to be filled with the Spirit. He wants us to walk wisely, understanding what the will of the Lord is (Eph. 5:15-18). God's will for us is to be sexually pure; to possess our own body in sanctification and honor, not in lustful passion (1 Thess. 4:3-5). God's choice for you is to be the husband of one wife, having children who believe. God directs us to be above reproach as His stewards, not self-willed, not quick-tempered, not addicted to wine, not pugnacious, not fond of sordid gain, but hospitable, loving what is good, sensible, just, devout, self-controlled, holding fast the faithful word of the Lord, and able to exhort sound doctrine" (Titus 1:6-9). "Do not be deceived; neither fornicators, nor idolaters, nor adulterers, nor effeminate, nor homosexuals, nor thieves, nor revilers, nor swindlers, shall inherit the kingdom of God" (1 Cor. 6:9-10). We cannot sow to the flesh and expect everlasting life with Jesus. We cannot live in sin, and die in Christ as a child of God. All have sinned, but we must be sanctified by the Spirit, cleansed, and reconciled to God, and made righteous in the sight of God and holy by the grace of God. The blood of Christ can cleanse from any sin. It is God's choice that we are changed into the image of Christ. God's will for our lives, Christian, will include suffering (1 Pet. 4:19), and discipline (Heb. 12:7-11) for our good that we may share His holiness and learn to trust and be established in Christ (1 Pet. 5:10; Heb. 12:10-11). We are to honor authority (1 Pet. 2:13). "Rejoice evermore. Pray without ceasing. In everything give thanks; for this is God's will for you in Christ Jesus" (1 Thess. 5:16-18). God's choice for us in life is to be spiritual and walk with Jesus. He would have us rejoice, pray, give thanks and quench not the Spirit (1 Thess. 5:19). The personality of God is rich in love. In this life, He chooses us to know eternal life in the blessings of redemption from His Son.

God is free to make His own choices. God has the sovereign right to choose whomever He wills to save and bless by His providential acts in this life. God has the sovereign right to reveal Himself to anyone in any way He chooses. God has the sovereign right to bless some folks with more of His presence and grace and knowledge. God has the sovereign right to deal with anyone in their physical and mental characteristics for their life in this world. In spite of giving mankind some knowledge of His power (Rom. 1:18-20), wisdom (Prov. 1:24-33), and holiness (Rom. 2:1-15), we still are responsible for the poor choice made in the garden of Eden. We need God's help through the work of the Holy Spirit to come to Jesus (John 6:44). The freedom of choice in a natural man, because he is considered spiritually dead, cannot receive, accept, and follow Jesus. Man is not righteous or seeks for God (Rom. 3:10-12). Man needs to be justified, that is, freed from the penalty of sin with God. Justification with God comes through the gift of righteousness from God by faith in Jesus Christ. We must be born again (John 3:3). This occurs in accordance with the grace of God, not of works, lest any man should boast (Rom. 4:13-16; Eph. 2:8-9). This is God's plan, way, and choice. Man has some freedom, but so does God. For some folks, the doctrine of election does not meet what they call rational human standards. They think that God is unfair in the freedom of His choice with the mercy of election, and they turn away from it and Him. This is their freedom of choice, and it comes with the weight of personal responsibility in their own decision, and unfortunately with tragic consequences. Like it or not, the Scriptures are the word of God (Ps. 138:2; 2 Tim. 3:16), and they clearly teach that God makes the choice in the doctrine of election (Rom. 9:16-23). The disagreement they have about election is with God, and not another man. Man is responsible to "be all the more diligent to make certain about His calling and choosing you" (2 Pet. 1:10). Man is responsible "to work out your salvation with fear and trembling" (Phil.2:12), and not just blame God or another man. The "work out your salvation" is a seeking and searching for God. Fear and trembling means with great care and serious consideration with a dependence upon the grace of God. Our attitude should be one of humility and vigilance. The immature Christian grows into trembling at God's greatness, holiness, justice, wrath, and grace. We strongly desire to do right. The power that compels us comes from the Spirit that indwells us. "God is at work in you, both to will and to work for His good pleasure" (Eph. 2:13). It is a blending that includes man's responsibility with God's divine resources. God's work becomes our incentive, and we discover His living presence. Some people prefer their own ease, safety, interest, and pleasure from the world, in place of God's truth, holiness, duty, and the honor of Christ's kingdom. Amen.

Divine election means it is by God's choice, and took place before the foundation of the world (Eph. 1:4,9). Divine election is a predestination to adoption as sons who have obtained an inheritance. Divine election is according to the kind intention and counsel of His will that He purposed in Jesus Christ (Eph. 1:5, 9, 11). Divine election was to save sinners (2 Tim. 1:9; 2 Thess. 2:13). Divine election was designed to honor and magnify the grace and glory of God (Eph. 6:1,12). We were chosen as a people for God's own possession to "proclaim the excellencies of Him who has called you out of darkness into His marvelous light" (1Pet. 2:9). We were chosen to receive mercy and to worship God. He first chose us, and He first loved us (Eph. 1:4; 1 John 4:19). The faith we have, Christian, is the fruit of God's willing choice of us. The repentance we undergo and the prayers we offer up are the fruit of election. The mysterious work of the Holy Spirit enables us to "seek first His kingdom and His righteousness" (Matt. 6:33). The church is the household of God filled up with the elect of God (1 Tim. 3:15). He chose us to become members of His body for "salvation through sanctification by the Spirit and faith in the truth" (2 Thess. 2:13). The wisdom of God was made known through the church to the rulers in the heavenly places (Eph. 3:10). Christ is the head over the church which is His body (Eph. 1:22). Divine election makes believers of the word of God that grow in faith when they read the Bible (Rom. 10:17).

We were not elected by God because we were holy, but that we might become holy. The call of God means you were "predestined to become conformed to the image of His Son" (Rom. 8:29). Whatever path you have journeyed on, "He called you through the gospel, that you may gain the glory of our Lord Jesus Christ" (2 Thess. 2:14). Whatever path you have journeyed on, the providential operations of the Spirit of God were effectual. The gift of faith from God (Eph. 2:8) comes with the power of God. You have been changed to be able to see His hand at work in your life. The joy and reality of true faith showers your heart at times and is the evidence for the proof of election. You become more certain about His calling and choosing you (2 Pet. 1:10). The proof of your election is in the fulfilled promise of a new heart and the obedience of faith. Your life becomes more holy with a sense of being blameless before Him (Eph. 1:4). The proof of your election comes in the manifestation of a new life with strength and knowledge for Jesus. Christ becomes the ruler in your heart and life (Col. 3:12). The Bible becomes the Word of God. You are spiritually hidden with Christ in God, and are protected and preserved by the loving kindness and power of God. Amen.

You are His workmanship created in Christ Jesus (Eph. 2:10). Because of election, your heart will know a strong belief in the profound truth of Jesus. Your life is being prepared for His presence by a very real sanctification. You will know that the glory you gain, He has purchased. The glory He possesses, in part, is communicated to those He chose to believe and obey the gospel. In the future, we shall be glorified with Christ, and see and share in His glory. Jesus said, "the glory which Thou hast given Me I have given to them; that they may be one, just as we are one" (John 17:22). The Father and the Son are one, and we will be glorified with them (Rom. 8:30). The spiritual union we have of being seated with Christ in heavenly places (Eph. 2:6), and chosen by God, has just begun. We were called to gain the glory of the Lord (2 Thess. 2:14). It was the prayer of Christ that we all be one, and that means we have unity. We are believers in one body, animated by the same Spirit, and knit together by having one heart for Christ. Every true Christian is inclined to love all true Christians. Believers are united by a divine nature. Believers are knit together by a bond of love and charity with one heart. Believers are one in their desires and prayers, having the same spirit of adoption. Believers are one, in their designs and aims for the glory of Christ. Believers are being changed into the same image of Christ (2 Cor. 3:18).

Christ emptied and humbled Himself by becoming obedient to the point of death. Therefore, "God has highly exalted Him, and bestowed on Him the name which is above every name, that at the name of Jesus every knee should bow and every tongue confess that

Jesus Christ is Lord" (Phil.2:9-11). He is Lord of all, by the design and choice of God the Father. He is exalted with honor and power and all authority, "to the glory of God the Father" (Phil. 2:11). The Lordship of Christ, by the choice of the Father, is the core of Christianity. The purpose of all creation, chosen by the Father, was to be glorified by the Son revealing the riches of the grace of God in Christ Jesus (Eph. 2:7). The name for Jesus Christ as Lord, is a title of majesty and sovereignty over all creation. The title of Jesus Christ as Lord declares His true character and dignity worthy of our worship. The exaltation of Jesus Christ is a great source of encouragement in our salvation and help in times of affliction and humility. The name of Jesus for us means grace, and a certain place to take heart about our future glory. The name of Jesus is a place of peace, faith, hope, and help. The name of Jesus is a place of surrender, forgiveness, and acceptance with God the Father. By the love, power, and choice of God, we gladly choose His Lordship for our life. God choose this incredible, eternal blessing for sinners like us to become vessels of mercy for His glory. Amen.

We are the chosen family of God. The spiritual presence of Christ in believers is both His glory and our glory. His presence is the source of the power and privilege and duty for being one and unified. We become one in the faith. We are united by divine grace and power through the providential actions of the Divine counsel. The life and soul of the new man in us gains a spiritual strength to love another Christian. Though we all may be quite different, and at times even annoying to one another, we are inclined by the spirit of Christ to be in unity and love one another. As believers, we are all called to trust the same glorious Savior, and share in the same glory. We believe the same truth, belong to the same Father, and share in the same witness of the Holy Spirit. God chose love to be the centerpiece in our behaviors toward one another. From the generous personality of God, "He willed to make known what is the riches of the glory of this mystery among the Gentiles, which is Christ in you, the hope of glory" (Col. 1:27). The mystery is; that it is because of Christ working in you, that there is true hope for the future in the glorious things to come. It is not a "pipe dream," it is the promise of God. We have been sealed by the Holy Spirit for the day of redemption (Eph. 4:30). Christ is in you by the Spirit's presence, finishing the work of sanctification in salvation, and securing the promise of God's glory. For us, the hope of glory is our conformity to Christ (Rom. 8:29). The hope of glory is in our resurrection by the same Spirit that raised Jesus from the dead (Rom. 8:11). The hope of glory includes a heavenly inheritance (1 Pet. :3-4). The reality of Christ living in you becomes the anchor that guarantees the promises of God. "The Holy Spirit of promise was given as a pledge of our inheritance, with a view to the redemption of God's own possession, to the praise of His glory" (Eph. 1:14). His presence means election, salvation, conformity to Christ, eternal glory, and an inheritance. "We are His workmanship, created in Christ Jesus for good works, which God prepared beforehand, that we should walk in them" (Eph. 2:10). By the grace of God, though the heart of every Christian was once dead, it has been made alive in Christ. God was never dead.

"He predestined us to adoption as sons through Jesus Christ to Himself, according to the kind intention of His will, to the praise of the glory of His grace which He freely bestowed on us in the Beloved" (Eph. 1:5-6). In eternity past, our adoption as believers was settled in the heart of God before He made the world and us. In love, He chose us for adoption as sons through His own Son. Our adoption is only realized in Jesus, and was the kind choice and intention of His will. We are secure in the Son of God. To be clear, we did not seek Him or ask for Him or even know how to find Him. He found us and has manifested Himself to us (Rom. 10:20; Isa. 65:1). Gentiles are fellow heirs, members, and partakers of the promise in Christ Jesus through the gospel (Eph. 3:6). It was God's own choice, His own free will, and the action of His own grace. Amen. The crucifixion of Jesus and the shedding of His blood was predetermined by the will of God. Evil men carried it out. Our conformity to the image of the Son of God was predetermined by the kind intention of the will of God (Eph. 1:3-12). God's wisdom, and how He makes His choices are a mystery (1 Cor. 3:7). God's sovereignty and man's responsibility coexist perfectly in the righteousness of God. God sits on a throne and is a perfect Master and King. The doctrine of election is the truth of God that man cannot completely understand. We understand it is righteous, because it comes from a perfect God that can only make perfect choices and decisions. We are asked to receive it by faith from the Bible that is inspired by God (2 Tim. 3:16). It is not necessary to understand it for the forgiveness of sin and salvation, and it is not something to argue about. Jesus saves. Nevertheless, some folks do not like this doctrine; they chafe at it, it is vexing to them and makes them angry. They resent the thought they may not be saved, find it annoying and unfair. They take no pleasure in it or the God who might make choices like this. God's desire is that all men would be saved and come to repentance (1 Tim. 2:4; 2 Pet. 3:9). God offers salvation to everyone (Titus 2:11), but we know that not everyone will choose to be saved by Jesus. People will be held accountable to God for how they lived their lives (Rom. 14:10-12). Though we have sinned in this life, in the ages to come, God will show the riches of His grace toward us in Christ Jesus (Eph. 2:7).

True believers have been born again as children of God (John 1:12). They are adopted as sons of God (Eph. 1:5). The adoption is a present experience in this life, as well as, a future reality. "For all who are being led by the Spirit of God, these are the sons of God. For you have not received a spirit of slavery to fear again, but you have received a spirit of adoption as sons by which we cry out "Abba! Father! The Spirit Himself bears witness with our spirit that we are the children of God, and if children, heirs also, heirs of God and fellow heirs with Christ" (Rom. 8:14-17). "Having the first fruits of the Spirit, we ourselves groan within ourselves waiting eagerly for our adoption as sons, the redemption of our body" (Rom. 8:23). We were adopted in the past when God predestined us, we presently groan within ourselves waiting for the redemption of our body. We were adopted; past, present, and future, with the Spirit guaranteeing our salvation. While we were yet sinners, Christ died for us (Rom. 5:8). Knowing from the beginning, we would be sinners, He still chose us. Knowing in time, we would be weak for sin, He kept His choice of us. We are never earning our salvation. We are discovering that God never gives up on a true believer. We can be confident, that He who began a good work will perfect it until the day of Christ Jesus (Phil. 1:6). To God be the glory. Predestination and election are grounded in God, and please Him as a kind intention (Eph. 1:5). The choice by God is a great benefit and reveals a good will toward the elect in the absolute love of us in His Son. The assurances of sonship are realized by us, from the Spirit leading us to the obedience of faith (Rom. 16:26), and love for the brethren (1 John 5:1-3). We develop a child-like confidence in God (Gal.4:6; Rom. 8:15), and an access to God, as a trusting Father, through Jesus (Eph. 3:12). We come to know a changed life (1 John 3:9-17). We know that the source of our adoption is God's choice, and that the path of salvation is God's choice, by grace through faith in Christ (Rom. 4:16; Gal. 3:26, 4:3-6). Amen.

Adoption admits man, by the choice and grace of God, into the family of God for eternity. It takes place the moment we believe in Jesus Christ (1 John 3:2; Gal. 3:26). We wait for all the privileges of adoption (Rom. 8:23). The blessings of adoption are numerous, they include; fatherly love, care, and comfort (John 17:23; Luke 12:27-33; 2 Cor. 1:4), and family name, likeness, service, and chastisement (1 John 3:1, 14; Rom. 8:29; John 14:23-24; Heb. 12:5-11). We become heirs by the grace of God (Titus 3:7; 1 Pet 3:7) with a promise (Gal. 3:29; Heb. 11:9). We become heirs through the righteousness of faith (Rom. 4:13). "God chose the poor of this world to be rich in faith and heirs of the kingdom, which He promised to those who love Him" (James 2:5). The love of God has been poured out within our hearts through the Holy Spirit (Rom. 5:3-5). We learn to love the Lord with all our heart, and more than our own life (Mark 8:35). We learn to live for Christ and endure temptations, in the power of the love of God (1 Cor. 10:13). We become His children, and He becomes our Father God. "The Spirit bears witness with our spirit that we are children of God" (Rom.8:17). The Bible tells us that if we are His children, that we are heirs of God and fellow heirs with Christ (Rom. 8:17).

The truth about adoption is that it involves an inheritance.

"After listening to the message of truth and believing the gospel of your salvation, you were sealed in Him with the Holy Spirit of promise, who is given as a pledge of our inheritance, with a view to the redemption of God's own possession to the praise of His glory" (Eph. 1:13-14). He predestined us to adoption as sons (Eph. 1:5). "We have obtained an inheritance according to His purpose who works all things after the counsel of His will" (Eph. 1:11). We are to work heartedly for the Lord, "knowing that from the Lord you will receive the reward of the inheritance" (Col. 3:23-24). To work heartedly means to be diligent and cheerful for the Lord as His servant, and not to earn a reward. It is an inheritance that is "imperishable and undefiled and will not fade away, reserved in heaven for you" (1 Pet. 1:4). The inheritance is for the righteous in Christ (1 Cor. 6:9; Eph. 1:11), the sanctified (Acts 20:32) and the transformed believer (1 Cor. 15:50). A place is being prepared for His adopted children (John 14:2-3) that will be all glorious (Rom. 8:17). Heaven with Jesus will be the main inheritance. The Holy Spirit in us now, is the earnest of that inheritance, both as a sanctifier and a comforter. The Spirit of God is holy, makes us holy, and is called the Holy Spirit of promise (Eph. 1:13). What it means to inherit eternal life will be revealed. We will have new bodies in a new sinless environment. Our inheritance will be to see the glory of Jesus. Our inheritance will be eternal joy, peace, and gratitude to God. Amen.

Our inheritance is reserved for us in heaven where it is secure. While we are living on earth, we are still on a journey of growing in grace and knowledge and serving the Lord. We have the promises of His presence (Heb. 13:5) and protection (Ps. 91:15). We are being kept by the power of God through faith. Amen. Most importantly, Jesus is before all things, and in Him all things hold together" (Col. 1:17). The Lord Jesus has dominion over all things and is the heir of all things (Heb. 1:2). He is the end, as well as the cause of all things (Rom. 11:36). Creation is kept together by the Son of God. Also, "the eyes of the Lord are upon the righteous, and His ears attend to their prayer" (1 Pet. 3:12). God exercises a providential affection and government over us. God has a special care and always hears the prayers of the faithful (1 John 5:14; Heb. 4:16). God designed our world as the place He would display His grace and wisdom in the choice to redeem lost sinners. He would reveal His purpose for the church and the magnificent role of Jesus (Eph. 3:11). To accomplish His purpose, God has governed our world from the beginning. He created all things for Himself and His pleasure (Prov. 16:4; Rev. 4:11). God sees and acts in our universe, and especially in our individual lives. The word "providence" means to supply or give sustenance to what is needed. The Lord will provide (Gen. 22:7, 14). Biblically, the word providence refers to God's foresight and power to see and watch over us, and protect and provide for our future (Matt. 10:29-31). God's gracious oversight of us is His providence. God's providence orchestrates the gift of faith in our lives to bring us to salvation and good works in Jesus Christ (Eph. 2:8-10). Nothing escapes His notice and He works in the smallest details, which at times might seem unusual. In His wisdom, God makes no mistakes, and in His power, He is always in control. We will make poor choices, but He will always have our best interest in His heart. God's work in our lives brings about what He wants at the right time for His glory, and to our greatest benefit. Nothing ever happens by chance.

The providence of God works from the choices God made for us. "The Lord has established His throne in the heavens; and His sovereignty rules over all" (Ps. 103:19). At all times, in all places, in all situations, and with all people, the Lord reigns. "God is the judge; He puts down one, and exalts another" (Ps. 75:7). We are always in His hands (Ps. 23; 139:10). The active energy of the will of God is always around us. The same power that caused us to exist, is required to maintain our existence. You know you are alive, but you had no choice about in what time or year, in what country, and who your parents would be. You had no choice about your sex, skin color, height, or physical features. We were created with a purpose by God, and not some random mechanism like evolution. We do not suddenly just appear in life, and acquire an awareness and conscience. God has been in all the details, especially in our ways with Jesus. We become a Christian and gain the Holy Spirit for our life, according to His grace. We read and gain confidence in the Bible as the word of God, trust in Jesus and grow into an obedience of faith, according to His loving kindness. We experience God's presence, believe in prayer, and rejoice in His work in our mind and hearts, according to His providence. You begin to know the truth, and the truth is setting you free (John 8:31-32). The truth delivers us from the darkness of spiritual death and emancipates us from a life of sin. By the providence of God, you are delivered from the penalty of the law and the wrath of God. You become a slave of righteousness, and are free to serve God (John 8:36; Rom. 6:17-18). You are the beneficiary of God's love and kindness and the work of His own hands in bringing you into a salvation experience that is God's choice and glory. Recognizing God's providence will strength your faith, and put peace and confidence in your heart that God is in control. You get a deep sense that God has entered your life, and hope to see and hear more of His presence. The whole world, including our country can look like they are falling apart, but rest assured, the providence of God is always working and cannot be extinguished. Everything has been ordered by Divine wisdom, power, and good and perfect will.

God is in every event, causing all things to work together for good according to His kind intention and perfect will (Rom. 8:28). When I was younger, I could not readily determine whether a particular event was arranged by Providence or not. As an older person, my guess might be a little better, but I still mostly lack the ability to know exactly what God may be doing or arranging by His providence. When I look back on my life, I believe I can better recognize God's voice and actions bringing me to be the believer in Christ I am today. God has blessed me to sense His presence sometimes, understand my life better, and in the process, confirm His faithfulness to me. My faith is strongly supported when I realize He was with me, and working out His good and perfect will. To God be the glory. This has become what I personally believe. Someone else may have a different experience, but they cannot take mine away from me. I have touched on this in previous books, and will just mention a few highlights here. I believe God stepped into my life a couple of times when I was young. I sense this from certain sporting events, but especially at eleven years old when I came to Christ and was baptized. I believe God stepped into my life a lot about being holy, which schools I would attend, the choice of my wife and even the house we were to purchase and live in for many years. I believe God protected me at work, around water, and in cars. The Lord was with me at work at work for successes and failures. The Lord has been with me choosing a church to regularly attend, teaching Sunday school classes and especially sharing the word of God in the jail. The Lord sent me into the Bible to read, study, share, and write about the love of God. Amen

God is always with us. By His choice, there will be times we become more consciously aware of His presence. In His time, God reveals facts about Himself and the Gospel to our mind and heart from the Bible. Certain scriptures take on a deeper meaning and importance than we initially harbored as we grow in grace and knowledge. We grow, by the grace of God, into a more personal relationship with the Lord. We become more informed. As we grow closer to Jesus in a deeper faith, we began to see more clearly the riches of God and how glorious and active He really is. He touches our hearts every day, in a way that keeps us mindful of His loving presence and our continuing need of holiness (Ps. 139). Christ lives within us (Gal. 2:20). Living with a sensitive conscience and awareness of His presence and power is His choice for us, and a great blessing. It is a gift of the grace of God. His mind is over our mind and His Spirit is over our spirit. The good news is that the providence of God makes it hard to sin.

God's presence is spiritual. It can be difficult to describe when God is present and moves, because the sense of it for us is new and a mystery. It is personal. A unique impression takes place that is holy. To me, I have a sense that a "clear cloud" has moved over my mind. Something has impressed me, but I feel outside of it. I feel free and peaceful and aware that something happened. I do not hear words with my ear or have a fear of what is going on. It is very short in time. Sometimes I sense God's presence when I responded to something I think was right, and sometimes when I think of doing something wrong. Sometimes I think it is an answer to prayer for someone else, to comfort me; or an answer to prayer by someone for me. Something bigger than me is sensed in my heart, and it is not just explained by good feelings. Sometimes, I have just an overwhelming sense of peace, comfort, or confidence that what just happened is the way to go in a particular decision. Sometimes, I think I heard a word behind me, "This is the way, walk in it" (Isa. 30:21). The voice of God for me may have been similar in sound or sense, but the circumstances and timing have always been different. I have no doubt that for each person and their situation, the voice will be special for them. God is providentially in control of His own presence with us, and therefore, He has His own chosen time and reason to speak. God may providentially choose to speak to your heart in songs, scriptures, certain people, in church or shopping, in His service or on your couch at home. You may be in a crowd or alone. "We are the temple of the living God; just as God said, "I will dwell in them and walk among them" (2 Cor. 6:16). He proves Himself in love with us by nurturing a special relationship with us. The word of faith is always near us. We believe in our heart and confess with our mouth that God raised Jesus from the dead, resulting in the salvation of our souls (Rom. 10:9-10). The word of faith matures in a believing soul that has been personally chosen for adoption unto salvation. I will be their God, and they shall be My people" (2 Cor. 6:16).

A choice is given to us by God to "enter by the narrow gate; for the gate is wide, and the way is broad that leads to destruction, and many are those who enter by it. For the gate is small, and the way is narrow that leads to life, and few are those who find it" (Matt. 7:13-14). Two roads are described here; one narrow road leads to eternal life, and the other broad road leads to eternal death. Where you will live for eternity is determined by which road you take. Deep down inside of us, we know that we are going to die and face a judgment, so the choice of the road we take will have eternal consequences. The idea that there is a right and wrong is real. "Strive to enter by the narrow door, for many, I tell you, will seek to enter and will not be able" (Luke 13:24). Do not delay or procrastinate, there is only one safe door, and it is through an intimate relationship with Jesus Christ (John 10:9). "He who believes in the Son has eternal life; but he who does not obey the Son shall not see life, but the wrath of God abides on him" (John 3:36). This is the word of God. He who ears to hear, let him hear (Matt. 13:9). If you do not like these words, I recommend you gently take that up with God. God's way of forgiveness and salvation is by grace through the shed blood of Jesus, and not your work (Eph. 2:8-10). You must receive Him to be saved.

The gate and the way are narrow because you can only make it through this passage having received the merit of Jesus Christ into your account. It is not easy and requires self-sacrifice; rather than ease, self-indulgence, and your own ideas about righteousness. Our salvation in Jesus may seem difficult and we strive; but it is not received by our work. It becomes ours only by the grace of God through personal faith in the gospel of Jesus Christ. It will cost you your natural love of sin and pride, and give you trouble from the world and Satan. You will agonize and groan within yourself (Rom. 7:14-23, 8:23-25). Many will try to enter heaven on their own terms, understanding or works, instead of God's terms. Walking with Jesus, God's way, becomes the greatest miracle and blessing in the living experience of a believer. It is not earned by our work, but we will exert an effort to humbly trust Christ, and fight the good fight of faith (2 Tim. 4:7-8). The broad way is easier, self-indulgent and requires little moral character, maturity, and sacrifice. The broad way is where you can appear religious, ignore God's truth, and think your sin is tolerated or not that bad with God. God may get some decent lip service now and then, but no change or fruit from the man's heart. On the narrow path through a narrow gate, a man wakes up to the serious offense to God that sin in his life is, and seeks forgiveness in Jesus. He undergoes moments of agonizing self-examination and feelings of helplessness and doom. He gives the ruins of sin in his life serious attention, and wants to be free. He is very interested in pursuing a course to be right with God. He humbly recognizes he needs help from God to be responsible and sincere to bring forth an effort to know and follow Jesus.

The Bible tells us that "He who has found his life shall lose it, and he who has lost his life for My sake shall find it" (Matt. 10:39). By denying Christ, we lose our life in an eternal death. By losing our life for Christ, we find it to our unspeakable advantage in an eternal life. Amen. We need to know that Jesus is the choice that God has made for us, and for that, we need the Lord to open our heart. There is a statement made in the Bible at the conclusion of the Parable of the Wedding Feast that should make you read your soul. It says, "Many are called but few are chosen (Matt. 22:14). A lot of people will hear the call of God coming from the revelation of Himself in the creation of the world, and especially, coming directly to their own hearts. They may hear the call of God to be holy in their conscience. They may hear the call of God during preaching and or the study of the word of God. Jesus said, "He who has ears to hear, let him hear" (Matt. 11:15). God gave us ears to hear, and strongly invites or calls us to consider and be mindful of the things of God. God's word should get our undivided attention, because it is from God and as such, it would be important. We should attend to God's word and pray for understanding. Way too many folks hear the word but fail to fully understand it. They think it sounds good, but do not respond with action. Some just check the box through Sunday attendance. Only a "few" are listening and responding which shows they have ears to hear. The "many" are invited but show little or no interest or concern, and some are downright hostile to the message of the Bible. The few that are chosen are the elect, they accept the call on God's terms. The positive response of the few comes from the grace of God. It is an effective calling because they respond from the true gift of faith from God (Matt. 11:27, 24:22, 24, 31). They were chosen in Him before the foundation of the world (Eph. 1"4-11). God draws the hearts of those chosen (John 6:44), and they become a new creation in Christ (2 Cor. 5:17). God grants repentance (Acts 11:18), gives faith (Eph. 2:8), and the gift of the Holy Spirit (John 14:16-17). They have spiritual ears and eyes to see and understand the power of God's truth and what it will be in the future (Rom. 8:28-30). The "few" respond with "fear and trembling" in their souls in their discovery of God working in them (Phil. 2:12-13). To the few, Christ becomes wisdom, righteousness, sanctification, and redemption from God (1 Cor. 1:30). The beneficial outcome of being "enslaved" by God is sanctification, eternal life and seeing the Lord (Rom. 6:22; Heb. 12:14). God completes the work (Phil. 1:6). The sinner is turned from sin to Jesus Christ to be forgiven and saved, by the choice of God. He becomes our peace (John 14:27). "All have sinned and fallen short of the glory of God" (Rom. 3:23). "For the wages of sin is death, but the free gift of God is eternal life in Christ Jesus our Lord" (Rom. 6:23). To God be all the glory and the gratitude. Amen.

The elect souls have been chosen by God, and are being sanctified by the Holy Spirit. They have been sprinkled with the blood of Jesus (1 Pet. 1:1-2), and are justified by God (Rom. 8:33). The obedience to God becomes a strong desire, hope and clear choice in a true Christian. The Christian is instructed to clothe himself with a heart of compassion, kindness, humility, gentleness, patience, peace, and gratefulness (Col. 3:12-15). The Christian is to let the word of Christ richly dwell within himself, and all that he does, in word and deed, be in the name of Jesus giving thanks to the Father (Col. 3:16-17). Sometimes in the scripture, the word used for "choice" can have the same meaning as the word used for "elect." For example, at His crucifixion, Jesus was referred to as "His chosen One" (Luke 23:35), and in another scripture as a "choice stone" (1 Pet. 2:6). In both cases, the word used for choice can mean elect. Jesus Christ is a precious and choice foundation stone. He is the promise of God for us now and in the New Jerusalem (Rev. 21). In this holy city, "the Lord God, the Almighty and the Lamb, are its temple. The glory of God illumined it, and its lamp is the Lamb. Nothing unclean will ever come into it, but only those whose names are written in the Lamb's book of life" (Rev. 21:22, 23, 27). "He who believes in Him shall not be disappointed" (1 Pet. 2:6). This is the Lords doing, Christian, and we will not be confused; Jesus Christ is our cornerstone.

We are a chosen people that belong to God with a Divine purpose. "We are His workmanship, created in Christ Jesus for good works, which God prepared beforehand" (Eph. 2:10). The Bible tells us that Paul endured all things for the sake of those who are chosen (ex. Elect) (2 Tim. 2:10). Paul was an apostle of Jesus Christ, and was faithful to write a lot of the New Testament. Paul was a bond-servant of God, "for the faith of those chosen of God and the knowledge of the truth which is according to godliness" (Titus 1:1). Paul had the honor of serving God in the gospel of His Son (Rom. 1:9). It is the glory of angels that they were chosen and "sent out to render service for the sake of those who will inherit salvation" (Heb. 1:14). Angels are ministers of divine Providence that do God's will. We are in God's hands. We cannot physically see God or angels, Christian, but they are present. God works in amazing ways. He transforms our hearts, and calls and enables us to spread the Gospel (Matt. 28:19-20). We take part in the glorious plan of salvation by the grace of God. By God's choice, we are to go and make disciples and baptize them in the name of the Father, the Son, and the Holy Spirit. The Lord promises to be with us. By God's choice, the church is to go to work to sound off the word of the Lord (1 Thess. 1:8). The gospel is the truth (col.1:5), which is after godliness, purifying the heart in the fear of God. Faith is the "choice" gift of God to His children. Faith is the first and enduring principle of our justification and sanctification. Faith does not feed our pride, but rather humbles a man. True faith rests on God Himself, and we will persevere, to the glory of God.

God chose to redeem a remnant of humanity for salvation, called vessels of mercy, before the foundation of the world (Rom. 9:23; Eph. 1:3-14). God's elect is always secure, and it is impossible to take us out of the Father's hand, or the hand of Jesus (John 10:28-29). Let the lost man seek and call upon the Lord while He may be found (Isa. 55:6). "Let the wicked forsake his way, and the unrighteous man his thoughts; and let him return to the Lord" (Isa 55:7). The Bible makes it clear that God's thoughts and ways are a lot higher than ours, and that His word will not return to Him empty (Isa. 55:8-9,11). Satanic deception and chaos and wars have been going on for a long time, and can be expected to increase in the last days of man. False Christs and prophets and signs and wonders will be so deceptive that even the elect will be tempted to believe the lies (Mark 13:22). We are to take heed and be aware of lying wonders. This might apply to reports of alien activity in our skies that goes beyond our technology. "Nevertheless, the firm foundation of God stands, having this seal, the Lord knows those who are His" (2 Tim. 2:19). Trials of sincerity, hypocrisy, confusion, and faith are permitted by God to let man discover what is really in him for Christ. We grow in grace and knowledge to be like Christ. The attacks of the powers of darkness cannot nullify the love, power, and promises of God. Christ is our firm foundation, and the devil cannot destroy the faith of the elect (1 Cor. 3:11). The seal of God is upon us. It is by His choice that we are secure in His ownership; we have been bought with a price (1 Cor. 6:20), and certified by the presence of the Holy Spirit as sons of God (Rom. 8:16). We hear the voice of Jesus and He knows us. By the grace of God, in this life we have taken in experiential knowledge and tasted of His goodness and assurance (Rom. 8:16). By the grace and choice of God, we know a separation from unrighteousness, and He remembers us back into His eternity.

He is mindful of us now, and will be for our future going into eternity to come. Just prior to the return of Jesus Christ, the Great Tribulation will be cut short for the sake of the elect (Matt. 24:22). He will send out His angels and they will gather His elect (Matt. 24:31). The called, chosen, and faithful (ex. Elect), will accompany Jesus Christ, the Lamb, when He overcomes those who wage war against Him (Rev. 17:14). As God's elect in this world, we will have some trouble with sin and opposition, but mercy will come at last like a great flood. The justice and honor of God will be fully vindicated from the disaster brought on after the entry of sin into the world. We love God because He first loved us (1 John 4:19). We choose God because He first chose us to be His people. A lot of people choose their lusts instead of God, and they would rather be rich in this world than rich toward God. They would rather have heaven on earth than heaven after they die. The choice He made of us will reveal His perfect knowledge, wisdom, power, justice, and lovingkindness. God's choices for us are, "Things which eye has not seen and ear has not heard, and which have not entered the heart of men, all that God has prepared for those who love Him" (1 Cor. 2:9). The wonderful and present possession of eternal life, revealed to us by the Holy Spirit, did not enter our eye, ear or heart until God revealed it to our souls. We would have never discovered the wisdom and goodness of God without a revelation from Him. Life and immortality were revealed in the Gospel (2 Tim. 1:10). It is impossible to know what God has prepared for our future as the bride of Christ. He will make the perfect choice. We wait on God. Amen.

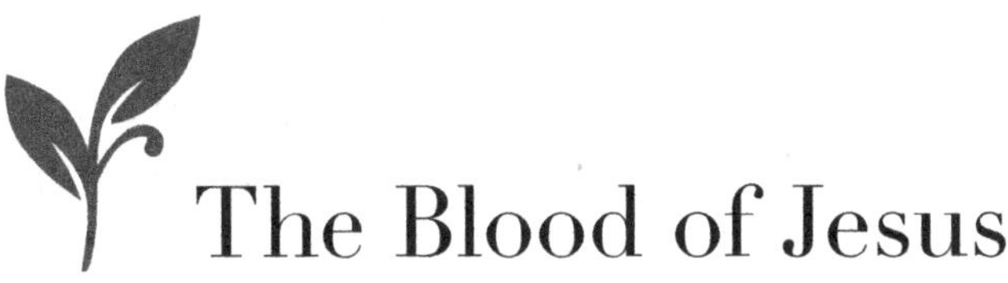

The Blood of Jesus

> "Be on guard for yourselves and all the flock, among which the Holy Spirit has made you overseers, to shepherd the church of God which He purchased with His own blood" (Acts 20:28).

Dear Christian,

The Bible tells us that "the salvation, and the power, and the kingdom of our God and the authority of Christ have come, for the accuser of our brethren has been thrown down, who accuses them day and night before our God. And they overcame him because of the blood of Lamb and the word of their testimony, and they did not love their life even to death" (Rev. 12:10-11). Take courage, Christian, Jesus has "overcome the world" (John 16:33). In this life, you will try hard to fix or get rid of guilt and any addiction you might develop to solve your own sin problems. You will try to understand yourself and help yourself, but you will not succeed. A time is coming when you will be ready to give up, and God steps in to teach you about His Son, and His grace and love. You were just wishing for freedom, but God has a lot more to give you. The call of God may take the form of a surrender, but it is not a defeat. God calls you because God is love (1 John 4:8). God's way to help you, forgive you of sin and save you, is by His gift of faith through grace, it is not by all your hopes and hard work (Eph. 2:8-9). "For God so loved the world, that He gave His only begotten Son, that whoever believes in Him should not perish, but have eternal life" (John 3:16).

The gift was not free. According to the Law, "without the shedding of blood there is no forgiveness" (Heb. 9:22). The blood is an act of presentation of life to God. It brings the thought to our minds that blood was shed for the remission of our sins. Since the blood of the Son of God is the only sufficient sacrifice available, our confidence then is only in the blood of Jesus. An animal's blood was used in the Old Testament as a "type" for the perfect blood of Jesus Christ, our Great High Priest, the mediator of a New Covenant. It is impossible for the blood of animals to take away sins (Heb. 10:4). The Law was a shadow of the good things to come and not the very form of things (Heb. 10:1). In place of being offered every year, the offering of the body of Jesus Christ was once for all time. "By one offering He has perfected for all time those who are sanctified" (Heb. 10:14). Christ did not enter the holy place of the earthly Tabernacle made with hands which represented a type. He entered heaven itself with His own blood to appear in the presence of God for us (Heb. 9:12, 24). He sits at the right hand of the Majesty in the heavens (Heb. 8:1). "He is the mediator of a better covenant, which has been enacted on better promises" (Heb. 8:6). He offered Himself without blemish to God, and can cleanse your conscience from dead works to serve the living God (Heb. 9:14). In the New Covenant, He puts His laws into our minds, and writes them upon our hearts. He promises to be our God, and we shall be His people (Heb. 8:10). The blood of Christ was infinitely precious. He offered Himself through the eternal Spirit, without the stain of sin in His nature or life. His blood reaches into our soul and conscience, and can purge out the uncleanness that has lodged in our hearts. His blood renews our soul to serve the living God by the purchase of the Holy Spirit (Heb. 9:14). He entered heaven as our Surety and Forerunner (Heb. 6:20). He honored God. It was the blood of His "Son" (Heb. 1:2-3), the blood of "God" incarnate (Acts 20:28), and called a precious blood by the Holy Spirit (1 Pet. 1:19). For this reason, He is the mediator of the New Covenant (Heb. 9:15).

Since the Bible is from God and spiritual, before you can receive its teachings, you must be born of the Spirit (John 3:6) and filled with the Spirit (Eph. 5:18). The Bible tells us that "a natural man does not accept the things of the Spirit of God; for they are foolishness to him, and he cannot understand them" (1 Cor. 2:14). A naturally born person does not believe the blood of Jesus can do what the Bible says it does. Only those born again see the kingdom of God, which "is not eating and drinking, but righteousness and peace and joy in the Holy Spirit" (Rom. 14:17). Only those born again, can worship and serve Christ in a manner acceptable to God (John 4:24; Rom. 14:18). Only those born again, will "have confidence to enter the holy place by the blood of Jesus" (Heb. 10:19). Only those born again, understand "Whoever wishes to save his life will lose it, but whoever loses his life for My sake shall find it" (Matt. 16:25). We must receive and have a relationship with the Lord Jesus to find eternal life from Him. He takes us where we have never been before by helping and sustaining our soul (Ps. 54:4). The Christian religion is the religion of sinners that will seek the continued pardon of their sin. "If we confess our sins, He is faithful and righteous to forgive us our sins and to cleanse us of all our unrighteousness" (1 John 1:9). The sinners without Jesus do not confess their sin or seek forgiveness. They end up trying to pay the penalty for their sin outside of God's plan. God's grace is only in His plan which requires the blood of Jesus as the payment for our sin. Our daily sin will affect our present fellowship with Jesus, but not our standing as being justified before Him, which is called justification, or just as if we never sinned. The appeal to Christ for forgiveness of sin includes our past, present, and future sin. Satan's accusations against the believer therefore can be seen as directed against the perfect righteousness of Jesus. The shedding of His blood on the cross revealed His love for us, and "released us from the penalty of our sins by His blood" (Rev. 1:5).

The Father "delivered us from the domain of darkness, and transferred us to the kingdom of His beloved Son" (Col. 1:13). The Son is the head of the church. It was the Fathers good pleasure to reconcile all things to Himself through His only begotten Son. The

Father made peace with us through the blood that was shed on the cross by Jesus Christ (Col. 1:18-20). God chose the shedding of blood to atone or make amends for our sin. We do not exactly know why God chose blood. The Bible does tell us that blood has life-giving qualities (Gen. 9:4), and that "the life of the flesh is in the blood" (Lev. 17:11). God says that "He gave blood for us on the altar to make atonement for our souls" (Lev. 17:11). The Bible tells us that "without the shedding of blood there is no forgiveness" (Heb. 9:22). The Bible tells us that "the Lord was pleased to crush or bruise Him if He would render Himself as a guilt offering" (Isa. 53:10). By His blood atonement, Jesus fulfilled many Old Testament types that pointed to Him. It was by blood sacrifices that men were to approach God (Gen. 4:4), that a covenant was established with Abraham (Gen. 15:8-19), and the Jewish people were to make it out of Egypt alive (Ex. 12:23). No one can come to the Father except through Jesus (John 14:6). We need the blood offering of Jesus to reverse the sentence of death for sin (Rom. 6:23). We need the righteousness of God, as a gift, that comes by faith through the sacrifice of Jesus (Phil. 3:9). We need a relationship with Jesus that casts aside our works and pride and opinions. We need to be covered by the blood of Jesus to be safe when He comes again. He came the first time as a Savior (Luke 2:11), and is coming again as a judge (Rev. 19:11; Ps. 98:9). He came the first time as the Lamb (John 1:29), and is coming again for salvation (Heb. 9:28) as the Lion (Rev. 5:5). "We must all appear before the judgment seat of Christ" (2 Cor. 5:10).

The first reference to the blood can be seen in the book of Genesis. After the fall of man in the Garden of Eden, God spoke to the serpent or the devil. He said, "I will put enmity between your seed and her seed; He shall bruise you on the head, and you shall bruise Him on the heel" (Gen. 3:15). Biologically speaking, a woman produces no seed, and the Bible only mentions the seed of men. The word "seed" means descendant. Therefore, the promised Seed would have to be miraculously planted to be the seed of the woman. This passage speaks of the virgin birth and the incarnation of Jesus in a prophecy. This is the first prophecy in the Bible, and has been called the protoevangelium or the first gospel message of good news. The battle between good and evil or the godly and the wicked has been going on since the beginning, and continues right up into our day. The world hates the Christians (1 John 3:13). The seed of the serpent will bruise the Messiah's heel, but the Messiah will crush the serpent's head. This prophecy, in part, was fulfilled at the cross, and will be complete when Satan is cast into the lake of fire and brimstone (Rev. 20:10). Through Christ's suffering, shed blood and death, Satan bruised the heel of the human nature of Jesus. Christ's feet were nailed to the cross. Satan may have thought that he killed God, but God cannot die. Satan continues to bruise the heel of Jesus in our lives by accusation and persecution (Isa. 53:4). Christ Himself bore our sins and griefs, and "took our infirmities, and carried away our diseases" (Matt. 8:17). Though Christ received a painful wound, He inflicted a mortal wound on the serpent, crushing his head. "The God of peace will soon crush Satan under your feet" (Rom. 16:20). Amen. "The Son of God appeared for this purpose, that He might destroy the works of the devil" (1 John 3:8). We are born into this world as natural men (1 Cor. 2:14) under the curse of death (Rom. 5:12), and then face a judgment before God (Heb. 9:27). The good news is that a natural man can become a spiritual man and overcome the curse of eternal death. The good news is that a dead man can become alive. The good news is that God is rich in love and mercy and grace. The good news is that God has made us alive and seated us in heavenly places. The good news is that we are saved by grace through faith, not a result of our work, it is the gift of God (Eph. 2:1-9; Rom. 6:23). Amen.

The principle of blood atonement was God's ordained remedy for the problem of sin. Forgiveness of sin was not possible without the shedding of blood (Heb. 9:22). In the Old Testament, the blood of an animal sacrifice to atone for the guilty could not take away sins, but it could cover them up for a time, until the new and perfect covenant through the blood of Christ was inaugurated (Heb. 9:11-15). The life of an innocent animal to atone for the guilty, foreshadowed the offering of Jesus Christ Himself to God.

Christ was acting in His mediatorial office (1 Tim. 2:5). No other kind of sacrifice could adequately represent the power, superior nature, and efficacy of the shed blood of Christ. The blood is the life (Deut. 12:23) and the life of the flesh is in the blood (Lev. 17:11). The blood is physical and material, while life is spiritual and immaterial. When the blood is shed, the life is drained away from the body and the soul departs bringing death. "For the wages of sin is death" (Rom. 6:23). Sacrifices are efficacious by virtue of the death. The blood of Christ, is to be understood as the atoning death of the Savior. Jesus Christ gave His life for us and He died for us, and the fear of our death passes away, and we receive the gift of eternal life God's way (John 3:16). The Bible tells us that "God will allot Him a portion with the great, because He poured out Himself to death, and He Himself bore the sins of many" (Isa. 53:12). The soul of Jesus was deeply grieved, to the point of death (Matt. 26:38). He willingly poured out His "life blood" completely emptying Himself unto death. About His life Jesus said, "No one has taken it away from Me, but I lay it down on My own initiative" (John 10:18). Jesus poured out His own soul (Isa. 53:11). Jesus was "delivered up by the predetermined plan and foreknowledge of God, and put to death on a cross by godless men" (Acts 2:23). The love, strength, and power of Jesus endured, and He overcame the bearing of our sin. The Resurrection and leaving behind His work in our life, guarantees we too will overcome, and have the victory over sin and death by His love. To God be the glory.

How can we be certain that the shed blood of Jesus was acceptable to God for the forgiveness of our sin, and the future blessing of eternal life? We were not present to see His death and resurrection, but we are alive to experience the consequences of the Fathers pleasure. The Holy Spirit is alive and spends time with us to teach us all things and be a Helper (John 14:16, 26). Jesus said, "It is the Spirit who gives life; the flesh profits nothing; the words that I have spoken to you are spirit and life" (John 6:63). Both God the Father and the Son, can give life (John 5:21). "That which is born of the Spirit is spirit, you must be born again (John 3:6-7). We must be drawn by God the Father (John 6:44, 65) and quickened to life by the Spirit (John 6:63). Jesus said, "He who believes in Me, as the scripture said, from his innermost being shall flow rivers of living water" (John 7:38). We will only be satisfied by coming to Christ because He alone can fill our spiritual emptiness. The Bible tells us in the next verse that "Jesus spoke of the Spirit, whom those who believed in Him were to receive; for the Spirit was not yet given, because Jesus was not yet glorified" (John 7:39). After Jesus predicted His betrayal and Judas departed from the room where they took the Lord's Supper, Jesus stated that His death on the cross was His glorification (John 13:21-31). Though the agony of death was before Him, it was no disgrace. The Son of God, as incarnate, the Son of Man, performed the greatest work in history. The last Adam was obedient and destroyed him who had the power of death, that is the devil (Heb. 2:14). He purchased for Himself all the elect of God, and glorified God (John 13:31). On the cross, He cried out "It is finished" and gave up His spirit (John 19:30). All things had been accomplished for the putting away of the sins of the people, providing for them a perfect righteous standing before God with a secure eternal inheritance. The power, justice, holiness, faithfulness, and love of God was glorified at the cross of Jesus Christ. "God loved us and sent His Son to be the propitiation for our sins" (1 John 4:10).

The gift of the Holy Spirit was made possible by the shed blood of Christ. The Holy Spirit was not given until the price was paid. Jesus said, "John baptized with water, but you shall be baptized with the Holy Spirit" (Acts 1:5). Jesus said to them that "they shall receive power when the Holy Spirit has come upon you; and you shall be My witnesses" (Acts 1:8). He had commanded them to not leave Jerusalem, but to wait for what the Father had promised them (Acts 1:4). After the resurrection, Jesus spent time instructing His disciples. He was seen by many people at different times, occasions, and locations in His resurrected body for forty days. One time there was over 500 people (1 Cor. 15:6), and then He ascended into heaven (Acts 1:9). Ten days later, on what we call the Day of Pentecost, the Holy Spirit descended upon the Apostles and other followers of Jesus Christ in a rush of wind and tongues of fire (Acts 2:1-4). The Church of the living God was born (1 Tim. 3:15). Amen

We "overcome the accuser because of the blood of the Lamb, and because of the word of their testimony, and they did not love their life even to death" (Rev. 12:11). The book of Revelation in chapter five tells us that "the Lion that is from the tribe of Judah, the Root of David, has overcome so as to open the book and its seven seals" (Rev. 5:5). John, the author sees a Lamb standing, as if slain, take the book from Him who sat on the throne (Rev. 5:6-7). Myriads of angels, living creatures and elders exalt the Lamb, saying with a loud voice, "Worthy is the Lamb that was slain to receive power and riches and wisdom and might and honor and glory and blessing" (Rev. 5:12). The One who dwelt among men in the flesh (John 1:14), the Messiah, Jesus Christ, is coming to judge the earth in righteousness (Ps. 96:11-13). Amen. The testimony of John the Baptist, the "voice of one crying in the wilderness" (John 1:23; Isa. 40:3) is clear and grabs at my soul. "Behold, the Lamb of God who takes away the sin of the world!" (John 1:29,36). The Bible tells us, "You were not redeemed with perishable things like silver or gold, but with the precious blood, as of a lamb unblemished and spotless, the blood of Christ" (1 Pet. 1:18-19). We are to be on guard "to shepherd the church of God which He purchased with His own blood" (Acts 20:28).

The scriptures clearly point to Jesus Christ as the Passover Lamb whose blood "covered" and protected the Israelites from the destroying angel in Egypt (Ex, 12:3-13). Paul clearly understood Jesus to be the Passover Lamb. "For Christ our Passover also has been sacrificed" (1 Cor. 5:7). The slaying of the Son of God was foreordained before the foundation of the world (1 Pet. 1:20; Rev. 13:8; Isa. 45:21). "God will provide for Himself the lamb" (Gen. 22:8). The atonement, made possible by the cross of Jesus, is presented to our hearts, Christian, in the picture of Abraham offering his only son Isaac (Gen. 22). The Bible tells us that the testing of Abraham was in the land of Moriah, three days journey from where he was living in the land of the Philistines (Gen. 22:2, 21:34). Mount Moriah was the place selected by David (2 Sam.

24:18) where Solomon built the temple in Jerusalem, and where the Lord appeared to David on the threshing floor of Ornan the Jebusite (2 Chron. 3:1). The second temple was built on the site of the first temple. Some scholars believe that Mount Moriah is the place, or at least close by, to that called Golgotha, where Jesus was crucified (Matt. 27:33-35). Jewish tradition claims that God created Adam on Mount Moriah, which would be near where the second Adam would die for God's elect. Moriah means "chosen by Jehovah." Mount Moriah is in Old City Jerusalem, and is a sacred place to Christians, Jews, and Muslims. The Bible suggests a third temple will most likely be built sometime before the tribulation, I assume near the site of Solomon's temple (Dan. 9:27). I know that God is in the details, and that nothing is impossible for God (Luke 1:37). Amen.

Jesus is the true Lamb of God who takes away the sin of the world (John 1:29). He was appointed by the grace of God. He must be received into your heart for salvation. In Jewish Law, one lamb was offered in the morning and another lamb was offered at twilight every day (Ex. 29:38-39). Another lamb was killed and eaten at the Passover to commemorate their deliverance from Egypt (Ex. 12:3-11). Jesus was the Lamb of God, provided by God and offered in atonement for sins, one sacrifice for sins forever (Heb. 10:12). We are redeemed by the precious blood of Jesus. He was the unblemished, spotless, and sinless Lamb of God who appeared that we might have faith and hope and believe in God (1 Pet. 1:19-21). Look to Jesus and be saved. Only the blood of this "Lamb" can take away sins. "He would render Himself as a guilt offering" and "bear their iniquities" and "He Himself bore the sin of many" (Isa. :10-12). John saw a lamb standing, as if slain (Rev. 5:6). The Lamb of God is referred to by Moses (Gen, 3:15), and prophesied by Isaiah (Isa. 53:4-12) and Jeremiah (Jer. 23:5-6). The Lamb of God was typified by Noah's Ark (Gen. 6-7; Heb. 11:7). The Tabernacle was a type of Jesus Christ (Ex. 25-40) and He was typified by the Passover lamb (Ex. 12:3-10). We are to behold the Lamb of God with seriousness, reverence, and with an eye of faith (Heb. 12:2). "Turn to Me and be saved all the ends of the earth" (Isa. 45:22).

Behold Jesus with an eye for repentance (Zech. 12:10), gratitude (1 John 4:10), and love (Rom. 5:8). When you "eat" of Jesus Christ (John 6:53-58), you will know the virtue of Him changing your heart (2 Cor. 5:17) and comforting your conscience (Heb. 9:14). Amen.

If you are alive, then you were born in what we call the first time, according to the flesh. That is, you had an earthly father and mother, were born as a natural person, and did not know the Lord. We are born without any saving spiritual life. We were born of blood, but not of God. We cannot accept the things of the Spirit of God; for they are foolishness to us and we cannot understand them (1 Cor. 2:14). We do not see the true, valuable, and better nature of Jesus Christ compared to anything else in the world. To see Jesus, and enter the kingdom of God, we must be born again (John 3:3). "That which is born of the flesh is flesh, and that which is born of the spirit is spirit" (John 3:6). The truth is, we did not choose anything about our first birth, that is, we did not choose the time or where in the world we would be born, or even our parents. We did not choose our sex, height, or skin color. God did. We do not create new life in our souls or control when we would be born again or how we would grow in grace either. God did. We are born again by the grace of God; it is a gift and a miracle (John 1:13). It is the sovereign, mysterious and loving work of the Holy Spirit of God (John 3:8; Eph. 1:3-14). Amen.

To know God, we must have new life. The Bible tells us that "when we were dead in our transgressions [God] made us alive together with Christ" (Eph. 2:5), that is, He gave us a second birth. The mysterious work of the Spirit is compared to the blowing of the wind (John 3:8). The world does not know the Spirit of truth, and men do not receive the teaching that the shed blood of Jesus means anything, especially about saving them from the penalty of their sins. Man is a fallen creature; a depraved being who is not spiritual but loves sin and rejects holiness. Man is too prideful and rebellious, and has a veil over his heart that prevents him from seeing or embracing God's love in Jesus. The Bible tells us that "God has shut all up in disobedience that He might show mercy to all" (Rom. 11:32). Man needs God's supernatural influence by the Holy Spirit to overcome his rejection and disinterest in the Gospel. In the Fall of man in the garden of Eden, man's heart was withdrawn from God, his understanding darkened, and his will hostile to God and enslaved to sin. The depth of man's depravity made it impossible for him to receive Jesus and accept the Gospel on his own. We have the freedom to say no thanks to Jesus, but not yes to God without God's help. This describes the condition of all natural men. In the case of those folks who receive the Gospel, the influence of God has "drawn" them to the Son. "No man can come to Me [Jesus] unless the Father who sent Me draws him" (John 6:44, 65). "It is the Spirit who gives life; the flesh profits nothing" (John 6:63). The "drawing" is the power of the Holy Spirit allowing our souls to hear a wake-up call from God. It is the beginning of God's children being taught of God (John 6:45; Isa. 54:13). By the grace of God, we begin a journey to know God. We are awakened to a great sense of need and a conviction that we are lost. The Lord is appearing in our soul. God says, "I have loved you with an everlasting love; therefore, I have drawn you with lovingkindness" (Jer. 31:3). God has always loved us, and when the Son of Man comes into our hearts, by the grace of God, it is our believing in Christ for eternal life (John 3:14-15, 12:32). Those being drawn by God are His children (Isa. 54:13). They are being drawn and taught by God into a conscious and believing experience from the gift of faith in His Son Jesus Christ. All who hear the Gospel do not respond positively to it, but the ones who do are the elect, chosen by God to trust Christ. We are called to know the power and goodness and wisdom of God in Christ (1 Cor. 1:24). The call of God is effectual and irrevocable because it comes with Divine power (Rom. 11:29). God's word does not return to Him empty without accomplishing what He desires (Isa. 55:11). It is to the glory of God that He has made both the hearing ear and seeing eye (Prov. 20:12). The kindness of God revealed in the shedding of the blood of Jesus Christ, led me to repentance (Rom. 2:4).

The creation of a new man (2 Cor. 5:17) is what being born

again is all about. We are drawn (John 6:44), quickened (John 6:63) and become partakers of the divine nature (2 Pet. 1:4) by the pleasure, will and power of God. God's word does not educate or fix the natural man to be holy. The grace of God imparts a new nature, which He feeds and fills with the Word of God. "He saved us not on the basis of deeds which we have done in righteousness, but according to His mercy, by the washing of regeneration and renewing by the Holy Spirit, whom He poured out upon us richly through Jesus Christ our Savior" (Titus 3:5-6). The devil wants you to focus only on yourself. He wants you to monitor and worry about your progress in holiness, good works, resolutions, baptism, and repentance. He wants you to believe that you are doing enough to earn the right to be saved. The key with God, however, is to focus on Christ and to seek Him first, and all these things shall be added unto you (Matt. 6:33). Faith in Christ is the beginning of wisdom and true godliness. Jesus saves. It is not the amount of your faith that saves you, but the look of faith, by the grace of God, out of your soul onto the Savior Himself. In His death, His blood was shed. The debt for the price of your sin was paid, and the promise of sending the Holy Spirit was fulfilled. The presence of the Holy Spirit with your soul is the "down payment" that God is at work (Eph. 2:10; Phil. 2:13). Your responsibility, in part, is fulfilled in your worship, fear, and gratitude to God for His inexpressible love. Jesus prayed that the Father would send us another helper to be with us forever (John 14:16). Would He have sent the Holy Spirit if the sacrifice of Jesus was in any insufficient? I think not. The Holy Spirit is the Spirit of truth, whom the world cannot receive (John 14:17). Jesus said, "The Helper, the Holy Spirit whom the Father will send in My name, He will teach you all things" (John 14:26). God sends you into His word to get the truth, and then gives you more understanding and peace and joy and obedience, along your journey back into His presence. The true testimony of Jesus is established in your heart by the grace of God, through the powerful work of the Holy Spirit. Amen. Jesus said, "When He [Holy Spirit] comes, He will convict the world of sin, righteousness, and judgment" (John 16:8). The testimony of the Holy Spirit is about Jesus. The testimony of the Holy Spirit is about holiness, eternal life, and the righteousness of Jesus. The testimony of the Holy Spirit is taking place when He calls you to look to Jesus. He wants you to be forgiven of your sin by the blood of Jesus, and receive Him into your heart for eternal life. This is love, "He first loved us" (1 John 4:19). Amen.

The restoration and spiritual regeneration of Israel during the time of the captivity in Babylon and shortly after was prophesied in Ezekiel and Zechariah. The nation of Israel has been miraculously preserved for thousands of years. God was in a covenant with Abraham (Gen. 15, 17). Though other nations have been destroyed, Israel was scattered and not absorbed into other nationalities. God proclaims that He will gather them out of all countries and return the Jews to their own land to vindicate, magnify and sanctify the holiness of His great name (Ezek. 36: 22-24). He promises to do a great work in them to qualify them for the work He planned for them. He will sprinkle clean water on them, give them a new heart and a new spirit, and put His own Spirit in them, so they would be careful to observe His ordinances (Ezek. 36:25-27). God makes all His people alive together with Jesus Christ, the Messiah (Eph. 2:5; Col. 2:13). "How blessed are the people whose God is the Lord" (Ps. 144:15). The literal fulfillment of these scripture verses requires a future millennial blessing to Israel after the coming of Christ (Jer. 23:5-8). God is saying that Israel will be born again. In Zechariah, the Lord proclaims a king is coming, endowed with salvation, humble, and mounted on a donkey (Zech. 9:9). The Lord says, "Because of the blood of My covenant with you, I have set your prisoners free from the waterless pit" (Zech. 9:11). A sinful state is like bondage in a dungeon where there is no water. The truth in these verses also clearly describe the New Covenant. New Testament conversion is a preview of the spiritual revival God has in store for all true Israel and Gentiles who are of the seed of Abraham and believe. As a natural man, we were in the pit with no water, but have been rescued by the grace of God. By the blood of the New Covenant of the Lord Jesus Christ, we have been saved. We have been sealed in the covenant by the blood of Jesus. The

New Covenant takes away guilt and gives a real rest to our hearts. We will be His people and He will be our God (Gen. 17:8; Jer. 24:7, 31:31-33; Ezek. 37:23, 27; Zech. 8:8; Heb. 8:10). He will counsel, guide, and protect us, and we will know Him and proclaim His excellencies. Amen.

The spiritual regeneration of Israel by the Holy Spirit, can also be applied in the New Covenant for the promises made to Christians (Ezek. 36:25-27). The promise of the Holy Spirit comes with gracious influences and operations for the sanctification of all of God's people. The Bible tells us that God will sprinkle clean water on you, which signifies, both the blood of Christ upon the conscience to take away guilt (Heb. 10:22), and the grace of the Spirit on the whole soul to purify it from corrupt inclinations (Ezek. 36:25). "Moreover, I will give you a new heart and put a new spirit within you" (Ezek. 36:36). "I will put My Spirit within you and cause you to walk in My statutes" (Ezek. 36:37). We cannot sanctify God's name or live to His glory but by His grace. A new heart and a new spirit with God's help are indispensable to walking in newness of life. A heart of flesh instead of stone will make us more conscious of God, with a desire to know and live according to His will. The Holy Spirit within us will give us wisdom, the will and power to be taught and guided into true faith in Jesus, and to do a good work (Phil. 2:13). The promise is, "you will be My people, and I will be your God" (Ezek. 36:28). God circumcises our hearts (Col. 2:11). This kind of spiritual surgery can only be done by God, and He does this initially by drawing us to Jesus (John 6:44). We need the love, power, and grace of God to move in us to be born again. "Unless one is born again, he cannot see the kingdom of God" (John 3:3). Because this is only a work that God can do, it is a humbling experience for the natural man with his pride to accept. "By grace you have been saved through faith; and that not of yourselves, it is the gift of God" (Eph. 2:8-9). Motivated by love, God softens our heart to come to Christ. God opens our minds to understand our sin and our need of Jesus as a Savior. God gives us the desire, hope and will to follow through in coming to Jesus for forgiveness. To God be the glory.

Although the work of the Holy Spirit cannot be seen with the eye, the evidence of His presence can be known or manifested by the new relationship that develops in your soul. The new heart with the gift of faith grows by God's grace and knowledge and more deeply embraces Christ as Savior and Lord. Jesus said, "It is the Spirit who gives life; the flesh profits nothing; the words that I have spoken to you are spirit and are life" (John 6:63). The Bible tells us that, "faith comes by hearing, and hearing the word of Christ" (Rom. 10:17). The Lord opens your heart (Acts 16:14), and sends you into His word to nourish your spiritual life and guide you into a closer walk with Jesus. The Lord has magnified His word according to all His name (Ps. 138:2). The Lord speaks to us by His word and by His Son (Heb. 1:1-2). His word quickens, sustains, and comforts us. His word tells us how our sins are pardoned and our souls saved. His word declares His glory, grace, love, goodness, faithfulness, patience, kindness, mercy, justice, holiness and all the perfections of God. His word will make you tremble (Isa. 66:2) and leap for joy (John 15:11). In the Bible are the words of spiritual life devoted to Jesus and used by the Holy Spirit to impart new life. "You have been born again not of seed which is perishable but imperishable, that is, through the living and abiding word of God (1 Pet. 1:23). "The word of our God stands forever" (Isa. 40:8). The Holy Spirit is the Spirit of the written word through which God moved men to write it (2 Pet. 1:21). The Holy Spirit is the Spirit of truth whom the world cannot receive, because it has not been born again (John 3:3, 14:17; 1 Cor. 2:14). The world is in a political mess, and a liar and opposed to God. It lies in the power of the evil one (1 John 2:16, 5:19). "In the exercise of His will, He brought us forth by the word of truth" (James 1:18). The Bible is the word of God that contains the true means of regeneration.

Some of the things that Jesus said or taught were hard to understand or accept by certain people, and as a result, they rejected Him altogether. The idea that a man cannot come to Jesus on his own, because of the depth of his natural depravity, and must be drawn by the Father, is difficult to accept. The decision to be saved does not entirely belong to them. Salvation lies in the lovingkindness and sovereignty of a perfect God and not in their work. The way is in humility and not their intelligence and pride. The way is in surrender and faith in Jesus, who to the natural man may be just another person. Jesus told us that His teaching was not His, but His who sent Him (John 7:16). The idea that God has acted by His supernatural influence to overcome the natural depravity in some folks, but not all people is troublesome to them. The sovereignty of God in salvation is a spiritual deep that took place before the foundation of the world in the counsels of God (Eph. 1:4-5). Our salvation "does not depend on the man who wills or the man who runs, but on God who has mercy" (Rom. 9:16). In this deep spiritual mystery, Christian, we must let God be God. We are still responsible, through fear and trembling, to discover His work in our hearts (Phil. 2:12). The Bible tells us, that our hope of salvation lies outside of ourselves, that it is in Jesus, and by the grace of God (Eph. 2:8-10). The Bible also tells us that this kind of teaching led many of His disciples to withdraw and not walk with Jesus anymore (John 6:66). God's word is the truth, and must be received above a man's pride, feelings, opinions, and ideas about what they think is fair or right. "God has shut up all in disobedience that He might show mercy to all" (Rom. 11:32). We all stand convicted of unbelief. Not every individual person will know the mercy of being brought to believe in Christ. We must receive the righteousness that comes by faith in Christ. The conversion of Gentiles is a mystery (Eph. 3:3-8). The Bible tells us that God chose "to make known the riches of His glory upon vessels of mercy, which He prepared beforehand for glory," and "endured with much patience vessels of wrath to make His power known" (Rom. 9:22-23). Our being made alive in Christ, was to show in the coming ages the surpassing riches of His grace toward us in Christ Jesus. The Holy Spirit helps us become as "little children" (Matt. 18:2). The disciples that left Him, may have called Him Lord, but their action proved they were spiritually dead and lost (Matt. 7:21). Jesus knows those who will not believe (John 6:64).

The new birth is not of the will of your flesh, but of God

(John 1:13). God works according to His own eternal counsel and sovereign pleasure (Eph. 1; Rom. 9). We should not expect it to be any other way. Because the nature of the natural man has not changed, the unbeliever is filled with hate against God, and the Christian who believes in God (Rom. 8:7). For the believer, spiritual intelligence comes into the heart by the grace of God. The nonbeliever lives by the worlds intelligence which thrives off the physical evidence alone. When we are born again, God gives us the grace of faith in our new heart to read and learn from the Bible (Rom. 10:17), and follow Jesus. In the exercise of faith, we will read the Bible, and understand the doctrine, get more faith, and follow on to discover and know the Lord (Hosea 6:3). Jesus becomes the bread of life for our soul (John 6:35), and we grow in the spiritual strength and the comforts that only He can provide. "By faith we understand" (Heb. 11:3). By faith, we perceive in our mind, God's infinitely creative genius, power, and lovingkindness. By faith, we sense His presence with us daily, and grow in believing His providential acts of kindness to us that bring us to Jesus in this life, and for the life to come. When we lean into Jesus, we gain a confidence that has a testimony that we cannot walk away from. We have been changed, we are saved, and by the grace of God will not go back to our old life. The Bible tells us that, "if any man is willing to do His will, he shall know of the teaching (John 7:17). "He who has My commandments and keeps them, he it is who loves Me" and "I will disclose Myself to him" (John 14:21). Faith in Jesus fixes our lives fully and forever on God. We have been blessed with the gifts of peace and truth. The gifts of God establish in our hearts that He is a rewarder of those who seek Him (Heb. 11:6). We work out our salvation with fear and trembling (Phil. 2:12). We will not be perfect in this life, but we will know, by the grace of God, a willingness and desire to do the will of God. We will be living with Jesus, by the grace of God, to please Him and glorify Him. The peace in faith will inform you of God's will. Faith may precede reason to confirm His presence, goodness, and glory. God takes our faith into obedience, which will be a comforting mark of His love and workmanship (Eph. 2:10).

Since the shed blood of Jesus was accepted by the Father for the payment of our sin, the Holy Spirit that He promised (Luke 24:49), was sent to comfort, teach, and help us to grow in Christ (John 14:16, 26). The influence of the Holy Spirit on the soul of a believer is evident. The plan of God also involved the presence of the Holy Spirit in the building up of the Church (Matt. 16:18). The Bible tells us that ten days after the Ascension of Jesus Christ (Acts 1:9), the Holy Spirit appeared in an upper room in Jerusalem filled with the twelve Apostles and probably another 120 disciples (Acts 1:12-15). "Suddenly there came from heaven a noise like a violent, rushing wind and it filled the whole house. There appeared to them tongues as of fire distributing themselves, and they rested on each one of them. They were all filled with the Holy Spirit and began to speak in tongues (Acts 2:1-4). The building of the Church was commenced by the power of the Holy Spirit energizing people. The same Holy Spirit is at work in us today to spread the Gospel and glorify Jesus. "Christ loved the church and gave Himself for her; that He might sanctify her, having cleansed her by the washing of water with the word, that He might present to Himself the church in all her glory" (Eph. 5:25-27). Have you been made spiritually alive and quickened? Do you have the Holy Spirit in your soul? Has "the law of the Spirit of life in Christ Jesus set you free from the law of sin and of death" (Rom. 8:2). Out of the new birth, with a new and living heart, a people would become free. Together, they would gather for worship and be called the Church. They would be vessels of mercy (Rom. 9:23) and love each other (1 Pet. 1:22). God's word would be fulfilled. The message of the second coming of Jesus is mentioned over 300 times in the New Testament, and it will be fulfilled. Amen. He is coming again to take the people of His church, that He shed His blood for, to heaven. Israel will be saved (Rom. 11:25-27). He is coming to sit upon the throne of David (Luke 1:31-33) and judge the nations (Matt. 25:31-46). He is coming to bring a righteous government to the earth (Heb. 1:8). "He is coming the same way they watched Him go into heaven (Acts 1:11). The scripture will be accomplished in your life by the grace of God. "He who began a good work in you will perfect it until the day of Christ Jesus" (Phil. 1:6). God's word from His mouth will not return to Him empty, but will accomplish what He desires and what He sent it for (Isa. 55:11). Amen.

The Holy Spirit is described as the source of spiritual life (Rom. 8:10-11; John 6:63). It is the Holy Spirit who becomes the Almighty Agent within the believer that secures our deliverance from sin (Rom. 7:24-25). Our deliverance is made possible through the death, burial, and resurrection of Jesus Christ. The Holy Spirit makes this a reality and an effectual experience in our life. The shed blood of Jesus was far superior to the Old Testament sacrifices. It was only done once to "perfect for all time those who are sanctified" (Heb. 10:14). The Son of God offered His own blood, without blemish, and not another animal's blood. The new nature, with the promise fulfilled of the Holy Spirit, provides for an intimate relationship with God. Our obligation is not to the Mosaic Law with its requirements, Christian; we are to follow the law of the Spirit of life in Christ (Rom. 8:2). The Bible tells us, that when we surrendered to Jesus Christ and received Him into our hearts, we died, and our life was hidden with Christ in God and Christ becomes our life (Col. 3:3-4). We still are in a conflict between the law of sin and the law of God, but we "joyfully concur with the spiritual law of God in the inner man" (Rom. 7:22). "If Christ is in you, though the body is dead because of sin, yet the spirit is alive because of righteousness" (Rom. 8:10). Because we have the righteousness of Jesus, there is no condemnation for us (Rom. 8:1). The Law of the Spirit of life in Christ Jesus (Rom. 8:2) is a "regulative" principle which exercises a loving and powerful influence in our lives. We can resist (Acts 7:51), quench (1 Thess. 5:19), and grieve (Eph. 4:30) the Holy Spirit, but God is faithful and still graciously works within us (Eph. 2:10). "God is at work in you, both to will and to work for His good pleasure" (Phil. 2:13). The principle of sin brings death (Rom. 7), but the operating principle of the Spirit of the life in Christ is more powerful (Phil. 1:6). The Christian has a new law or principle of life in his inner man. "The path of the righteous is like the light of dawn, that shines brighter and brighter until the full day. The way of the wicked is like darkness; they do not know over what they stumble" (Prov. 4:18-19). The life of the righteous is from grace to grace, to see more of God's goodness and mercy. All my life, God has been patiently preparing me for His presence. To God be the glory.

Our new spiritual life is no longer earthly, but is with the life of the One who shed His blood and rose again. He walks with us and talks to us, and our lives are regulated by His lovingkindness. The Spirit is resident within us, and when we grow in grace to learn His new laws, heaven comes to us. When we get saved, we are going to heaven. When we surrender and submit, by the grace of God, the Lord discloses more of Himself to us (John 14:21). The closer we get to Jesus, the more convicted we are about the truth of His life. The closer we get to Jesus, the more convicted we are about the truth being in the Bible. Jesus died and shed His blood. He rose from the dead and is coming again. I believe by the grace of God. Being alive in Jesus is a life changer. In the Spirit of life in Christ Jesus, we are to "bear one another's burdens, and thus fulfill the law of Christ" (Gal. 6:2). We are to exercise patience and compassion towards others, which agrees with the law of love (Rom. 13:8; James 2:8). "You shall love your neighbor as yourself" fulfills the royal law (Matt. 7:12). We are being justified as a gift of God's grace in Christ Jesus. God displayed Him publicly as a propitiation, or the way to regain favor with Himself. The way of salvation is through faith in His perfect sacrifice. The shedding of His blood demonstrated a righteousness in Him, that is imputed to us by the grace of God. No flesh will boast. The Lord is our righteousness (1 Cor. 1:30). It is all God's glory. Faith is a depending and self-denying grace that casts every crown before His throne. Faith is a law and a working grace that depends solely on Jesus Christ (Rom. 3:24-28). The law of faith is another way of saying the principle of faith. The basis of our justification is based on believing what Jesus Christ has done for us. We are saved by grace through faith, not of works (Eph. 2:8-9).

The Law of liberty is described in the book of James. "The one who looks intently at the perfect law, the law of liberty, and abides by it, will be blessed in what he does" (James 1:25). The law of the Lord is perfect, restoring the soul (Ps. 19:7). Obeying the law of God is the way to discover your God-given destiny. In Jesus, we are in a state of freedom in opposition to bondage to sin (Rom. 6:16) and the Law (Gal. 2:4). Freedom is enabled by the indwelling Spirit (Rom. 8:2). Because Jesus shed His blood in dying and was resurrected, the Spirit was sent and we could be born again to new life. True liberty is living as we should, and being captive to the word and law of God. To learn and love Christ is to be blessed with freedom. We will be judged by the law of freedom at the Bema seat of Christ (2 Cor. 5:10). This is where the judgment of only the believers works take place, and is not about salvation, which took place on Calvary for the believer (Rom. 8:1). "If therefore, the Son shall make you free, you shall be free indeed" (John 8:36). "Mercy triumphs over judgment" (James 2:13). Let the scriptures be your standard, Christian, and love be your law. Amen.

The main effects the Spirit produces are in our hearts. The life it brings confirms the truth about Jesus. We were not present to see Him alive, but the life the Spirit works in us through gift of faith is enormous. In being alive, our conscience is awakened, and more sensitive and inclined to seek and do the will of God. We find ourselves putting off the old man and putting on the new man (Eph. 4:22-24). The natural man is lost, dull and disinterested about God. Spiritual things like faith are foolishness to him (1 Cor. 2:14). All those who have the Spirit are led by God into the scriptures to grow in the grace of faith (Rom. 10:17). We were blind and ignorant, but the Spirit of truth teaches us all things (John 14:16, 16:13). We begin to know and grow, live, and enjoy the essentials of true religion. We will delight in Bible study (Ps. 1:2). God removes the veil of prejudice, bias and misunderstanding, and shines truth into our hearts. A lost person will not care about Jesus, or study the Bible. A lost person will choose to remain where he is; believing he is already right and feeling complete with the little bit of sin he thinks he has, without the need of Jesus. A person with the Holy Spirit becomes rich with God. The person with the Holy Spirit rejoices in Jesus. He is like the people who found the lost coin and the lost sheep, and recognize that they were once like the prodigal son (Luke 15). A person who has the Holy Spirit knows what the conflict is like between the Spirit and the flesh (Gal.5:17). A person who has the Holy Spirit knows that the principle of evil is in him, but joyfully concurs with the law of God in the inner man (Rom. 7:22-23).

The blood of Jesus opened the way for our forgiveness and acceptance with God. The blood of Jesus released the truth that sets us free. Because of the shed blood of Jesus, we can receive the Holy Spirit and be changed into a new man by the grace of God and the work of the Holy Spirit. A lost person will not know the burden of his sin, is a servant of sin, and does not experience the inward conflict of the Lord saving his soul. A lost person will not see the merits of the shed blood of Jesus preparing their heart for eternity in God's presence. All who have the Holy Spirit have been led to Christ for salvation, by the grace of God, as a vessel of mercy (Rom. 9:23). He teaches us that nothing but the blood of Jesus can atone for sin. He unfolds the doctrines of justification and sanctification in our minds by the grace of faith (Rom. 5:1-5, 8:1-4; 1 Cor. 1:30). He is called the spirit of holiness (Rom. 1:4). We have strong desires to be free from sin and walk closely with the Lord. The Holy Spirit leads us into the fruit of the Spirit; which is love, joy, peace, patience, gentleness, meekness, faith, and kindness (Gal. 5:22-23). We live and walk by the Spirit, and we love the brethren (1 John 3:14). We all are children of the same King. A person who has the spirit of adoption, will cry "Abba Father" (Gal. 4:6). The Holy Spirit teaches us to pray, whereas the lost person does not know how to pray. The lost person knows nothing about faith in Christ, living a holy life, or being comfortable with people who know the Lord. The presence of the Holy Spirit can be discerned, by the grace of God, by a Christian in himself, and sometimes sensed in another believer. The fruit of the Holy Spirit in you, in part, is evidence you are a child of God. Nevertheless, we are to "be diligent to make certain about His calling and choosing you" (2 Pet. 1:10). Those who have read the word of God and recognize they have grown in grace and knowledge will know Jesus, and that by God's grace, they have eternal life (1 John 5:13). Amen.

"The wages of sin is death, but the free gift of God is eternal life in Christ Jesus our Lord" (Rom. 6:23). We deserve to die because of sin, but eternal life is a merciful gift from Jesus that we will release eternal gratitude in our eternal souls. It is Christ Jesus Himself that purchased it for us. The blood of the Lamb of God is good news. We have come to the city of the living God, "and to Jesus, the mediator of a New Covenant, and to the sprinkled blood, which speaks better than the blood of Abel" (Heb. 12:24). The sprinkled blood of Jesus graciously forgives us instead of crying out for vengeance as the blood of Abel's did (Gen. 4:10). In the Old Testament, the blood of sprinkling could mean preservation (Ex. 12), confirmation of a covenant (Ex. 24), purification (Heb. 9:21), and sanctification (1 Pet. 1:2). The sprinkling of the blood of Jesus has made us kings and priests. He accepts us and encourages us to draw near to God (Eph. 2:13). We have confidence to enter the holy place by the blood of Jesus (Heb. 10:9). When we believe God's testimony for the blood of Jesus, we are safe and protected by Christ, our Passover Lamb (Ex. 12:13). Let us draw near with a sincere heart in full assurance of faith having our hearts sprinkled clean from an evil conscience (Heb. 10:22).

The blood of the Lamb contains life. "Unless you eat the flesh of the Son of Man and drink His blood, you have no life" (John 6:53). The sacrificial death of Christ must be received into the heart by faith. We were not present to see Christ, but others were, and they gave a strong testimony. We also have the word of God that testifies to the truth about Christ, and the study of the Bible is the source of a growing faith. Most important is the testimony of the Holy Spirit, which applies the power of God to the healing of our hearts in this life. The death of Jesus becomes a new life for us. By the grace of God, we continue to receive Christ into our hearts every day by study, prayer, and obedience. He nourishes our souls every day. Eating the flesh and drinking the blood means believing in Jesus. We hunger and thirst after Christ for righteousness and safety for spiritual growth and eternal life. Being spiritually with Jesus is the foretaste of heaven on earth. Jesus lived His life in a dependence upon the Father, and when we eat and drink Jesus, we are living with a dependence upon Him (John 6:57). When we dwell with Jesus every day, then the soul is refreshed and the truth will set us free (John 8:32). He told us, "The cup which is poured out for you is the new covenant in My blood" (Luke 22:20). In the Lord's Supper, the juice we drink from the cup is the symbol of the blood of Jesus. It represents the seal of our everlasting covenant of peace with God (Heb. 13:20; Isa. 54:10). Partaking of the Lord's Supper becomes a deep humbling spiritual experience, confirming for us that by the blood of Jesus, we belong to God. The strong foundation that our faith rests upon is the blood of Jesus Christ. We will be forever safe; beyond the possibility of sin, disobedience, and trouble forever. Amen.

"God is light, and in Him there is no darkness at all" (1 John 1:5). "If we walk in the light as He Himself is in the light, we have fellowship with one another, and the blood of Jesus His Son cleanses us from all sin" (1 John 1:7). The blood of Christ will cleanse your conscience from dead works to serve the living God (Heb. 9:14). The word "purging" is also used for cleansing sometimes. David prayed to God, "purify me with hyssop, and I shall be clean; wash me, and I shall be whiter than snow" (Ps. 51:17). We are cleansed of the guilt of sin, and the defiling consequences of sin in our soul. We are cleansed in conscience and heart; body, soul, and spirit by the blood of Jesus. The word "hyssop" is an herb, but it means God's grace in this passage. We are cleansed by the blood through the power of the Spirit (1 John 1:7, 9). In the book of the Revelation, the saints are clothed with white robes and have palm branches in their hands (Rev. 7:9). The white robes speak of holiness, being justified and sanctified, from our victory in Jesus. We have been purged and cleansed by the grace of God, to be a fit bride for the Son of God (2 Cor. 11:2; Rev. 19:7). The blood of the Lamb contains our forgiveness (Heb. 9:22) and our peace (Col. 1:20). "He Himself is our peace" (Eph. 2:14). We have been bought with a price (1 Cor. 6:20). The whole Church, and God's work of grace in spreading the Gospel, was purchased by Christ with His own blood (Acts 20:28). Amen.

By God's love, grace, sovereign pleasure, and Christs act of righteousness (Rom. 5:18-19), we were justified by His shed blood (Rom. 5:9). While we were still helpless and dead in our sins, He died for the ungodly (Rom. 5:6). The blood of the Lamb is the atonement, that is, the blood forgives sin in our soul so that it becomes indiscernible by God Himself. The result of the forgiveness of sin or atonement, is that God is favorably disposed toward the sinner and the result is reconciliation with God. Atonement means redemption from the wrath of God. We are "justified as a gift by His grace through the redemption which is in Christ Jesus" (Rom. 3:24). To demonstrate the righteousness of God, He passed over our sins previously committed and reconciled us to Himself by the blood of Jesus through faith (Rom. 3:25). "Through the obedience of the One, many will be made righteous" (Rom. 5:19). It appears that many, but not all, will be saved. Some folks will not understand the Son of God, regard the blood as unclean, and insult the Spirit of grace (Heb. 10:29). The righteous will overcome the accuser by the blood of the Lamb (Rev. 12:2), be sanctified through His blood (Heb. 13:12), and with Him, resurrected to eternal life (John 6:54; Rom. 6:5; 2 Cor. 4:14). A price was paid, atonement was made and the chosen of God are redeemed by the blood of the lamb (Eph. 1:7, 14). Amen. The Bible tells us that God says, "I will be merciful to your iniquities, and I will remember your sins no more" (Heb. 8:12). The promises in the New Covenant are far superior to the Old Covenant. The complete pardon of sin by God, and the promise of purity in our hearts, is only possible because of the shed blood of Jesus. He wipes out our transgressions for His own sake, and will remember them no more (Isa. 43:25; Ps. 103:12). Our sins will never be held against us. Forgiving ourselves is not found in the scripture. God's forgiveness is much greater and means more. To God be the glory. Amen.

The blood of Jesus Christ is precious and sufficient to cleanse us from all sorts of sins. The blood from the spiritual fountain of Jesus Christ is a perfect help and hope against all despair that might try to lodge guilt in your soul. The blood of Jesus has purchased for us a liberty and peace to come close to the Father in our prayers (Eph. 2:13-14). He inaugurated a new and living way through the veil, that is His flesh, and a confidence by His blood to enter the Holy of Holies (Heb. 10:19-20). Without the work of Christ, we are without the presence of God. Because of Jesus, we can draw near to God's throne of grace (Heb. 4:16). We overcome by the blood of the Lamb (Rev. 12:11). The Lord gives His best gifts to His children. He gives light (Eph. 5:14), repentance (Rom. 2:4; 2 Tim. 2:25), His Spirit (Rom. 5:5), and His blood (Rom. 3:25). The Son of Man came "to give His life a ransom for many" (Matt. 20:28). The blood of Christ is called precious blood not only because it was the blood of God (1 Pet. 1:19), but because it was the blood of His heart (Eph. 5:25). Amen. The blood gives the pardon of sin, grace, peace, promises and glory (Acts 5:31; 2 Pet. 1:4; John 1:16, 10:28, 14:27). He gave freely (Rev. 21:6).

The majesty and dignity of Jesus was so infinite in value, that He could give it once for the whole multitude of man to be forgiven of sin. His sacrifice was the result of God's love, not the cause of it. God sees the blood which gives the power of intercession to the Lord Jesus Christ for our benefit. In the Old Testament, the blood of the bullock was sprinkled before the veil on the four horns of the Golden Altar of sweet incense before the Lord (Lev. 4:7). When the Father sees the blood of Christ, He desires to fulfill the eternal covenant to forgive and save the people chosen to be redeemed by His blood. After Jesus shed His blood on the cross, He was raised for our justification and ascended into heaven to intercede for us with the Father. Jesus is always pleading our case before the Father (Heb. 7:25). It is to our great comfort, consolation, and security that Jesus works governing our universe, the church, and intercedes for us by praying for our perseverance in faith. Praise God.

When Jesus was pierced for our transgressions (Isa. 54:5), there flowed both blood and water (John 19:34). "This is the one who came by water and blood, Jesus Christ; not with water only, but with the water and the blood" (1 John 5:6). The blood takes away the guilt of sin, and the water removes the filth. We are pardoned for past sins, and delivered from future sins. The flowing of blood and water from the side of Jesus confirms the fact that He died. The blood stands for atonement, forgiveness, and our justification before God. The water stands for purification, regeneration, and our sanctification before God. No bone was broken (Ps. 34:20; John 19:36). The scripture was fulfilled in His death and will be completely fulfilled in the future. The Bible tells us that in the future, "They shall look upon Him whom they have pierced" (Zech. 12:10; John 19:37; Rev. 1:7). God was and always will be in complete control. We are made fully righteous by Jesus. "If we confess our sins, He is faithful and righteous to forgive us our sins and to cleanse us from all unrighteousness" (1 John 1:9).

The free and complete forgiveness of all our sin by the shed blood of Jesus seems too good to be true, but God's Word is true (2 Pet. 1:4). Jesus paid a high price for our redemption, healing, and deliverance from sin. Never forget that "no man will be justified by the law in the sight of God, it is evident; for, the righteous man shall live by faith" (Gal. 3:11). Never forget that salvation is a gift of God; "we are saved by grace through faith" (Eph. 2:8). This great promise from God, who cannot lie (Heb. 6:18), for the forgiveness of our sins is through the shed blood of Jesus Christ. The Bible tells us "There is forgiveness with Thee, that Thou mayest be feared" (Ps. 130:4). We have redemption and forgiveness through His blood, according to the riches of His grace (Eph. 1:17). Our conscience is cleansed (Heb. 9:14), and God's power released for us, through the blood of His Son. We are rescued from a life of eternal death, into a relationship with God to live in His purpose forever.

The believer is blessed with understanding, and an awesome fear of God's love, kindness, and power. We experience the mercy of God and the fear of losing His lovingkindness. We have come to know God, Christian, by the shed blood of Jesus. "The fear of the Lord is the beginning of wisdom; A good understanding have all those who do His commandments" (Ps. 111:10). Amen. God's presence through fear and trembling is part of our responsibility, work, and discovery on the path of salvation through the shed blood of Jesus (Phil. 2:12). God's presence, and the grace of reverence and fear, takes us to the awesome place of worship with understanding and gratitude in a loving and merciful God. It is only possible in

Jesus because He paid the price required for us to receive the Holy Spirit to be comforted and taught the truth of God. He paid the price for us to know the fear of God. He paid the price by shedding His blood, for us to obtain an obedience of faith, and experience a true praise in worship. The love and mercy of God the Father stepped in between the sinner and destruction. The love and sacrifice of God the Son, willingly shedding His blood, paid the price of our redemption. The Holy Spirit graciously gives us Christ Jesus and every blessing He has secured. Our salvation was purposed by the Father, accomplished by the Son, and applied by the Holy Spirit. Our justification, sanctification and assurance of salvation was secured by Jesus Christ and applied and worked in us by the Holy Spirit. Salvation is a divine work and a divine gift. Our salvation is in Christ alone, and by His Spirit alone. Our responsibility is to follow Jesus by reading the Bible, and discovering the work He has done for us in shedding His blood, that we might come to know forgiveness and a walk by the obedience of faith. God has chosen for His children to behold their salvation in the heart and mind of their soul. In salvation, "God pardons all your iniquities and heals all your diseases" (Ps. 103:3). God forgives us as a judge and cures us as a physician. "Though your sins are as scarlet, they shall be white as snow" (Isa. 1:18). When we die and pass into the mysteries of the spiritual world, Christian, our sins do not follow us and are forgotten (Heb. 8:12; Isa. 38:17; Micah 7:18-19). By the blood of Jesus, the great mercy of our forgiveness is a sign of divine favor, election, and happiness. To God be all the glory. Amen.

The Plan of Salvation by God

> And the angel of the Lord said to them, "Do not be afraid: for behold, I bring you good news of great joy which shall be for all the people; for today in the city of David there has been born for you a Savior, which is Christ the Lord" (Luke 2: 10-11).

Dear Christian,

There are many passages in the Bible that tell us about the causes and means of our salvation. It is a great work that starts with the love of God. Salvation is ascribed to God the Father. God "has saved us, and called us with a holy calling not according to our works, but according to His own purpose and grace which was granted us in Christ Jesus from all eternity" (2 Tim. 1:9). The Father chose us to be in Jesus Christ before the foundation of the world (Eph. 1:4). Wherever the gospel is an effectual call, it is found to be a holy call. The origin of our salvation is in free grace for the eternal purpose of God. God the Father initiated the process of salvation by "granting" (John 6:65) and "drawing" us (John 6:44) to Jesus by the power of the Holy Spirit. "To you it has been granted to know the mysteries of the kingdom of heaven" (Matt. 13:11). Since we are morally unable to effectually hear God, we first need Divine power and grace to work in us to come to Christ.

We cannot and will not come to Christ in the will of our old man, we must be born again of God (John 1:12-13, 3:3). We are drawn by the Holy Spirit. He gives us a new and powerful conviction that we are lost, but can be rescued or saved by Jesus. Our depravity is overcome by God and we "see" Jesus and the truth of the Gospel. Our humble cry for help to believe and trust Christ to be saved, is to be "quickened" by "the Spirit who gives life" (John 6:63). Jesus said, "All that the Father gives Me shall come to Me" (John 6:37). The calling from God sets us apart from our sin to our Savior. The reason for God's action does not lie in us, but rather in His own heart of love. God sovereignly designed salvation for what is called the elect. God initiates, sustains, and completes the work of salvation (Phil. 1:6). The plan of salvation includes the atonement of Christ, which means He makes a reconciliation of the guilty with God by divine sacrifice (Rom. 3:23-26; 1 Pet. 1: 18-21). Jesus is the One "who will save His people from their sins" (Matt. 1:21). It was from the merit and satisfaction on the cross that Christ received from the Father, that would be the foundation to send the Holy Spirit of God for us. The Holy Spirit would work in the elect the benefits proposed by God and purchased by Christ (John 14:16-17, 26). The operations of the Holy Spirit would convict the world concerning sin, and righteousness, and judgment. The Holy Spirit would guide believers into all the truth, and glorify Christ (John 16:8, 13-14). "He saved us, not on the basis of deeds we have done in righteousness, but according to His mercy, by the washing of regeneration and renewing by the Holy Spirit" (Titus 3:5). We are delivered from our miserable condition by the grace of God, the merit of Christ and operation of the Spirit. This is all in God's plan for you to understand and experience His love for you on the way to everlasting life.

Salvation is also ascribed to the means of the Word. "In humility receive the word implanted, which is able to save your souls" (James 1:21). The Word is a chief means employed in coming to Christ, because faith comes by hearing the word (Rom. 10:17). "For by grace you have been saved by faith; and not of yourselves, it is the gift of God" (Eph. 2:8). Faith is not the cause of the new birth, but the consequence of the new birth. As a result of the Spirit's operations, and His application of the Word, we grow in grace to repent and believe in Jesus Christ. "We have been born again not of seed which is perishable but imperishable, that is, through the living and abiding word of God" (1 Pet. 1:23). The Holy Spirit will use pastors, other ministers of Christ, fellow believers and many situations and circumstances to speak to your heart about Jesus. Baptism and the Lord's supper are important ordinances that, by the grace of God, confirm true repentance, and faith in us for Jesus. In summary, God the Father elected certain ones to salvation, God the Son died for the elect, and God the Holy Spirit quickens the elect. They work in agreement, and in order, with harmony. The Word is appointed for conversion and the ordinances for confirmation. Our faith and repentance are wrought in us by the Holy Spirit. Christ came to bring us to the Father (1 Pet. 3:18). Christ came to demonstrate the Father's goodness (2 Cor. 5:19) and righteousness (Rom. 3:25). The honor that gave us the benefits we come to possess, belongs to the Lamb that purchased it for us. "In Adam all die, but in Christ all shall be made alive" (1 Cor. 15:22). If we ascribe our conversion to our own strength, we wrong the Holy Spirit. Christ's blood made the way and opened the door for us to go to heaven. The new nature is being wrought in us by the Holy Spirit. "Be ye doers of the word, and not hearers only" (James 1:22). The Bible tells us that faith without works is dead (James 2:17). The examples it gives is Abraham offering up his son Isaac, and Rahab protecting the messengers (James 2:21, 25). "Abraham believed God, and it was reckoned to him as righteousness" (James 2:23). When faith was working with the works, faith was perfected (James 1:22). We are justified by faith without works with God (Rom. 3:28, 4:5-6, 5:1), and justified before man by works and not faith alone (Rom. 4:2; James 2:24). Paul's ministry before men was justified by works (1 Thess. 1:2-5, 2:3-10).

Some of the final teachings of Jesus from the Sermon on the Mount are a warning to us, that after hearing His words, we should go forth and practice them. He tells us "To enter by the narrow gate, for the gate is wide, and the way is broad that leads to destruction, and many are those who enter by it. For the gate is small, and the way is narrow that leads to life, and few are those who find it" (Matt. 7:13-14). Where you will end up in eternity depends on the road you take. There is a right road and a wrong road relating to the entrance you take to eternal life. In another passage it says, "strive to enter by the narrow door" (Luke 13:24), where strive means to agonize. This does not suggest works for salvation, but emphasizes the value of it being the most important matter in your earthly life. Salvation is a miracle to experience on God's terms. "Fight the good fight of faith" (1 Tim. 6:12). The narrow gate is not self-righteousness, frivolous curiosity, or mindful speculations: but as Christ is the door (John 10:9), we recognize our responsibility to live for Him whose grace delivered us from our sins and saved us. It is a way of self-denial and humility, repentance, and personal faith in Christ leading to a life of holiness. It is a loving and personal relationship. The broad way and the wide gate are the way to destruction. It is not the loss of being, but the loss of well-being. The natural or lost man will not have the witness in his conscience and mind of an agonizing brutal conflict about sin. He may not want the consequences of sin, but does not see Jesus as the answer. The natural man will not be striving to enter through the narrow door. The importance of dealing with his sin, and the value of eternal life in Jesus are not lodged in his thoughts.

In the closing words of the Sermon on the Mount, Jesus tells the parable of two kinds of builders (Matt. 7:24-27). One was wise and one was foolish. The wise man dug deep and laid the foundation for his house on a rock. The foolish man built quickly and laid the foundation for his house on the sand. The rock is Christ and the sand is self. The wise builder is the person who puts the words of Jesus into practice. The foolish builder is the person who only pretends or professes faith, or holds only an intellectual commitment to Christ, but does not build his life on the words of Jesus. Both builders hear the words of Jesus Christ and build houses that look similar, but have a different foundation. When the rain, floods, and wind blew, which means when the troubles of life come, only the house built upon the rock or the words of Jesus did not fall. Our faith will be tested to reveal to our own hearts whether it is genuine. Our spiritual life must be built with trust and obedience, by the grace of God, upon the fulness of Christ's merit. Building upon a rock requires hard work, great care, diligence, and a lot of struggle and pain. This is not a work to save yourself, but rather a journey of discovery, that the truth of your election and calling by God are realized as certain (2 Pet. 1:10). A wise builder is preparing for another world, while the foolish builder, builds only for this world. A wise builder talks and walks with Jesus, and grounds his hope, forgiveness, and future salvation on Jesus (1 Tim. 1:1). We are God's fellow workers, God's field, and God's building (1 Cor. 3:9). A foolish builder will have no regard for the Word of God or the church. A foolish builder with a foundation of sand will have no godly concern for obedience and purity of heart. Religion to them is external and not a matter of something happening in their heart and soul.

True salvation involves hearing the word of God and following up on it, by the grace of God, with obedience. Jesus said, "If you love Me, you will keep My commandments" (John 14:15). When we are born again, we receive the gift of faith with trust to believe and love Jesus. The Holy Spirit's presence with us gives rise to obedience and the love necessary to keep His commandments. If you are falling in love with Jesus, then you will begin to keep His commandments. The obedience we experience builds a confidence that we belong to Jesus. The obedience of faith is a gift from God, and is powerful evidence for us from God, that we truly love Him. We do not work up a great love for Jesus on our own that leads to obedience, and then get some kind of credit from Him. He chose and loved us before we chose and loved Him (Eph. 1:4; 1 John 4:19). Since we love Him, we will keep His commandments. For a weak and struggling Christian who loves Jesus, these words of promise to keep His commandments are encouraging. This is the glory of the covenant of grace, that God accepts and esteems of sincere obedience as perfect obedience. A Christian will know the conflict of the two natures, the principle of evil or the law of sin, and the law of God. Thanks be to God through Jesus Christ that we joyfully concur with the law of God in the inner man (Rom. 7:18-25). Amen. Oh Lord, help us to dig deep. Help us to deal with our desperate spiritual condition, and repent, and by your grace live up to the knowledge you have given us for the glory of Jesus Christ. "For many are called, but few are chosen" (Matt. 22:14). These words of Jesus appear at the end of the parable of the Marriage Feast (Matt. 22:1-14). The many called includes folks who are hypocritical, not concerned with religion, and those who only make a profession but their life is a contradiction. The few, on the other hand, are those chosen for salvation, by sanctification of the Spirit. They are traveling through the small gate on the narrow road, by the grace of God, that leads to life.

The knowledge and evidence that you are saved, and that in the future it will go well for your precious soul, is a comforting gift from the Lord. Saving grace appears in the soul of an elect individual by the grace of God, in His time, through the work and power of the Holy Spirit. God Himself and His presence becomes the assurance in your heart of the precious and convicting knowledge of eternal life. One of the first works of the Holy Spirit is to have you look at your sin as an enemy to fear because the forces behind it are trying to kill you. The Holy Spirit turns you to be willing to get rid of sin. Your mind, conscience and will become very weary of sin. You develop an enmity against all your sins, and recognize they are only present to steal, kill and destroy you (John 10:10). Sin is present to keep you separated from God. These kinds of thoughts, and the desire to escape the clutches of sin, become strong and habitual. The desire to be right, serious, and sincere with God, begins to dominate your decision-making and will. This is the plan of God in your salvation at work. Your heart will be looking to give Him your heart (Prov. 23:26). The heart that abandoned God in the garden of Eden, is drawn by the Lord God back to Himself, revealing the great mercy and grace of God to choose to forgive and save. When you are willing to not continue in sin, you have discovered the saving grace and work of God in giving you a new heart for your soul. Though sin has afflicted your life, you are now more focused and willing to be rid of sin, because of hearing God's voice. It is about your sin and not your afflictions. The Bible gives us the examples of Pilate who was unwilling to condemn Jesus (Matt. 27:22-24), Herod who was unwilling to behead John the Baptist (Mark 6:26-27), and Darius who was unwilling to cast Daniel into the lion's den (Dan. 6:14-17), yet the prevailing part of their wills had a bias towards the wrong thing. You will cry out to God for help to do the right thing. Oh Lord, let me outlive my sins. You cry out to God for your life to be healed, your lusts subdued and you soul cleaned out. In the plan of salvation is a humble plea for God to help you be godly, and to fear and respect Him, in the way He truly deserves. God's grace will sound like David did, "search me, O God, and know my heart; try me and know my anxious thoughts; and see if there be any hurtful way in me, and lead me in the everlasting way" (Ps. 139:23-24). Amen. A man with God's grace will sound like Paul did in the conflict of serving the law of God in his mind and the law of sin in his flesh (Rom. 7:14-25). By the grace of God, Christian, we wake up to the fact that sin took our heart, without consent, and violated our souls like a criminal. The grace of God has saved me from myself. I'm learning to love God. God is all good. He becomes our Shepherd. The plan of God is for us know His presence, and the plan of our salvation by His grace. Thank you, Jesus.

A truth in the saving power of God's grace, is that it goes after all your sins, and especially the secret ones. It does not just go after the sin that was causing your greatest affliction, but it seeks out everything that separates you from God. A sincere heart of grace from God goes after the sins of the body and the heart. Both the outside and the inside of a man need cleansing. The conflicts, striving, and groanings because of sin will make you become very weary of your life. The Christian life will have victory and defeat; but the seed of God, as a principle of grace abides despite the war in your soul that takes place. The battle for your heart is evidence that you are standing against the evil nature of sin. The more your heart rises against sin, and you experience the separation from sin to God, the more you will know the true presence of God in the battle. To God be the glory. God's plan all along was to save you by His grace and not your hard work. A person with true grace abhors sin because sin is fighting against God's holiness for your present and eternal life. The nature of sanctification is personal for each person. The miracle of God's grace is for your personal salvation. How can we continue in sin against such a good and great creator God. You will shun all appearances of sin (1 Thess. 5:22). True grace will make you stand against your favorite sins. Your greatest hopes are to have more of God's grace and to live a holy life. A man with true grace will always be inclining his heart for God and His statutes (Ps. 119:112). We will not be perfect, Christian, because grace now only weakens sin, but glory in the future annihilates all sinful practices. Amen. "Having these promises, beloved, let us cleanse ourselves from all defilement of flesh and spirit, perfecting holiness in the fear of God" (2 Cor. 7:1). "Do not lose heart in doing good, for in due time we shall reap if we do not grow weary" (Gal. 6:9). Keep relying on the Spirit to work in you and through your life. Never give up, Christian, God has His way and time to bring joy into your life and glory to His name. Stay on the path of obedience to the Lord.

One of the ways that God gives the assurance of His presence, and the assurance of your salvation is through the grace of obedience. Once we become a Christian, and more aware of holiness and what God desires for our life, we try hard to work out His will in our life. We believe we know Jesus and are sincere, yet we are weak to grow in the obedience we know would please Him. In the covenant of grace, "God is at work in you to will and to work for His good pleasure" (Phil. 2:13). God builds an inner awe and a holy experience by the power of His grace, in His time and way, for our obedience, and deserves the glory. We could not and cannot work our way by our own effort at obedience, it is the gift of God. The glory of the covenant of grace is not by our keeping the law in any legal way, but by God accepting a sincere obedience as perfect obedience. This acceptance is defined as an evangelical sense. "We work out our salvation with fear and trembling" (Phil. 2:12), and God infuses us with grace that inclines our soul to fall in with every command He presents to our hearts. From our desires and will we choose the Lord. From our affections and hopes we choose the Lord. From our understanding and respect, we choose to keep and do the words of the Lord (Rom. 8:18, 7:12; Ps. 119:173, 97, 163, 127). From the obedience of faith, we obey God in the spirit as well as the letter. We bring our hearts to a sincere obedience of all the commands of God, no matter how important they may seem. We discover this work of the Lord going on in our soul. The obedience of faith from God is learned and grows by reading the word of God. The obedience that springs from true faith, Christian, is the obedience of a son that is free and not forced obedience like a slave. True obedience that accompanies salvation changes us from impurity and sin to purity and holiness. We become humble and heavenly minded in place of pride and an earthly mind (Rom. 12:1-2). We become new creatures (2 Cor. 5:17) through faith, by the grace of God. Our assurance of salvation derives from the Lord's work in us because we sense the miraculous nature of it. It does not occur as the result of our best efforts. We strive, in fear and trembling, at the discovery of God's lovingkindness. A hypocrite will only express an interest in religious duty when he is under some affliction, or distress in his conscience, and or realize a profit in some way. The obedience of faith is the path that God has chosen for us to recover the image of God, and to make you know that your calling and election are for sure (2 Pet. 1:2-11). The path is not for obtaining salvation, but for obtaining the assurance of salvation. God's glory is the end of all our obedience of faith in Jesus.

All the grace that flows into your life through Jesus Christ will make you strong (2 Tim. 2:1). Through Him the Gentiles received grace, "to bring about the obedience of faith, for His name's sake" (Rom. 1:5). Through Him, the secret knowledge of the mystery of the gospel and the preaching of Jesus Christ has been made known to all the nations, leading to the obedience of faith (Rom. 16:26). The plan of God all along has been for you to receive the gift of faith when you were born again. The grace of faith is the pathway that God would use to lead us into an obedience of faith necessary for walking with the Lord. Obedience springs from faith, and faith comes from hearing the word of God (Rom. 10:17). The Bible tells us that "God has granted to the Gentiles also the repentance that leads to life" (Acts 11:18). The obedience of faith is very important to God, and saving faith will make you obedient to Jesus Christ. Do not let your soul settle with or accept unholy practices with the Lord. "Those whom the Lord loves He disciplines" (Heb. 12:6). God's plan for your salvation is not for you to work harder, but to know the "peaceful fruit of righteousness" that comes to those who have been trained by His discipline (Heb. 12:11). God's plan in salvation is for you to know "the repentance that leads to life" (Acts 11:18). Amen. Repentance is also a gracious gift of God. Repentance is not self-energized, but "granted by God leading to the knowledge of the truth" (2 Tim. 2:25). The changing of our minds by repentance, is from the kindness of God (Rom. 2:4). With true faith, God plants true repentance. Repentance in salvation is not trembling, almost being persuaded, fearing Hades, and making a confession to God. Repentance is a hatred of sin, and a turning from sin with a determination in the strength of God to forsake it. Like faith, we never get perfect repentance, but we will be sincere. Repentance is a grace. God gives the salvation Himself to those whom He will (Rom. 9:15-16). Pray for repentance. You will know sorrow for sin, and by the grace of God you will bring forth a permanent and practical repentance in your life. You will desire holiness and to be like Christ. God's grace makes men willing to be saved, and by divine mercy, repentance is in His plan. In God's plan of salvation, for us to repent by God's grace, we first learn, believe, and think about Jesus.

The Bible tells us that Israel was not completely cast away. "But by their transgression salvation has come to the Gentiles to make them jealous" (Rom. 11:11). God's plan was to make the Jewish people jealous to draw them back to Himself. The Bible tells us, that "once we were disobedient to God, but now have been shown mercy because of their disobedience, so these also have been disobedient, in order that because of the mercy shown to you they also may be shown mercy. For God has shut up all in disobedience that He might show mercy to all" (Rom. 11:30-32). "A partial hardening has happened to Israel until the fulness of the Gentiles has come in" (Rom. 11:25). The fulness of the Gentiles is thought to mean the spread of the gospel throughout the whole world. This would mean the time between Nebuchadnezzars conquest of Jerusalem in 588 BC through the present time. When the Jewish people rejected God, they were cut off from the blessings of a relationship with God. When the time is right, God will restore the nation to faith in the Messiah, that is, Jesus Christ (Luke 13:35).

The survival of the Jewish people and the nation of Israel over many centuries is a testimony to God's providence and faithfulness. The devil wants to stop the spread of the gospel and prevent Jesus from coming again. The devil is spiritually active against both Christians and the Jews, teaching hate in the hearts of unbelievers. The practice of discrimination or anti-Semitism targeting the Jews was present in the Greco-Roman world and even from early Christians. It continues up into our present day. The Jews were thought to be associated with evil, killing Jesus, and spreading disease. They suffered during the Crusades and were blamed for the Bubonic plague. They were not allowed to get good jobs or own land. They had to wear distinctive clothing and live in ghettos. They were found to be useful in the founding of financial markets and lending money, which earned them the reputation as greedy and money-hungry. They were expelled from England, Spain, France, Germany, and Russia. They had no land of their own. Over time, they experienced numerous pogroms, and eventually the Holocaust as an effort to specifically eliminate the Jewish people in World War II. Some people thought they had too much power and were not loyal to the countries they lived in. Eventually they found allies in England and America, allowing them to flourish and eventually gain a homeland in the Middle East. Currently, they are still under attack by Islamic states with the purpose of destroying them all. The signals in the world for the end of time for humanity seem to be appearing. The Iranian leaders think the same thing, and are hastening a nuclear apocalypse to bring into the world their own messiah. God will soon call the Jewish people back home, and the time of the Gentiles will end (Rom. 11:25). Jesus is coming again; the will of God will be done. Amen.

It is the Spirit of God who works in us to will of His own good pleasure (Phil. 2:13). It is the Spirit of God that works in us the desires for grace. Jesus said, "It is the Spirit who gives life; the flesh profits nothing; the words that I have spoken to you are spirit and are life" (John 6:63). Wherever God designs to give life, He gives repentance. He takes away our old heart of stone and replaces it with a new heart of flesh. To believe Christ died for you, and to draw strength against sin and comfort in trials from this doctrine, is the spirit and life that God intended for you to know in this life. In salvation, God planned for you to hear His voice in the study and hearing of His word, and then to behold your new life in praise for His grace. True desires after Christ for salvation, holiness, and grace, is in the plan of your salvation by the grace of God. The desire to believe, obey, fear, repent and serve the Lord are marks of God's grace for the well-being of your soul in the future. "Blessed are those who hunger and thirst for righteousness, for they shall be satisfied" (Matt. 5:6). It takes grace to desire grace, and we can only desire grace after we have already tasted of it. A natural man does not know or desire grace, but a man born again will desire sanctifying grace. A natural man lives without God, Christ, the Holy Spirit, the church, and hope (Eph. 2:12). The wisdom of the natural man is without understanding and at enmity with God (1 Cor. 2:14; Rom. 8:7). The natural man cannot desire saving grace. We all used to be a natural man (Eph. 2:1-3). The saved man, on the other hand, desires to honor God, deny himself, grow in grace, improve his mercies, and glorify God.

The grace of God is the glory of God we begin to know in this life. It will become full in heaven. The seed of God enables believers to see the justice and excellency and beauty of grace, whereas the carnal heart sees nothing in grace that is desirable. The natural man is blind and cannot see God's work in the world or even in his own soul, because he does not have spiritual eyes. To the Christian, grace is the image of God. Grace is the delight, honor, and glory of God. Grace is the purchase of Christ, the work of the Spirit, and the pledge and assurance of the glory of man with Christ. Grace preserves the Christian, and fits him for fellowship with the Father, Son, and the Holy Spirit in this life. Grace allows a man to behold his salvation in his own mind, and lets him know that he is accepted of God (2 Cor. 5:9). The growth of grace in our souls promotes faith and holy desires, and fixed resolutions for our home in heaven. No man can love his brothers and sisters without God's grace (1 John 3:10, 4:6-11). All our graces and the evidence of them reveals the favor of God's love from heaven. Grace in your heart is in God's plan, for you to discover the wisdom of Christ's work in saving your soul.

A main way you can know you have the saving grace of God's life in your heart, is to look at your heart and watch it and keep it for Jesus. The Psalmist declared "Thy word I have treasured in my heart that I may not sin against Thee" (Ps. 119:11). Solomon tells us "My son, give attention to my words; incline your ear to my sayings. Do not let them depart from your sight; Keep them in your heart. For they are life to those who find them, and health to all their whole body. Watch over your heart with all diligence, for from it flow the springs of life" (Prov. 4:20-23). This passage is about life and death, and the importance of keeping our understanding, will, and the affections of our soul well-guarded. The evidence for saving grace is to keep our heart in a patient and gracious frame. We are to be humble, serious, repenting, in a believing frame of life. God measures us by our wills and not our works. "If there is a willing mind, it is accepted according to what a man has, not according to what he does not have" (2 Cor. 8:12). The Christian watches his heart, while the hypocrite watches his lips.

In the heart of God's children lies the saving graces of repentance and confession. "The sorrow that is according to God produces a repentance without regret, leading to salvation; but the sorrow of the world produces death (2 Cor. 7:10). True and saving repentance includes grief in your heart for sins committed. This is also called godly sorrow and a broken and contrite heart (Ps. 51:17), and a mourning heart (Zech. 12:10). "Blessed are those who mourn, for they shall be comforted" (Matt. 5:4). Godly sorrow is a spiritual grief for sin that displeased the Lord our God. Godly sorrow releases a deep mourning from a forgiven and saved soul. We have sinned against God (Ps. 51:4), been foolish and presumed on His goodness. The saving grace of God breaks the bond between the sinner's heart and sin. Godly sorrow means the love and favor of God for you. The mourning in our life is a looking in faith to Christ, and believing in Christ. It speaks of the goodness of God and the joy yet to be revealed. Godly sorrow produces a longing for freedom, a fear of sin, a wake-up call to action, anger to sin and a zeal for the Lord (2 Cor. 7:11). We become weary of sin and fearful of falling into it. When we do sin, and we will (1 John 1:8), we sincerely confess our sins from our broken heart by repentance, in hope for a restored relationship with the Lord.

The promise by God in the gift of confession to a Christian is forgiveness and cleansing (1 John 1:9). This becomes a very precious gift in God's saving grace, because of the peace it provides. It establishes that God is still accepting us, despite our weaknesses. The lost man sees no reason to come to God in confession. The saving grace of God brings a Christian to the Lord seeking mercy that arises from a true sight and sense of sin. "If we confess our sins, He is faithful and righteous to forgive us our sins and to cleanse us from all unrighteousness" (1 John 1:9). God is merciful, and helps us come sincerely with a confession of specific sins with our mind, heart, and soul. We have rebelled against God and departed from the knowledge we have of His teachings. We are humbled and sorrowful, with an eye of faith on God's pardoning grace. Help us Oh Lord to see our sins the way you see them, and to confess them all to you. Confession is a deep root of spiritual life; it is personal, trusting, and valuable. God is faithful and righteous, that is, He is true to His holy word and holy nature. God fulfills the promise of forgiveness and remains righteous to the covenant He made with His Son and us. We experience two important spiritual benefits. Forgiveness is remission of sin's guilt and punishment, and cleansing is remission of sin's defiling presence. Sin separates us from God, and God's grace restores our fellowship. The miracle that takes place in confession of sin in the heart of a child of God,

Christian, is part of the treasure found in our earthen vessel (2 Cor. 4:7). The high price required by God, and necessary to pay for our forgiveness and cleansing, was the precious blood of Jesus (1 Pet. 1:18-19). In His time, God delivers us from the power and practice of sin. In the plan of God, we learn the forgiveness of God that we may worship Him with gratitude and fear (Ps. 130:4). Amen.

It is to your immeasurable advantage, no matter where you are at, spiritually speaking, to have your heart and the eye of your faith always fixed on Jesus. Jesus is a free, rich, and sovereign gift of God. Jesus is a perfect expression of the grace of God. By free grace, we understand the good will and favor of God. The lovingkindness of God is better than life (Ps. 63:3). The people of God were foreknown, predestined, chosen, called, justified, reconciled, adopted, and conformed to the image of His Son. The people of God are saved, glorified, obtain an inheritance, and are predestined according to His purpose, who works all things after the counsel of His will (Rom. 8:29-30; Eph. 1:4-11). By grace you have been saved, not of works (Eph, 2:8-9). God's grace is the foundation for all our spiritual and eternal mercies and comforts. "In the ages to come, God will show the surpassing riches of His grace in kindness toward us in Christ Jesus" (Eph. 2:7). God was always at work to save your soul; you are His workmanship (Eph. 2:10; Titus 3:5-7). To the end, that your hope in Christ would be to the praise of His glory (Eph. 1:12). God's grace is your safest city of refuge. The Bible tells us, "The Law came in that the transgression might increase; but where sin increased, grace abounded all the more" (Rom. 5:20). Grace is greater than my sin. The Law of Moses could not prevent sin because it was too weak, the Law could only condemn and make the transgression of Adam more evident (Rom. 3:20). God fully knows us (Ps. 139:1-4), and searches our hearts with the purpose of helping us (Rom. 8:27). The Bible tells us that "God is greater than our heart, and knows all things" (1 John 3:20). Regardless of some of this knowledge, He chose to give us a new heart and save us by grace (Ezek. 36:26; Eph. 2:8). Our new heart, by the grace of God, in the plan of salvation, is the evidence He has saved us.

In God's plan, He brought forth a mediator in the Person of Jesus, who paid the price for our sins by His death, and then imputed to us His righteousness that justified us before the Father. The Lord becomes our righteousness (1 Cor. 1:30), that completely justifies us before the throne of God. In God's plan, the Lord Jesus becomes our crowning comfort and spiritual refuge. We triumph in the righteousness of Christ. As saved sinners, we are never alone because Christ will always be standing with us. The righteousness of Christ answers all our fears, doubts, and conflicts. We belong to Him, and He becomes our life and purpose. By the grace of God, we become His people and He becomes our God (Ezek. 36:28). We are to love, trust, mourn, repent, confess, and grow in grace (Ps. 92:12-14). We are to hold out and persevere to the end (1 Cor. 15:58). "Those who wait for the Lord will gain new strength; they will mount up with wings like eagles, they will run and not get tired, they will walk and not become weary" (Isa. 40:31). Its amazing grace, that God stands engaged to us in the covenant of grace, to give us what we need and to do for us what we cannot, to secure our salvation. Nothing is impossible with God (Luke 1:37).

The covenant of grace by God means our salvation is secure. God planned it and wrote it down in the Bible for us to read. We are to read the Bible and grow in faith, and trust and in His grace. "For of His fulness we have all received, and grace upon grace" (John 1:16), and "faith to faith" (Rom. 1:17), and "life to life" (2 Cor. 2:16). "I will be your God and you shall be My people" (Jer. 32:38). "For as many as may be the promises of God, in Him they are yes; wherefore also by Him is our Amen to the glory of God through us" (2 Cor. 1:20). The promise of our salvation is only in Christ. The promise of grace for salvation was sealed by His own oath, "in which it is impossible for God to lie" (Heb. 6:18). Salvation has been sealed by the witness of the Holy Spirit in our hearts (John 14:16; Eph. 1:13). He chose you in the beginning to receive His love and grace (Eph. 1:4), and He still loves you for His choice. The covenant of salvation for us is everlasting with God (John 3:16). "I will make an everlasting covenant with them that I will not turn away from them, to do them good; and I will put the fear of Me in their hearts so that they will not turn away from Me" (Jer. 32:40). God has ratified the covenant of grace with us by the death of His only begotten Son. The death of our mediator in the covenant makes it like a last will and testament, settling the covenant of grace whereby it cannot be altered. The inheritance designed by God, for the "called" of God, was meant to be eternal (John 3:16). When the evidence of salvation in your heart may seem somewhat meager, Christian, recall that God stands with you in a covenant of grace. In this great covenant, God has declared and accepted sincerity over perfection. In God's eyes, we are perfectly righteous in Christ (Heb. 10:14). God pities His people under their weakness, rather than rejecting them for their weakness. God has chosen to judge His people by the frame of their hearts and inward disposition and will, rather than by their work (Acts 13:22; 2 Cor.8:12). The covenant with God is amazing. It reveals the mercy and gracious ways of God. He gives a new heart (Ezek. 36:26) and a will that works for His good pleasure for our salvation (Phil. 2:13). He will provide a holy bride for His Son (Rev. 19:7-8).

In the covenant of grace, God performs perfectly His side of the agreement. He also does the "heavy lifting" on our side of the agreement, by giving us a new heart of faith. We are responsible to "work out our salvation with fear and trembling" (Phil. 2:12). The covenant of grace is based upon the oath of God and the precious blood of Christ. The blood of Christ is called the blood of the eternal covenant (Heb. 13:20), and the blood of the New Testament for the remission of sins (Heb. 9:15). With the gift of faith, we are implanted into Christ. In Christ, we discover our implantation by our sanctification and imitation of Christ. We are justified by imputation of the righteousness of Christ, and sanctified by the impartation of the righteousness of Christ. The imputed righteousness, that is, our Justification is God's experience of our righteousness, legally placed into the account of the sinner. Imparted righteousness, that is our sanctification is our own experience through the work of the Holy Spirit in our hearts (2 Cor. 3:18; 2 Pet. 1:4; Rom. 7:14-25). The new nature we have from God is evidence of true salvation. "We know we have passed out of death into life, because we love the brethren" (1 John 3:14). A saved man will give up his heart, affections, will and life, and venture his whole soul upon Christ. A saved man will be cleaving to Jesus and His righteousness in the face of anything else. "Though He slay me, I will hope in Him" (Job 13:15). O Lord! I have been weak and overcome by sin. I was blind and could not see, I was lost and could not be found. You rescued me and brought me to Jesus. You know you have changed me and I have given my heart to Jesus. You saved me, forgave me of my sin and I desire to be obedient in Jesus' name.

The sovereignty of God and man's responsibility to God in salvation are plainly set forth throughout the scriptures. The sovereignty of God described in the scripture is absolute, irresistible, and infinite. "Thine, O Lord, is the greatness and the power and the glory and the victory and the majesty, indeed everything that is in the heavens and the earth; Thine is the dominion, O Lord, and Thou dost exalt Thyself as head over all" (1 Chron. 29:11). God is sovereign in the exercise of His power, mercy, and grace. "Grace reigns through righteousness" (Rom. 5:21). God is sovereign and dispenses His favors as He pleases. "The Lord has made everything for its own purpose" (Prov. 16:4). "Salvation is of the Lord" (Jonah 2:9). He is the Potter and we are the clay (Isa. 64:8). By nature, we are children of wrath (Eph. 2:3). "God has shut up all in disobedience that He might show mercy to all" (Rom. 11:32). The ultimate destiny of every individual is decided by the will of God. He assigns the eternal destination of His creatures; some are vessels of mercy prepared unto glory, while others are vessels of wrath fitted for destruction (Rom. 9:22-23). So then salvation does not "depend on the man who wills or the man who runs, but on God who has mercy" (Rom. 9:16). We "become children of God who believe in His name, who were born not of blood, nor of the will of the flesh, nor of the will of man, but of God" (John 1:12-13). "As many as were ordained to eternal life believed" (Acts 13:48). "By the grace of God, I am what I am" (1 Cor. 15:10). God makes the difference between the elect and the non-elect (1 John 5:20). "For whom He foreknew, He also predestined to become conformed to the image of His Son; and whom He predestined, these He also called; and whom He called, these He also justified; and whom He justified, these He also glorified" (Rom. 8:29-30). "God has chosen you from the beginning for salvation through sanctification by the Spirit and faith in the truth" (2 Thess. 2:13). You were chosen by the foreknowledge of God for the sanctifying work of the Spirit (1 Pet. 1:2). He called and saved us according to His own purpose and grace which was granted us from all eternity (2 Tim. 1:9). The cause of His choice lies within Himself and not the objects of His choice. Faith is the gift of God whereby we learn, grow, enjoy, experience, and understand we are saved by grace (Eph. 2:8). To God will be all the glory. Amen.

The Bible clearly teaches God's sovereignty and that everything is fore-ordained (Eph. 1:5, 11). The Bible also teaches that man is responsible, and that "each one of us shall give an account of himself to God" (Rom. 14:12). The Bible also tells us that man is free to act, does what he pleases, and will reap what he sows (Gal. 6:7). We are taught in another place that God's compassion "does not depend on the man who wills or the man who runs, but on God who has mercy" (Rom. 9:16). The fact that God predestines, and that man is still responsible is a truth that most people cannot understand, accept, or believe. Some people see the combination of sovereignty and responsibility as unfair to man and a contradiction. This becomes especially problematic to human reason, when we remember that man is totally depraved, enslaved in sin and spiritually destitute, and at the same time accountable to God. Man, when he was created was endowed with full capability to meet God's requirements, but fallen man possesses no power in his nature to do any spiritual good. How then can he be expected to be without excuse in connection with the sins he commits? After the Fall, man retained all his faculties which makes him still responsible, but he is in bondage and spiritually weak by the separation from God. Man had the power to reject Christ but not the power to receive Christ. After the Fall, man had a mind that was at enmity with God (Rom. 8:7) and hated Him (John 15:18). Man chooses according to his nature, and in his fallen state, he chose self and sin. Before he will choose Christ, he must be born again (John 3:3). Some people see the truth of God's sovereignty and man's responsibility as two parallel lines of truth that do not cross in our minds in this life. I believe that we will meet in eternity in heaven where a better understanding of all truth will come from the Lord. God is just and perfect and righteous and has acted according to His pleasure. Our responsibility is to let God be God.

God is first in the matter of our salvation. All that is good or ever will be good in us, was preceded by the grace of God. All our fears, hopes, desires, interest, and convictions become ours by the grace of God. The effect of God's powerful grace is the cause of our salvation. It is a gift from God that allows our hearts to grow in grace and knowledge and receive Jesus for forgiveness of sin and salvation. We are not saved by what we want or do, Christian, God's reason is a mystery to us. The reason He saved you belongs to His good pleasure from the eternal counsels of God (Eph. 1:4-6; Phil. 2:13). God's choices will stand. The grace of God is unmerited by you, and you will know it. Before coming to Jesus, you were in the flesh, ignorant of God and not interested in Him. However, now you rejoice that God is doing a work in you, and tremble about the life you had before your conversion to Christ. The grace of God wakes you up for salvation. The grace of God puts cries into the lips of those that cry out for Him. He saves men that do not seek Him (Isa. 65:1). He goes after the lost sheep (Luke 15:1-7). If you are seeking for God, it is because He has already been seeking for you. The reason we cry out and begin to pray, is because God has been at work. There is a motion of the Holy Spirit in our hearts before we know we want or need it to move closer to God for forgiveness and eternal life. God's mercy is a miracle, and way beyond our understanding of what is good. It was God who struck the effectual blow of grace into Saul on the road to Damascus (Acts 9:3-5). It was God who set the alarm bell in your own life to wake you up about Jesus. Amen. The sovereignty of God is taught in the word of God, which was inspired by God (2 Tim. 3:16). The sovereignty of God will take you away from working to pay the penalty for your sin, and leave you in the humble and grateful place of worship and service to God Almighty. God seeks us and entreats us to be saved. God made us into a being that becomes humble and contrite of spirit, who trembles at His word (Isa. 65:2). He draws and invites us to come and lay hold of spiritual life in Christ. Jesus said, "Come to Me, all who are weary and heavy-laden, and I will give you rest" (Matt. 11:28). God calls your soul to come to Jesus. You are invited to "taste and see that the Lord is good; how blessed is the man who takes refuge in Him!" (Ps. 34:8). A life of faith finds good food in everything. Your life will not become full and complete, until you have Jesus at the center of it.

Alongside the truth of God's sovereignty is the truth of man's responsibility. Although we lost our power to meet God's requirements, He does not forfeit His rights over us as our creator. We are still accountable and responsible for what is impossible for us to do. We did not lose our faculties, but we lost the power to use them right. From the beginning, man's responsibility never rested on anything within himself, but was always based solely upon God's rights over him. God always had the right to command us and the right to be obeyed. The faculties of man, including his intelligence, conscience, and volution, qualified the man and gave him the strength to be fully responsible. Man was made upright (Eccl. 7:29). Man was made in the image of God (Gen. 1:27). Man had a heart created in him for righteousness, holiness, and for the glory of God. Man was spiritually enlightened to love the Lord his God and render Him a sinless obedience. He could be responsible to God. However, Adam was a creature made mutable, which means he had the ability to change. He was put on probation under a covenant of works, and tested about his love to God by Satan in the garden of Eden. Adam rejected God's authority and fell from his original estate. In the beginning of the history of man, God, in His wisdom and justice, made Adam our federal head and the legal representative of all his posterity. The consequences of Adam's disobedience fell on us. "Through one man's disobedience the many were made sinners" (Rom. 5:19), and "in Adam all die" (1 Cor. 15:22). We are still responsible subjects of God's creation and accountable for our actions; to love, serve and improve the opportunities that the Lord gives us (Matt. 25:14-30). Depravity does not invalidate or provide an excuse for falling short of our obligations to God.

Almighty God, the Creator, has the absolute right to control the creatures that appeared in life by His omnipotence and will. "Come, let us worship and bow down; let us kneel before the Lord our maker. For He is our God, and we are the people of His pasture, and the sheep of His hand" (Ps. 95:6-7). God created us and preserves us and has every right to govern us in the present time and in the eternity to come, when time will be no more. The will of God will be our responsibility. We are not now, and never were, and in the future never will be living under our own authority. We will be alive in the future with obedience and joy in the moral government of God. He has the right to command and we have the obligation to obey. A penalty for disobedience upholds the authority of God. Our conscience becomes a guide that God is righteous. "God causes all things to work together for good" (Rom. 8:28). Man was not originally commanded in ignorance, he knew that by disobedience, he would incur the displeasure of God (Gen. 2:16-17). The wage of sin is death (Rom. 6:23). We reap what we sow (Gal. 5:7). The lake of fire is not a joke, the second death is for everyone whose name is not written in the Lambs book of life (Rev. 20:14-15). The world does not know God, and is not afraid of transgressing His teachings. Man is still under obligation to obey and acknowledge God's authority and dominion, and love Him with all their heart and strength (Matt. 22:37).

Once we know who God is, and what our relationship to Him in Jesus means, we recognize His authority and our responsibility. We belong to God. Our sole purpose and duty in life is to glorify God. God is the owner of all sinful men, and one sinless man for a short time called Adam. Our inability proves our rebellion to God. Our spiritual death from Adam did not kill any part of our being, but separated and alienated us from fellowship with a holy God. We lost spiritual purity and power. We became ignorant and blind (Eph. 4:18). They that are in the flesh cannot please God (Rom. 8:8). We are like prodigal sons (Luke 15). When the prodigal son finally came home, the father said, "this son of mine was dead, and has come to life again; he was lost, and has been found" (Luke 15:24). The son was not physically dead, but he was separated from his father. The conversion of a soul from sin to God, spiritually speaking, is the raising of the soul from death to life. The Christian knows Jesus, and the ignorance and blindness about Jesus has been removed by the grace of God. You have been changed. You are not the man you used to be, and you know it. God is standing with you. We possessed moral faculties before conversion, but because of our depravity, and enmity in our mind, and perversity in our will, we failed to use them for the glory of God. The natural man can love, he just cannot love God. The natural man cannot please God. The natural man is responsible for the sickness in his own heart and mind. We would have fallen in the garden of Eden if we had been present. Adam was made upright and failed, and serves as our representative. We are responsible for the enmity, the depravity, and the corruptions against God. Man is guilty.

Man's inability to obey God is not because he lacks the necessary faculties. Man cannot blame the presence of a hostile power outside of himself forcing him to act against his own desires or inclinations. A man ponders the motives set before his mind, and chooses what he prefers, and this is what makes him accountable. Man chooses evil with his faculties intact and not being a victim of a power outside of himself. Man follows his desires and rejects the good, instead he chases evil and is guilty. He voluntarily misuses his faculties and sins deliberately. Man, not only will not, but he cannot please God. The eyes and the understanding of a fallen man's heart cannot tolerate spiritual light, until God heals them. Man has no natural ability to receive God's truth for the saving of his soul. The mind of the natural man is deranged. His heart and mind and will are blind and wicked (Eph. 4:18), and opposed to the light of convictions. The unregenerate man has been disabled by sin, but he remains responsible to glorify God. The unregenerate voluntarily chooses evil, even though he is a rational creature with the power of choice. The natural man lacks a good heart. Man's conscience testifies to him both about his responsibility to be right with God, and the criminality of his wrong doing. We have a sense that we will be giving an account of ourselves (Rom. 14:12) and that we are guilty (Rom. 3:23).

"Whoever shall call upon the name of the Lord shall be saved" (Rom. 10:13). The way to be saved is narrow but not exclusive. The Gospel is for "whoever" calls upon the name of the Lord. The Word of faith brings salvation. The way to be saved points to the importance of witnessing. God is patient (2 Pet. 3:9), and desires all men to come to the knowledge of the truth and be saved (1 Tim. 2:4). According to the word of God, the lost must have a witness to hear, hear to believe, and then call upon the Lord Jesus to be saved. They must begin to understand and believe that Jesus died for their sins, was buried, and raised on the third day according to the scriptures (1 Cor. 15:1-4). The lost must hear to gain some knowledge and faith to believe about Jesus. They must get the sense that God hears them calling upon Him to be saved through the forgiveness available to them in Jesus. Reading the word of God is a kind of hearing and learning, by the grace of God, that brings forth an awareness and trust in the truth of faith that Jesus loves them and will save them. Amen.

What about the Christian that has been born again, and his way of doing things that are displeasing to God? Before conversion, he is as likely to sin as the natural man, and we know also that after conversion, he will have moments of weakness. We know that without Jesus we can do nothing (John15:5), but the Christian will confess his sins, and he will pray for God's help and strength. "The flesh sets its desire against the Spirit, and the Spirit against the flesh; for these are in opposition to one another, so that you may not do the things that you please" (Gal. 5:17). The "may not" in the New American Standard Bible is the word "cannot" in the King James Bible. This passage speaks of a problem with the Christian's spiritual ability and the extent of his responsibility. Regeneration and being born again, is only the beginning of His good work in the elect (Phil. 1:6). We are all imperfectly sanctified in this life (Phil. 3:12). There is a great difference between the unregenerate, who are dead in sin; and the regenerate who have passed from death to life. One is a slave to the devil, while the other has been translated into the kingdom of Jesus Christ (Col. 1:13). One rejects and despises Christ; while the other loves and desires to serve Him. The Christian cries out, "I do believe; help my unbelief" (Mark 9:24). A Christian will praise his Savior one moment, and the next, he may be groaning before Him in weakness and sin. Deep in his soul, the true Christian cries out in faith for help, recognizing his inability to do the right thing with God. At the same time, he knows that God's goodness and grace have already done a great work for him in the way of salvation. In His time, the work of God shines brighter and brighter, and He becomes our strength for obedience. The regenerate has been given knowledge and understanding to know the Son of God and eternal life (1 John 5:20; John 17:3). The Christian has a light shining in his heart revealing the glory of God in Jesus (2 Cor. 4:6). The light lets him know that he is "being transformed into the same image from glory to glory" (2 Cor. 3:18). Amen.

The metamorphosis of a Christian is first inward and takes some time. Each person is different, and God is at work personally and individually to reveal to you the truth in Jesus. In a Christian, the will has been freed from the dominion of sin in the old nature, to God working in him to will and to work for His good pleasure (Phil. 2:13). The affections are changed to delight and enjoy the things of God, while sin becomes a great sorrow. The conscience becomes more sensitive and aware of the sinful nature of certain practices that you try to avoid. Although we are a new creature in Christ, we have a life in which old ways are passing away and new things are coming (2 Cor. 5:17). We are "like newborn babes, long for the pure milk of the word, that by it you may grow in respect to salvation" (1 Pet. 2:2). The Christian grows in grace and knowledge because he has the principle of spiritual life in being born again. The Christian will know spiritual inability, and by the grace of God will learn humility, and patience for himself, as well as the goodness, power, and the faithfulness of God. The unregenerate remains ignorant, blind, and lost, and sadly, does not know it, because he is not alive in Jesus. In a spiritually growing Christian, the commands of the new nature are not burdensome (1 John 5:3). The believer is growing in faith and obedience, and knows the rewards of being with God are peace and assurance (Prov. 3:17). "The Lord makes me lie down in green pastures" and "restores my soul." We gain the confidence that He is guiding me in paths of righteousness for His names' sake" (Ps. 23: 2-3). I do not have the answers to everything, but I have enough of God's presence to know of His goodness and lovingkindness for my soul in Jesus. We can be moved by God to know we are saved. Amen.

Christ lives in the regenerate soul in a way that the old man of sin is dying. We can say with Paul, "I have been crucified with Christ; and it is no longer I who live, but Christ lives in me; and the life which I now live in the flesh I live by faith in the Son of God, who loved me, and delivered Himself up for me" (Gal. 2:20). A natural man always lives like the old man and remains unregenerate. However, in a new man in Christ Jesus, "the old things passed away; behold, new things have come" (2 Cor. 5:17). The new things come with new responsibilities. "From everyone who has been given much shall much be required" Luke 12:48). The Holy Spirit helps us (Rom. 8:26). As one alive from the dead, we are to grow in grace and knowledge of Christ and the Bible. We are required "to make no provision for the flesh" (Rom. 13:14), and "to not love the world" (1 John 2:15). We are to use our spiritual gifts, and employ our talents (1 Pet. 1:10). Our life is hidden in Christ (Col. 3:3), and so is the conflict of the two natures between the flesh and the spirit (Rom. 7:15). "A righteous man falls seven times, and rises again, but the wicked stumble in times of calamity" (Prov. 24:16). The Christian will delight in the law of God after the inward man (Rom. 7:22), and when he sins, he will confess his sins for forgiveness and cleansing (1 John 1:9). The new man has been freed from the love, guilt, and penalty of sin, but not its presence, and all our corruptions at one time (1 John 1:8). God has promised us that sin shall not be master over us (Rom. 6:14). God intimates that the older man, that is unregenerate, shall serve the younger man, that is the regenerate. "Younger, because he appears later in our life, while we are born the first time naturally as an older man (Gen. 25:23). God is always at work in His children.

Sin will always be with us in this life, but will diminish by the grace of God. God may allow us to learn the demoralizing effects of sin to keep us humble, and dependent upon Him for grace. We groan under sin and feel unworthy of God's goodness. He knows our frame and that we are but dust (Ps. 103:14), and that we must lean upon Him for grace to live up to the knowledge He has given us in Jesus. The sense of God's continuing presence with us is a source of great encouragement to a Christian. A Christian is on a journey of discovery to know God. It is our responsibility "to work out our salvation with fear and trembling; for it is God who is at work in you, both to will and to work for His good pleasure" (Phil. 2:12-13). In salvation, God really gets your attention. Your "work" becomes important and you think about it with the utmost care. You will take pains to be diligent. What is in your heart starts showing up in your life. You will grow in grace and knowledge. It is a life of God's sovereignty appearing in man's responsibility. The plan of God will always depend on the grace of God. To God be the glory for His mercy, grace, and truth in the gift of salvation for our souls. In this life, salvation by faith is true when it rests on God alone. "My soul waits in silence for God only; from Him is my salvation. He only is my rock and my salvation, my stronghold; I shall not be greatly shaken" (Ps. 62:1-2). To wait upon and for God, Christian, is the place of true faith, sincerity, and a spiritual purity. To eventually have our soul possessed in this way, only comes to us by the grace of God. "Salvation belongs to the Lord" (Ps. 3:8). "Salvation is from the Lord" (Jonah 2:9). By the power and mercy of God, Christian, we see the salvation of God in our heart. We behold His work to save our souls (Eph. 2:10). All glory be to God. Amen.

The New Birth by God

> "But as many as received Him, to them He gave the right to become children of God, even to those who believe in His name, who were born not of blood, nor of the will of the flesh, nor of the will of man, but of God" (John 1:12-13).

Dear Christian,

"In the beginning God created the heavens and the earth" (Gen. 1:1). Creation was a supernatural event, and the natural explanations presented by man make no contribution. No man was present when creation occurred, and I know the word of God in the Bible is true. God created the heavens and the earth and all that is within them in six literal twenty-four days just like the Bible says (Gen. 1). It appears that God created a mature universe. The idea of old age and millions and billions of years to make our world is a myth. The idea that humans evolved is mostly from the influence, starting around two-hundred years ago or so, of secular scientists primarily in the fields of Geology and Biology. Man is too complex to have evolved, no matter how much time you try to add into it. The idea of millions and billions of years for creation to occur is no where to be found in the Bible. Some folks have tried to fit the idea of millions of years between Genesis chapter one and two, but the Bible text makes no assertion of long ages. Any ideas about what must have happened in this proposed long-time frame is pure speculation. Remember "Nothing is impossible with God" (Luke 1:37). Do not let man be your authority over the word of God. "God spoke, and it was done" (Ps. 33:9). Let God speak for Himself.

There is no doubt that the narrative in Genesis chapter one and the big-bang model disagree. The big-bang model claims the sun came before the earth and the Bible states the earth came before the sun (Gen. 1:2-9,16). I have had problems with the results of dating methods, interpretations about light from space and time, and the absence of transitional forms in the fossil record. Most people think that evolution is a scientific fact. Some people think evolution is objective and rational and connected to being intelligent. Some people think that religious thinking is all faith, irrational, subjective, and not intelligent. A good study of evolution will show you it contains a lot of circular thinking which is not evidence or scientific. The model of evolution is impossible chance with no God, and misleads people about the origin of man. We are very complex creatures, physically, mentally, and spiritually, such that, I think, it is impossible for man to evolve by natural laws alone. This is true to me no matter how much time you think you must add to the process to secure some credibility. This area of study is still important. To believe in evolution draws people away from God and His word and blocks the path to a faith experience with Jesus. Each person needs to do their own diligent study and draw their own personal conclusions.

Though we are born into the world through parents, the Bible reveals that the first man and women were created by God, complete and functional (Gen. 1-2). "Then God said, Let US make man in our image, according to Our likeness," and "male and female He created them" (Gen. 1:26-27). God said to them, "Be fruitful and multiply and fill the earth and subdue it" (Gen. 1:28). "The Lord God formed man of dust from the ground, and breathed into his nostrils the breath of life; and man became a living being (Gen. 2:7). Man was created with dust, in God's image by God Himself. Adam and Eve were created upright (Eccl.7:29) and with intelligence (Gen. 2:19). As they came out of God's hands, they were rational, good, and upright, or determined to follow God. Man was created superior to animals (Matt. 10:31) and given wide dominion over them (Gen. 1:28). Man was fearfully and wonderfully made (Ps. 139:14). Man was created for God's pleasure and glory (Isa. 43:7; Rev. 4:11). We exist because of God's will, ability, and pleasure to create. "The Lord has made everything for its own purpose, even the wicked for the day of evil" (Prov. 16:4).

Man, meaning both male and female, is the crown of creation. In God's image means they were like God in mind, will and emotion and with an ability to reason. In God's image includes spiritual qualities like self-consciousness and God consciousness. In God's image means man was good and sinless. I think the phrase "in Our image" was to glorify the Father, Son, and the Holy Spirit. Mans creation was distinctive, in that it involved the Godhead and His image. Every man is made in the image of God but the image was marred. Through the fall of Adam, man lost his original righteousness (Rom. 5:18-19). Though a great deal was lost, man still had a mind and a conscience. Man became what the Bible calls a natural man, and lost true spiritual knowledge (1 Cor. 2:14). Man can be rational and mentally competent, and at the same time ignorant, disobedient, and defiant of the Gospel message. Man knows that murder, theft, greed, and sex crimes are wrong, but he cannot always do right. "Professing to be wise, they became fools" (Rom. 1:22). They became futile in their speculations, and their foolish heart was darkened" (Rom. 2:21). Since creation of the world; His attributes, power and divine nature has been clearly seen, yet they do not give thanks and honor God (Rom. 1:20-21). The god of this world has blinded the minds of the unbelieving that they cannot see the light of the Gospel of the glory of Christ, who is the image of God (2 Cor. 4:4). Thus, they will not have this God rule over them. They think they have God figured out and do not fear Him. They think they are not that bad to deserve Hades or experience a poor judgment from the kind of life they lived. God should be kind, and act in a way that seems fair to them. They know that they have made some mistakes, but everyone has, and they think some folks are a lot worse than they are. The idea that they might need a savior to cover their sin seems unnecessary. Their sin is not sin, or it does not bother them to have to do anything more about it. They get their "light" from understanding the world and their feelings, and consider that as meaningful as compared to what the Bible might have to say about Jesus and eternity. They live with a gamble about God. They think that science cannot be all wrong about the age of the universe and the earth and the Bible right. The thought of creation conflicts with their sinful lifestyle, while evolution takes God out of the equation of life. The world by wisdom does not know God, and their foolish heart darkens their spiritual faculties. Fallen man retains a sense of beauty in music, art and literature and can experience precious relationships with other people, but not communion with God. We were made for communion with God, and no substitute, no matter how precious, can give the rest or make known a man's purpose to himself than God Himself.

What was truly distinctive in the creation of man was that God "breathed into his nostrils the breath of life; and man became a living being" (Gen. 2:7, KJV). From God's Spirit, we receive the spirit or breath of life and become a living soul. The workmanship of God of breathing into us exceeds the nature of the dust He used to make us. The soul of man came from God. The dust will return to the earth and the spirit will return to God who gave it (Eccl. 12:7). Man is a steward of His soul and will give an account for it. The life He breathes into us, should breathe after Him. Jesus Himself, breathed on His disciples, saying, "receive the Holy Spirit" (John 20:22). God can make a new soul. Man is different from the other creatures. God breathed His own breath into the nostrils of Adam. He is the potter and we are the clay (Isa. 64:8). "Let everything that has breath praise the Lord" (Ps. 150:6).

"He chose us in Him before the foundation of the world, that we should be holy and blameless before Him. In love He predestined us to adoption, as sons through Jesus Christ to Himself, according to the kind intention of His will, to the praise of the glory of His grace, which He freely bestowed on us in the Beloved" (Eph. 1:4-7). This great passage of the Bible in Ephesians is the definition of election. In the Bible, election is an act of God before creation in which He chooses "vessels of mercy" to be saved (Rom. 9:23). They are chosen not on account of any foreseen merit in them, but only because of His sovereign good pleasure. They were chosen in the counsel of God from eternity. They were chosen before they had a being, and chosen to be holy according to the good pleasure of His will. "The gifts and the calling of God are irrevocable" (Rom. 11:29). The glory of God is His own end. "God shuts up all in disobedience that He might show mercy to all" (Rom. 11:32). God shuts up even His elect, so that they display their true nature as sinners, before He shows them His mercy (Rom. 11:30-32). The outworking of election for people who deserved wrath (Rom. 1:18), reveals the greatness of God's grace. The sovereign choice of God takes place before any works of a man (Rom. 9:11). "God's choice does not depend on the man who wills or the man who runs, but on God who has mercy" (Rom. 9:16). God leaves some sinners as they deserve with hardening of their heart for sin (Rom. 9:18), and selects others to be vessels of mercy, upon which He makes known the riches His glory, which He prepared beforehand for glory (Rom. 9:23).

The great wonder is that God chose to be gracious to anyone. When the Gospel is preached, some people respond because they have been drawn (John 6:44). God, by His Spirit, calls the elect to respond with faith to believe. When a man comes to a true and active faith in Christ, it proves their election to be a reality (1 Thess. 1:2-5; Titus 1:1; Acts 13:48). God's choice was an act of predestination and eternal purpose (Eph. 1:5, 9, 11). God chose those who would be sprinkled with His blood (1 Pet. 1:2) before the foundation of the world (Eph. 1:4). The Christian is chosen to be saved in Christ, bear His image, have a holy conduct, and share His glory in eternity. God chose us to be redeemed from the guilt and stain of sin, through the atoning death of Christ, and the gift of the Holy Spirit (Eph. 5:25-27; 2 Thess. 2:13). Our union with Christ by faith means everything to the believer. Our salvation, from first to last, is found in Christ alone by the grace of God. It is an eternal security of love that nothing can separate us from (Rom.

8:35-39). We have an inheritance reserved in heaven, "protected by the power of God through faith for a salvation ready to be revealed in the last time" (1 Pet. 1: 5). We are to "be diligent to make certain about His calling and choosing you" (2 Pet. 1:10). The fact of election is no license to sin (Eph. 5:5) or presume on the goodness of God (Rom. 11:19-22). The fact of election by God is our great incentive to be humble, joyful, and grateful. "Rejoice that your names are recorded in heaven (Luke 10:20). Those who have been chosen by God, are to put on a heart of compassion, humility, and patience forgiving each other. They are to let the peace of Christ rule in their hearts to which they were called (Col. 3:12-15).

What is the evidence in your soul for the proof of election? First, remember election was not an arbitrary choice made by God. The basis of His choice is in the mystery of His will (Eph. 1:9). It was according to His purpose (Eph. 1:11). It was to make known the majesty of His grace and mercy, to the praise of His glory (Eph. 1:6, 12;2:7). We were chosen to "proclaim the excellencies of Him who called us out of darkness into His marvelous light (1 Pet. 2:9). God's choice was pleasing to Him and in perfect harmony with His love and justice. Believing the Bible and receiving the gift of faith is the fruit of election. Repentance is produced in the heart of an elect person by the sovereign work of the Holy Spirit. Election does not depend on human will but God's will and mercy (Rom. 9:16). "Everyone who beholds the Son and believes in Him, may have eternal life" (John 6:40). God is completely in control, and we have personal responsibility for our choices. Though humans might be stumped understanding how both, God's sovereignty and human choices can be true and exist together, God is not stumped. Salvation is offered to all men (Titus 2:11), so that all men are without excuse (Rom. 1:19-20). God will have all the glory for salvation. I believe that God carried my soul for Jesus, at times and in ways, that I cannot fathom, yet I believe He was at work (Phil. 2:13). In my heart, a miracle has taken place. Fulfilling my responsibility to work out my salvation with fear and trembling (Phil. 2:12), is not a work that I can glory in. The Bible is alive, and faith comes by reading God's word (Rom. 10:17).

The testimony from my life and heart is that the truth can be found only in a personal relationship with Jesus. The testimony of God lies not in the model of evolution, but the truth of creation and being born again. The testimony of God is in the call to holiness. The testimony of God lies in receiving Jesus, putting on the new man, and walking by the Spirit. The testimony of the scripture is for Jesus. We must be born again to know we have a new heart, and realize the power of God. To God alone belongs this glory. The experience of being born again and saved is personal. Each person is unique, and will be personally drawn by the love of God. The one aspect that will not be different, is the response of the individual to Jesus Christ. Your hope, trust, and confidence will always be in Him. "There is no other name under heaven that has been given among men, by which we must be saved" (Acts 4:12, 10:43; Matt. 1:21). In salvation, your heart will be changed. "The Spirit bears witness with our spirit that we are children of God" (Rom. 8:16). To begin to know your election, you must first know you are being saved, and God only makes this true connection in Jesus. "Whoever will call upon the name of the Lord will be saved" (Rom. 10:13). The way is narrow and God opens the door (Rev.3:20). Our call to God for help goes out with a believing expectation of an answered prayer. Our call to God for help goes out in complete dependence upon Jesus believing that He can and will save us. The Bible tells us, "That if you confess with your mouth Jesus as Lord, and believe in your heart that God raised Him from the dead, you shall be saved; for with the heart man believes, resulting in righteousness, and with the mouth he confesses, resulting in salvation" (Rom. 10:9-10). The gift of faith to trust Christ, Christian, is from God. Faith becomes a conquering grace for which God gets all the glory. The Spirit of truth has been abiding with you. The Spirit of truth has been sent for you in the name of Jesus, and He will be teaching you all things (John 14:16, 26).

Inside your election, Christian, will be the gifts of faith, love, and affection for Jesus. True love is practical and flows forth with obedience to the commandments of Christ. Obedience to the commandments of Christ will be the result of your love to Him (John 14:15). This is powerful evidence that God has been at work in your heart. Amen. Our comfort and peace about being chosen by God follows when we are faithful and diligent in our duty. Do not despair, you will never be perfect (1 John 1:8). Do not let your sin get a strong grip and tell you that because you still sin that it means you do not love Jesus. Since you love Him, you will keep His commandments (John 14:15). We learn to love Jesus and grow in grace and knowledge. "We love Him because He first loved us" (1 John 4:19). God is patient (Ps. 103:8). For those whom the Lord loves, He disciplines, and it is for discipline that you endure (Heb. 12:6-7). We need the power of the Holy Spirit to be living within us to love the Lord and to be obedient. We will know that the Lord is at work, and give Him the glory, and not pat ourselves on the back. Be diligent, and with fear and trembling work out your salvation (Phil. 2:12). It is from the principle of love to Jesus that we keep His commandments. It may take some time, experience, and knowledge to discover the true love for Christ in your soul. It takes growth in grace to recognize God's lovingkindness that will lead you to run after Him in love. It becomes our greatest blessing to be in love with the Lord. It is the evidence we have been born again. It confirms the choice He made for us. To God be the glory. "May the Lord direct your heart into the love of God and into the steadfastness of Christ" (2 Thess. 3:5). We wait in Christ for faith in Christ to believe that indeed He came once in the flesh, and will be coming again in glory. God blesses us with progress in knowing Jesus, and opens a path for us that allows our heart to move deeper and deeper into the love of God. A closer walk with Jesus is the assurance of being born again and inheriting eternal life (John 17:3).

"But as many as received Him, to them He gave the right to become children of God, even to those who believe in His name, who were born not of blood, nor of the will of the flesh, nor of the will of man, but of God" (John 1:12-13). Here we are told that we must receive Him, and then we are born of God. Salvation comes to a sinner by "receiving" Christ, that is, by "believing on His name".

We respond to God's offer of grace in Christ (John 3:16). We agree with the facts about Jesus and welcome Him into our hearts by faith for a personal relationship. We need to be born again to have spiritual life (John 3:5). "That which is born of the flesh is flesh, and that which is born of the Spirit is spirit" (John 3:6). In that moment you believe, He gives you new birth as a child of God. You were dead and guilty of sin as a natural man, and God quickens you from death to life and removes the guilt of sin (John 1:29). The drawing and quickening by God to faith in Christ is by His grace and you become a spiritual man by being born again from above (John 6:44). God gave, based on the decision of His will, the desire and right to become children of God. It is a gift of God's sovereign grace, without any merit or work on your part (Eph. 2:8-9). "See how great a love the Father has bestowed upon us that we should be called children of God" (1 John 3:1). We are brought supernaturally into God's family. "The Spirit bears witness with our spirit that we are children of God" (Rom. 8:16). We know Christ. Amen. We believe in His name. To God be the glory. To believe means we have moved closer to Christ from our heart and soul and find rest in Him. He is God with us (Matt. 1:23). The name of Jesus is powerful, Christian; in His name we have the forgiveness of sin, salvation, and eternal life in heaven. God's gracious intention all along has been to save you, and bless you with glory in the future as the bride of Christ. The evidence that comes along with being born again is a growth of faith in Christ, new life, peace in the conscience, love, and increased holiness. The assurance of your salvation comes in not how much you know, but the One you know. "Thanks be to God for His indescribable gift" (2 Cor. 9:15).

Those who receive and truly believe on Christ have been born again by a supernatural birth from heaven. "Whoever believes that Jesus is the Christ is born of God; and whoever loves the Father loves the child born of Him. By this we know that we love the children of God, when we love God and observe His commandments" (1 John 5:1-2). "If you know that He is righteous, you know that everyone also who practices righteousness is born of Him" (1

John 2:29). If we know intuitively that God is righteous, then you know experientially that His children practice righteousness. "The Spirit Himself bears witness with our spirit that we are children of God" (Rom. 8:16). In God's perfect will, Christ was to suffer and rise again from the dead on the third day, before He entered glory (Luke 24: 26,46). After this, repentance for forgiveness of sins was to be proclaimed in His name to all the nations, beginning with Jerusalem (Matt. 24:37). By the grace of our all-glorious God, this became the foundation for our faith in being saved. Thank you, Jesus. Believing in Christ is evidence we have been born again and that God has given us new life. We cannot take the credit for our faith in Christ as some sort of wise decision we made on our own. God imparted new life and deserves all the glory (1 Cor. 1:26-31; Eph. 2:1-10; Acts 13:48). We have the evidence by the new Witness of the Holy Spirit in our hearts (1 John 5:10-13), by the love we have for one another (1 John 4:7-11), and by a life of righteousness (2 Cor. 5:17; 1 John 2:29). "No one who is born of God practices sin, because His seed abides in him; and he cannot sin, because he is born of God" (1 John 3:9). A born-again individual has two natures in him, the old and the new. The power to live a righteous life is not found in the old nature. The power to live a righteous life is only found in the new nature. Since God cannot sin (1 John 3:9), the new nature that issues from His holy seed cannot sin (2 Pet. 1:4). The old nature is still present and can sin, if you let it sin (Rom. 6:12). If you yield to the desires in the old nature, you will live a defeated Christian life. It may take some time, but the old life has been delivered a death blow, and the new man will grow stronger and stronger and eventually sit alone on the throne of your heart. To God be the glory.

The new birth is a Divine work not left to chance. It is clear, that all people do not choose to receive Christ. The new birth is accomplished by the Holy Spirit (John 3:8) applying the Word in living power to your heart. It is not of blood, the will of the flesh or of another man, but of God (John 1:13). Your birth into God's family has nothing to do with your parents, that is, the blood or your genetics. Your parents may have been exemplary Christians, with great influence and prayed over you, but God still makes the choice. We cannot "will" ourselves into the family of God, your flesh will never go there. Our personal effort and desire, does not bring about the new birth. The will of friends, family members, and preachers have no power to bring about the new birth in another person's life. "There is none who understands, there is none who seeks for God" (Rom. 3:11). The Bible also tells us that "all men are under sin, that the promise by faith in Jesus Christ might be given to those who believe" (Gal. 3:22). "God has shut up all in disobedience that He might show mercy to all" (Rom. 11:32). "All have sinned and fallen short of the glory of God" (Rom. 3:23). "The wages of sin, is death, but the free gift of God is eternal life in Christ Jesus our Lord" (Rom. 6:23). The scripture declares that all, both Jew and Gentile are in a state of guilt, and unable to attain to righteousness and justification by the law. "The Law has become our tutor to lead us to Christ, that we may be justified by faith" (Gal. 3:24). Failure to keep the Law drives us to Jesus, who gives us rest (Matt. 11:28). God has promised you new life in Christ. Faith in Christ frees you from the bondage of the Law. Only the Spirit of God can remove spiritual blindness. Only the Spirit of God can give us eyes with the power of faith to see that Jesus saves. Amen.

We must be drawn by the Father (John 6:44) to receive Jesus and be born again by the Spirit (John 3:6). We must have spiritual light and power to see Jesus, and be in the family of God. This all happens by the plan, grace, and mercy of God. God knew that we would need to be born again to seek Jesus, otherwise, our natural born man would have preferred sin and passed on the offer to receive Jesus. "The hearing ear and the seeing eye, the Lord has made both of them" (Prov. 20:12). God gives both the natural eye and ear to see and hear physically, and the spiritual eye and ear to see and hear spiritually. He gives the ear that hears God's voice and the eye to see the beauty of Christ. God opens our understanding with gratitude for being born again in Christ. We cannot "will" ourselves into the family of God. It may be hard to accept, Christian, and I think a lot of people stumble at this, but our personal effort and determination does not bring about our supernatural birth. The natural man is opposed to God (1 Cor. 2:14). Wishful thinking, strong desires and hard work does not make you a child of God. The will of your earthly family members and well-meaning church workers cannot produce a child of God. The miracle of the new birth is of God. The people and circumstances of your life may be tools in His hands, but only God can bring forth a true believing child of God. True believers live under the power of His regeneration, growing in grace to the obedience of faith (1 John 3:1; James 1:27; Rom. 1:5, 16:26). "As many as were ordained to eternal life believed" (Acts 13:48).

Salvation is a gift to be received, not a reward to be achieved. Jesus said, "Everyone who has heard and learned from the Father, comes to Me" (John 6:45). It is through the Spirit informing our heart about the love of God, bringing us out of darkness into His light and creating a new man. It is through the Spirit overcoming our self-righteousness and convicting us of our lost condition. The Holy Spirit moves upon the Father's choice and the Son's obedient love. God draws us into a New Covenant and communion with Himself by the influences of the Holy Spirit. "He loved us with an everlasting love; and drawn us with lovingkindness" (Jer. 31:3). It is a powerful love that nothing can separate us from (Rom. 8:38-39). It is rich in grace and peace, and makes us careful and fearful to please Him. God works an affection in us that makes us glad. He writes His law upon our hearts, and tells us, He will be our God and we will be His people (Jer. 31:33). Those born of God, will know God, because God will reveal Himself to His own children. The Holy Spirit will make us hungry for the bread of life which came down out of heaven (John 6:32). We never get hungry or thirsty again, because in Jesus, we have complete satisfaction. Our soul is nourished and our spiritual life fulfilled. Since it not natural, it can only mean that God has been at work in us for us to have been born again. We discover God's love in our soul.

In the victory of Christ by His obedience unto death, souls would be born again. "As Moses lifted up the serpent in the wilderness, even so must the Son of Man be lifted up; that whoever believes in Him have eternal life" (John 3:14). In another verse, "and I, if

I be lifted up from the earth, will draw all men to Myself" (John 12:32). What is being meant here, Christian, by being "lifted up" is the crucifixion of Jesus on the cross. The precious blood the Son of God shed in dying for us, would be the means of obtaining the forgiveness of sin and our reconciliation with the Father. He paid our debt for sin in full. The sacrifice of Christ gets the believer's attention. The sacrifice of Christ resulted in the release of God's power to draw men to Himself. Jesus is "lifted up" in our hearts by the Holy Spirit, which draws us closer to Him. The drawing of our soul to be saved is ascribed to the Father (John 6:44) and the Son (John 12:32). Our soul is made ready in the day of His power (Ps. 110:3). The gospel had power in men's souls and in the church, and both grew mightily after the death and resurrection of Jesus. Drawing is the power of God to do something you could never do on your own, and that is come to Christ. He overcomes our selfish pride, self-righteousness, fear, ignorance, and unholy desires, to see our greatest need. We are taken up into the arms of God by His love. We grow by the grace of God in gratitude and learn to love the Lord. We discover more of His presence with fear and trembling (Phil. 2:12), and spending more time being fed by His word. We find ourselves willing, not forced, to live according to the will of God. We sense a great wisdom, a beauty in holiness and the fresh air of freedom. "Where the Spirit of the Lord is, there is liberty" (2 Cor. 3:17). Truth liberates, whereas unbelief or ignorance, even in believers can leave them stunted in growth. Godliness is a light in the soul and God's goodness is realized and welcomed as a spiritual beauty. We are God's people by purchase (1 Cor. 6:20) and effectual calling. The Lord opened our heart (Acts 16:14). We have been born again and belong to the Lord, never to go back to being a natural man. Amen.

"No one can come to Me, unless the Father who sent Me draws him; and I will raise him up on the last day" (John 6:44). Man uses his free choice and will to rebel against God. We have sinned and fallen short of the glory of God (Rom. 3:23). We must be born again and receive a new heart before we will ask for mercy from God. Being drawn by God is indispensable in our coming to

Jesus, that is, we will not and cannot do it on our own. We need God to open the eyes of our heart, and when He does, we will come to Jesus (John 6:37). "It is the Spirit who gives life, the flesh profits nothing; the words that I have spoken to you are spirit and are life" (John 6:63). "He who is of God hears the words of God" (John 8:47). "My sheep hear My voice, and I know them, and they follow Me" (John 10:27). All people are not drawn and made willing to hear the voice of God. They may not be of God and cannot believe (John 12:39). It is comforting and assuring to the believer's soul that the Lord Himself, of His own free will, has freely drawn you to Himself. He drew you and will keep you with His omnipotent power. Those He called, He justified and glorified (Rom. 8:30). They were predestined and ordained to eternal life (Acts 13:48). "In the exercise of His will He brought us forth by the word of truth" (James 1:18). We are born again of incorruptible seed, by the word of God (1 Pet. 1:23). The words of God are spiritual truth and powerful, and by the Spirit impart life. It is our responsibility to read the word, open our mind to see ourselves, and engage our hearts in faith for the light to shine in a way that permits us to discover and see our own salvation. "Everyone who is of the truth hears His voice" (John8:37). The sheep follow His example. Amen. We come to Jesus as a sinner with nothing to be saved, except our soul, and He saves it. This is God's sovereign and underserved grace for us given to Christ in eternity past. The gift of faith to believe is humbling. "Not to us, O Lord, not to us, but to Thy name give glory because of Thy lovingkindness, because of Thy truth" (Ps. 115:1).

In the creation of human beings, God gave Adam and Eve a free will. They were mutable and not robots, and could make their own choices and decisions. They could either obey God or disobey Him. God warned them that if they ate of the tree of the knowledge of good and evil, they would die (Gen. 2:16-17). They disobeyed God, and sin entered the world, and death spread to all men (Gen. 3; Rom. 5:12). To will is to choose and to choose is to decide between alternatives. The will is motivated to "make a decision" by the strongest influences in the mind. The will is the servant of the mind. The scripture teaches us to "watch over your heart with all diligence, for from it flow the springs of life" (Prov. 4:23). God, who gave us our souls, commanded us to watch over them. God wants us to do His will from our heart (Eph. 6:6). Fill your heart with the word of God. Guard your eyes and ears because they are gates to your thoughts which influence your heart and will. Figuratively speaking, the heart is the control center of your being. The heart is considered a place of emotions, knowledge, wisdom, conscience, moral character, rebellion, and pride. The heart includes your thoughts, desires, words, and actions. The heart describes your inner being, and is the place Satan and sin will try to invade and control. A man cannot understand his own heart (Jer. 17:9). We need a new heart, and at regeneration when we are born again, God gives us a new heart (Ezek. 36:26). Our true conversion turns the heart from Satan, self, and sin, to God, Christ, and holiness. We are called to seek God with all our heart (Matt. 22:37). Our heart is what makes each of us unique individuals, and out of the heart, we decide what we will do. The heart has also been used to describe an individual's personality. A man is what his heart is, and God "looks" into it to see if we are faithful. God has called us to take care of our hearts. It is our duty, and at the same time, it is God who gives the enabling grace to do it. The course of our life with a new heart, seeks the mind and heart of God. We seek obedience to the will of God, and His glory when we have been born again. Amen.

The Bible tells us that after Creation, "God saw all that He had made, and behold, it was very good" (Gen. 1:31). In Adam and Eve, the will was free to do good and to do evil. They were free to be obedient or disobedient. When they fell into sin, their human nature was profoundly altered. In the fall, human nature lost its freedom to not sin. "Just as through one man sin entered into the world, and death through sin, and so death spread to all men, because all sinned" (Rom. 5:12). Through one mans disobedience and transgression, many were made sinners, resulting in condemnation to all men (Rom. 5:18-19). A sinner is born the first time with a heart that is "more deceitful than all else and desperately sick" (Jer. 17:9). Man has a strong bias toward evil. Man became a natural and unspiritual man that will not come to Christ on his own (John 5:40). "A natural man does not accept the things of the Spirit of God; for they are foolishness to him, and he cannot understand them because they are spiritually appraised" (1 Cor. 2:14). The mind of the flesh is hostile toward God and cannot please God (Rom. 8:7-8). Man, in a natural state, suffers from the bondage of the will. The will of fallen man shows no interest in accepting Christ, never reads the Bible or prays. The man will develop addictions and fail to consider death or eternal life seriously. Independent of man's bondage, he still is responsible to God to repent, believe, and receive Christ. Most people think that responsibility should go along with ability. Though we are unable to receive Christ as Savior because of sin, we still are responsible to God and susceptible to judgment. God does not just throw away His standard of holiness because man sinned, but He chose the way of grace in His Son for man to be forgiven and reconciled to Himself. God is good. Amen.

A born-again Christian will experience conflict between the grace of God and corruption in His heart. When we are born again, a struggle occurs between the new heart from God and the remainders of indwelling corruption. The Bible tells us that "The flesh sets its desire against the Spirit, and the Spirit against the flesh; for these are in opposition to one another, so that you may not do the things you please" (Gal. 5:17). Paul said, "I was not practicing what I would like to do, but I am doing the very thing I hate" (Rom. 7:15). My personal testimony is that I struggled in the conflict of two natures (Rom. 7:14-25). True grace in me strived against these sins and corruptions, and my soul mourned and groaned under them as a great burden. I knew I was obligated to live right before God, but could not. I suffered for a time in my conscience and felt powerless to make the change to live for God. I was blind, blocked, stressed and weak. I could not convert myself. I knew I could not be perfect (1 John 1:8), but I surely knew that I should be better than I am. Paul writes about this conflict when he says "Wretched man that I am! Who will set me free from the body of this death?" (Rom. 7:24). The reality is that we are born with a fallen nature, and because of sin, will reach a point that is miserable and distressing in mind and heart (John 8:34; Rom. 6:20). Failure in the Christian life is discouraging. I did not fully understand my weakness, get help, or have any previous experience with my predicament. I lived inside the trouble of my soul with fear. I felt alone. I felt honest to myself with God and wanted to be free, but getting free was bigger than me. I always felt responsible and thought for a long time I could rescue myself. I was wrong. I cried out to God and I believe He helped me in His time. He sent me more deeply into His Word, the Bible, which became my pathway to freedom. When I got stronger and gained some ground against my sin, I knew it came from outside of me. It came from the Lord as a result of Bible study. The Bible is a powerful book, I believe the Holy Spirit changed my life. God was working in me to will and to work for His good pleasure (Phil. 2:13). For me, the word of God became alive (Heb. 4:12).

Let me give you a short review of what the Lord has done for me. I came to Jesus at eleven years old at a revival meeting in our church and was baptized shortly after. The Lord moved me to come forward, and I have never forgotten His hand upon me at this time. I believe I was born again, but I remained mostly ignorant of what was in the Bible. I went to church, but failed to mature for almost twelve years. The old man in me was still strong and the world was waiting for me when I went to college. I got entangled in sin, and over time grew worse, until I started going back to church in graduate school. The Lord sent me to work in the church, gave me a helpful wife, and opened the Word of God to my heart. I especially studied the books of Ephesians, Romans, and the Gospel of John. I was directed by some good folks into Bible commentaries by Arthur Pink, Watchman Nee, Thomas Brooks, Charles Spurgeon, and Matthew Henry. I began to teach and share Jesus. God gradually made me more alive in Christ. I needed the Lord to grow in grace and knowledge. After retiring from work, I wrote four books about the Lord. God saved me from myself. To God be the glory.

Sin is a tough taskmaster, but no match against the grace, power, and love of God for our souls. There is no such thing as luck and chance at work in the salvation of our souls, but there is the loving providence and work of God. We are drawn by God to come to Jesus (John 6:44). We are born again by the Spirit (John 3:3, 6). We are given a new heart, a new spirit, and the Holy Spirit to be careful to observe the ordinances of God and walk by the Spirit (Ezek. 36:26-27). "We are His workmanship, created in Christ Jesus for good works" (Eph. 2:10). We are exhorted to "work out our salvation with fear and trembling; for it is God who is at work in you, both to will and to work for His good pleasure" (Phil. 2:12-13). My great need and inability were taken care of in God's time and way in the saving work of Jesus Christ. I know myself to be a "vessel of Mercy" (Rom. 9:23). I believe in God's love and sovereign actions to save my soul. "Thanks be to God through Jesus Christ our Lord!" (Rom. 7:25). God was patient with me. He gave me a faith unto obedience through His Son, to God be the glory (Rom. 1:5, 16:26). "I am not ashamed of the Gospel, for it is the power of God for salvation" (Rom. 1:16). I know that the righteousness of God has been revealed in my heart from faith to faith (Rom. 1:17). I know the riches of His kindness and forbearance. I know that the kindness of God has led me to repentance (Rom. 2:4). The fact that I learned I was powerless against my sin, and needed the grace of God in Jesus to give me freedom is a strong basis for my gratitude. The necessity of the grace of God confirms in my thinking the depravity in man as a result of the fall. I do not boast of my works, my salvation is a gift of God (Eph. 2:8-9). Amen.

The Gospel of Jesus Christ is all about the grace of God. The doctrines of grace reveal God's love and mercy and have been remembered by some folks by the acronym of TULIP, which originated from the work of John Calvin (1509-1564). It is also called the five points of Calvinism. It is based on God's word and focuses on God's sovereignty. The "T" stands for Total Depravity and means that since Adam's fall, human beings have inherited a sinful nature. The heart, mind, will, affections, and body of man have been corrupted. We are completely lost and cannot save ourselves. We cannot choose God, but God chooses us and sanctifies us in Christ to come into His presence (Jer. 17:9; Mark 7:21-23; Eph. 2:1,3; Rom. 6:16-20; 1 Cor. 2:14). The "U" stands for unconditional election. This means that God chooses or elects people to be saved based on His will alone, and nothing worthy in the person (Eph. 1:4,11; 2:4; Rom. 9:11,16; Isa. 43:7). The "L" stands for limited atonement which means that not everyone who ever lived will be saved, but only the elect or chosen of God. The blood of Christ was sufficient for all to be saved, but not everyone's sin was imputed to Christ. Sin is a debt paid by Christ on the cross (Matt. 6:12; Col. 2:14; 1 Pet. 2:24; 1 John 2:2). The "I" stands for irresistible grace and takes the view that it is the act of God making the person willing to receive Christ. The choice and mercy of God depends on God's desire, not man's ability (Phil. 2:12-13; John 6:29; Rom. 9:16). The "P" stands for perseverance which takes the view that we are secure in Christ. Because salvation is the work of the Triune God, it cannot be lost. We cannot be lost or perish. Those who leave the faith were never believers to begin with (John 10:27-28; Phil. 1:6; 1 Cor. 10:13; 1 John 2:19). The five points of Calvinism are arranged in a logical order. As a natural man, we are totally depraved because of sin. We need the Lord to choose to bring the elect forth by His grace. Not all will come. God must call us and make salvation secure and safe by the powerful and effectual work of the Holy Spirit. To God be the glory for His grace.

The spiritual condition in the natural fallen man cannot understand God (1 Cor. 2:14). The defilement and stain of sin corrupted who we are and what we do. The depth of the damage of sin has penetrated our entire being to the point we cannot know God, unless God chooses to reveal Himself to us. We need God for everything, and especially to be born of God to have spiritual life. It is not that some people cannot be honest and do good deeds, but that their nature is in rebellion to God, and they seek the things of sin and self. What they do and think is only natural or normal to them, and expected, hence, they are called natural men (1 Cor.

2:16). We are born with a nature that is depraved. "All of us have become like one who is unclean, and all our righteous deeds are like a filthy garment" (Isa. 64:6). The good news is, that God by His supernatural influence, acted against human depravity and drew us to His Son (John 6:44). We cannot be repaired by fixing the old man, we must be born again (John 3:7). After the fall, the will of man became enslaved in the natural man, and his only hope to be freed is by Divine help. We must acknowledge our helplessness and cry out to God for help. A man with an unchanged mind and heart will not and cannot come to Christ, hence he is totally depraved. Some folks prefer a lighter sounding language, like total or moral inability. The fact remains that without Jesus, our heart is "deceitful and desperately wicked" (Jer. 17:9). Because of this condition, man is considered born dead (Ps. 51:5, 58:3; Eph. 2:1-5), and must be born again to know God. A sinful lifestyle seems right and feels good. "There is no fear of God before their eyes" (Rom. 3:12). In drawing us to Jesus, the Holy Spirit supernaturally overcomes us, and wakes us up to our lost condition. On our own, we cannot, do not, and will not, seek to know, please and love God. We would remain lost. According to the Bible, Adam, by God's design represented us, and when he fell, we were linked to him (Rom. 5:12, 18).

Depravity means we became sinners by choice from a mutable nature. I believe if I was in his situation, I would have acted just like Adam. When we are born again in Jesus, God gives us a new heart, a new spirit, and His own Spirit within us to save us from ourselves and for Himself (Ezek. 36:25-27). We are freed from the power and penalty of sin, and made alive with a spiritual life to please God and follow Jesus. Our old sin nature is considered dead, but its sinful desires are not completely eradicated. We have been defiled, but now able to grow in grace and knowledge and holiness. We confess our sins to be forgiven and cleansed of all unrighteousness (1 John 1:9). In place of commanding us to do something we cannot do, God confounds and breaks us, and makes us ready for the grace to come to Jesus and be saved. God rescued us by His own sovereign grace. He did this "that He might make known the riches of His glory upon vessels of mercy, which He prepared beforehand for glory" (Rom. 9:23). Total Depravity means that the human ability to choose Christ by "free will" is a myth. The doctrine of total depravity is clearly taught in the Bible (Rom. 11:32; Gal. 3:22). You can do nothing to save yourself from God's judgment for sin, except to respond to the call to come to Jesus to be saved. We despair of ourselves, our will and our ability, and trust Christ alone for salvation. For this to occur, the Holy Spirit has been at work to draw and convict you that this is God's plan for your life. Our prayer is for God to be merciful to us as a sinner (Luke 18:13). Our pride is no where to be found. When I see that I deserve the wrath of God, and He gave me grace and mercy to be saved, I freely give God the "praise of the glory of His grace which He freely bestowed upon us in the Beloved" (Eph. 1:6). Amen.

For a long time, Christian, I desired to have more assurance that I was indeed born again, forgiven, and saved. At the same time, I was ignorant of a lot of scripture. I had good church attendance, tithing and service in the church, but lacked a good Bible knowledge and a more complete obedience of Faith. I had some peace and the hope of heaven, but not a perfect practice of holiness and the privilege of joy in worship. I was sincerely striving against my corruptions, but did not have the sufficient grace for a more holy victory. God will not be mocked or presumed upon, whatever we sow is what we reap (Gal. 6:7). God was patient to break my old heart and get me into His word. Based on the objective facts of Christianity, I was saved, but a deeper personal assurance was an agonizing struggle in my faith. My weak faith left me with a weak assurance. I was worried about some scriptures, because I knew I should have a better testimony. For example, "If you love Me, you will keep My commandments" (John 14:15). I was keeping some commandments, but not all. I struggled and suffered, and spent too much time fighting for me to get right with God. I wanted to keep God's commandments and love Jesus and the Father. I wanted Jesus to disclose Himself to me (John 14:21), so I could have more peace, obedience, and assurance. I needed the grace of God. I had been a Christian for a while, but was missing out on the abundant life part. In God's time and with His mercy, I found out what I was missing. I was missing the word of God. "Faith comes by hearing, and hearing by the word of God" (Rom. 10:17). Why it took me so long to grasp the truth is still a mystery to me, but not God. Bible study became my life. Amen.

Jesus said, "Come unto Me, all who are weary and heavy-laden, and I will give you rest" (Matt. 11:28). Jesus said, I am the way, and the truth, and the life; no one comes to the Father, but through Me" (John 14:6). Our assurance comes from looking to Jesus and the union we have with Him. In the Word, God enlightens the eyes of our heart in His time. In the Word is the convicting knowledge of the hope of His calling and the glory of His inheritance for the saints (Eph. 1:18). A natural man does not accept the things of the Spirit of God that come to him from a sincere study of the Bible (1 Cor. 2:14). The god of this world blinds our minds from seeing the light of the Gospel of the glory of Christ, who is the image of God (2 Cor. 4:4). The Holy Spirit gives the gift of sincerity for us to learn and fear the Lord, and see through the deceptions. The Spirit of God shines a light in our hearts through the preaching and reading of the Word, that makes faith in Christ powerful and real (2 Cor. 4:6). The word of God is living and active (Heb. 4:12), and does not return to Himself void (Isa. 55:11). The truth of Christ speaks with spiritual authority in our minds, stirs our affections and makes more of His presence our assurance. Amen. God's gift of the grace of faith with assurance may take a while, but it is the rightful inheritance of His children.

"The firm foundation of God stands, having this seal, the Lord knows those who are His" (2 Tim. 2:19). The reality is the world is full of a lot of trouble, chatter, and perverse behaviors; nevertheless, Christian, the Lord is in control and preserves His own children. The foundation lies in the power and character of God. The gates of Hades shall not overpower the promises of Christ (Matt. 16:18). God knows you and you know Him. He chose you before the foundation of the world, and predestined you as a son (Eph. 1:4-5). He brought us forth by the word of truth (James 1:18). Salvation began with the original plans and continues in the execution of

Gods abilities. We have been sealed by the Holy Spirit of promise (Eph. 1:13). The seal means ownership, protection, holiness, and the guarantee of our security. The Son of God knows the born-again genuine believers, and will separate the believing "wheat" from the non-believing "tares" (Matt. 13:24-30). "The Spirit bears witness with our spirit that we are children of God" (Rom. 8:16). Assurance is a life-long discovery, and a gift to be patiently received from God. When we know we are new creatures in Christ (2 Cor. 5:17), the firm foundation of assurance becomes clearer to us. "My sheep hear My voice, and I know them, and they follow Me" (John 10:27). The hearing ear is made and given to us by God (Prov. 20:12). We are known personally and affectionately by God for eternity. As we follow on to know the Lord, He manifests to us more of His glorious reality. He knits Himself to us. Our spiritual life is always on a journey and we grow in grace and knowledge. The Christian life at different times, will show the innocence of childhood, the prime of manhood, and the experience of maturity (1 John 2:13-15). Our lives are not perfect, but we are forgiven because Jesus was perfect. We still deal with sin, but our trust and assurance, is always in what Christ has already accomplished for us. For me, the genuine path as a Christian, for knowing Jesus and walking in obedience, has been progressive. To God be the glory.

I believe we learn to be a Christian by the grace of God. I have learned the love, patience, goodness, and truth of the Lord out of the trials of sin in my life. In my deepest time of troubles with sin and in the groaning of my soul, I have the sense He heard me and helped me with His love. Over my whole life it seems, and certainly in times of weakness, God has been faithful and stayed the course with me. In it all, was the call to be holy and walk with Jesus. The direction that God has always given me, is to into His word. The result was to see His hand at work in my life. At one time, I thought I was sincere enough, but I was not serious enough, and the Lord patiently changed my heart. Instead of my will to sin, God gave me a will to be holy. From trying hard to please God, reading the Bible turned me to be grateful and worship Jesus. The way of the scripture turned me into the way of God's sovereign grace. For me, I think the path was learning about surrender and following Jesus in obedience. I became a Christian at a young age. In fact, the song the church sang when I came forward was "I surrender all," which still resonates in my heart to this day. I was young and did not really understand what it meant to surrender to the Lord. Throwing up your hands and arms, and yelling I surrender had a spiritual depth that I was blind to. Eventually, I was lured away from God by the world and myself, and it was the wrong decision and my fault. I waded into a world of sin, and it took me a while to wade back out. In the process, I learned about the love and patience of God. I learned about the incredible gift of forgiveness and reconciliation with God because of the sacrifice of Jesus. There were a few times when I gave up and surrendered to God, and pleaded for mercy and help. He heard my cry (Ps. 18:6, 120:1). The prayer of faith that God gave me, Christian, was answered by God's grace bringing forth my liberty (Ps. 118:5). As a result, I believe Jesus is the Christ, the Son of the living God (John 3:16). God revealed the life of Jesus to me (Matt. 16:17). God taught me the truth, and made me willing to do His will (John 7:17). All these blessings mean His presence with me, and I have been born again. To God be the glory.

Jesus Himself experienced a "surrender" when He yielded His will to His Father. His soul was deeply grieved to the point of death in the garden of Gethsemane (Matt. 26:38-39). As a result of the anguish of His soul and because He poured out Himself to death, He was allotted a portion with the great (Isa. 55:11-12). He was poured out like water and His heart melted like wax (Ps. 22:14). The full price of our redemption was paid. Jesus was expended, in love, for our souls. We find that Paul wrote from Phillippi about being poured out as a drink offering upon the sacrifice and service of their faith" (Phil. 2:17). He was expended for their souls (2 Cor. 12:15). Paul also wrote to Timothy about being poured out as a drink offering as the time of his departure had come (2 Tim. 4:6). A Christian is brought to a place of surrender, and by the grace of God, is broken of himself. A Christian has been chosen to be emptied of self, and then filled with faith to believe and trust the truth that Jesus saves. We are blessed to learn the affection of Jesus for our souls. He promised that we would be His people and that He would be our God (Ezek. 11:20). It was because of the obedience of Jesus that the Holy Spirit was sent, and became a powerful influence in our souls. I believe in Jesus, by the grace of God. Jesus was poured out as a sacrifice of atonement, whereas Paul was poured out to honor the truth of God. The war in your soul for Jesus, Christian, is a worthy fight. Keep the faith, and welcome the grace of God to pour out your soul as a living sacrifice for Jesus (Rom. 12:1). The victory has already been won. I pray that you will finish the race with great joy and comfort. I pray that you will receive the crown of righteousness (2 Tim. 4:8) and the crown of life (James 1:12), that the Lord has promised to all those who love Him. The crown of life is for those who persevere in faith through temptation, tribulation, and persecution. The crown of righteousness is for those who were made righteous, and look for the return of Jesus Christ. The crowns were purchased by the righteousness of Jesus Christ, and will be given to those who have the love of God reigning in their hearts. You are the child of a King. Amen.

The responsibility of Man to God

> "Work out your salvation with fear and trembling; for it is God who is at work in you, both to will and to work for His good pleasure" (Phil. 2:12-13).

Dear Christian,

An important topic about the plan of God for our salvation becomes the requirement of both God's sovereignty and man's responsibility. How does the sovereignty of God and man's responsibility work together? The Bible is very clear about God's sovereignty in our salvation. We were chosen before the foundations of the world (Eph. 1:4), and must be drawn to Christ by God (John 6:44). We must be born again (John 3:3). We are saved by grace, and not our works (Eph. 2:8-9). We are His workmanship (Eph. 2:10). After Adam, every man comes into the world a fallen and sinful creature. "We are dead in our trespasses and sins" (Eph. 2:1). God is rich in mercy and love, and "even when we were dead in out transgressions, made us alive together with Christ" (Eph. 2:5). God's grace unlocks and opens our soul, and the spiritual life He implants results in our union with Christ. Being born of God, we begin to live a life of sanctification. We are delivered from the guilt of sin and the fear of death by His justifying grace. The great love of God flows out of His heart and He supernaturally makes us alive in Christ. Thank you, Lord.

According to the Bible, we come into the world in a "fallen" spiritual condition in which the only cure is God's plan of redemption in Jesus. The Bible teaches this truth which is called total depravity. Our depravity is called total because without God acting for us, we would never come to Him. Sin has made a mess of our mind, will, and emotions. "There is none righteous, not even one; there is none who understands, there is none who seeks for God" (Rom. 3:11). Anything not done for the glory of God, and not by faith in Him, is not acceptable. It does not mean that man is without a conscience or sense of right and wrong. Nor does it teach we cannot do some good things, but the problem is, we are motivated by our self-interest and not God's glory (Heb. 11:6). God overcomes man's depravity by His own grace. He infuses spiritual life into a dead sinner, and he is born again by the Holy Spirit (John 3:3). We are born again "not of blood, nor of the will of flesh, nor of the will of man, but of God" (John 1:13). The doctrine of total depravity destroys self-righteousness and a man's ability to work from his own free will to be saved. The Bible tells us that God has shut up all men in disobedience that He might show mercy to all (Rom. 11:36). Some men do not like this teaching because it makes them feel helpless about themselves, and lets them know that they need help to be acceptable to God. A Christian knows that sin was ruining his life and that God alone rescued him from bondage. "Wretched man that I am! Who will set me free from the body of this death?" (Rom. 7:24). The purpose of the Bible is to help make God become known to us. The purpose of the Gospel is to bring sinners unto Christ to find our responsibility according to God's will for us in salvation. "Thanks be to God through Jesus Christ our Lord! (Rom. 7:25).

The Bible tells us that God created man in His own image. God is a trinity in unity; as the Father, Son, and Holy Spirit. Man is a unity in body, soul, and spirit (1 Thess. 5:23). Although man is an infinite distance from God, he was made upright (Eccl. 7:29). Man was finite and a creature made by God. God "breathed into his nostrils and man became a living being" (Gen. 2:7). He was made to rule over the works of His hands (Gen. 2:15, 19; Ps. 8:6). Adam was holy and had no sinful depraved nature. God blessed Adam, and he was well-equipped for his fitness as our federal head. He was still a creature whose soul was held in life by God (Ps. 66:9). Being only a creature, he had the potential to fall. Although he had high moral excellency, he was not omniscient. Also, he was not immutable like God (James 1:17), who cannot be tempted with evil (James 1:13). Adam had the capacity to be tempted to sin and change his ways, whereas God cannot be tempted to sin and fail in being holy in Himself. Adam was a rational creature with a freedom of his will, and the power to choose. He could choose to keep his integrity with God or comply with temptation to sin. Adam was made by God, and therefore was responsible to serve and please God. The test of obedience was made to determine whether the will of God was important to him. A test of Adams loyalty and obedience to his creator was made to see if he would remain holy and enjoy God's favor. Adam was put on probation (Gen. 2:16-17). God had every right to assert His authority as Creator to gain evidence and enforce man's relationship to Himself. Today, man has the pride, arrogance, and ignorance to believe in his own mind, that he deserves a free and fair conversation with God.

The Bible tells us that God established a garden in Eden. He planted trees good for food and to look at, as well as a tree of the knowledge of good and evil (Gen. 2:8-9). God also established a covenant of works with Adam (Gen. 2:16-17). He could eat freely from any tree in the garden, "but from the tree of the knowledge of good and evil you shall not eat, for in the day that you eat from it you shall surely die (Gen. 2:17). Then God blessed the man by giving him a helper, named Eve, suitable for him (Gen. 2:18, 21-23). Man's character had not yet been confirmed in righteousness. Regrettably, Adam and Eve failed the test, and evoked the displeasure of God. Some folks think Adam and Eve turned aside and fell rather quickly from God. After the Fall, God's presence left them, and man's nature became inclined to sin. Man is called the "slave of sin" (John 8:34), and a subject of its dominion. It pleased God to leave Adam and Eve without His help, and to the freedom of their own will and mutability. God is not the Author of their sin, nor did He provide them with the natural means of failing. The Bible tells us that "God made man upright" (Eccl. 7:29). It is impossible that sin should come from the Father of light, so we cannot blame God for the origin of our depravity. Man is a fallen creature. The Bible tells us that man himself is to blame for his depravity. We ruined ourselves by our apostasy from God. As a result of the Fall, in every generation throughout the world, every child is born with a depraved nature and cannot please God. The heart becomes deceitful above all things, and desperately wicked (Jer. 17:9). Depravity shows itself in pride, envy, malice, revenge, and sensual lusts. The signs of depravity are seen in war, murder, disease, and death. Depravity is seen in liars and crooks and especially in the contempt for Christ. The world is full of jealousy, cruel behaviors, and hate. The deep stain and defilement of mankind with total depravity from the Fall cannot be fixed or changed by man. Our rebellion against God's authority and the deserting of His way, cast us all into a deep gulf of wretchedness. This was the origin of human depravity. We need a miracle of grace from God to be reconciled back to God.

The Bible gives us the account of how sin entered the world. "Now the serpent was more crafty than any beast of the field which the Lord God had made" (Gen. 3:1). The tempter in the likeness of a serpent, was the malignant spirit of Satan. He was the first sinner and rebel against God's dignity that attacked Adam and Eve (Rev. 12:9, 20:2). Satan was a sinner, traitor, and tempter enraged against God and His glory, and jealous of man's happiness in Christ. Satan's great sin was pride (Isa. 14:13-14). The serpent tempted Eve first. Most likely in the absence of her husband she transgressed, and probably became the seducer of her husband (Gen. 3:1-6). Eve did not blame Adam, and the Lord did not charge Adam with any complicity in Eve's crime. The serpent was probably beautiful, stood erect, and may have eaten the apple himself and spoke to her without dying. Eve should not have talked to the serpent and fled; instead, she played with the temptation and believed his lie. She saw "the tree was good for food, and that it was a delight to the eyes, and the tree was desirable to make one wise" (Gen. 3:6). The Bible says, "she ate of the fruit, and she gave also some to her husband, and he ate" (Gen. 3:6). The serpent deceived Eve, but Adam was not deceived (1 Tim. 2:14). Adams guilt was greater because God made the covenant with him (Gen. 2:16-17). Adam listened to the voice of his wife (Gen. 3:17). Adam and Eve may have been uncertain about the kind of death God spoke to them about, that is; spiritual, physical, or eternal. Regardless, they sinned by disobedience and sin entered the world. The Bible tells us that "each one is tempted when he is carried away and enticed by his own lust. Then when lust has conceived, it gives birth to sin, and when sin is accomplished, it brings forth death" (James 1:14-15). Man is not now as God first made him. He has lost the glory of his creation and landed in a place of sin and misery. The history of mankind in wars, disease, and death is a testimony of the ways of sin.

The fact is, the whole human race was put on probation by God in the person of Adam; he is our legal representative and covenant head (Gen. 2:16-17). The fact is, the whole human race has sinned and fallen short of the glory of God (Rom. 3:23). The wage of sin is death (Rom. 6:23). God has shut all up in disobedience that He might show mercy to all (Rom. 11:32). The Bible tells us that by the offense of one, judgment came upon all men to condemnation (Rom. 5:18). Therefore, each person is not individually placed on trial, but we were on trial in one person as our representative head. The example given by others, was that Adam was like the root of a tree, with all the offspring being the branches. Kill the common root and all the branches die. What Adam did, we in effect would have fallen like he did. Adam was more richly endowed than we are and he failed the test, the idea is we would have failed it also. From all eternity, it was foreordained that the first man, Adam, should prefigure in some way the incarnate Son of God. The first man was made a living soul on earth, the last Adam, that is Christ, was a quickening spirit from heaven (1 Cor. 15:45-49). Amen. God knows all things and has planned all things. The plan of God is all about the glory of Christ. Both Adam and Christ transacted as the one for the many. The principle of imputation, that is, the righteousness of Christ, reckoned to the account of a believer was not new. Imputation was the principle upon which God acted from the beginning. "So then through one transgression there resulted condemnation to all men, even so through one act of righteousness there resulted justification of life to all men. For as through one man's disobedience the many were made sinners, even so through the obedience of the One the many will be made righteous" (Rom. 5:18-19). Thus, in Adam we see disobedience, transgression, sinners, and condemnation; while in Christ we see obedience, righteousness, justification, and eternal life. If God kept Adam from sinning, Adam would have been our savior. The honor was way too much for a creature to bear, only the Lord from heaven was worthy. God's plan, before the foundation of the world, was to reveal the fact of imputation: first in Adam and his disobedience; then in the last Adam, that is Jesus Christ, and His obedience. Though some people truly hate this teaching, God can only be just. What finite human being can understand the justice of the infinite God? He has decided to bring forth vessels of mercy to make known the riches of His glory (Rom. 9:23). The Lord is righteous in all His ways, and kind in all His deeds" (Ps. 145:17). Amen.

It appears that Adam's great sin was against God's majesty and more guilt fell upon him than Eve. He was not deceived (1 Tim. 2:14) or weak, but in defiance of God, he presumptuously sinned against God. Adam had no sacrifice, and there is no record in the scripture that he repented. He may have been ungrateful and unbelieving, and preferred his own will and way. Adam broke the covenant he made with God (Gen. 2:16-17). Adam acted in defiance of God and His authority and the threat of death. He tried to be independent of God. The life of God had departed from his soul after he sinned, and he tried to hide from an omniscient God. He blamed God for giving him a wife (Gen. 3:12). She could tempt him but not force him to sin; no attempt at self-justification was acceptable with God. The eyes of their conscience were opened and they knew they were naked (Gen. 3:10-11). They lost the image of God. The Spirit of righteousness that had covered them had departed, and they sensed guilt and shame which filled their souls. They were exposed to the wrath of God. They tried to hide their shame and true character. The sense of God's displeasure made them dread the presence of God. Instead of being as god's (Gen. 3:5), they were fearful and trembling criminals. They became like a natural man without understanding (1 Cor. 2:14). They tried to preserve their self-respect with effort to sew fig leaves together as a religious exercise. They tried to hide from God speaking to them. We do this today by not reading the Bible, or going to church. The outcome for the serpent was to be crushed; the outcome for Eve was sorrow and servitude; and the outcome for Adam was sorrow, toil and sweat, "and to dust you shall return" (Gen. 3:15-19). The Bible tells us that "the wages of sin is death, but the free gift of God is eternal life in Christ Jesus our Lord" (Rom. 6:23). We have a Savior, Jesus (John 3:16), and the promise of forgiveness and cleansing if we confess our sins (1 John 1:9). We have His presence. He has taken hold of our hand to lead us through the shadows of death into His presence that we might worship Him in His glory. We have a great high priest who can sympathize with our weaknesses (Heb. 4:15). We are encouraged by the Lord to buy gold and white garments to clothe ourselves that the shame of our nakedness may be covered (Rev. 3:18). We are to rejoice greatly in the Lord who has wrapped us with a robe of righteousness, and clothed us with garments of salvation (Isa. 61:10). A child of God in Jesus is not cast out.

The results of the original sin were inherited by the descendants of Adam and Eve. What God declared after the Fall was said to all of mankind. The calamity of sin and evil would descend upon the world. A child born into the world would be called a natural man (1 Cor. 2:14), with a depravity of nature in his soul, unable to know, understand and please God. They are inclined to lies and wickedness. They are spiritually cut off from the Lord (Ps. 58:3). By nature, indulging the desires of the flesh and mind, dead in trespasses and sins, children of wrath before birth (Eph. 2:1-3). We are born children of wrath because of our federal union to Adam, who fell under the wrath of God. "God has shut all up in disobedience that He might show mercy to all" (Rom. 11:32). The sin of Adam was imputed to us. "Foolishness is bound up in the heart of a child" (Prov. 22:15). "The scripture has shut up all men under sin, that the promise by faith in Jesus Christ might be given to those who believe" (Gal. 3:22). The Law was added because of transgressions and to convict us of our sins. The Law was added to lead us to Christ. We are to look, hear, receive, and believe the Gospel (Gal.3:19-26). The promise of salvation comes only through the gift of faith in Christ (Eph. 2:8). Christ Jesus is the only Mediator available to us, and the only One God accepts that has a righteousness necessary to bring us to salvation. He is all we need. From the Fall until now, all men have been born dead in sin, and the objects of God's displeasure. The way of deliverance for man from the curse of the Fall and the penalty of sin, is by faith in Christ. Amen.

All men are made in the likeness of fallen Adam. David declared, "Behold, I was brought forth in iniquity, and in sin did my mother conceive me" (Ps. 51:5). Jesus said, "that which is born of the flesh is flesh" (John 3:6). All men that are propagated by a fallen man are depraved. Our very nature has fallen, and our sin flows from our heart with enmity for God. We are not sinners by accident, Christian, but by a depravity lodged in the innermost desires of our soul. We are of the flesh, sold by ourselves into bondage to sin (Rom. 7:14). We have a law in the members of our body, waging war against the law of our mind and making us a prisoner of the law of sin and death (Rom. 7:23). The corruptions of nature are transmitted to the offspring. Our nature is contaminated with a carnal bias (Rom. 7:14). We are mankind, which is fallen with a depraved human nature, commonly referred to in the Bible as the flesh. We are born as flesh, an old nature, that serves the law of sin (Rom. 7:25). The new nature in Christ cannot commit sin (1 John 3:9). The nature of human depravity was not to die physically, but Adam died in his relationship with God, and so did we. The spiritual death of Adam was not the destruction of his spirit, but it was separation from God. We were dead in trespasses and sins (Eph. 2:1). Natural man walks "in the futility of his mind, being darkened by their understanding, excluded from the life of God, because of the ignorance that is in them, because of the hardness of their heart, having become callous, have given themselves over to sensuality" (Eph. 4:18). They cannot understand spiritual issues about God. They still had the ability to reason and distinguish between right and wrong in their conscience. Man had a will, but the manner of its use makes the action sinful. The malignant influence of sin, as a disease, made him blind and foolish, rebellious, and insensitive to spiritual things. The image of God was marred in man.

After the Fall, man retained his rational powers to choose and the freedom of his will, within the rule of divine providence. The will is still influenced by the mind and desires. The natural man chooses to please himself and not God. Scripture attributes the alienation from God in a fallen man, to "the ignorance that is in them" (Eph. 4:18). Scripture speaks of a new man as "being renewed to a true knowledge according to the One who created him" (Col. 3:10). The natural man will not and cannot believe, and therefore chooses to remain ignorant and in the dark about God. He does not understand the truths of God, and therefore cannot believe them. The world and its teaching, like evolution, are favored over Bible study and the knowledge of God, which leaves their mind darkened. It is a willful ignorance based on the rejection of God's revelation of Himself in nature (Rom. 1:18-24). A defiled and corrupted nature is no longer free to do that which is good and holy. His freedom is a bondage to sin that he fails to see because of blindness and understand because of ignorance. The spiritual nature of the Bible becomes a foolishness in his mind and heart. Being in bondage to sin and a captive of the devil is being depraved. Being greedy and morally unclean in thought, word, and deed, is being depraved. The natural man cannot see or believe the devils at work in his life. Although the Fall cast us out of God's favor and imputed to us a depraved nature, we remain responsible to

God. God created us, and is still the owner of a sinful man. We are creatures and subjects of a rightful Lord. The Fall did not change the relationship between the creator and the creature. Our duty is still to glorify God. Our duty is to submit to His authority with all our heart and strength. This all does not seem fair to the natural man. The truth is, we still depend upon God for every breath we take. God did not lose His right to claim and command us, just because we lost the power to obey Him. Man, on his own, cast away the power to meet His requirements; we remain His subjects. Before salvation, a man will think this is unfair, but after salvation, when he is a new man, he accepts God's truth. A saved new man will own himself as a sinner without excuse, is humbled, and seeks God in prayer, Bible study and repentance. The conscience of a saved man will agree with God and runs to Jesus.

From the Fall, man lost the moral image of God which made him a spiritual being. God is holy (1 Pet. 1:14-16). God made man upright (Eccl. 7:29). Being upright shadowed forth the moral excellence, that he lost in the Fall. In regeneration, God writes His laws in our hearts and puts them in our minds, and makes us willingly subject to His authority (Ezek. 36:26-27). This is the great miracle in being born again. Adam had a holiness before he fell, but he lost it when he disobeyed God. By regeneration and sanctification, Christian, it is restored in the elect who are made "partakers of His holiness" (Heb. 12:10). Holiness develops from the new birth, as we grow in grace and knowledge of the Lord. Adam's holiness allowed him to "see God" spiritually by the Holy Spirit indwelling him. Again, Adam lost this knowledge of God in the Fall, but it is restored to the elect at regeneration. God said, "light shall shine out of darkness, is the One who has shown in our hearts to give the light of the knowledge of the glory of God in the face of Christ" (2 Cor. 4:6). The illumination of the Spirit of God shines in us by the grace of God. The glory of God in Jesus is the great knowledge that enters the heart of believers. This truth makes us believers. The treasure of gospel light into our earthen vessel converts the soul, cleanses the conscience, and rejoices the heart by a power that you know had to come from God. You do not create this light, Christian, it is the gift of God. The light is life. The light is the truth of Christ. Knowing that Jesus is alive in you is the greatest motivation for godliness. It is a life worthy of the calling you have received because it is from God (Eph. 4:1). The light does not shine in a depraved soul unless God has been at work. By the Fall, man lost the life of God. "He that hath the Son hath life" (John 5:12). God is the "fountain of life" (Ps. 36:9). "His favor is for a lifetime" (Ps. 30:5). "Thy lovingkindness is better than life" (Ps. 63:3). By the Fall, man lost his interest in God, love for God and communion with God. The depraved individual cannot worship the Lord in spirit and truth (John 4:24). The depraved individual cannot worship the Lord with fear and love, and an obedience of faith, with the hope of righteousness (Gal. 5:5-6). In this dreadful condition of depravity, we cannot deliver ourselves. Unless we are born again, we are unfit for God's presence.

In the book of Genesis, the Bible tells us that after the creation, "God saw all that He had made, and behold, it was very good" (Gen. 1:31). After the Fall, when men began to multiply on the face of the land, the Bible tells us that God saw something else. "The Lord saw that the wickedness of man was great on the earth, and that every intent of the thoughts of his heart was only evil continually" (Gen. 6:5). Man became defiled and corrupt, and a totally depraved object, and God saw it. As soon as sin was conceived, evil followed. "The intent of man's heart is evil from his youth" (Gen. 8:21). Sin is likened to a dead and rotting body (Rom. 7:24), putrefying sores (Isa. 1:5-6), a canker, or gangrene (2 Tim. 2:17), the dung of filthy creatures (Phil. 3:8) and the vomit of a dog (2 Pet. 2:22). Sin is a species of practical atheism. Sin is pictured as Leprosy, an unclean thing (Isa. 64:6) and produces opposition to God. "The carnal mind is enmity against God (Rom. 8:7). The mind set on the flesh is hostile toward God. The person whose mind is only set on the flesh is lost. All the behaviors of a fallen man have the nature of sin in it, and come short of the glory of God. Total depravity means your nature is rotten to the core. It is God who gives the wake-up call to the person that recognizes this condition for themselves, and shows them the way to be saved in

Jesus. The knowledge of Christ and the principles of faith, love, and forgiveness, are yours Christian, by the grace of God. The glorious saving work for you was accomplished by a miracle of divine power in your soul by a wonderful Creator. We are His workmanship (Eph. 2:10). Do not trust your own feelings and opinions that will appear as logical to a natural man as hearing from God. We are not born again by our will, but of God (John 1:13). Humble yourself to reading the Bible. It is where the true power of faith, and living hope with the mercy of God may be found to be born again (Rom. 10:17; 1 Pet. 1:3, 23). God has many ways of leading you to Christ, and into the heart of Christianity. His gracious way, is to lead you into holiness from depravity, and to let you behold the difference in your heart. You will have a terrific conflict between your conscience and your lusts. God desires you to be free from the consequences of sin, and to rejoice in the freedom of walking with Jesus. The Holy Spirit of God is at work in you to produce a hatred of sin, and a repentance without regret leading to salvation (2 Cor. 7:10-11). The new relationship you develop by the grace of God, will enable you to move responsibly toward Him, with fear and trembling (Phil. 2:12).

Corruption has invaded every part of man's nature, and especially ravaged his inner man. The Bible tells us our "minds are blinded" (2 Cor. 3:14) and our "understanding darkened" (Eph. 4:18). The Fall corrupted and depraved our soul, but a lot of people are not aware of it. The Bible says, "both our mind and conscience are defiled (Titus1:15). Even though they knew God from the creation of the world, as well as creating themselves, they did not honor Him or give thanks and their foolish heart was darkened (Rom. 1:20-21). "Professing to be wise, they became fools" (Rom. 1:22). "There is a way that seems right to a man, but its end is the way of death" (Prov. 14:12). What the sun is for natural things, like plants on the earth; the word of God is for spiritual life for man to know God. The influences and consequences of darkness on the unregenerate mind leaves it corrupt and rebellious to the truth (1 Tim. 6:4-5). The affections and will are rooted in our understanding, and they misunderstand godliness. A change of mind comes from God. Amen. When we do not know God, we choose the pleasures of sin. God's grace is revealed to us when He teaches us to know Himself (Jer. 31:33-34). If a man remains ignorant of God, and chooses worldly and fleshly wisdom, his false reasoning and judgment will be the motivation to continue in sin. Christ has delivered us from the power and domain of darkness Col. 1:13). Once I was blind, but now I can see (John 9:25). Darkness fills the mind with enmity against God, and turns our affections and wills to "mind earthly things" (Phil. 3:19). A natural man will regard the highest wisdom of God as foolishness. We become bias and prejudice and habitual in sin. We fail to make a true inspection of our heart. Gratification of ourselves fills our imagination and becomes a stronghold. The love and power of God in a Christian pulls down the strongholds for sin, and makes us willing to follow Jesus in the day of His power (Ps. 110:3). We must be renewed in the spirit of our mind to discern the nature of God in Christ. We would search in vain forever to discover the love and peace of God, unless He is pleased to reveal it to us (Matt. 16:17). We would remain a vain natural man pursuing the shadows and miss the substance. We would prefer what we think and want even if they are lies, instead of the truth. We would not know the difference between the truth and lies, unless the Lord gives us light to be spiritually sensible. The natural man of the world prefers the shadows and lies and turns the truth upside down. The natural man runs for and after himself, instead of the Lord, our God.

The Bible tells us to "watch over your heart with all diligence, for from it flow the springs of life" (Prov. 4:23). The heart of an unregenerate man has been described as a rock (Jer. 23:29) and stony (Ezek. 11:19). A hard heart has not learned about God's goodness, authority, or majesty. A hard heart does not realize the power of God's anger and wrath or fear it, because of the obstinacy in his fallen nature. The folks with a hard heart are not moved by God's call or harken to God's word. The natural man is married to his lusts. The doctrine of repentance does not find a home in a hard heart. The heart of a saved person, however, longs to read and hear God's word and to know His will, so that when he learns it, he knows what to follow. The heart of a saved man will know and understand his responsibility in living and about salvation is to God.

The affections of a man are thought to be the sensitive faculty of the soul. The understanding discerns, the affections allure and the will executes the final decision of the mind, carrying it into action. Before man fell. His affections were directed toward God. After man fell, his mind, including the understanding, affections and will were separated from God, and became self-love. After the Fall, Adam and Eve attempted to hide from God (Gen. 3:10). Sin caused man to depart from the living God (Heb. 3:12) and forsake the fountain of living water (Jer. 2:13). He, who was to be the delight of our souls was abandoned. We ended up seeking the things of self, sense, friends, and money, as our delights and chief good. We lost the knowledge to honor and enjoy the Lord, and instead chose our own way to be glad. The unregenerate turned away from God for power, and greed (Col. 3:5) and a craving after evil things (1 Cor. 10:6). The body and our own soul became more important than God. Our clothes and earthly pleasures were preferred before spiritual life and the things of God. Man's carnal desires were more important, and ruled the soul by lust, rather than a desire for spiritual well-being. The knowledge of God being holy, and the consequences of our being unholy had little bearing on what we wanted to do. The wisdom of God was viewed as foolishness (1 Cor. 2:14), or not considered at all. The idea of becoming as "little children" seemed kind of embarrassing (Matt. 18:3). The natural man stubbornly embraces anti-God prejudices, and faith is seen as dangerous and a leap into the dark. They live by their lusts and senses, more than reason and a relationship with God. They are buried in a deep hole and are not looking for help to get out of their desperate situation, which they cannot even see. The pathway to hear and walk with God is not registering in their hearts. They do not seriously consider the future consequences of avoiding God. They think the future, if there is one, will turn out good for them, because they are not that bad in their mind. They are being deceived when they act as their own judge.

The scripture speaks of lust as worldly (Titus 2:12), fleshly (1 Pet. 2:11), foolish (1 Tim. 6:9), and deceitful (Eph 4:22). The imagination in the thoughts of a fallen man from his heart is evil (Gen. 6:5). Affections for sin in our fallen nature precede the act of transgression. The source of temptation lies within a fallen man; something inside him is unsatisfied and he is willing to be influenced by the devil. We are carried away and enticed by our own lust (James 1:14). Lust in us has power and produces a covetous way within us, a craving, that when conceived brings forth sin (Rom. 7:8; James 1:15). Temptation is not sin. Conception occurs when the desire of our old nature joins with the outward temptation and we act. When the will yields to lust, then it is sin. When you are tempted, Christian, call upon the Lord to help you. Let the thoughts of His goodness enter your heart. Remember that the wages of sin and death were paid for by the work of God's love in Jesus for you. God's grace in God's time will always be sufficient to give you the victory. We will fight many battles. His victory is our victory. To God be the glory. You will try hard to be right with God, but God's way is to reveal His grace in His timing with His power. When God picked us up in Jesus from our fallen state, He came with the power and authority to save you. Your Christian life is a matter of the will and not your hard work and feelings. You will know that God is at work, "both to will and to work for His good pleasure" (Phil. 2:13). There is a big difference in your heart between what you think you accomplish, and what God preforms on your behalf. We are headed into God's glory, by the grace of God. His presence means everything. We fear and tremble and strive as a child, while our heavenly Father delivers us into the victory of Christ. God gives us the gift of faith in Christ, and the gift of assurance of faith in Christ. Amen.

The Fall hardened man's heart, blinded his mind, and contaminated his conscience, affections, and will. The Bible tells us that nothing good dwells in us (Rom. 7:18). The Bible tells us that "the whole head is sick, and the whole heart is faint. From the sole of the foot even to the head, there is nothing sound in it" (Isa. 1:5-6). The fallen and depraved creature is ignorant and without knowledge. Man does what he does in the world because of what he is. We have all been shut up in disobedience (Rom. 11:36). Only by God's grace, can we be raised to know the mercy and truth that can set us free (John 8:32). Only by God's graceful work in us can we know salvation from the natural state of total depravity. We are lost, but we can be found. "With men this is impossible, but with God all things are possible" (Matt. 19:26). Man's nature is already corrupt and dead, and he is insensitive to it, in fact, he loves it. Man is guilty and the wrath of God abides on him, and he is without strength to do anything about it (Rom. 5:6). The pride in a natural man does not accept this kind of assessment of his being. He believes this kind of thinking, if true, reveals a God that he is not that interested in pursuing a relationship with. Some natural man might try to repent, show contrition, and beg for mercy from God. Although this might sound right, a man's work will not save him. The antidote necessary, because of the nature of the depravity, means the miracle of a changed mind can only come from God.

Our redemption is from sovereign grace and mercy (Eph. 1:3-11, 2:8). It takes a miracle. It takes the surpassing greatness of God's power toward us who believe that He raised Christ from the dead, and seated Him at His right hand in the heavenly places, far above all rule and authority and power and dominion as head over all things to the church (Eph. 1: 19-22). The power of God must overcome the malice of Satan, remove the hold the devil already has on us, and rescue us from our depravity. God's wisdom, strength, and amazing grace together bring forth His elect as living stones (1 Pet. 2:5). We are His workmanship (Eph. 2:10). A part of mankind was to know redemption and be rescued as "vessels of mercy" (Rom. 9:23). Another part of mankind would know the standard of divine justice by the infliction of the threatening punishment of disobedience, as "vessels of wrath" (Rom. 9:22). As the supreme judge of the earth, the honor of God's righteousness, mercy, grace, and the glory of His holiness would be made manifest. Our redemption is the answer to the great dishonor of God, becoming a great glory to God. God was dishonored when man, that was created in His image, revolted, and sinned against Him. God's holiness was slighted when Adam gave allegiance to Satan, but God gained the victory in Christ. He did not repair the damage by simply clearing the guilty or declaring sinners righteous. To vindicate His justice, glorify His holiness and magnify His name, the plan was to pay the penalty and secure our forgiveness through the work and sacrifice of His only begotten Son. The Son of God, our Deliverer took on the human nature of Adam (Rom. 5:12-21; Heb. 2:14). He was to be the seed of Eve to bruise Satan on the head, and have a life of flawless obedience. No mere creature would be right, he had to have infinite value, dignity, wisdom, and be capable of meriting an infinite blessing. He must be possessed of infinite love and mercy and dear to God. No ordinary man or creature qualified.

The person and work of Jesus Christ in the Bible is referred to as "the wisdom of God in a mystery which God predestined before the ages to our glory" (1 Cor. 2:7), meaning salvation. The eternal Son of God was predestined to be our God-man Mediator (Eph. 3:10-11). He is called the wisdom of God (1 Cor. 1:24) and the Word of God (Rev. 19:13). The origin of our Mediator was in the Divine counsels (Prov. 8:22-23). Christ was God's first Elect (Isa. 42:1), and the church was chosen in Him (Eph. 4:1). Though the Man, Christ Jesus, had no historical existence, He had a covenant subsistence as the second Person of the Trinity with the Father. "He was in the beginning with God. All things came into being by Him. In Him was life, and the life was the light of men" (John 1:2-4). Christ was appointed to be our Mediator, and from everlasting He was established (Prov. 8:23). The subject of wisdom in Proverbs 8 has personal properties, that can refer to no other person than the Son of God Himself. He was present in Creation and worked beside the Father as a master workman. "He was rejoicing in the world, His earth, and having My delight in the sons of men" (Prov. 8:31). He delighted in saving sinners. He delighted to do the Fathers will (John 4:34; Ps. 40:8). God's choice in the Person of Christ to be the Restorer of His honor, vanquish Satan and save His fallen people was perfect. The body of Christ was supernaturally made by the operation of the Holy Spirit in a virgin. He would be one Person with two natures. The incarnate Son preformed a wonderful work for His people. A miracle of grace was needed to make us worthy of everlasting glory. We needed to be quickened into new life, darkness dispelled, love of sin destroyed, with a mind and will to be holy. The truth is, Christian, we will not come to Christ unless the Spirit draws us (John 6:44). The wisdom of God is evident in the work that the Son was commissioned to perform, and in the tasks assigned to the Holy Spirit. The miracles of regeneration and sanctification mean our salvation.

For all eternity, God planned the earth to be the stage, where He would display His perfections in creation, providence, and redemption (Eph. 1:4-12). He foreordained everything which comes to pass, shaping everything to the promotion of His grace in glory (Rom. 11:36; Eph. 1:11). For wise and holy reasons God allowed the introduction of evil. He allowed the Fall to make a more complete revelation of His glorious attributes. In fact, the shedding of the blood of Jesus for our redemption "was foreknown before the foundation of the world, but has appeared in these last times for the sake of you" (1 Pet. 1:19-20). It was God's will to have Eve and Adam tempted unto sin, for a higher manifestation of His glory. The Law came in and sin increased, but "grace abounded all the more" (Rom. 5:20). Sin reigned in death so grace might reign in righteousness to eternal life through Jesus Christ (Rom. 5:21). God could have prevented the Fall; as evidenced by what He did with Abimelech (Gen. 20:6), and Balaam (Num. 23:20). Adam and Eve were free to exercise their own will and nature and became accountable to God. God was not the Author of their sin. God does not tempt any man (James 1:13). God overrules evil for good (Gen. 45:8) and is sovereign over sin and Hades and holiness and heaven.

"The Lord is righteous in all His ways, and kind in all His deeds" (Ps. 145:17). He stands in no way in need for instruction or judgment about His deeds. He has magnified Himself by bringing forth redeemed and clean saints by His grace and providence, that were unclean sinners and rebels destined for Hades. The way of our salvation was determined by His amazing and wonderful grace. The Trinity of God was at work. The Father appointed the redeemer and accepted the price of redemption. The Son was the Redeemer by offering up Himself, and through His obedience, the Holy Spirit was sent to comfort us and communicate the truth to us. The Father made many promises to the incarnate Son that insured His success (Isa. 42:1-7. 49:1-7; Ps. 16:8-10). Christ was made a curse for us, "that we might receive the promise of the Spirit through faith" (Gal. 3:13-14). It is through the gift of faith in Christ (Eph. 2:8), that we become accepted, righteous, happy, peaceful, and entitled to eternal life in heaven. He called us according to His own purpose and grace in Christ Jesus and saved us from all eternity (2 Tim. 1:9). He convicted us of all our sin and imparted faith to us. "God chose us from the beginning for salvation through sanctification by the Spirit and faith in the truth" (2 Thess. 2:13). He saved us according to His mercy, by the washing of regeneration and renewing by the Holy Spirit, whom He poured out upon us richly through Jesus Christ our Savior" (Titus 3:5-6). To God be all the glory for a good, great, and perfect plan. The Lord Jesus obtained our redemption and sanctification.

The Spirit was sent to earth to glorify Christ (John 16:14). The presence of the Spirit in your life is a witness to the exaltation of Jesus, and the sure promise that He is coming again. The Spirit of God builds a great hope in the truth of the rapture of God's people before the tribulation. We are "to wait for His Son from heaven, whom He raised from the dead, that is Jesus, who delivers us from the wrath to come" (1 Thess. 1:10). The Rapture can be realized in the illustrations in the Old Testament where God rescued both Noah from the flood and Lot from the destruction of Sodom (2 Pet. 2:5-7). In the letter to the church in Philadelphia, the Lord promises to keep them from the hour of testing that is coming upon the whole earth (Rev. 3:10). "God has not destined us for wrath, but for obtaining salvation through our Lord Jesus Christ" (1 Thess. 5:9). We will suffer persecution for living godly in Christ Jesus (2 Tim. 3:12; John 15:18, 16:33), but we will not suffer the wrath of God that will fall upon the earth and unbelievers. My opinion, is that the rapture of believers in the air may be described In Revelation 4:1 with the door standing open in heaven. Some believers do not believe in the rapture because the word is not found in the Bible. The church is not mentioned as being present in the tribulation described in Revelation chapters 4 to 18. The church does appear again until Revelation 19 at the end of the tribulation, describing the second coming of Jesus. The church is mentioned as the bride at the marriage supper of the Lamb (Rev. 19:7-9), just before the second coming of Christ (Rev. 19:11-16). In the wisdom and amazing grace of God's plan for us, He is not only going to save us, but will bless us further with greater discoveries of His love and glory. We will be holy creatures, members of His body and heirs of God (Rom. 8:17, Eph.1:11). The Lord through the grace of God in the Gospel heals all our diseases by fixing our hearts on the Son of God. "The Lord knows how to rescue the godly from temptation" (2 Pet, 2:9). In His time, the Lord draws us closer and closer to Himself, and we behold His glory and our salvation as the best and most important miracle in our heart and mind. We are changed by the grace of God, and we believe in Jesus, and look forward to seeing Him. We are in the last days, Christian, where evil is surrounding us with ignorance and blindness. It is almost criminal to be a Christian. Look for the coming of Jesus and a new earth in which righteousness dwells. "Be diligent to be found by Him in peace, spotless and blameless, and regard the patience of the Lord to be salvation" (2 Pet. 14-15).

In the penal affliction that came upon man after the Fall, he lost no moral or spiritual faculty, but rather the power to use them correctly with and for God. The wages of sin were death, but death here means the separation from God. Adams soul and our soul were separated and alienated from God (Eph. 4:18). By way of explanation; this is why the lake of fire is called the "second death (Rev. 20:14). Those who reject Jesus will pay the penalty of eternal separation "from the presence of the Lord" (2 Thess. 1:9). The Bible tells us that death came by sin, and that death passed to Adam's posterity because all have sinned (Rom. 5:12). We shared in the great transgression of Adam, and the same punishment was inflicted upon us. Adam, as our representative was in the strongest position to succeed. He had the graces of God, and more enablement from God than we would have had if we were in his position. In other words, we would have failed the temptation and sinned against God in the garden of Eden. The Bible tells us that when Adam was 130 years old, "he became the father of a son in his own likeness, according to his image and named him Seth" (Gen. 5:3). This scripture tells us that Seth became a son in the image and likeness of Adam, and is different to Adam's being created in the image of God (Gen. 1:27). Adam's first son, Cain, gave evidence of being morally depraved when he brought the wrong sacrifice to God and ended up killing his brother (Gen. 4:3-8). Man is born depraved in his moral nature and does not accept the things of the Spirit of God (1 Cor. 2:14). Man needs to be born again by God. Even after regeneration, man still needs God's grace to be acceptable to God. Jesus said, "apart from Me you can do nothing" (John 15:5). When our fellowship with Jesus is interrupted by sin, and or we are not depending upon Him, then we are not abiding in Him. He that lives upon His promises, and is led by the Spirit in love and faith, will bring forth much fruit.

Before the Fall, Adam was endowed with all the ability to do whatever was required of him. After the Fall. He lost his power to please God, but God did not lose His authority over Adam. The fact that he fell and lost his ability, by his own folly, did not cancel his obligation to his Maker. All the world is accountable to God (Rom. 3:20). After the Fall, man lost the ability in his soul to know, love, and choose spiritual good. The corruption in his soul made him blind, insensible, and opposed to spiritual good. As a sinner, he had an enmity against God that made him unwilling to come to Christ. Man had faculties after the Fall, but not the power to use them for right. In the Fall, man's body, mind, and morals, experienced a decline and change because of the displeasure of God. "By one man sin entered the world, and death by sin" (Rom. 5:12). Disease, sickness, weakness, aging, and physical death impacted the physical powers of man. Man has a diminished mental state because of the Fall. He walks in the futility of his mind, "being darkened in their understanding, excluded from the life of God, because of the ignorance that is in them, because of the hardness of their heart" (Eph. 4:18). Adam and Eve's ignorance was revealed when they tried to hide from God. Fallen man cannot overcome the foolishness and ignorance in his own heart. The true knowledge of God escapes him. There is a defect and inability in his mind to receive the things of God (1 Cor. 2:14). A spiritual and saving knowledge of Jesus is beyond their thoughts and reasonings. The natural man has not experienced the miracle of illumination and regeneration which is from the Spirit of God (1 Cor. 2:12). The natural man has the power to think, but he cannot discern the things of the Spirit. The eyes of his heart have not been enlightened to hear the Spirit calling him to know the hope in the riches of the glory of God in Christ (Eph. 1:18). "The light of the knowledge of the glory of God in the face of Jesus Christ" (2 Cor. 4:6) is not shining in his heart.

The moral powers of man have been crippled by the Fall. The ability to choose between right and wrong, and good and evil, with the proper motives, has been disabled. With ignorance and darkness in the mind, and the affections misplaced, the lost man's view of things is worldly and selfish. After the Fall, man became disinclined to choose the good, and chose evil because his heart was biased toward sin and self. The ways of our world are the facts that support the corruption. In our world, the Lord is rejected and despised by folks, and loved and embraced by others. No sinful natural human being can change his moral perception of truth because he walks in darkness. "The gospel is veiled to those who are perishing" (2 Cor. 4:3). Unless the sovereign God is pleased to have mercy on them, the moral darkness continues and they are lost forever.

In the Fall, man did not lose his intelligence, but did lose the ability to reason in a wise manner. Man did not lose the faculties that made him rational, moral, and responsible, but he did lose the principle of holiness. He gained the principle of sin, and lost the ability to act in a spiritual manner. After the Fall, man was unable "to love the Lord your God with all your heart, and with all your soul, and with all your mind, and with all your strength" (Mark 12:30) and his neighbor as himself (Mark 12:31). Love is a holy nature with holy dispositions, and God is love (1 John 4:8). We need the Lord, Christian, in our heart to make spiritual choices from spiritual perceptions that will give us the ability to do good, and then truly know spiritual delights in Jesus. Jesus once said, "the ruler of this world is coming, and he has nothing in Me" (John 14:30). The enmity in the serpent was coming for Jesus, but he had nothing in Him for Satan to fasten upon. There was no corruption in Christ, the purity of His nature was above the possibility of sinning. Unfortunately, because of the Fall, Satan could find something in Noah, Abraham, David, Peter, and us, but Christ was the Lamb "without blemish"" (1 Pet. 1:19).

When the principle of sin entered man's soul, corrupting his whole being, he was incapable of obeying spiritual motives. The natural man became bias toward evil. The change in man after the Fall, which was the result of his own choice, or was voluntary, and therefore deliberate and willful, makes man guilty and responsible. The natural man acts according to what is in his mind and affections, which are free, but biased because of the corruptions in his heart. His heart must be changed before he can and will choose God. He must be born again (John 3:3). Make no mistake here, Christian, all have sinned and all are still responsible to God for the stewardship of their soul. Satan's power has access to the moral faculties of our soul; to confuse, delude, incline our understanding to his will, and make secret suggestions to our hearts. He wants to gain our consent, but he cannot change our nature. Sinners are free to sin. We condemn ourselves the way God condemns us, when we are on the path to salvation in Christ. Shifting the blame or guilt onto Adam or someone else, or even on God, in a way of offering excuses for your sin is not acceptable to God. Man ruined himself by the free exercise of his own faculties. It is a fact that we are born ignorant and insensible of God. It is a fact that we love and live for ourselves, with no delight in God. We do not see the wisdom in the justice of God. It is a fact that God is "holy in all His ways, and righteous in all His works" (Ps. 145:17). In the day of judgment every mouth will be stopped (Rom. 3:19). We are without excuse (Rom. 2:1). The natural man does what is consistent with his corruptions. Jesus said, "he who is of God hears the words of God; for this reason, you do not hear them, because you are not of God" (John 8:47). Jesus said, "you believe not, because you are not of My sheep" (John 10:26). Jesus said, "Everyone who is of the truth hears My voice" (John 18:37). Jesus said, "No one can come to Me, unless the Father who sent Me draws him" (John 6:44). The natural man sticks with his corruptions; while he who has the Holy Spirit, is being drawn by His supernatural activity that overcomes the depravity in coming to Jesus. The sinner is awakened, humbled, and broken before God. The new nature reveals to his heart that he is without excuse, in fact, he is guilty of sin against God. He needs help to be saved. By the grace of God, he can see Jesus. Amen.

The law of sin is an indwelling law, deep in a man where dwells no good thing (Rom. 7:18). The law of sin brings ignorance and darkness into the mind to contend with our understanding. The law of sin brings spiritual deadness and stubbornness into the will. The law of sin brings vanity and defilement into the affections. The seat of the law of sin is the heart (Prov. 4:23; Mark 7:23). That which is called the carnal mind is the same as the law of sin. "The mind set on the flesh is hostile toward God, for it does not subject itself to the law of God, for it is not even able to do so" (Rom. 8:7). If you are alive and following your flesh, you are not pleasing God. The friendship of the world is enmity with God (1 John 2:15-16). When the Bible uses the phrase "in my flesh," it means "in me by nature" that is corrupted. The extent of hostility or enmity toward God appears in the whole of the carnal mind opposed to God. The natural man's deep-rooted enmity against God appears in the affections, will, and the practice of sin in his life. For God has shut up all in disobedience that He might show mercy to all (Rom.11:32). All men have been shut up under sin that the promise by faith in Jesus Christ might be given to those who believe (Gal. 3:22). We are wretched men and wonder who can set us free from this body of death (Rom. 7:24).

The Bible is clear that we are God's workmanship (Eph. 2:10), and that God works in us both to will and to work for His good pleasure (Phil 2:13). The Spirit opens the heart (John 1:12, 3:16, 16:7-14). We have the responsibility to humbly cast ourselves before Him in fear and trembling (Phil. 2:12). We are responsible to be serious and sincere. We are responsible to strive, improve and grow in the gifts and graces that God has given us. We discover our responsibility by working out what God has already put into us for salvation. When we read our Bible and learn about God, we are to open our hearts and let God, be God. Our new heart from God comes with an honest faith and a deeply rooted determination to be obedient. Spiritual intelligence and understanding comes to the heart by faith (Heb. 11:13). The exercise of faith in Jesus manifests assurance to us from the path of obedience. We follow on to know the Lord (Hosea 6:3). In humility with fear, and trembling with vigilance, we discover God's loving presence. We discover a willingness to know the Lord and His teaching, and to do His will (John 7:17). We discover our loving the Lord and have deep desires to live in the obedience of faith. "A good understanding have all those who do His commandments" (Ps. 111:10). God makes His Word shine in our mind and heart to discern the glorious reality of Jesus. By the grace of God, we come to realize He has disclosed Himself to us (John 14:21) with the grace of responsibility. Amen. God's grace and mercy has been revealed in our soul. It has been the Lords doing. To God be all the glory.

How does God deliver us from our indwelling corruption and awful bondage to sin? First, at our regeneration, He makes good on the promise, "I will put My law within them, and on their heart, I will write it; and I will be their God, and they shall be My people" (Jer. 31:33). We are born again. Second, in our present Christian life, His law becomes powerfully alive in us with the knowledge of Christ. "The mind set on the flesh is death, but the mind set on the Spirit is life and peace" (Rom. 8:6). The awful enmity inbred in every one of Adam's posterity, Christian, dominates every faculty of their being and is against God. But now in Christ Jesus you who were formerly far off have been brought near by the blood of Christ (Eph. 2:13). For He Himself is our peace, by abolishing in His flesh on the cross, the enmity between man and God. God now grants us grace to be saved through faith, and to grow in righteousness as free gifts (Eph. 2:8). Salvation is God's gift and work for man (Eph. 2:10, Phil. 2:13). Man, by the grace of God, discovers the work of God, in fear and trembling (Phil. 2:12). We are responsible to strive and be diligent in the work of securing our souls. We work at our salvation by setting our mind and heart on it with great care. We are to maintain an attitude of fear and trembling in absolute dependence upon God's grace. We tremble with holy awe and fear to offend such a great God. We are to imitate Christ. It is God's sovereign enablement that makes it possible for man to fulfill his responsibility. It is a divine balance with our responsibility blended with God's divine resources. For those chosen by God for salvation as a vessel of mercy, we discover His goodness and love, power, and faithfulness. We learn to follow the Lord in obedience. We learn that we are responsible to use every means available to us in Bible study, prayer, service, and fellowship to gain experiential evidence, with fear and trembling, that the grace of God is with us. Another way of saying all this, is that the start of our spiritual life entirely requires the grace of God drawing us to be born again. Once this happens, our growth is accomplished by God's grace and man acting responsibly, working together. You will know the truth and the truth will set you free (John 8:32). In being made willing to do His will, you shall know of the teaching (John 7:17). By the grace of God, we keep His commandments, proving the Lord has disclosed Himself to us (John 14:21). In salvation, we discover His awesome presence. Amen.

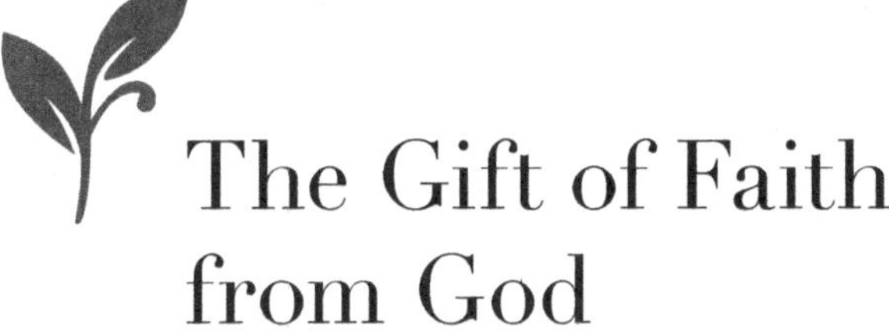

The Gift of Faith from God

> "Let us run with endurance the race that is set before us, fixing our eyes on Jesus, the author and perfecter of faith, who for the joy set before Him endured the cross, despising the shame, and has sat down at the right hand of the throne of God" (Heb. 12:1-2).

Dear Christian,

God has chosen to reveal Himself to us through a few descriptive titles in the Bible. No single title can describe everything about God, but each one can reveal a different part of His character. I have selected just a few titles of God to describe in this letter, with a primary focus on the names for Jesus. God is all good. We reach out to Him for help and comfort and peace for the forgiveness of sin and acceptance in our future. Our hearts can safely hide with the Lord. The meaning of the names can be a shield for protection and holding His truth. The glory of God is great, and humans can only know it as a wonder. The wonder begins when we come to Jesus, by the grace of God, and are born again to see the kingdom of God (John 3:3). "In the exercise of His will He brought us forth by the word of truth" (James 1:18). We "have been born again not of seed which is perishable but imperishable, that is, through the living and abiding word of God" (1 Pet. 1:23). The grace of regeneration is conveyed by hearing and reading the gospel. The word of God is a living word (Heb. 4:12) and the means of spiritual life. The word of God has been like a seed in me that grew slowly. The Holy Spirit convinces the soul it is lost, and furnishes the graces of faith (Acts 15:9), hope (1 John 3:3), fear of God (Ps. 34:9), and the love of Jesus Christ (1 Pet. 1:8). The truth has set you free (John 8:32). You will search more of the Bible for Jesus. The Bible tells us, "Thou hast magnified Thy word according to all Thy name" (Ps. 138:2). Without a doubt, the clearest manifestation of God comes to us from His word, which will never pass away (Matt. 24:35). What God promises in His word is faithfully performed.

"We are to run with endurance the race that is set before us, fixing our eyes on Jesus, the author and perfector of faith, who for the joy set before Him endured the cross, despising the shame, and sat down at the right hand of the throne of God" (Heb. 12:1-2). We are to fight the fight of faith, on the facts of Christ's precious and humble death and wonderous resurrection. We are to run with endurance laying aside any encumbrance and sin which so easily entangles us. We are to be diligent to press forward to the upward call of God in Jesus. We must lay aside the fondness and inordinate cares of this life which can be dead weights to reading God's word and putting your faith into action. We must lay aside the sin which we nourished; knowing at one time we were unwilling to part with it. The sin which has the most power over us, that we cannot or will not give up, is most likely spoiling our conscience and ruining our testimony for Jesus. The sin can be external, like an overindulgence of something in the world, or internal like a fleshly lust waging war against the soul (1 Pet. 2:11). There must be a sincere turning from self (Matt.16:24) and the world, and a sincere turning to the Lord (Isa. 55:7). We must lay aside the old self and put on the new self and be renewed in the spirit of our mind (Eph. 4:22-24). We must not be conformed to this world, but be transformed by the renewing of our mind to prove the good will of God (Rom. 12:2). We must deny ungodliness before we can live godly in the present age (Titus 3:12). "Even so consider yourselves to be dead to sin, but alive to God in Christ Jesus" (Rom. 6:11). We are called by God to pursue personal holiness. To run the race, we need the strength and power in the grace of God. We need a relationship with Jesus because He is the author and perfector of our faith (Heb. 12:2). We must learn to trust Jesus and walk by the Author of our faith.

The Bible tells us that the life of faith begins when we look to the Lord Jesus and trust Him for salvation (Isa. 45:22; John 3:16; Acts 4:12). The life of faith continues to grow as we keep our eyes of faith fixed on Him. The eyes of faith become sight when we see Him in all His glory (1 John 3:1-3). The secret to gaining faith, which is defined as the assurance of things hoped for, the conviction of things not seen (Heb. 11:1), is found only in Jesus. He is our example (1 Pet. 2:21) and the Person the Holy Spirit will glorify and disclose to our hearts as the Savior (John 16:13-15). Jesus lived in dependence upon God (John 6:57), in communion with God (John 8:29), in obedience to God (John 15:10), and in confidence that He had overcome the world (John 16:31). The born-again Christian has a new heart and becomes a new man, by the grace of God, with a spiritual mind willing to learn more about Jesus. The gift of faith from God empowers and thrills the soul with the vision of Jesus. The new heart has a passion and grateful thoughts for Jesus and His glory. The power of forgiveness releases freedom in the mind to love God. "There is no other name under heaven that has been given among men, by which we must be saved" (Acts 4:12). The Lord Jesus has the honor of having the greatest name ever in and under heaven, and He has become our righteousness (1 Cor. 1:30). The new birth with faith is the imparting of Divine life on dead men, for which the "Son of man must be lifted up" (John 3:14). "Lifted up" means not to sit on a throne, but to die lifted up on a cross. There is a story in Numbers 21 about a brass serpent that the Jewish people could look up at for healing, when they were bitten by serpents. This look mirrors the look of faith for Christians being saved by looking unto Jesus, the author and perfector of their faith. We look at Christ, not our good works, feelings, and resolutions or baptism experience to be saved. "The Son of Man came to seek and to save the lost" (Luke 19:10). We look to Jesus as the Author of our faith and the Perfector of our faith (Heb. 12:2). We are helped by Him in the beginning, the middle, and the end of our race with a faith that is victorious. Our faith is a gift from a wonder-working God.

"For by grace you have been saved through faith; and that not of yourselves, it is the gift of God" (Eph. 2:8). When we were saved by God's grace, we received the supernatural gifts of faith and hope. The Bible also says, in hope we have been saved (Rom. 8:24). Faith respects the promise of God, and in hope we continue to trust God for the good things to come. Grace through faith is the instrument of salvation, where hope refers to a good future. Both faith and hope are supernatural gifts from God for encouragement in the truth. They both work by God's love (1 John 4:19). Amen. "Faith is the assurance of things hoped for, the conviction of things not seen" (Heb. 11:1). Christ is the object of our faith and hope. The gifts of faith and hope mature, by the grace of God, and seal up a strong persuasion in the soul that God is true. They are not opinions, rather they are spiritual truths and experiences in our heart of God's reality of holiness and goodness. Christ dwells in the soul. Faith and hope in Jesus become facts of life. Christ fills the soul, and becomes a kind of possession that gives the believer a joy inexpressible and full of glory. "Though you do not see Him, you believe in Him and love Him" (1 Pet. 1:8). "Having been freed from sin and enslaved to God, you derive your benefit resulting in sanctification" (Rom. 6:22). You concur with the law of God in the inner man (Rom. 7:22). The reality of the new man in you builds the conviction that Jesus is the Christ, the Son of the living God. The promise from God for the outcome of your faith will be conformity to Christ, and the salvation of your soul (1 Pet. 1:9). Faith in your life will prove to be a conquering grace over all that is in the world, the lust of your flesh and the boastful pride in your life. You will know in your conscience, that it will be impossible to please God without faith. You will know and "believe that He is, and that He is a rewarder of those who seek Him" (Heb. 11:6). You will learn that the Lord God is your strength, and that the righteous man will live by his faith (Hab. 2:4, 3:19). You will choose to walk with God, and walk in and after His promises. In the Gospel, "The righteousness of God is revealed from faith to faith" (Rom. 1:17). It is not from faith to works. The Bible tells us, that "Abraham believed God, and it was reckoned to him as righteousness" (James 2:23). The Bible tells us that, "faith was working with his works, and as a result of the works, faith was perfected" (James 2:22). We "behold as in a mirror, the glory of the Lord, are being transformed into the same image from glory to glory" (2 Cor. 3:18). It is by the persevering grace of faith in Jesus that we continue to press forward. Our failures and weakness do not steal our salvation, and we do not lose God's love. In God's plan, we learn to trust Him by faith and gladly grow in grace and knowledge. Faith is being perfected.

Faith in Jesus delivers a confidence to your heart that He is "the way, and the truth, and the life" (John 14:6). You choose to keep close to God and honor Jesus by the way you live your life. In this way, you will experience the justification by faith that brings forth, by the grace of God, a life of sanctification (Rom. 5:1-5; 1 Cor. 1:30). You have been forgiven and are being separated from your sin. You desire to "see" more of the glory of God yet to be revealed (Rom. 8:18). God has the time and can do the kind of work appointed to complete this vision, which because it is in your heart, nothing and no one can deny it. "Those who wait upon the Lord will mount up with wings like eagles" (Isa. 40:31). The gospel blessings of grace and peace that are in your conscience and bless your soul, are from His Spirit. Faith is in the beginning and remains present in all the progress of your Christian life. The gift of faith initially engrafts us into Christ, and then we live and walk with faith by virtue of being in Him. God has stepped into my whole life, and faithfully worked His lovingkindness to grow me in the grace of faith. Amen.

My testimony is that God is faithful. He has faithfully called me to be holy and to shun sinful habits. He has faithfully protected me at work, around water and in cars. He has providentially directed my life in the schools I attended, the lady I married, the jobs I took and even the home we purchased. The Lord has faithfully directed us to the churches we attended and the service we participated in through the years. At the time of many of these events, the presence of the Lord in the work was not as clear to my heart as it is today. I remember the grace of God faithfully working in me my salvation and sanctification. I remember turning to the Lord, and hearing from the Lord. My conversion was not an illustrious or miraculous one-time experience, but a steady growing in grace and knowledge. Nevertheless, it is miraculous to me. I believe Jesus Christ came into the world to save sinners like me (1Tim. 1:15). I believe that faith without a work in your heart, soul, and body; being by itself, is dead (James 2:17). I believe, that to be able to remember the mercy, kindness, patience, and power of God, from our journey of faith, is by the grace of God. To God be the glory for those times He was present, and in my ability to remember His goodness to me. He forgives all our sins, heals all our diseases, redeems us from the pit, crowns us with love and satisfies our desires with good things. The Lord performs righteous deeds in us and through us (Ps. 103:3-6). "The eyes of the Lord are toward the righteous, and His ears are open to their cry" (Ps. 34:15). He made us physically and spiritually alive, and then made us more alive in Jesus in His way and time. Amen.

Faith is a powerful gift from God (Eph. 2:8-9). Jesus spoke a parable in the New Testament about faith and the small mustard seed (Matt. 13:31-32). The small seed grows into a huge tree. The small beginnings of faith, when it is true, can grow to be a lot more meaningful as we mature through life. The mustard seed reflects the omnipotent nature of God, and symbolizes the potential of faith in our lives when it grows after its small beginning. With God, nothing will be impossible (Luke 1:37). An active faith in Christ, figuratively speaking, means nothing will be impossible for a Christian. Faith in God allows us to get over our greatest difficulties. The more God blesses us in Christ, the more we earnestly desire to increase our faith in Him. The greater discoveries of faith, makes the delight of faith more pleasing in our hearts. The discovery of faith increases our desires and dedication to live a life of strength from it to please the Lord Jesus. Never forget, that God moved spiritual "mountains" by His power, wisdom, and love to save your soul. Humble people understand their weakness, Christian, and depend completely upon God. He is "able to do abundantly beyond all that we ask or think, according to the power that works within us" (Eph. 3:20). Real faith becomes the key to unleashing God's unlimited power according to His will and pleasure. The source of faith is the word of God (Rom. 10:17). Faith is important because it honors the God who gave it as a gift. You will know that God honors faith, by the victories you will have in living the Christian life. Faith enables you to overcome evil with good (Rom. 12:21). Faith enables you to overcome the world (1 John 5:4). The shield of faith enables you to defend yourself against temptation (Eph. 6:16). God is a shield to those who put their trust in Him (Prov. 30:5). We take up the shield of faith by believing what God has said. It gets easier to pick up a strong shield when we grow in grace and knowledge and learn more of the scripture. The Holy Spirit reminds us that Jesus, the author, and perfector of our faith, forgives us of all our sins. "There is therefore no condemnation for those who are in Christ Jesus" (Rom. 8:1). He helps us live by faith and walk by faith. He helps us gain the victory of faith for this life and our life to come, for His glory.

"This is the work of God, that you believe in Him whom He has sent" (John 6:29). We have received a gift of faith by the righteousness of Jesus Christ. God works in us and on us a faith in Christ and quickens our soul to working for Him. "He who began a good work in you will perfect it until the day of Christ Jesus" (Phil. 1:6). "He chose you in Him before the foundation of the world. He predestined you to adoption as a son. In Him, you have redemption through His blood. He made known to you the mystery of His will in Jesus. You believe the message of the gospel of salvation and have been sealed in Him with the Holy Spirit of promise (Eph. 1:4, 5, 7, 9, 13). You have been called to be conformed to the image of His Son and will be glorified (Rom. 8:29-30). It began for you when God drew you to be born again in Jesus, and receive the supernatural gift of faith (John 6:44, 3:3; Eph. 2:8). You are His workmanship, created in Christ Jesus for good works, which God prepared beforehand (Eph. 2:10). The word of faith is in your heart and in your mouth for believing and confessing that Jesus is Lord, and that God raised Him from the dead. You shall be saved (Rom. 10:8-10). Your faith has come by hearing the word of Christ (Rom. 10:17), a miracle from God. The Holy Spirit was present to birth faith in the gospel message in your heart and mouth. Christ is exhibited within you. The kingdom of God is within you (Luke 17:21). Christ is in your mouth by your reading the Bible daily and in your heart by your seriously thinking about it daily. The word of faith is all about Jesus; we believe God raised Him from the dead resulting in our righteousness, and confess Him as Lord resulting in salvation. We give God our souls by believing in our heart, and we give God our bodies be confessing with our mouth. Faith in Christ is a trust that cannot be disappointed because it is a gift of God. This is the plan of God that comes from God, that no man can work for it or boast about it. Amen. True saving faith involves persuasion, trust and surrender to the truth of Jesus, and includes the conduct of a new man with a changed lifestyle. The man that God gives true faith to will believe, repent, and obey. He will remain knitted to the promises of Christ his whole life. He will grow in grace and knowledge and holiness because faith is a conquering grace. God will send you into His word for the rest of your life to bless you. The Holy Spirit will engender a growth from faith to faith in your life because there is a righteousness in the progress of faith (Rom. 1:17).

God is faithful to begin and finish His work (Phil. 1:6). "It is God who is at work in you both to will and to work for His good pleasure" (Phil. 2:13). It is your responsibility to worship and praise God from whom all blessings flow. He opened your heart to see and hear the truth. You are to "work out your salvation with fear and trembling" (Phil. 2:12). It is God's sovereignty and man's responsibility together for salvation that is Divine truth. What God has done inside us, must come outside. It is a marvelous truth indeed that God lives in us and desires to work through us. God's work and our walk are both necessary ingredients for the witness of Jesus Christ. We ought to walk as He walked (1 John 2:6). We ought to live in obedience, surrender, and dependence on the Holy Spirit. We work out what was already worked into us by the Spirit. We are to work out our salvation with the attitude of fear and trembling. The gift of faith has conquered our souls for Jesus. The fear of the Lord is to walk in His ways. "The fear of the Lord is the beginning of wisdom; A good understanding have all those who do His commandments" (Ps. 111:10). We are spiritually weak and can still stumble at the power of temptation to sin. We are to distrust ourselves and fear to offend such a good and holy God. Sin is deceitful (Heb. 3:13). Fear and trembling means to walk with humility and holy reverence. It is not about losing our salvation, but about honoring God. The thought of God makes me tremble; God was patient with me and let me grow into trembling about Himself. Meeting God will be the most important event in time, and for eternity we will ever know. By the grace of God, I have chosen to live by faith in Jesus. By the grace of God, I have chosen obedience. The more I read the Bible, Christian, the more I understand what God has done for me in Christ. The more I prayed and served in His church, the more I sensed His presence feeding me to desire more of Jesus. I want to be ready to see Jesus. I am an old man now, so I know that this event is not very far away for me. The good news is, that God has given me grace to prepare me for His presence. He blessed me through the years with a faith in Jesus. It has been a progressive and true faith, that has revealed a victory in Jesus. Jesus is the Prince of Peace (Isa. 9:6). To God be the glory.

We are to fix our eyes on Jesus, the author and perfector of our faith (Heb. 12:2). The scripture says that, "God highly exalted Him, and bestowed on Him the name which is above every name" (Phil. 2:9). At the name of Jesus every knee should bow, and "every tongue confess that Jesus Christ is Lord, to the glory of God the Father" (Phil. 2:10-11). Our Lord bears the human name of Jesus, commanded by angels from heaven (Matt. 1:21; Luke 1:31), and not by Joseph and Mary. It was a common name, but people used "Jesus of Nazareth," where He grew up, to distinguish Him from other folks. Jesus means "Yahweh saves" and was the Greek form of "Joshua." In the Old Testament, Joshua leads the His people to victory over the Canaanites (Joshua 1-12). In the New Testament, Jesus leads His people to victory over sin. The promised land is a type of eternal rest for the saint's inheritance in the kingdom of God. Jesus rescued us from the spiritual evil that alienates us from God (Matt. 18:11).

Jesus was also called Immanuel, which means "God with us" (Matt. 1:23; Isa. 7:14). This is not a personal name, but rather indicates His role bringing God's presence to man. God was gracious and faithful to send the Messiah, to be with us, and be our Deliverer. He is the Savior and there is no other (Isa. 43:11). The Helper, the Holy Spirit, whom the Father sent in Jesus' name will be with us forever. The Spirit of truth abides with us and is in us (John 14:16-17). He teaches us all things and brings to our memory what Jesus said. God is close by us and is faithful. To God be the glory. Jesus' title of "Christ" is not a surname, but means He is God's "Anointed One" or "Chosen One" sent from God to be a King and our Deliverer (Dan. 9:25-26; Isa. 61:1). Christos is the Greek equivalent of the Hebrew word for Messiah. Thus, Jesus Christ means "Jesus the Messiah" or "Jesus the Anointed One." Ancient Israel thought that their Messiah would deliver them from pagan nations like the Romans, but Jesus came to deliver them from the power and penalty of sin (Luke 4:18; Rom. 6:23). God anointed Jesus with the Holy Spirit and with power (Acts 10:38). Jesus fulfilled Old Testament prophecies and rescued sinners (1 Tim. 1:15). He will be the King over all the earth (Zech. 14:9). The name of Jesus is peace in my soul. The presence of Jesus in my soul releases power and purpose for my life. The presence of Jesus reminds me of God's goodness and grace to save me. "There is salvation in no one else; there is no other name under heaven by which we must be saved" (Acts 4:12). This is the honor of Christ's name, the Lord our righteousness (Jer. 23:6). Healings and miracles are performed in the name of Jesus (Acts 3:16). We pray in the name of Jesus (John 14:13). We pray that God will count you worthy of your calling, fulfill your desire for goodness and do the work of faith with power (2 Thess. 1:12). "Whatever you do in word or deed, do all in the name of the Lord Jesus, giving thanks through Him to God the Father" (Col. 3:17). We live in the name of Jesus. Amen.

The Old Testament predicted the coming of the Messiah, and the New Testament reveals the Messiah to be Jesus of Nazareth. The Old Testament prophecies tell us the Messiah would be born of a virgin (Isa. 7:14) in the town of Bethlehem (Micah 5:2). He would be "a priest forever according to the order of Melchizedek" (Ps. 110:4), a King (Isa. 11:1-4), and a son of David (Matt. 22:42). He would perform miracles (Isa. 35:5), and suffer crucifixion (Matt. 27) before resurrection (Isa. 53:10; Hosea. 6:1-2; Ps. 16:8) and glory (Isa. 53). Jesus fulfilled the requirements of being the Messiah. He was born to Joseph and Mary and called Christ, which means Messiah (Matt1 :27). He was born to a virgin (Matt. 1:23) of the tribe of Judah (Luke 3:30) in the town of Bethlehem (John 7:42). He performed miracles by "curing many people of diseases and afflictions and evil spirits: and He granted sight to many who were blind" (Luke 7:21). Jesus was rejected by the religious leaders as well as a lot of the people (Matt. 21:42; John 19:12-16). He suffered a crucifixion for sinners between two robbers (Matt. 27:38). He was despised and forsaken of men, pierced through for our transgressions, and by His scourging we are healed (Isa. 53:3-5). This prophecy was fulfilled in the death of Jesus, identifying Him as the Messiah (Matt. 27:27-60). Jesus was recognized by many folks as the Christ (Matt. 16:16; Luke 2:26-32, 4:41; John 11:27). Christ died for our sins according to the scriptures, and that He was buried, and that He was raised on the third day, according to the scriptures" (1 Cor. 15:3-4). After His resurrection (Matt. 27:9, 22-23), He remained on the earth for an additional forty days, and was seen on a dozen different occasions, one time with over five-hundred people being present (1 Cor. 15:6).

Jesus Himself unequivocally stated that He was God. (John 8:49-50; John 10:30). The Jewish people did not recognize Jesus as their Messiah because they were looking for an earthly king, not the ruler of a spiritual kingdom. Jesus suffered and died for our forgiveness of sin and salvation. The Bible tells us that the Messiah, "Who for the joy set before Him endured the cross, despising the shame and has sat down at the right hand of God (Heb. 12:2). The motivation for Jesus was the joy He would have in our salvation. The motivation for Jesus was to satisfy the injured justice of God. He rejoiced to see peace between man and God. He rejoiced to be the Mediator, and seal the covenant of grace to open the way for sinners to eternal life with God. He would have the reward of the highest honor to sit at the right hand of the Father. "In Thy right hand there are pleasures forever" (Ps. 16:11). He would have the power and influence to make intercession for us (Heb. 7:25). The joy that abides deep down in the heart of the believer is a part of God's essence and presence with us. The outcome of the finished work of Jesus on the cross, would be the joy of presenting sanctified believers to the Father in glory. He had the joy of redeeming, from endless woe, all the sinners that God had chosen for eternal life. He had the joy of lavishing His perfect love on those eternally lost. He had the joy of revealing the Father's heart of love to save sinners (John 3:16). He loved us while we were yet sinners (Rom. 5:8). God loves and God gives us life, to the point He spared not His only begotten Son. "A great love the Father has bestowed upon us, that we should be called children of God" (1 John 3:1). The love of Christ surpasses knowledge (Eph. 3:19). We can know the faithfulness of His love, by the guidance and comfort He faithfully gives us every day. We can grow, by the grace of God, to know more deeply His love, but the truth is, the riches of Christ for us and the church are unfathomable (Eph. 3:8). We can come to know some of the width, length, height, and depth, of His love (Eph. 3:18), but the essence of love in the Father and the Son is incomprehensible and surpasses our knowledge. Thank you, Lord for your infinite love.

Jesus said, "I am He who bears witness of Myself, and the Father who sent Me bears witness of Me: (John 8:18). Jesus said, "the very works that I do, bear witness of Me, that the Father has sent Me" (John 5:36). The Father bore witness of the Son in the prophecies of the Old Testament. The prophecies were fulfilled in the character, teaching, and actions of Jesus. We have the testimony of John the Baptist (John 1:19-34). We have the witness of the

Father at His baptism (Matt. 3:17) and on the mountain of the Transfiguration (Matt. 17:5). We have the great and precious witness of the Holy Spirit that Jesus said the Father would send in His name to help us (John 16:7-15). The physical presence of Jesus was to be gone from them, to be replaced by the spiritual presence of the Holy Spirit. The witness about Jesus is from God. Amen. The witness of Jesus from God is in the conscience and the heart of the believer. The believer has been drawn by the Father (John 6:44), and born again by the Holy Spirit to see the kingdom of God (John 3:3). The believer has a new heart, a new spirit, and God's Spirit with Him to make it possible to see Jesus (Ezek. 36:26-27). The believer is able, by the grace of God, to overcome the world, the flesh, and the devil (1 John 3:16). The believer sees Jesus as the way, the truth, and the life (John 14:6). A believer begins to live with a clear conscience and a cleansing from all unrighteousness (1 John 1:9). The witness from God in our hearts tells us that the Bible is the word of God, and cannot contain errors. The gift of faith becomes a conquering grace.

The name of Jesus becomes a mighty tower of strength and refuge (Ps. 61:3). We take a strong stand for Jesus, and remain with our Christian experience throughout life. The change that we experience is not in words but in deeds, not in words but in power. God births a cry in us and for us from our soul for His help. We have a hearing ear and a seeing eye. (Prov. 20:12). God comes near, and picks up on where we are, and what good He will do for us. "The Spirit helps our weakness", and "intercedes with groanings too deep for words" (Rom. 8:26). God searches our hearts, "knows what the mind of the Spirit is, and intercedes for the saints according to the will of God" (Rom. 8:27). The Christian does not understand exactly how the Lord is working for us in this spiritual way, but He knows this action is beyond his means. It is the grace of God at work revealing His presence, goodness, and love. We are saved by grace through faith and not our works (Eph. 2:8). He chooses us to be a vessel of mercy (Rom. 9:23). To my heart, He has made known the riches of His glory. To my heart, He has made known a call to holiness and acceptance in Jesus. To my heart, He has blessed me with a gift of the obedience of faith. He gave me the ear to hear His voice (John 10:27), and the eye that sees the beauty of His glory. He opened my understanding and enabled me to follow Jesus. He is the God of all grace (1 Pet. 5:10). Amen.

It is a difficult thought, Christian, but not all people want His word abiding in them, and do not believe in Jesus (John 5:38). For whatever reason and or excuse, the word is not treasured or hidden in their heart, and they will not trust and honor God and come to Christ. The carnal mind is enmity against God (Rom. 8:7). They stand against Jesus Christ, who is God. The natural man is unwilling to come to Jesus for life (John 5:40). They fail to see the trouble ahead and do not flee to avoid the wrath to come. Perhaps it is too humbling, and they decide they just want to keep their sin, which may be more fun to them. Perhaps, faith is not intellectually satisfying to them; and they accept the world's views of science instead of the Bible, which they have trouble believing. God knows. The true Christian has usually passed through a time of helplessness, with sighs of hope, that God came to his rescue in Jesus. The grace of God shows us Jesus as our eternal Shepherd, and in the day of His power, He becomes our everything. We were weak, foolish, and lost, and God became our Savior, Redeemer, and Provider. "He makes me lie down in green pastures: He leadeth me beside the still waters. He restoreth my soul: He leadeth me in paths of righteousness, for His name's sake" (Ps. 23:1-3). I shall not want anything because He perfectly supplies all my need. He gives me the truth and leads me by love. When I do not feel good or right, He always restores my soul. I have a renewed heart, and can be led in the way of holiness. It is to my privilege and His honor, that I am able, to walk in a path of righteousness for His sake. He is with me. Amen.

Jesus declared Himself to be the "I am" (John 8:58). God had earlier used these words to describe how He would be known when He commissioned Moses to bring His people out of Egypt (Gen. 3:10-14). Jesus identifies Himself as the self-existent and eternal One, and equal with Jehovah. He was the Messiah, the Son whose name shall be called Wonderful Counselor (Isa. 9:6). He was making Himself equal with God, that He was God Himself. Jesus said, "Before Abraham was born, I am" (John 8:58). The Jews picked up stones to throw at Him (John 8:59). From the self-sufficient, blind, and self-righteous and vain man, the Lord Jesus passes out of the temple hidden from them. In the New Testament gospel of John, Jesus elucidates the deeper meaning of His calling Himself "I am." He is our Immanuel, God with us (Isa. 7:14). Jesus said, "I am the bread of life; he who comes to Me shall not hunger, and he who believes in Me shall never thirst" (John 6:35). Jesus said, "I am the living bread that came down out of heaven" (John 6:51). There is no spiritual life apart from satisfying our hunger and quenching our thirst by faith in the testimony of Jesus. He is the Divine food from heaven that fills and saves our souls for eternal life. By Him, we are alive when we daily feed on Him. Against temptation and for cleansing, we partake of His presence to fill our needs. Again, Jesus spoke to them, saying, "I am the light of the world; he who follows Me shall not walk in the darkness, but shall have the light of life" (John 8:12). God is love (1 John 4:8), God is spirit (John 4:24), and God is light (1 John 1:5). Believers are light in the Lord (Eph. 5:8). If you follow Jesus, you have the light of life. Jesus is a moral light for all men, and a spiritual light for believers only. We can be said to follow Him as Lord, if we are committed to Jesus in doctrine and conduct. Light means true knowledge, happiness, and holiness; while darkness is ignorance and error, guilt, and misery. The world, including America, is in spiritual darkness. They have some light of conscience and intelligence, but do not have the grace to see the Lord and will be without excuse (Rom. 1:20). The believer is in a place, by the grace of God, where the true light of life in Jesus has been turned on. He can see the character of God, the worth of souls and the future.

In the parable of the good shepherd, Jesus tells us, "I am the door, if anyone enters through Me, he shall be saved, and go in and out and find pasture (John 10:9). In the same parable, Jesus says, "I am the good shepherd; the good shepherd lays down His life for the sheep" (John 10:11). By nature, because of sin we are alienated from God, but the "door" leads us into the presence of God for salvation. We were far away at one time, Christian, but now we are made close by the blood of Christ (Eph. 2:13). Jesus also said, "I am the way, and the truth, and the life; no one comes to the Father, but through Me" (John 14:6). Apart from Jesus, we can do nothing (John 15:5). The Lord Jesus lays us on His shoulders like wounded sheep and brings us home (Luke 15:5-6). The Father draws us (John 6:44), and brings the lost sheep home (Luke 15:6). To go in and out and find pasture expresses our perfect freedom and rest in Jesus. Jesus came that we might have abundant life (John 10:10). God is with us. He becomes our Immanuel by His presence in our hearts. We find peace and rest, holiness, and healing, and a pasture with light to see our lives by we never knew existed. The Author of our faith has become to us wisdom, righteousness, sanctification, and redemption (1 Cor. 1:30). We have gained a great truth, that is, we have been born again, we have been changed and chosen by God to be the bride of Christ. God is true, Jesus is alive, and the Holy Spirit is at work in our hearts. We are believing in Christ, and know the future of mankind is in His hands. The new nature is spiritual and the work of our Divine Shepherd, who laid down His life for ours. Jesus is the way to the Father, the truth, forgiveness, heaven, and eternal life. His glory will be the most glorious. We know that the thief came only to steal, kill, and destroy (John 10:10). We know that the thief's work was to bring ignorance, prejudice, error, blindness, hardness of heart and darkness about the goodness of God in Jesus. Those who refuse to heed the call to follow Jesus will know judgment and separation from God because of their sins for eternity. Believers will know a judgment as sons (Rom. 14:10), but not sinners, because their sins will have already been judged, forgiven, and forgotten (Isa. 43:25). Believers will know that they are vessels of mercy to the glory of God.

Jesus said, "I am the resurrection and the life" (John 11:25). The believer will know by faith that his heart and mind is in eternal life. The believer will know for sure that the plans God had for him were for his "welfare and not for calamity to give you a future and a hope" (Jer. 29:11). The believer will see Jesus and the assurance and convictions of faith, which will be the facts. The believer will know what Jesus meant when He said, "I am the true vine" (John 15:1). Most importantly, we will be full of joy and gratitude for Jesus, who forever secured the way for our forgiveness of sin, and for holiness, and acceptance with the Father. The strength to be holy and the comfort derived from moving closer and closer to Jesus will be ours because of His righteousness (Rom. 8:10). He will have given life to our mortal bodies through His Spirit which indwells us (Rom. 8:11). The renewed image of God upon your soul is resurrection and life. "Because I live, you shall live also" (John 14:19). The Lord is for the body; and though it is broken, defiled, and despised at times, the body will be reunited to the soul and be a glorified body that will be imperishable (1 Cor. 15:42-44). The eternal life of the soul will be in the vision of God. "I shall behold Thy face in righteousness; I will be satisfied with Thy likeness when I awake" (Ps. 17:15). Now, we only get a glimpse of God's glory, the full feast of joy, gratitude and worship is yet to come. It will be "joy unspeakable and full of glory" (1 Pet. 1:8).

God's light in our soul fills it now with acceptance, peace, joy, and hope. God's light in the future will allow us to see His Son and ourselves at great peace and joy as His children. Our God "will be called Wonderful Counselor, Mighty God, Eternal Father, Prince of Peace" (Isa. 9:6). Our mighty God was born as a child, made flesh and became our Savior. We know and worship Him as a Wonderful Counselor. Great was the mystery of godliness for His whole life (1 Tim. 3:16). He is the mighty One in strength and wisdom, love, and goodness. As a King, He preserves the peace, because He is our peace (Eph. 2:14). A peaceful government will forever be on His shoulders. It is true, the closer we walk with Jesus, the more peace and safety we enjoy. The glory of the Father, the Redeemer and the redeemed will continue forever. The Prince of Peace will be our glorious Prince of life in this life, and all throughout the life to come (Acts 3:15). Jesus Christ is the true vine to life and peace in this life, and eternal life and peace forever. Amen.

Salvation is only found in the name of Jesus (Acts 2:21,4:12).

He is the only truth, the only life, and the only way to come to the Father (John 14:6). The Bible was "written that you may believe that Jesus is the Christ, the Son of God; and that believing you may have life in His name" (John 20:31). Our peace is only in the Person of Jesus Christ, and you must find yourself getting hold of Him to obtain it. Sin is a volitional act of disobedience against the revealed will of God. Sin is a force to destroy you, a fact to condemn you and the wages of death. It is a falling short of the glory of God (Rom. 3:23). To be forgiven of sin, and be saved from its penalty, will only happen by the almighty power and love of God (John 3:16). The offer and the plan for salvation in Jesus is from God, and we must be born again to receive it (John 3:3-7). We are God's choice, "by grace through faith, and not of yourselves, it is the gift of God (Eph. 2:8). The gift of faith from God can be discovered by hearing and or reading the word of God (Rom. 10:17). By the grace of God, a relationship develops with Jesus by faith, in which Christ gives and maintains His presence as the Prince of Peace (Isa. 9:6). Sometimes, before He gives strength, we must be made to know our weakness. He produces peace in our alienated minds. A heart of rest is only found in Jesus. In His sacrifice, was the Almighty spiritual power, love and grace of God released and able to deliver us back into His own life with peace. The exclusive nature of the spiritual power of God in Christ irritates and disturbs some folks, but not the Christian. The grace of peace is God's own to give. The evidence in the soul of true peace is not found in the world. The evidence of the forgiveness of sin and the washing away of guilt is only found in Jesus, our Peacemaker, and not the world. The Bible was written that we might have life in His name (John 20:31). The Bible was written that we might believe in Jesus as the Son of God, the Christ, the Messiah, the Savior, and that we might have faith and life through His name.

"He Himself bore our sins in His body on the cross, that we might die to sin and live to righteousness; for by His wounds, you are healed" (1 Pet. 2:24). Jesus our great High Priest bore our sins as our substitutionary sacrifice. He brought about an atonement for our sin and made peace with God. Jesus carried Himself up to the cross in His body and offered Himself for us, like it was an altar. When we learn He died for us, we try to live for Him, which seems right in our minds. When we try to do this on our own, we learn to live with failure. We keep trying because it feels right, because He still deserves our obedience. This becomes a work, and is a natural way of thinking. We may have a little success, but it is not empowered by God. Jesus said, "If anyone wishes to come after Me, let him deny himself and take up his cross and follow Me" (Luke 9:23). What we desire in Jesus does not come to us by trying harder to be righteous, which will always seem right, but rather, we must die. The desire to deny yourself and come after Jesus is energized by the Holy Spirit. Denying yourself involves faith and repentance. We turn from ourselves and sin, and God's grace enables us to walk obediently with the Lord. Dying to self is not a burden, it means being humble and patient. Do not let anger arise in your heart. Be content when your advice is ignored and your opinion ridiculed. You are content to be alone and glad when your brothers prosper. When you are dying to self, you make no plans for yourself, but rather look to see what Jesus wants you to do. We must endure the hardships and contradictions of life. Jesus left us an example we are to follow to be in His steps (1 Pet. 2:21). Let the secular world go. The change we undergo will not be accomplished by repairing our old man, but by becoming a new man (Eph. 4:22-23; 2 Cor. 5:17). The Spirit in the new man will not strengthen the old man to try harder to follow Jesus, but will lead him to die (Rom. 6:6) and put on Jesus (Rom. 13:14). We must be born again and have the help of the Lord to die to self.

"Therefore, holy brethren, partakers of a heavenly calling, consider Jesus, the Apostle and High Priest of our confession" (Heb. 3:1). The high priest's main duty was to make sacrifices for the people's sins once a year on the Day of Atonement (Lev. 16). He would take the blood of an animal sacrifice and sprinkle it on the mercy seat of the Ark of the Covenant in the Holy of Holies, for the sins of the congregation. Jesus is the ultimate High Priest (Heb. 2:17, 3:1, 4:14-15, 10:10-12). Since our sin was imputed to

Christ and His righteousness was imputed to us (2 Cor. 5:21), we have access to God's presence, without an animal sacrifice, with hope that we may find mercy and grace in our time of need (Heb. 4:16). He was sent from God to go between God and us as a High Priest. The Bible tells us that "He had to be made like His brethren" to become a "merciful and faithful high priest" and to "make propitiation for the sins of the people" (Heb. 2:17). Since He was tempted and suffered, "He is able to come to the aid of those who are tempted" (Heb. 2:18). "Since we have such a great high priest who has passed through the heavens, Jesus the Son of God, let us hold fast our confession" (Heb. 4:14). "Let us draw near with confidence to the throne of grace, that we may receive mercy and may find grace to help in time of need" (Heb. 4:16). Jesus was designated by God as a high priest (Heb. 5:10). We have been called to salvation according to His purpose (Rom. 8:28). We have been called by grace (Gal. 1:6), through the gospel (2 Thess. 2:14), out of darkness into light (1 Pet. 2:9). Consider the importance and faithfulness of the Holy Spirit to point us to Jesus, the High Priest of our confession resulting in salvation (Rom. 10:9).

The Lord Jesus is ready and willing to be merciful and helpful for us in times of temptation. He completely understands us and is faithful to be compassionate with us, and provide grace in time of need. Jesus Christ made propitiation for us by turning away God's wrath. Jesus Christ made atonement for us with God by the cancellation of our sin. The Lord Jesus offering Himself to die on the cross, satisfied the righteous demands of God's justice. It was His willingness to be humbled that resulted in the mercy we received. We were in the joy that was set before Him to despise the shame and endure the cross (Heb. 12:2). "Through His own blood, He entered the Holy Place once for all, having obtained eternal redemption" (Heb. 9:12). "How much more will the blood of Christ, who through the eternal Spirit offered Himself without blemish to God, cleanse your conscience from dead works to serve the living God? (Heb 9:14). He always lives to make intercession for us (Heb. 7:25). Our Great High Priest, that is Jesus, speaks to the Father on our behalf. He lives with the purpose of seeing us come back home. Our hope and faith for eternal life rests upon Jesus. The fact that He is now interceding for us, guarantees the security of the believer in the promises of God. The intercession of Christ confirms the truth of our sanctification. He prayed for us (John 17:13, 15), and we live to see His faithfulness in our lives. I have confessed my sin, and by the grace of God, have come to experience a cleansing from unrighteousness (1 John 1:9). My prayers are limited, but God's love in Christ surpasses knowledge and goes beyond whatever I could ask or think, according to the power that He works within us. To God be the glory (Eph. 3:19-21). This means that we cannot and will not be separated from the Lord.

Jesus is sitting at the right hand of the Father (Acts 2:33). It is not by our might, Christian, but God's kindness through intercession that we have the victory over sin, the world, and the devil. "Not by might nor by power, but by My Spirit, says the Lord of hosts" (Zech. 4:6). The Spirit of the Lord of hosts is mighty in the conscience of a man. The conscience is the place, given by God, where we testify to ourselves guilt or innocence. The conscience is the place we apprehend the will of God. The conscience is the organ of faith for us, by which we realize our sincere decisions for Jesus. The blood of Jesus purges the conscience of dead works (Heb. 9:14). The renewed soul can serve the living God. A renewed soul with a cleansed conscience is a blessed person at peace with God. He grows in grace and gratitude with the Lord. Faith matures into action from the soul into the body. He studies the Bible and seeks a church for worship and purpose to serve the Lord. He lives to glorify God. The holy obedience of Jesus gave the blood of Jesus great value. By the mercy of God, we present ourselves as a holy and living sacrifice, which is acceptable to God, and is a spiritual service of worship (Rom. 12:1). Our lives become empowered by the Holy Spirit which makes us alive for a living work. We become more aware of ourselves, and are more strongly gripped and held by the truth. A clear conscience becomes a "must" when we decide to follow Jesus and avoid sin. A clean conscience is a wonder, and a supernatural gift from God, that lets the light of truth outshine falsehoods in the soul. "Conscience is the candle of the Lord" (C. H. Spurgeon).

"All of us like sheep have gone astray, each of us has turned to his own way; but the Lord has caused the iniquity of us all to fall on Him" (Isa. 53:6). As natural men, we were easily deceived and strayed from spiritual truth. Mankind lies under the stain of original sin, and as a natural man does not accept the things of the Spirit of God (1 Cor. 2:14). In our conscience, we turn from the voice of the Lord and choose to go astray and follow stubbornly our own heart after sinful appetites. The way of sin for us becomes a way of grief and sorrows, and a way of habits and fears, which puts our conscience into a war of pain. We are saved from this ruin by coming to Jesus and receiving Him into our hearts. He was pierced through, crushed, chastened, and scourged that we might be healed (Isa. 55:5). Thank you, Jesus. He draws us (John 6:44), we are born again and sanctified by the work of the Holy Spirit (John 3:3-7), all through the shed blood of Jesus Christ for eternal life (John 3:16). God continues to work in us, "both to will and to work for His good pleasure" (Phil. 2:13). In the counsels and providence of God, He determined to begin a good work in us, and will perfect it until the day of Christ Jesus (Phil. 1:6). We were helpless and deceived, dim-witted, ignorant, spiritually weak, and prone to stray like sheep without a shepherd (Matt. 9:36). We "were continually straying like sheep, but now, by the grace of God, have returned to the Shepherd and Guardian of our souls" (1 Pet. 2:25). Saved and unsaved individuals, by grace through faith in the Gospel of Jesus, return like sheep to the Shepherd. We daily need to repent and return to Jesus, the Shepherd and Guardian of our souls. We need a divine Overseer because the war against our souls is continual, and Jesus watches over our souls. God has access to what is going on inside us and "intercedes for the saints according to the will of God" (Rom. 8:27). The Spirit helps our weakness, with groanings too deep for words, and the Father, who searches our hearts, knows what the mind of the Spirit is, and gives us the victory. I believe we also groan too deep for words (Rom.

8:26-27). The Guardian of our souls is at work guarding His sheep (John 10: 27-28).

Our Great High Priest, sooner or later, sends us into the word of God for a deeper walk of faith in Jesus. The Bible is the word of God, and when the Bible is speaking to us, we are hearing from God. Men were moved by the Holy Spirit to write the Bible. Jesus is called "the Word of God" (John 1:1; Rev. 19:13). The living Word and the living Lord are mysteriously linked in our time and eternity by the grace of God. When you receive Jesus, you receive the Word of God and the Father. If you reject Jesus, you reject the Word of God and the Father. The Bible is the written revelation of God. "The Word of the Lord is a light to guide you, a counselor to counsel you, a comforter to comfort you, a staff to support you, a sword to defend you, and a physician to cure you. The Word is a mine to enrich you, a robe to cloth you, and a crown to crown you" (Thomas Brooks). "The scriptures teach us the best way of living, the noblest way of suffering, and the most comfortable way of dying" (John Flavel). The Bible itself tells us that the "word of God is living", and can pierce between the soul and the spirit and "judge the thoughts and intentions of our heart" (Heb. 4:12). We have a great High Priest in Jesus, who has passed through the heavens, and can sympathize with our weakness (Heb. 4:14-15). God can easily reach the place in our being that gets our undivided attention, to call us and conform us to Jesus according to His perfect will. The supernatural power of God saves us, and becomes the source of the grace for our victory in Christ. In His time and way, the supernatural power of God acting for us, caused all things to work together for good according to His purpose (Rom. 8:28). "Faithful is He who has called you, and He also will bring it to pass" (1 Thess. 5:24). God's word penetrates between the soul (psyche) and the spirit (pneuma), producing conviction and emotion about our thoughts. The word 'pneuma" for the human spirit focuses on our spiritual life and God, whereas the word "psyche" focuses more on a man's life. The penetration of God's word exposes our deceptions, delusions, and moral sophistries. It leads a child of God to cry out for help. The division of the soul and the spirit is a controversial topic. Some folks think the spirit is man's Godward consciousness, and the soul is the man's earthward consciousness. Some think that the spirit refers to the whole person, whereas soul and body refers to the persons immaterial and material parts (1 Thess. 5:23). The word of God or the sword cuts open the soul and the spirit of a man exposing his inner man. There is a piercing to the depth where "all things are open and laid bare to the eyes of Him with whom we have to do" (Heb.4:13). God sees everything. We have the experience of being wrought upon, and learn some things, but not everything. I learned I was weak and ignorant of God. I learned I had to suffer and be humbled. I learned I was a sinner and needed help to be saved. I had no place to run to. I found mercy and grace because the Lord found me. I have been pierced by the word of God, Christian, not to bleed to death, but to wake up to life. Read the word of God for yourself to discover yourself. The Spirit of God uses the word of God to lead His people to a more intimate and faithful relationship with Jesus. Amen.

"God is the One who has shown in my heart to give the light of the knowledge of the glory of God in the face of Christ" (2 Cor. 4:6). I have "been enlightened and have tasted of the heavenly gift and have been made a partaker of the Holy Spirit, and have tasted of the good word of God and the powers of the age to come" (Heb. 6:4-5). As a newborn babe, I have longed for the pure milk of the word, that by it I may grow in respect to salvation. I have tasted the kindness of the Lord (1 Pet. 2:2-3). God gave me a hunger and a thirst after His word. God put a desire in my heart to know more about Jesus, enlightened my mind, gave me the Holy Spirit and a taste of His goodness. You will not grow, spiritually speaking, without feasting on the word of God. You will know impulses to feed on the word of God. The desire to read the word of God comes from tasting the word of God. A true Christian will desire more of the word of God, that he may increase in the grace and knowledge of our God and Savior and High Priest, the Lord Jesus. Every day we get up and go forward to honor and follow Jesus. The Bible tells us that we come to Him as a living stone, choice and precious in the sight of God, being built up as a spiritual house for a holy priesthood (1 Pet. 2:4-5). The Bible tells us, that "we are a chosen race, a royal priesthood, a holy nation, a people for God's own possession, that you may proclaim the excellencies of Him who has called you out of darkness into His marvelous light" (1 Pet. 2:9). We are the people of God who have been shown mercy, and saved by His love and power. The priesthood of Jesus will know of no failure. He gave us life, twice, and knows the good plans He has for our future (Jer. 29:11). He is the author and perfecter of our faith, and caused us to be born again and grow in grace into a living hope (1 Pet. 1:3). We learn to live through Him (1 John 4:9). The Lord becomes my rock, and fortress and deliverer (Ps. 18:2). The church of God is a spiritual house, sacred to God, endowed with believers as a holy priesthood offering our bodies, souls, affections, prayers, and praises through Jesus Christ to God. We are, figuratively speaking, living stones alive to God by the power of His Holy Spirit. The cleft in the Rock of ages is a safe place. Christ is our precious cornerstone (Isa. 28:16; 1 Pet. 2:6). We have been appointed to a privileged position in a royal priesthood (Ex. 19:5-6), made possible by our great High Priest. "He made us to be a kingdom, priests to His God and Father; to Him be the glory" (Rev. 1:6). In God's eyes, we are royalty. Amen.

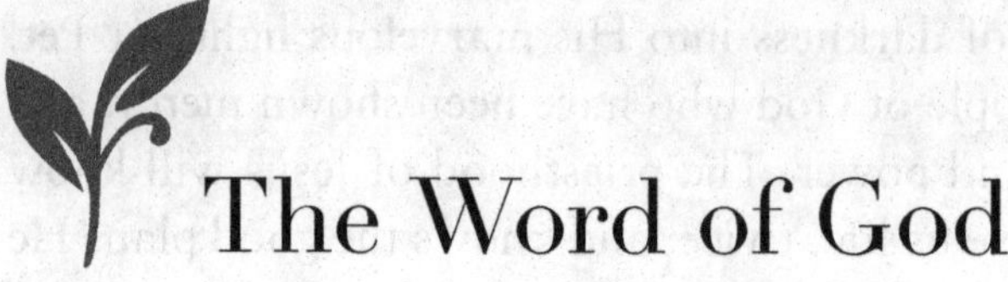

The Word of God

> "All scripture is inspired by God and profitable for teaching, for reproof, for correction, for training in righteousness; that the man of god may be adequate, equipped for every good work" (2 Tim. 3:16-17).

Dear Christian,

The history of Christianity owes a great debt of gratitude to God for the preservation of the Bible. Thank you to the Catholic Church and individuals such as Augustine (354-430), Martin Luther (1483-1546) and John Calvin (1509-1564) for the expansion and reformation of the Christian religion. Calvins impact was indispensable for the spread of Protestantism in France, and across Europe into England and finally the United States. Calvin taught the absolute sovereignty of God. He also taught that election and justification by faith was the work and will of God and the Holy Spirit. The doctrines he taught, along with human responsibility, are clearly biblical principles (Eph. 2:8-10; Phil. 2:12-13). In the nineteenth century, the developments in science, and a changing world brought conflict with the authority of the Bible and its relevance to society. The result was compromise and uncertainty by the church, and the rise of liberalism in the world. The disparagement of the Christian doctrines about depravity and election from a secular world conflicted with biblical truth. The people of God believed the Bible was without error and divinely inspired (2 Tim. 3:16-17). God does not make mistakes or lie (Heb. 6:18). Liberalism believes that Christianity is outmoded and that supernatural miracles, based on natural scientific analysis, are impossible. They trust their humanistic ideas and values and accept a subjective relativism. They decided that God was dead, and therefore should not be feared or believed. The casting out of God, Jesus, the Bible, and the church as being relevant in our society, has left man spiritually naked with his own thoughts. Today, we have a world with a lot problems, despair, and without faith; searching for peace, happiness, freedom, and the meaning of life. Traditional Christianity is threatened. The liberal trend of humanistic reasoning is a heresy of God's truth, that will experience the catastrophe of Divine judgment. Our personal freedoms are losing social and governmental credibility, but the story is not yet complete. God, though seemingly hidden at times, according to the scripture is coming again in Jesus Christ (Rev. 19:7-16). Amen.

The Bible can be a difficult book to accept and understand, because it is a spiritual book. The Bible comes to us from a loving, infinite, and unlimited spiritual God. We are finite, limited, and natural men that need God's help to grasp His goodness. "A natural man does not accept the things of the Spirit of God; for they are foolishness to him, and he cannot understand them, because they are spiritually appraised" (1 Cor. 2:14). As a result of the original sin in the garden of Eden, we became a natural man. We are unable to know God, know about sin, be forgiven and saved without God's help drawing us to Jesus (John 6:44). The natural inclinations and principles of the unregenerate natural man make him unwilling to enter the mind of God. The wise man of the world lives after the flesh, and receives nothing by faith or think they need supernatural assistance. The Bible is spiritual and inspired by God (2 Tim. 3:16). God reveals the great truths of the Gospel to us through the Spirit, who searches all things, even the depths of God (1 Cor. 2:10). Before you can receive its teachings, you must be born of the Spirit (John 3:6) and filled with the Spirit (Eph. 5:18). Without the Spirit's illumination, we cannot understand the Word. The supernatural enablement of the Spirit gives us the desire and power to understand the message of the cross. The deep things of God have been partially revealed to believers, whereas our science and the natural soulish man are blind and without a clue about the Spirit's inspiration. The promise of the Holy Spirit was made by Jesus (John 16:7) and fulfilled on the day of Pentecost (Acts 2). The work of the Holy Spirit was to "convict the world concerning sin, and righteousness, and judgment" (John 16:8) and to guide believers into all the truth (John 16:13). The Spirit was given to be our guide (Rom. 8:14). The Spirit not only shows us the way to Jesus, but goes along with us with providential influences and comforts.

The Spirit of God sends us into the Word of God to grow in grace and knowledge, and discover the Bible's inspiration from God. We are taught by God. We learn to believe and grow in the faith of obedience by the grace of God (Rom. 1:5, 16:26). We learn to love Him because He first loved us (1 John 4:19). The saved welcome and feel God's truth in their heart. Jesus is the living Word (John 1:1, 14) and the Bible is the written word (Ps. 19:7-11, 138:2). Both Jesus and the Bible are true (John 14:6, 17:17), and are light (John 8:12; Ps. 119:105) and bread (John 6:48; Matt. 4:4). The natural man can gain knowledge for his soul by study, but the spiritual man gains wisdom for his spirit, as a gift of grace from God by looking to Jesus. The Spirit of God, I know guided the thoughts and the pens of all the men that wrote the scripture. To be accurate and true, they required the grace of inspiration from God. "No prophecy was ever made by an act of the human will, but men moved by the Holy Spirit spoke from God" (2 Pet. 1:21). The Bible is complete, we have "all the truth" and are warned to not add to it (Rev. 22:18).

The importance and value of all the doctrines in the Bible are based on the Divine inspiration by God. The Christian religion is a Divine communication from God. To the true believers of the Lord, the Bible is the Word of God. The Bible is inerrant and infallible. "Forever, O Lord Thy word is settled in heaven. Thy faithfulness continues throughout all generations" (Ps. 119:89-90). The grace of God gives our hearts a very comfortable knowledge of the word of the Lord. God's word is fixed, it cannot be any other way. I know God is faithful by the grace and glory of His patience. God's word keeps the world in its place, and the spiritual creation of you in your place. Amen.

"In the beginning was the Word, and the Word was with God, and the Word was God. He was in the beginning with God. All things came into being by Him, and apart from Him nothing came into being that has come into being. In Him was life, and the life was the light of men" (John 1:1-4). The Bible tells us, "The Word became flesh and dwelt among us; and we beheld His glory, full of grace and truth" (John 1:14). The Word existed in the beginning. The Word always was, and has eternal existence. The Word has an essential Deity and because the Word was with God, it must have had a distinct and eternal personality. Jesus was the Son of God before He came to earth. The Word of God was not called Jesus before He came as a man. In the Old Testament, the Word of the Lord was called the Son (Ps. 2:7,12). On more numerous occasions He was called the Angel of God (Gen. 21:17). And the Angel of the Lord (Gen. 22:11). The preincarnate appearances of the Son of God are called Christophanies. The examples include His appearances to Abraham (Gen. 12:7-9, 18:1-33), Hagar (Gen. 16:7-8), Jacob (Gen. 32:24-30), Moses (Ex. 3:2), Joshua (Judges 2:1-4) and David (1 Chron. 21:16-18), among others (Ex. Elijah, Daniels friends, and Zachariah). They are shadows of the incarnation and support the idea of God among us (Matt. 1:23). Not all people agree about the appearance of a preincarnate Christ, but they prefer the appearance of angels. Be encouraged, Christian, Christ is in you and with you. Christ is living to make intercession for you (Heb. 7:25). I believe His heart is always present to help and protect His children. The change you have experienced in your heart, is the evidence of His loving presence for you. "Old things have passed away; behold, new things have come (2 Cor. 5:17). To God be the glory for His presence with us. Amen.

"I am the Alpha and the Omega," says the Lord God, "who is and who was and who is to come, the Almighty" (Rev. 1:8; Isa. 4:4). Jesus Christ was with us in the beginning and will be with us in the climax of Divine revelation. What God thought came into being, that is, our universe, earth, what we see, and even ourselves. When we die, we will discover the greater depths of His love. The Christian message, the logos, which means the word with reason, is a gift from God that tells us about God. It is a message we can receive through the study of God's word, but primarily becomes alive to us out of a personal relationship with the Lord Jesus. It was not until John's description that the Word was identified as an actual Person, named Jesus (John 1:1, 14). The Word of God is the personification or the means of representing or revealing the Fathers invisible spiritual nature to His creation (Heb. 1:1-3). The word purifies us (1 Tim. 4:5), and judges us in a way of responsibility and privilege (John 12:48). Through the word comes the opportunity to hear and believe (Acts 4:4), and be born again (1 Pet. 1:23). The logos or the message of the Gospel must be heard, received, retained, and lived by (Matt. 13:20; Luke 8:13; John 8:31,51). The message must be witnessed about (Acts 4:29, 8:25) and taught (Acts 18:11). The word involves obligations and can lead to failures. The word can be disbelieved (1 Pet. 2:8), snatched away (Matt. 13:22), corrupted (2 Cor. 2:17) and rendered ineffective (Mark 7:13). The Christian message is the truth (John 17:7); it is a word of righteousness (Heb. 5:13), reconciliation (2 Cor. 5:19), salvation (Acts 13:26), the cross (1 Cor. 1:18), and the life to hold fast (Phil. 2:16).

Christ is the final spokesman of God (Heb. 1:2). The name of Jesus as the Word of God is the conveyor of the deepest, highest, and greatest wisdom of God in the Bible. The Word of God has creative power. "In Him was life, and the life was the light of men" (John 1:4). We have physical and spiritual resurrection, and eternal life from Him. All men "show the work of the Law written in their hearts and their conscience also bearing witness, and their thoughts alternately accusing or else defending them" (Rom. 2:15). The light constitutes them responsible human beings. The judgment of our day will be in the hands of Jesus Christ (Ps. 98:9; John 5:22). Jesus was the source of our physical life when we were first born, and the source of our spiritual life when we were born again. We have a law of nature in us that witnesses against sin. As the light of the world (John 8:12), Jesus reveals to us the will of God, our sins and fallen condition, and the salvation He provides for us in Himself. God's will, is that we might become sons of light (John 12:35-36), that is, have spiritual life in Him (Col. 3:4).

The Bible tells us, "It is the Spirit who gives life; the flesh profits nothing; the words that I have spoken to you are spirit and are life" (John 6:63). The Spirit that draws us and gives the regenerating power to be quickened, and gives life is the Holy Spirit (John 6:44, 63, 65). We are born again not of blood, nor of the will of the flesh, nor of the will of man, but of God (John 1:13). The life of God does not come to us through our heredity, or our good will or the will of others; it is a Divine work by the Holy Spirit applying the Word in living power to our heart. Amen. We are born again of incorruptible seed, "by the word of God" (1 Pet. 1:23). The words of God are spiritual and employed by the Holy Spirit to impart life. Our responsibility is to search God's word for ourselves, and sincerely seek the Lord to be saved. God is in the work to be sincere (Eph. 2:13), and provide the grace to be saved (Eph. 2:8). Some men prefer the darkness and hate the light of God, and will not seek Him in the way of repentance and surrender. They want to stay in control of their life. It is also true that God overcomes the depravity in "vessels of mercy" according to His eternal counsel and pleasure (Rom. 9:18-23; Eph. 1:4-11). This work of God offends the natural man, and today, as well as in the time of Jesus, "many of His disciples walked with Him no more" (John 6:66). When we read the written word, we can learn about God and His ways and acts, and His plan for the salvation of mankind. We will never completely understand the mind and heart of God, but we will know enough to realize we are being called to trust Him and believe in Jesus to be saved. By the grace of God, the "vessel of mercy" will let God be God.

There are different words to denote the Spirit of God. "Ruach" is the Hebrew word found in the Old Testament, whereas "Pneuma" is the Greek word in the New Testament that denotes the Spirit of God. They are both invisible forces that mean "wind," "breath," or "spirit" as the energy behind the force. God's Spirit is the source of life (Num. 27:16). It was promised that the Messiah would be empowered by the Holy Spirit (Isa. 11:12, 61:1; Matt3:16). Job said, "The Spirit of God has made me, and the breath of the Almighty gives me life" (Job 33:4). In being born again, God gives us a new heart, a new spirit, and His own Spirit in order to teach, guide, and lead us into paths of righteousness for His name's sake (Ezek. 36:25-27; John 14:16, 26; Ps. 23:3). The meaning of life becomes clear from our relationship with God. The wind blows, where, when, and how it pleases, so it is with the Spirit (John 3:8). Being born again we know we have new life, but it is a mystery to us how the Holy Spirit operates upon our soul. God knows.

There are two different Greek words that refer to the word of God. One is "logos" and the other is "rhema." Logos refers principally to the total inspired Word of God and the living Word who is Jesus (John 1:1; Luke 8:11; Phil. 2:16; Heb. 4:12). The word rhema is used to refer to the instant, personal speaking of God (Luke 1:38, 3:2; Acts 11:16; Eph. 6:17; Rom. 10:17). I have no doubt that God continually speaks to us today. God uses His "logos" Word to speak His "rhema" Word to us, and they never contradict each other. We know God objectively by what we read in the Bible or the written word (ex. Logos), whereas we can experience God in a more subjective and personal way by Him speaking to us in our situations (ex. Rhema). The personal speaking of God to my heart confirms the inspiration of the scripture. We read and pray with the logos or written word so the Lord can speak rhema to impart life (John 6:63) and wash us (Eph. 5:26), to fulfill His purpose and plan for our life. The word of God speaks to us every day. Both logos and rhema are important in our Christian life. We must know the "logos" to correctly perceive the "rhema." The word of God may be silent for many of the decisions we make in this life. The Holy Spirit gives rise to spiritual gifts (1 Cor. 12:1-11), and in the last days shall be poured out again (Acts 2:17). The times we believe that God has spoken to us, however, in the present and in the past, are precious, fulfilling, and confirming of the faith experience we are living in Jesus in this life. Amen.

From John 1:1-2, the Word, with a capital W, is a title for the Lord Jesus Christ. God is a communicator, and in these last days, has spoken to us through His Son (Heb. 1:2). Since Jesus embodied the message of God, He is called the "Logos" or "Word" of God (Col. 2:9). The word "logos" is also used many times to refer to the written message of God (John 17:17; Col. 1:25). The word of God is living and active (Heb. 4:12). Jesus is the Word of God, and the subject of the written word that is spiritually coming to us. We read the Bible with fear and trembling because it is the essence of God Himself speaking to us. God sends us into His word for faith (Rom. 10:17). God's words become God's Word in our hearts, which speaks to us abundant life (John 10:10). The life of a sinner goes no further than the body. Whereas the saint is spiritually alive by the grace of God in the soul, where he has the new nature, with a living spirit because of the righteousness of Christ (Rom. 8:10). The body has been appointed to die. The righteousness of Christ imputed to you secures the soul for eternal life. We have this great treasure in our earthen vessel (2 Cor. 4:7). The glory of God is revealed within us. From within us, God's plan is to call us by grace to reveal more of Christ within us. (Gal. 5:15-16). "I have been crucified with Christ; and it is no longer I who live, but Christ lives in me; and the life which I now live in the flesh I live by faith in the Son of God" (Gal. 2:20). I live in the exercise of God's grace in a state of dependence and union with Christ. That I have been changed, proves to my heart the power and inspiration of the Bible.

"The Word became flesh and dwelt among us, and we beheld His glory, glory as of the only begotten from the Father, full of grace and truth" (John 1:14). The incarnation is a central Christian doctrine. The Son of God assumed a human nature in the flesh and became a man named Jesus Christ. Christ was truly God and truly man. Jesus has explained God (John 1:18). The Bible explains our beginning in life and our future in eternity. The Bible explains the way to God, the truth about God and a life with God (John 14:6). The Bible explains God's plan for us to be forgiven of sin, and reconciled back to Himself by receiving the gift of His Son's righteousness. It is a salvation that you discover by God's grace and calling, through fear, trembling and diligence (Phil. 2:12). The Bible tells us that without the shedding of blood, there is no forgiveness of sin (Heb. 9:22). Only the Son of God could accomplish this great task for us, because He was a perfect sacrifice, holy and willing ((2 Cor. 5:21; Heb. 10:1-18). By faith, we understand and surrender our will to Jesus and take God at His word (Heb. 11:3; Rom. 8:28). By faith, men of old gained approval (Heb.11:2).

The Bible tells us we are saved by grace through faith, it is a gift of God (Eph. 2:8). The Bible tells us that faith comes by hearing and or reading the word of God (Rom. 10:17). Therefore, it is important that you gain the confidence that the Bible was inspired by God for training in righteousness (2 Tim. 3:16). The Holy Spirit is the author of the Bible (2 Pet. 1:21) and that Jesus is the author and perfector of our faith (Heb. 12:2). "God is at work in you to will and to work for His good pleasure" (Phil. 2:13). When you are "changed" by the power of God, then you will more deeply believe that everything the Bible has to say is accurate and trustworthy and can only have been inspired. The Bible says that "you have been born again not of seed which is perishable but imperishable, that is, through the living and abiding word of God" (1 Pet. 1:23). The word of God is living (Heb. 4:12). God has willed to make known to you the glory of this mystery, "which is Christ in you, the hope of glory" (Col.1:27). Amen.

The word of God is like a Divine mirror. When you read it, it reads you. It is alive, and able to discern and reveal the thoughts and intentions of your heart to yourself (Heb. 4:12). The word of God convicts men of their guilt, that they are in trouble and lost about salvation. God's word has the power to deliver a man from the penalty of the wages of sin. The love and patience of God comes out of the word, and inspires a search for wisdom, freedom, forgiveness, and peace. God's word can make you tremble, but at the same time is attractive like a magnet and imparts a sense of healing. "The unfolding of Thy words gives light; it gives understanding to the simple" (Ps. 119:130). God's word shines in our heart the light of the truth of knowledge, instruction, and direction. God's word gives the understanding "of the glory of God in the face of Jesus Christ" (2 Cor. 4:6). From the Bible, we are taught the truth about Jesus by the Holy Spirit (John 14:6, 26). We know that all things work together for good (Rom. 8:28) and that one day we shall be like Him (1 John 3:2). The Bible fully persuades us to trust Christ (2 Tim. 1:2) and know that we have passed from death unto life (1 John 3:14). The Christian conscience has passed from the lost world to a regenerate life with God. John tells us that he has written to us "who believe in the name of the Son of God, in order that you may know that you have eternal life" (1 John 5:13). "The one who believes in the Son of God has the witness in himself (1 John 5:10).

Following regeneration in the believer, there develops an inner conviction that the Bible is true and that "God is at work in you, both to will and to work for His good pleasure" (Phil. 2:13). "The Spirit Himself bears witness with our spirit that we are children of God" (Rom. 8:16). We "have received a spirit of adoption as sons by which we cry out, Abba! Father!" (Rom. 8:15). We have an inner conviction from the Lord that we have passed from death to life and are His children. Our reception as sons of God must be based objectively on the written word of God, and then, subjectively, on the fact of the Holy Spirit's witness with our spirit. Feelings are not facts and we can be deceived by them. We are saved by grace through faith according to God's word (Eph. 2:8). The Holy Spirit comforts us, draws us to prayer and loving others, and reproofs us for our choice to sin. "The inward seal of adoption is testified by the outward seal of sanctification" (Octavius Winslow). The idea of God adopting us as His children may be a difficult truth to be fully assured of. The assurance of our salvation will be strongly attacked by Satan. It can stagger our mind, plus our past sins and present carnal ways make it seem impossible and undeserved. By the grace of God, the Holy Spirit knows our weaknesses and has chosen to be our comforter. The fact is, the scripture makes it clear that God chose us before the foundation of the world, and predestined us to adoption to the praise of the glory of His grace bestowed on us in the Beloved (Eph. 1:4-6). The Holy Spirit, by His acceptance, confirms the true seed of faith in our hearts. The pant after holiness is the Spirit's inspiration and confirmation of God's love (John 3:16). It is personal, and in your conscience, you recognize the Bible's truth and the Saviors love, and thirst after righteousness. "Those whom the Lord loves He disciplines" (Heb. 12:6). The Christian, even in trial, should see a proof of the Father's loving care and concern for our highest good. Discipline is designed to cultivate Christian virtues. The Bible tells us that when God begins a good work in you, He will perfect it (Phil. 1:6). God's word is our assurance. Amen.

The Bible claims to be the inspired word of God (2 Tim. 3:16). God is the author of the Bible, and God cannot lie (Heb. 6:18). The Bible has been read by a lot of folks, and impacted more people's lives than any other book. The message of the Bible offers salvation by God's grace through faith, and not something we earn or work for (Eph. 2:8-9). We must be born again (John 3:5). "Whoever believes that Jesus is the Christ is born of God" (1 John 5:1). "Everyone who loves is born of God" (1 John 4:7-11; Rom. 5:5). "Everyone who practices righteousness is born of Him" (1 John 2:29). Whatever is born of God, overcomes the world by faith (1 John 5:4). "There are three that bear witness, the Spirit and the water and the blood; and the three are in agreement" (1 John 5:8). Although there are different interpretations for this passage, the most likely is that the water is a reference to the baptism of Jesus at the beginning of His ministry, and the blood is a reference to His death on the cross. God bore witness to His Son at His baptism (Matt. 3:17), at His death (Matt. 27:51-53) and the Spirit descended on the church at the Day of Pentecost (Acts 2:1-4). The Bible tells us that God is love (1 John 4:8), God is light (1 John 1:5), God is a consuming fire (Heb. 12:29), and God is spirit (John 4:24). "The Lord God is compassionate, gracious, slow to anger, and abounding in lovingkindness and truth" (Ex. 34:6). God is omnipotent, omniscient, omnipresent, and immutable (Isa. 46:9-10, Jer. 32:27,23:24; Ps. 147:5; Heb. 13:8). The Bible tells us that God's words will not pass away (Matt. 24:35). The Bible tells us that, "He who believes in the Son has eternal life, and he who does not believe will not see life but the wrath of God abides on him"

(John 3:36). Faith in God's Son is your assurance of salvation. "He who has the Son has the life" (1 John 5:12). There are only two kinds of choices; two ways (Ps. 1:6), two gates (Matt. 7:13-14), and two foundations (Matt. 7:24-27). It is your choice, eternal death, or eternal life. Choose to follow Jesus. The Gospel is both a Person we receive and a life we live. The Gospel is not perfection but a sincere direction. Are you growing in grace, knowledge, and obedience? You can know what you have chosen. God bears witness to you by signs, wonders, miracles, and gifts of the Holy Spirit, according to His good and perfect will (Heb. 2:4). You will not escape if you neglect such a great salvation (Heb. 2:3).

The Bible, from Genesis to Revelation, was written over a period of 1600 years. It includes 66 different books written by 40 different Jewish authors "commissioned" by God. The men selected by God were from all walks of life. The Bible shows remarkable unity and accuracy. Thousands of skeptics and kings have failed in their attempts to silence the Word of God. The mastermind of the Bible was God. It contains one rule of faith and one plan for salvation. The Bible characters were praised for their accomplishments; and the fact that their sinful activities were not covered up reveals the Bible was honest about their lives. Thus, Jacob was a deceiver (Gen. 27), Moses was a murderer (Ex. 2:12), and David was a murderer and an adulterer (2 Sam. 11).

Though the Bible is not a textbook, it does demonstrate historical, geographical, and scientific accuracies. For example, the Bible mentioned the Hittites whose existence was called into question for a long time. Today, we know the Hittite Kingdom formed in ancient Anatolia (ex. Modern Turkey) around 1600 BCE. They had conflicts with Egypt, worshipped a storm god, and produced the world's first known peace treaty. They were pioneers of the Iron Age and are famous for their role in the battle of Kadesh in 1274 BCE. The Bible reflected accurate scientific knowledge thousands of years before modern times confirmed it. For example, the earth was round (Isa. 40:22) and is suspended in space (Job 26:7). The Bible states the number of stars is vast (Gen. 15:15), and pointed out that there are currents in the seas (Ps. 8:8).

The Bible has many insights into good health. For example, the Bible distinguishes between clean and unclean animals, treating Leprosy, cleaning houses and bodily discharges (Lev. 11-15). "A cheerful heart is good medicine, but a crushed spirit dries up the bones (Prov. 17:22). The Bible explains why the universe has laws, design, and order. The Bible explains why we have love, justice, and truth. The Bible explains why we have evil and the way of salvation by God's grace. The Bible describes our reality and the truth in a much better way than what the worlds secular-humanists have tried to hoist upon us. The idea that we are the result of billions of years of time and chance of molecules creating human beings, with no purpose or significance in a dying universe is both meaningless and worthless. The Bible describes that God's work of creation, salvation, and spiritual life in the soul of the human nature is filled with reality and purpose, and He supports this with His continued guiding presence in our hearts.

The Bible can tell the future because it was inspired by God. God is able to do anything, Christian, and He alone is able to tell you the future before it happens. He alone is able to declare the end from the beginning. He can bring to pass whatever He has planned. The Bible is a word of prophecy that proves the sovereignty of God. Jesus told us things before they happened, so that when they did happen, you would believe that He was the Savior sent from God (John 13:19, 14:29). The Bible contains hundreds of detailed prophecies about our world, and in particular, the nation of Israel and the Messiah (Gen. 49:10; Deut. 28:15-68; Isa. 42:1-9, 49:1-13, 50:4-11, 52:13, 53:12; Ezek. 36). Fulfilled prophecy is evidence of inspiration. He is God (Isa. 41:22). Peter was an eyewitness to the fulfillment of the prophecy of the coming of the Lord Jesus Christ (2 Pet. 1:16-21). In your own heart, Christian, is the testimony that Jesus is coming again, which is the spirit of prophecy (Rev. 19:10). In your own heart, Christian, is the testimony of God providentially drawing you, at numerous times in your life, to believe and trust in Jesus. The Holy Spirit brings to our memory when the Lord was present to help us, and protect us, and guide us in paths of righteousness. The power of God was faithfully present, in His way and time, to deliver us from temptation and the power of sin. The grace of God has progressively educated and grown me over time, all about Jesus. It has been the Lord's work that has transformed and saved my soul. I can confidently say, to God be all the glory. Only God can foretell the future. God is not "living in time" as we know it. He is eternal, and exists outside and above "time", so that all things are always present. The fulfilled prophecies in the Bible, and the testimony of my own life, attest that the scriptures are the inspired, infallible, inerrant word of God. Amen.

The Bible tells us that, no one can snatch us out of the hands of Jesus and the Father (John 10:28-29). All our time is in His hands (Ps. 31:15). The reality of the Christian experience is that we will not always feel worthy and at peace with the Lord. The truth is, we are in a covenant relationship with God. It is a covenant relationship where He easily keeps His side of the agreement. He also provides the grace for us to be acceptable in keeping our side of the covenant. We grow in grace, knowledge, love, and obedience. He has said, "I will never desert you, nor will I ever forsake you" (Heb. 13:5). No matter what the circumstances are of any situation you are in, Christian; pray, read, and sing for His hands of grace, to cover you with faith, trust, and His presence. God's love does not fail in the heat of any furnace or lion's den. In the New Covenant, He has put His laws in our minds and written them upon our hearts. He will be our God and we shall be His people (Heb. 8:10). We are "letters of Christ" written with the Spirit of the living God on the tablet of our heart (2 Cor. 3:3). Our names are written in the Lamb's book of life (Rev. 20:15, 21:27), they are recorded in heaven (Luke 10:20). The prophecy for us, is that when we see Jesus, we shall be like Him, and see Him just as He is (1 John 3:2). We will see Jesus in heaven as "I am the Alpha and Omega, says the Lord God, who is and who was and who is to come, the Almighty" (Rev. 1:8). The vision John has is new to him, but he does say he saw, "one like the Son of Man" (Rev. 1:13). The vision was of Jesus, and reveals that Christ is God (Rev. 1:12-16). The Bible tells us that Jesus said "Do not be afraid; I am the first and the last, and the living One; and I was dead, and behold, I am alive for evermore" (Rev. 1:18). Jesus prophesied His death and resurrection (Matt. 16:21, 17:23; Luke 9:22). The Old Testament prophesied that the Messiah would have His hands and feet pierced (Ps. 22:16). Crucifixion was the Roman method of execution, reserved for crimes against the state. As king of the Jews, Jesus challenged Roman supremacy. We know from the crucifixion of Jesus that He was nailed to the cross, and that the evidence of scars on His hands were visible after the resurrection (John 20:24-29). In Isaiah the Lord says, "Behold, I have inscribed you on the palms of My hands; your walls are continually before Me" (Isa. 49:16). He will not forget the Jewish people or us. He died a cruel and cursed kind of death. Some have thought that the scar He received from the spear may remain in His glorious body, to show at His second coming to those who pierced Him (John 19:37; Zech. 12:10; Rev. 1:7). He was pierced for our transgressions (Isa. 53:5). Believers of all generations will see their names inscribed on the hands of Jesus and rejoice in His love, mercy, and grace. God is faithful to the Church, and His eyes are always upon her "walls," that is our lives, to remind us of His love. He is the master Architect of our cares and safety; we are His workmanship (Eph. 2:10). Our hope in Jesus will not be disappointed. Hope grows into assurance, because God is all powerful, generous, and trustworthy.

The Bible provides the knowledge that leads to salvation through faith which is in Christ Jesus. The journey is for your lifetime, from childhood to adulthood and through your senior years. "The scripture is inspired by God and is profitable for teaching, for reproof, for correction, for training in righteousness (2 Tim. 3:16). The Bible will "draw" and "tug" at you to read and study the meaning of passages, and to go all in with Jesus. By the love and grace of God, the "crown of righteousness" has been laid up as your reward. God declares that He will look "to him who is humble and contrite of spirit, and who trembles at His word" (Isa. 66:2). The word of God will make clear to your mind and heart that you are a vessel of mercy, fully convinced of the sovereignty and love of God to save your soul in salvation.

You will tremble with an awe of God's majesty and dread of His justice and wrath. This kind of heart is a living temple where the Lord rests. The presence of the Lord will make you aware of His conviction, inspiration, and determination. Read the Word of God to know God.

"Be diligent to present yourself to God as a workman who does not need to be ashamed, handling accurately the word of truth" (2 Tim. 2:15). The Word of God commands the believer to study the scripture. "Like a new born babe, long for the pure milk of the word, that by it you may grow in respect to salvation, if you have tasted of the kindness of the Lord" (1 Pet. 2:2-3). The Bible says that if you abide in My word, then you are truly disciples of Mine; and you shall know the truth, and the truth shall make you free (John 8:31-32). Enduring to the end is evidence we have passed from death to life (Matt. 10:22). Those who continue in His word, will be more informed, conformed and believe in the certainty of it. We may not know everything, but we will know enough that is needful and profitable. We will know and understand the truth regarding the salvation of men. The true disciple of Jesus will have the promise of knowing the truth and the liberty of being changed by it. We learn that the Gospel truth of being free from the guilt and bondage of sin is a great freedom. We learn that the Gospel truths of justification and sanctification in Jesus have power to liberate us from the tyranny of sin. Jesus was anointed by God to preach good news of deliverance to the captives, sight to the blind, good news to the afflicted, bind up the broken-hearted, and give freedom to prisoners (Isa. 61:2; Luke 4:18). The words of scripture have been fulfilled in my life. My spiritual experience is forgiveness and freedom from the penalty, bondage, and power of sin. I have been set free to behold my salvation by faith (Eph. 2:8) and serve God (1 Cor. 7:22). I have been set free to know the Lord makes me lie down in green pastures, leads me beside quiet waters, and restores my soul (Ps. 23:2-3). I have been set free to know and to live the rest of my days in an obedience of faith in Jesus (Rom. 1:5, 16:26). To God be the glory. My testimony is about the grace, love, and the power of God in the Gospel of Jesus Christ. My testimony is exactly as it is described in the Word of God. God sends you into His word with a purpose. Your diligence in Bible study has the great rewards of faith and obedience for your soul inside of it. God knows what He is going to do with the call for your life from His word. From your study, the Holy Spirit will make it possible for you to receive all the enabling grace and faith you will need to honor and glorify His name. Amen.

"Watch over your heart with all diligence, for from it flow the springs of life" (Prov. 4:23). "Be diligent to make certain His calling and choosing you" (2 Pet. 1:10). We are commanded to guard closely what goes around and into our hearts. The world, the flesh, and the devil are strong enemies that try to take over your heart. You are responsible to watch over your heart because it is where God looks and helps, and it is where your thoughts and feelings determine your conduct. Temptation to sin knocks at the door of your heart, and if received, will enter your soul's inner chambers to take up residency. God's word is to be kept with our whole heart (Ps. 119:69). The promise to us is, "the steadfast in mind Thou wilt keep in perfect peace, because he trusts in Thee" (Isa. 26:3). To keep the heart, which is our duty that God enables, means striving to live in conformity to the Word of God. The striving is not to save ourselves, but rather the time to experience the reality of discovering the grace of God at work in your life. What is in your heart comes out in your life. In being born again, the new heart becomes the seat of the Lord of life to feed the faculties of our soul. Reading the word of God is a great aid to keeping our heart. The influence and comforts of the Spirit from Bible study become more fixed in the decisions your heart makes for your life (Rom. 10:17). The faith you grow and gain in overcomes your corruptions and the enemy and, by the grace of God, gives you the victory (1 John 5:4). The nature of your spiritual victories in Jesus will be provocative to you because of their success. The power of God to bless you will establish in your heart His presence, and confirm to you the inspiration of the scripture by God.

The diligent pursuit of God in the scripture, releases His lovingkindness in your soul, and the truth of hope in Him that

He is setting you free. It confirms that you have been called and chosen by God for salvation. You are a vessel of mercy (Rom. 9:23). You have discovered that you are His workmanship, and that He has been at work in you, both to will and to work for His good pleasure (Eph. 2:10; Phil.2:13). God's assurances are the greatest springs of life. You have been called according to His purpose (Rom. 8:28). The bottom line is that God has effectually called you to Jesus through the words of truth in the Gospel, and brought you to faith and obedience by the blessings of His grace and peace. The gifts and the calling of God are without repentance and are irrevocable (Rom. 11:29). The truth promotes holiness and comfort and the potential to go to work for Jesus. The truth promotes gratitude for spiritual blessings, a great hope in Jesus and a prayer life. The truth promotes patience, integrity, and self-sacrifice. The evidence of being born again is unmistakable in your own heart. The stranger to the Gospel is frustrated, careless and unhappy. His conduct looks no different than the world, though he might claim differently. The Christian will be diligent to scrutinize his own heart. The Christian is being made to know he is being sanctified, which makes him grateful to God. The faith and hope he has is only resting on the glorious work of Christ. The evidence for a true calling is growth in Christian virtue. Applying all diligence, in your faith supply moral excellence, knowledge, self-control, perseverance, godliness, brotherly kindness and love (2 Pet. 1:5-7). "If these qualities are yours and are increasing, they render you neither useless nor unfruitful in the true knowledge of our Lord Jesus Christ" (2 Pet. 1:8). Amen.

The Bible is the inspired word of God. In the Bible we are commanded to listen to Jesus. "He who ears to hear, let him hear" (Matt. 11:15). The divine identity of Jesus was revealed at the Transfiguration, where we were also summoned to "listen to Him" (Matt. 17:5; Mark 9:7; Luke 9:35). The Bible tells us that "if you will receive my sayings, and treasure my commandments with you, make your ear attentive to wisdom, incline your heart to understanding; for if you cry for discernment, lift your voice for understanding; if you seek her as silver, and search for her as for hidden treasures; then you will discern the fear of the Lord, and discover the knowledge of God" (Prov. 2:1-5). "Whoever is of God hears the words of God" (John 8:47). The Bible has great rewards inside it, but you must travel through it. Amen. In the Bible, we hear the words of the Son of God about forgiveness of sin and inheriting eternal life. The consequences of listening are to be able to read the mind of God in the death of Jesus. This message concerns our future welfare and most solemn interest. Of all the things we hear in this life, the most important will be the Holy Spirit speaking to us about Jesus. We hear the love of God in the Gospel (John 3:16). We hear that it is His righteousness that justifies us before God. We hear that we are saved because of His obedience even unto death. Jesus paid it all, for our salvation. Quit thinking about how to earn your salvation. Quit hanging your head about your failures, and instead lift it in praise to God that has managed our weaknesses. By the grace of God, we hear and believe the Gospel. By the grace of God, we are blessed by an obedience of faith in His time. By the grace of God, we are sanctified for service in teaching the Bible, and being useful in the church and to fellow believers in sharing the Gospel. Bible study becomes important and an indispensable life-line to grow in grace and knowledge, and to hear from the Lord. Amen.

The Bible shows us God's lovingkindness and faithfulness, alongside a gracious and holy character. Reading the Bible should have a high priority and be done in a regular and respectful manner. The Bible is your spiritual life line to Jesus; you were born again by it (James 1:18), and grow in grace by it (1 Pet. 2:20). It should be highly prized by your soul. We should be humble and ready to learn when we read it with an open heart. What you learn should be put into practice (Ps. 119:105). You should meditate on what you read (Ps. 119:15) and, by the grace of God, remember and apply what you read to your life (Ps. 119:52). You will find that the word will speak to your heart about your circumstances, situations, and temptations. The word of God will comfort and guide you. The word of God will instruct you in your affliction (Heb. 12:7; John 14:1-3; 2 Cor. 4:17), and sin (James 1:15; Gal. 5:24; 1 Pet. 2:11;

Heb. 8:12) and unbelief (Isa. 26:3; 1 John 5:10; John 3:36). The scripture knows how to "hit home", and will touch your soul with conviction, faith, and peace.

The Bible provides ample examples of the lives of people in the Bible as living sermons to you about punishments and mercies (2 Sam. 12,24; Dan. 4; Acts 5; Luke 19:1-10, 15:11-24). Be humble and honest with God when you read the Bible and open your heart to hear His teaching. God can revive and strengthen you (Ps. 119:93) and warm your heart like He did for the disciples on the Road to Emmaus (Luke 24:32). Pray that He will give you understanding to see His goodness and grace (Ps. 119:18,73; Isa. 48:17). Be serious (Deut. 32:47) and do not let distractions keep you from this most important time with the Lord. Be careful to receive and trust God in all the commandments that you hear, as much as the promises that you may extract more comfort from. I recommend you read the whole Bible, but think it is best to read the New Testament first. Do not get bogged down in minor details. You will not get all the answers about life, but you will get enough to believe and trust in Jesus. The Bible is not like any other book, Christian, it will convict your conscience. It will pierce your soul (Heb. 4:12), and trouble your heart. Keep reading. You will feel the judgment of your sin and, by the grace of God, sense your great need and gratitude for a Savior like Jesus. The world does not want, in fact deplores, the idea of being judged for their sin. They will turn away from Jesus because it is not what they want to hear.

God is holy; and to inherit eternal life with God, the Bible teaches we must be born again, receive the Holy Spirit, and trust the righteousness of Jesus for our acceptance with God. We must grow in grace into the obedience of faith through our relationship with Jesus. It is our responsibility and duty to take up the Bible to hear from God. It is our responsibility, by God's grace, to walk with Jesus on the path that He has graciously laid out for us. It will be God's way or no way. We must let God be God. God is love (1 John4:8). "Thy hands made me and fashioned me; give me understanding that I may learn Thy commandments" (Ps. 119:73). "Remember the word to Thy servant, in which Thou hast made me hope" (Ps. 119:49). "This is my comfort in my affliction, that Thy word has revived me" (Ps. 119:50). John tells us that, "These things have been written to you who believe in the name of the Son of God, in order that you may know that you have eternal life" (1 John 5:13). I recommend that you read the various scriptures carefully to get the meaning about the love of God in Jesus. Read all the scripture as the Lord leads you, letting the the Bible itself interpret itself. Give thanks to the Lord for His truth. The Bible tells us that God has magnified His word according to all His name (Ps. 138:2). For me, I went back and forth between the Gospel of John and the letters written by Paul, particularly Ephesians and Romans. Mix in the lives of the Old Testament Patriarchs and draw upon numerous conservative commentaries. By the grace of God, in His time, God gave me the blessing of understanding the scripture in my mind and heart. To God be the glory. It has been a long journey, but knowing Jesus means everything to me. "The Lord God is my strength, and He has made my feet like hind's feet, and makes me walk on my high places" (Hab. 3:19). The God of our strength for this world, is the God of our salvation in the world to come. By the grace of God, I outrun my troubles and walk with Jesus in the high places of joy and triumph. Thank you, God, for making your Word the treasure in my heart, that I might not sin against Thee (Ps. 119:11). Amen.

The Old Testament Types for Christ

> "You search the scriptures, because you think in them you have eternal life; and it is these that bear witness of Me" (John 5:39). "And beginning with Moses and with all the prophets, He explained to them the things concerning Himself in all the scriptures" (Luke 24:27). "Behold, I have come (in the roll of the book it is written of Me) to do Thy will, O God" (Heb. 10:7).

Dear Christian,

The testimony for Jesus as the Messiah is clearly outlined in the Bible. Early on, John the Baptist proclaimed about Jesus, "Behold, the Lamb of God who takes away the sin of the world" (John 1:29), and in the book of John, the Apostle says. "And I have seen Him, and have borne witness that this is the Son of God" (John 1:34). Jesus said the Old Testament was about Him (John 5:39). A way we can know that Jesus was the Messiah is in the fulfillment of prophecies about Him (Gen. 49:10; Isa. 50:6, 53:7, Hosea 11:1, Zech, 9:9 and many more). The primary way though that we know the truth in Jesus, is by the work of love He performs in our heart. Amen. In addition, another way we learn that Jesus was the Messiah, is by the shadows and types described in the

Old Testament, that are revealed in the life of Jesus in the New Testament. The shadows and types were used in the Old Testament to describe and identify the Messiah when He came. They are representations of Someone to come. They were designed by God to prefigure some aspect of the person of Jesus Christ. Shadows are not a perfect reality because they have no substance, but they can be prophetic in the scripture about Jesus. The substance and reality belong to Christ (Col. 2:17; Heb. 10:1). The "types" in the scripture are people like Isaac, or things such as the temple, or events like the Passover. For example, Adam is called a "type" of the One who was to come (Rom. 5:14). Both were called the son of God and entered the world sinless. Adam as head of the old creation, is an obvious counterpart to Christ, head of the new creation. All humanity is viewed as being either "in Adam", in whom "all die", or "in Christ", in whom all are to be "made alive" (1 Cor. 15:22, 45). Christ is referred to as the antitype, and the relevance of the type to the antitype can then be appreciated. This letter expands on this topic, which I have found supports the inspiration of the scripture by God.

The Bible has a few images or shadows to hold up in your mind's eye to take a deeper walk with Jesus in the scriptures. One of these images is as a horn of salvation (Luke 1:69). It is not a horn to make music, but rather the horn of a wild ox as a weapon to beat back the enemies of your soul. Jesus stands guard to protect you against the wiles of the devil. His name can be a powerful weapon. In the New Testament, it appears in the prophecy Zacharias gave at the time his son, John, was born and named (Luke 1:57-79). The prophecy sounds like it might be for Israel and John the Baptist, but it is about Jesus and the redemption of His people. He says, God "has raised up a horn of salvation for us in the house of David His servant" (Luke 1:69). He speaks of John being called the prophet of the "Most High;" for you will go on before the Lord to prepare His ways (Luke 1:76). John's message was to give "His people the knowledge of salvation by the forgiveness of their sins" (Luke 1:77). John was a voice crying in the wilderness (John 1:23), he was not the horn. John was not of the house of David. The horn was a sign of strength and a club as a means of victory (Micah 4:13). God fights for Israel in the Old Testament and for us in the New Testament (Rom. 8:27). David called God his rock, shield, savior, refuge, and the horn of his salvation (2 Sam. 22:3). The horn was a deadly and powerful weapon against enemies. Jesus is the horn of our salvation because He secured our salvation. Jesus destroys the enemies of our soul today, and will complete the miracle when He comes again (Rev. 19:15-21). In Jesus, we have the horn of salvation protecting our hearts, and we "overwhelmingly conquer through Him who loved us" (Rom. 8:37). "The Son of God appeared for this purpose, that He might destroy the works of the devil" (1 John 3:8). He defeats all the roaring lions in your life. Thank you, Jesus. Nothing is impossible with God and nothing is stronger than God (Luke 1:37). The world wants a military savior, but God gives us something greater, that is, a Savior that conquers our sin for eternal life. We cling to the horn of our salvation, and are advanced with spiritual blessings for eternity, and our Redeemer is glorified.

Another type of image for Jesus, that again speaks of His strength to save us is when He is called the rock of our salvation. "O come, let us sing joy to the Lord; let us shout joyfully to the rock of our salvation" (Ps. 95:1). God is our abiding, immutable and mighty rock, and in Him we find a solid foundation for forgiveness, acceptance, safety, and eternal life. "While we were yet sinners, Christ died for us" (Rom. 5:8). The promises of God become a strong fortress in a saved soul, because Jesus is the rock of ages. In the wilderness, the Jews were fed bread in manna (Ex. 16:35) and drank water from a rock on two different occasions (Ex. 17:1-7; Num. 20:14). Paul says that they drank from a spiritual rock that followed them in their journeys, and that rock was Christ (1 Cor. 10:4). The Jews in the wilderness were miraculously supplied with bread and water, and the source was Christ. We share these privileges in the wilderness wanderings in our life. Jesus said, "I am the bread of life; he who comes to Me shall not hunger, and he who believes in Me shall never thirst" (John 6:35). "The water that I shall give him shall become in him a well of water springing up to eternal life" (John 4:14). Amen.

The spiritual rock of Jesus is always with us, to nourish and provide for our souls to trust Christ, and to cause all things to work together for good (Matt. 28:20; Rom. 8:27-28). We are strangers in the earth surviving by His gracious mercies. By the grace of God, we are filled with Christ and we build our house upon Him as our rock of salvation (Matt. 7:24-25). By the grace of God, our hearts confess that Jesus is the Christ, the Son of the living God (Matt. 16:16-17). The truth about Jesus was not worked up in our hearts to believe by natural means, but was revealed to us supernaturally by the Father in heaven (Matt. 16:17). The veil that blocked our understanding of Jesus and prevented us from recognizing His identity, was removed by the Father. The experience of knowing and walking with Jesus is life's greatest blessing, originating in the sovereignty of God (John 6:44). The freedom to choose Jesus was in the gift of faith from God (Eph. 2:8). The confidence to trust Christ, and the assurance to believe required God. Our zeal for Jesus, though weak at times, is real to the praise of God's glory and grace. Our confession of this knowledge, lodged in our hearts by the grace of God, is the rock upon which Jesus would build His church; and the gates of Hades shall not overpower it (Matt. 16:18). The "rock" refers to Jesus Himself, and the confession of faith in Jesus that true believers give. We build and trust our souls on the rock of our salvation, and not the shifting sand of the world. Jesus Christ is the head and the cornerstone of the church (Eph. 1:22, 2:19-20, 4:15, 5:23). The saints are called out to be the body of God's household, being fitted and growing together into a holy dwelling of God in the Spirit (Eph. 2:21-22). Amen.

The image of salvation as being a strong, secure, and stable rock because it is founded on Jesus, is also represented in scripture by God as being the cornerstone. The Bible tells us that God laid in Zion a precious cornerstone for those who believe. For those who disbelieve and reject the precious stone, it will become a stone of stumbling (1 Pet. 2:6-8). Those who believe will not be disappointed (1 Pet. 2:6) or disturbed (Isa. 28:16). The church or the Gospel-temple will be built "not by might nor by power, but by My Spirit, says the Lord of hosts" (Zech. 4:6). The Spirit of the Lord, Christian, silently works with power in men's souls and their conscience. Most of the time, if not all the time, no one else knows when God is doing something for your soul, except you. You may only know that something is happening, but you are not sure what it may be. The conclusion you will draw from the outcome, is that the power to be holy and serve God in a specific way was from God. By the nature of the change, you will know it was not from you. The gift of faith will let you know that the way of the Lord was being prepared. Every valley will be lifted, mountains and hills made low, rough ground become a plain, then the glory of the Lord will be revealed (Isa. 40:4-5). "The scepter shall not depart from Judah, nor the ruler's staff from between his feet, until Shiloh comes, and to him shall be the obedience of the peoples" (Gen. 49:10). The Lord will bring forth the head-stone and lay the foundation with shouts of grace (Zech. 4:7). Nothing is too difficult for the Lord. "He who testifies to these things says, yes, I am coming quickly. Amen. Come, Lord Jesus" (Rev. 22:20).

It is the grace of God that finishes the work of faith that He began in you when you first came to Christ (Phil. 1:6). The grace of God fills up our understanding with conviction, occupies our prayers and leads us in worship and praise. We have tasted of the kindness of the Lord (1 Pet. 2:3). Any crown we might have will be cast at the feet of free grace. We "come to Him as a living stone, rejected by men, but choice and precious in the sight of God" (1 Pet. 2:4). "We also are being built up as living stones as a spiritual house for a holy priesthood, to offer up spiritual sacrifices acceptable to God through Jesus Christ" (1 Pet. 2:5). We keep coming to Christ our whole life for personal and intimate fellowship. We keep drawing nearer and nearer to Him, and grow up in all things because of Him. We have a long way to grow, and the best is yet to come. "Things which eye has not seen, and the ears heard, and which have not entered the heart of man, all that God has prepared for those that love Him" (1 Cor. 2:9). We are born again to a living hope (1 Cor. 2:9) through the living word of God (1 Pet. 1:23). Christ is a Living Stone who gives us life; a life that will be revealed with Him in glory (Co. 3:4). We live through

Him (1 John 4:9). Believers are also living stones; in fact, believers are living temples of God, that the Holy Spirit dwells in (1 Cor. 3:16). We will live in the wonder of amazing grace. "How blessed is the one which Thou dost choose, and bring near to Thee (Ps. 65:4). God works graciously in us, attracts us with His love and power, and subdues our unwillingness so we can abide with Him as His sons forever. We become living stones in Jesus by grace through faith. We become partakers of the divine nature (2 Pet. 1:4) by grace through faith. We will always be living stones joined to Christ who is alive in us (Gal. 2:20) by grace through faith. "The Lord is my rock and my fortress and my deliverer, my God, my rock in whom I take refuge; my shield, and the horn of my salvation, my stronghold" (Ps. 18:2).

God has appointed and destined us for salvation through our Lord Jesus Christ (1 Thess. 5:9). We are sons of the light and the day and encouraged to be alert and self-controlled by obedience to the Holy Spirit. We are to live close to Jesus and "put on the breastplate of faith and love, and as a helmet, the hope of salvation" (1 Thess. 5:8). We do not merit salvation, but we do live with a good and lively hope, by the grace of God, for eternal life. Wearing the hope of salvation as a helmet protects the mind from considering the pleasures of sin, which stab at the joys in hope. When we follow Jesus, the hope of salvation is nourished with peace in our mind. Hope in Jesus is called the blessed hope (Titus 2:13) and is a certainty. A living hope from the Holy Spirit is a looking hope, that keeps looking no matter what, it cannot give up. The hope fixed on Jesus sustains courage, by the grace of God, and keeps us from surrendering to sin. We are being purified, rescued, and preserved at the same time (1 John 3:3). The Lord God is your strength and song and is becoming your salvation. You will be joyously drawing water and being refreshed from the springs of salvation (Isa. 12:2-3). The springs or wells of water that Jesus gives are living and spring up to salvation in the soul becoming eternal life (John 4 :14). Jesus Christ is a fountain of living water, that by faith, is always available to give forth waters of joy for renewed life. We give ourselves to God as living sacrifices (Rom. 12:1) and rejoice in God's goodness in rescuing our souls from eternal death. Amen.

"Behold, the Lamb of God who takes away the sin of the world" (John 1:29). Behold is a command to look and see. When the word "behold" is used in the scripture, it signifies something very important. In this case, we are to look and see who the Lamb is and what the purpose of the Lamb is. The Lamb is Jesus, and His purpose was to come to earth and die as a man to pay the penalty for our sin that we may inherit eternal life. The sacrificial lambs offered in the old dispensation or Old Testament for the atonement of sin were to be replaced by the one-time sacrifice of Christ. "One sacrifice for sins for all time" (Heb. 10:12). The Pharisees and Jewish people were looking for a savior in the way of a worldly king to deliver the people from the Roman yoke. The Jews wanted both freedom and power in the world, and to keep their sin. They missed seeing Jesus because they did not yearn for a Messiah and Savior as a sacrifice for their sin. The animal sacrifices of the Old Testament foreshadowed Christs substitutionary sacrifice in the shedding of innocent blood (Acts 8:32; 1 Pet. 1:19). The lamb first appears in the sacrifice made by Abel (Gen. 4), and we see it again where Abraham said to Isaac, "God will provide Himself the lamb for the burnt offering (Gen. 22:8). In a memorial of redemption called the Passover when the Jewish people left Egypt, a lamb was slain and the blood applied over the doorposts to protect the Jews from the last plague. When God passed through the land of Egypt, He struck down the first-born of man and beast, except He passed over the Jewish home where the blood of the lamb had been applied on the doorpost (Ex. 12). Later, we would learn that the lamb would be a man. "Like a lamb that is led to slaughter, and like a sheep that is silent before its shearers, so He did not open His mouth" (Isa. 53:7). Finally, we have the Lamb presented to Israel identified as a man named Jesus (John 1:29). He would take away the sin of both Jews and Gentiles. John gives the testimony of Jesus as existing before him, seeing the Spirit descend and remain on Him and that He was the Son of God (John 1:30-34). Paul testified that Christ, our Passover lamb has been sacrificed (1 Cor. 5:7).

Jesus when He instituted the Lord's Supper said, "this is My blood of the covenant, which is poured out for many for forgiveness of sins" (Matt. 26:28). In dying for us, Christian, Jesus proved His sincerity. In sending the Holy Spirit to comfort and guide us, the Father proved the purity of Jesus, and His pleasure to love us. God is good and great to give us a gracious heart for Jesus.

The sacrifices of the Old Testament covenant could not make atonement for the lost sinner, but the sacrifice of the Lamb of God brought eternal redemption. A man's blood could not atone, but the pure and perfect blood of God was able to make atonement for us. "Christ appeared as a high priest of good things to come" (Heb. 9:11). When Christ appeared, it was God taking the form of humanity in a miraculous virgin birth (Matt. 1:18). He was not just another human being, He was "God with us" (Isa. 7:14; Matt. 1:23). The scepter was in the hands of the Romans, not Judah, when Shiloh, that is, Jesus the Messiah would come (Gen. 49:10). The power of government came into the tribe of Judah with David and continued until the coming of the Messiah in Jesus, when Judea was a province of the Roman empire. Shiloh was not a town, but a reference to the Messiah. Four- hundred years before the actual appearance of the Messiah, a messenger was predicted to appear to clear the way for the Lord (Isa. 40:3; Mal. 3:1). This prophecy was fulfilled by John the Baptist when He proclaimed, "I am a voice of one crying in the wilderness, make straight the way of the Lord" (John 1:23). The good things to come were eternal redemption and a cleansed conscience (Heb. 9:11, 14).

The great distinction between Christ and the other high priests is that He was the Son of God and brought His own blood as the sacrifice. His sacrifice was perfect and motivated by love. He secured our redemption on the cross through His shed blood, and entered heaven in a glorified human body with the virtue of sacrificing Himself. When He was on the cross and died in the shedding of His blood, the veil in the temple was torn in two from top to bottom (Matt. 27:51). The blood that was shed for us, paid the debt for sin we owed but could never pay. Our debt was paid in full when Jesus stated, "It is finished" (John 19:30). Amen.

Jesus Christ was the veil to the Holy of Holies, and through His death, the veil was torn away and we have confidence to enter the holy place by the blood of Jesus. He inaugurated a new and living way for us through the veil, that is, His flesh. He becomes our merciful and faithful great high priest over the household of God, which is the church of the living God (Heb. 10:19-21). He was made like us to make propitiation for the sins of the people (Heb. 2:17). The Word of God encourages us to "draw near with a sincere heart in full assurance of faith, having our hearts sprinkled clean from an evil conscience and our bodies washed with clean water (Heb. 10:22). "To Him who sits on the throne, and to the Lamb, be blessing and honor and glory and dominion forever and ever" (Rev. 5:13).

There is a description of Jesus in the scripture that is the opposite of a lamb. He is also described as a lion, the lion of Judah (Rev. 5:5). There is mention of a book or scroll with seven seals containing God's judgment, but no one is found worthy to open the scroll. Jesus was found worthy because He lived a perfect life and in shedding His blood, defeated sin, and death. The lion has triumphed because He first became a Lamb. "Behold, the lion that is from the tribe of Judah, the Root of David, has overcome so as to open the book and its seven seals" (Rev. 5:5). The Lamb is seen standing, as if slain, and taking the book to open the seals (Rev. 5:6). At this scene, great joy and thanksgiving fills heaven. God has not dealt with us through His power and strict justice, but with grace and mercy through our Redeemer. He created us and saves us. To God be the glory of His grace. The genealogies for Jesus in Matthew and Luke record that Jesus was a descendant of the Tribe of Judah. Matthew starts with Abraham, in whom all the families of the earth are blessed, and brings the lineage to Jacob, the father of Joseph, the husband of Mary and the supposed father of Jesus (Matt. 1:1-17). Luke on the other hand traces the pedigree of Jesus from Eli, the father of the virgin Mary, back to Adam to show that Christ was from the seed of the woman to break the serpents head (Luke3:23-38; Gen. 3:15). Jesus was both by father and mother's side the Son of David, a descendant of the Tribe of

Judah. Interestingly, it is not possible today to trace the lineage of any person that might come along and claim to be the Messiah. The records were destroyed when the Romans burned the Temple to the ground in 70 A.D. Based on Jacob's blessing, the lion is the symbol of the tribe of Judah (Gen. 49:8-9). A lion symbolizes fierceness, majesty, and strength, and is called the king of the beasts. The tribe of Judah was a leader among the other tribes and won battles over those that opposed the Jewish people. Ruling our eternal kingdom will be Jesus, the Messiah, the Lion of the Tribe of Judah. He will bring to fulfillment all the promises of scripture.

The scriptures present our Lord Jesus Christ as the true God, who in grace became a true man for our redemption and His glory. Jesus Christ was one Person, with two full, distinct, and complete natures. He was fully God and fully man. "No one knows Jesus except the Father," (Matt. 11:27). "The Son can do nothing of Himself, but what He sees the Father do" (John 5:19). The Lord Jesus was set apart to become the servant of the Father's glory and man's blessing. Jesus was equal with God in essence and He became subordinate to the Father's will. For the creature, this is a depth we cannot plumb. He was the Son of God, that many times referred to Himself as the Son of Man (Matt. 20:28). He was the Son of God in the sense of His divinity (fully God) among humankind (Luke 1:35). He was the Son of Man by virtue of being born of a human mother (fully man) (Matt. 1:21-23), and He is the Messiah who comes from heaven (Dan. 7:13-14). He was called God by the Apostle John (John 1:1), by the Apostle Thomas (John 20:28), and by God the Father (Heb. 1:8). He claimed to be God before the world was made (John 17:5) and before Abraham (John 8:56-58). He received worship (Matt. 14:33) and forgave sin (Mark 2:10-11). By Him, all things were created (Col. 1:16), and He upholds all things by the word of His power (Heb. 1:3). He claimed to have all authority in heaven and on earth (Matt. 28:18). He healed the sick (John 5:5-9), raised the dead (John 11), fed five thousand people (John 6:9-14) and walked on water (John 6:15-20), among many other miracles. The Father called Jesus, His beloved Son, on two different occasions, at His baptism and when He was transfigured

(Matt. 3:17, 17:5). The Bible tells us that "in Him all the fulness of Deity dwells in bodily form" (Col. 2:9). The personality of God and the divine nature, including the attributes and perfections, in the fullest and permanent sense dwell in Christ. Amen.

Jesus was also a fully human man. He "was tempted in all things as we are, yet without sin" (Heb. 4:15). The idea that Jesus was human was evident that He had a human body (Matt. 26:12), a human soul (Matt. 26:38), a spirit (Luke 23:46) and increased in wisdom and stature (Luke 2:52). He had human parents (Matt. 1:19, 2:11). He knew the infirmities of the human nature. He was thirsty (John 19:28), weary (John 4:6), hungry (Matt. 4:2), wept (John 11:35) and was tempted (Heb. 4:15). He was God in human flesh. The two natures of God and man in Jesus are bound together in such a way that the two became one, having a single will and consciousness. Each nature, that is God and man, remain distinct and did not change into some kind of new nature. He was one person. The Word became flesh and dwelt among us, and we beheld His glory (John 1:14). The Son was sent in the likeness of sinful flesh (Rom. 8:3). The mystery of godliness was revealed in the flesh (1 Tim. 3:16). He was born of a female and partook of the same kind of flesh and blood that we do (Heb. 2:14). "Every spirit that confesses that Jesus Christ has come in the flesh is from God" (1 John 4:2). As a man He could die, but as God He could not die. "Through death He might render powerless him who had the power of death, that is, the devil" (Heb. 2:14). The devil was the first sinner, the first tempter to sin and the cause of death. He is said to have the power of death because he leads men to sin and fear death. Christ destroyed him who had the power of death, and delivered His people from the fear of death. Our manner and time of death is in the hands of Jesus Christ. He loves us and comforts us, and takes away the troubles of our soul.

The important test for us is, have we been touched and born again by the Holy Spirit? Do you know if you have a relationship with the Holy Spirit of God? The Holy Spirit of God will lead you into understanding the truth about Jesus. The Spirit of God will lead you to know and confess the importance and presence of Jesus for your soul. The Spirit of God will lead you to confess Jesus as Lord and develop hopes of holiness to follow Him and glorify Him. We do not fully understand it, but the incarnation of Jesus is important. "In the beginning was the Word, and the Word was with God, and the Word was God (John 1:1). "The Word became flesh, and dwelt among us, and we beheld His glory, glory as of the only begotten from the Father, full of grace and truth" (John 1:14). Confession with your mouth that Jesus is Lord, and believing in your heart that God raised Him from the dead, results in righteousness and salvation, by the grace of God (Rom. 10:9-10). Our mind and heart have been supernaturally instructed and enlightened by the Spirit of God. Nothing is impossible with God (Luke 1:37). Amen.

Through the insight of the Holy Spirit, the prophets were given prophecies about the birth and ministry of the Messiah. The Bibles prophetic testimony separates it from any other book, and strongly distinguishes the Person of Jesus Christ as the Messiah. "No prophecy was ever made by an act of the human will, but men moved by the Holy Spirit spoke from God" (2 Pet. 1:21). There are numerous prophecies, written hundreds of years before Jesus Christ was born, that were fulfilled and recorded in the New Testament. Since the completion of the scriptures, prophecy can only proclaim what has already been revealed in the scriptures. The Bible was divinely inspired. "Behold, a virgin will be with child and bear a son, and she will call His name Immanuel" (Isa. 7:14). This prophecy was fulfilled in the conception and birth of Jesus (Matt. 1:18-23, Luke 1:26-31). He will go forth as One from God from the days of eternity, born in Bethlehem Ephrathah (Micah 5:2). This prophecy was fulfilled in the birth of Jesus in Bethlehem (Luke 2:4-7). "The Lord said to Me, Thou art My Son, today I have begotten Thee (Ps. 2:7). This scripture is a noble proof of the glorious Divinity of our Immanuel, that is, Jesus. This great truth is our great mercy. It was fulfilled by the voice of God, at His baptism (Mark 1:11) and later at the transfiguration of Jesus (Matt. 17:5). On both occasions the Father said, "This is My beloved Son, with whom I am well pleased; listen to Him! (Mark 1:11; Matt. 17:5).

Miracles were predicted in the Old Testament to be performed by the Messiah for the blind, deaf, lame, dumb and dead (Isa 35:4-6). According to the New Testament, they were fulfilled by Jesus (Matt. 11:26, 15:30; John 11). The people knew that the power behind the miracles was of God and glorified the God of Israel (Matt. 15:31). The religious leaders and government officials, for the most part, did not know what was happening, but a lot of the people, by the grace of God, did.

The reign of the Prince of Peace was prophesied in Isaiah 9 and proclaimed for Jesus in the New Testament (Eph. 2:14). It was prophesied that a righteous reign would spring from Jesse and the Spirit of the Lord would rest on Him (Isa. 11:1-5, 61:1-3). These passages are fulfilled in our hearts by Christ Jesus, who becomes to us wisdom, righteousness, sanctification, and redemption, which are the great substances of our peace (1 Cor. 1:30). In Jesus, God has given us power, love, discipline, and an enlightened heart (2 Tim. 1:7; Eph. 1:18). "Therefore, having been justified by faith, we have peace with God through our Lord Jesus Christ" (Rom. 5:1). Our salvation has always been about God's grace in searching for man. After the fall of man in the garden of Eden, God declared war on Satan and gave the first promise of our Savior (Gen. 3:15). Satan would bruise Christ on the heel, but Christ would bruise Satan on the head. This prophecy meant the defeat of Satan, which was fulfilled at the cross of Jesus Christ where Satan thought he could kill God. The first gospel sermon was preached by God. The final blow will be delivered when Satan is defeated and cast into the Lake of Fire (Rev. 20:10). Satan inflicted a painful wound on Christ, who was called the Suffering Servant, the Messiah, that is, Jesus Christ our Lord and Savior. He was despised and afflicted, carried our griefs and sorrows and smitten by God. He was scourged, crushed, and pierced through, yet did not open His mouth. He was cut off out of the land of the living, assigned with wicked men and buried in a rich man's tomb. In bearing the sin of many and rendering Himself as a guilt offering, He was allotted a portion with the great (Isa. 53:1-12). Amen. When the fulness of time had come, God fulfilled this prophecy by sending forth His

Son to put an end to the Law, and redeem us that we might receive adoption as sons (Gal. 4:4-5). God gave His only begotten Son to shed His blood and die for us, that the penalty of sin would be paid and that we might gain eternal life (John 3:16). Amen.

In His life, Jesus Christ fulfilled the messianic prophecies that were written 700 years before He walked the earth. Jesus also fulfilled the prophecies about the death and resurrection of the Messiah. All this is most clear from the passage cited above in Isaiah 53, but details are also written into the Psalms. The Messiah would have His hands and feet pierced (Ps. 22:16), which was fulfilled in Jesus' life (John 20:25). The Messiah's bones would not be broken (Ps. 22:17) which was fulfilled in in Jesus's life (John 19:33). Men would cast lots for the Messiah's clothing (Ps. 22:18) which was fulfilled in Jesus's life (Matt. 27:35). In addition to prophecies about His death, His resurrection was also foretold. David tells us that the soul of the Messiah "would not be abandoned to Hades; neither will Thy Holy One undergo decay." "Thou wilt make known to Me the path of life" (Ps. 16:10-11). Both Paul and Peter quoted this Old Testament scripture of Psalm 16 when they declared that God had raised Messiah Jesus from the dead (Acts 2:24, 13:33-35). Isaiah tells us that the Messiah "will see His offspring" and the Father will "prolong His days" (Isa. 53:10). The good pleasure of the Father will prosper in His hands. "As a result of the anguish of His soul, He will see it and be satisfied" (Isa. 53:11).

Christ will see the fruit of the travail of His own soul in the great satisfaction of saving souls and the growth of His church. Christ is satisfied in being brought through grace to glory. He has been given the nations as His inheritance (Ps. 2:8). He makes us conquerors over our lusts and enemies, and makes us victorious as priests to God in prayer. The joy of the Lord comes by providing forgiveness, righteousness, and heaven for His children. He died for you. He willingly poured out Himself to death for us (John 10:18). Jesus said, "The Son of man is going to be delivered into the hands of men; and they will kill Him, and He will be raised on the third day" (Matt. 17:22-23). Jesus Himself foretold His disciples that He would be betrayed, killed by men, and raised again the third day. The disciples did not quite understand these words of Jesus, but later after the resurrection, they remembered (Luke 24:6-8). The Holy Spirit assists us to remember His Word (John 14:26). The Holy Spirit is faithful to remind us of the principles that should rule our behavior, and provide the words of comfort and promise that bring peace when we are needy. He can make our hearts burn within us from the scripture we have stored that we might not sin against God (Luke 24:32; Ps. 119:11).

In the Old Testament, there are “signs” that serve as “prophecies” of the death, burial, and resurrection of Jesus. The first one that comes to my mind is the story of Jonah. Jesus gave the religious leaders of His day the sign of Jonah who wanted to see a miracle from Him to prove His divine mission (Matt. 12:38-40). Jonah essentially died and was buried in the stomach of a great fish for three days and nights (Jonah 1:17). The Bible tells us that Jonah, while in the whale, remembered the Lord; and while he was fainting away in his distress after three days, Jonah was essentially “resurrected” when he was vomited up onto dry land (Jonah 2:2, 7, 10). In his despair, faith and hope, God rescued him to preach repentance to Nineveh (Jonah 3:1). Another likely prophecy of Jesus’ resurrection on the third day occurs in Hosea. The writer mentions about the people returning to the Lord after He has rebuked them (Hosea 5,6). He says, “come let us return to the Lord. For He has torn us, but He will heal us; He has wounded us, but He will bandage us. He will revive us after two days; He will raise us upon the third day that we may live before Him” (Hosea 6:1-2). Although this passage is about Israel being raised, it takes our hearts to the complete fulfillment of all God’s people to Jesus, who was raised on the third day (1 Cor. 15:4).

Another likely prophecy that foreshadows Christ’s death and resurrection can be seen in the story of Abrahan and Isaac (Gen. 22). The Bible tells us that on the third day, Abraham saw the place where he was to take his only begotten son and offer him as a burnt offering. Isaac does not die, and God provides a ram for the offering in the place of his son. I think the story is figurative, and foreshadows the reality of Jesus's death and resurrection on the third day. Isaac was received back as a type (Heb. 11:17-19). Isaac was offered up as an only son (Gen. 22:2), and Jesus was offered as the only begotten Son of God because of our transgressions, and was raised because of our justification (Rom. 4:25). Abraham considered Issac dead and received him back as a type in the manner of a miracle. Abraham was going to sacrifice Isaac as God instructed, but God provided a substitute. Abraham believed that if he sacrificed Isaac, God would have to raise Isaac again in order to keep the promise that he would be the father of many nations (Gen. 15:4). Abraham "believed in the Lord; and He reckoned it to him as righteousness" (Gen. 15:6). "Faith was reckoned to Abraham as righteousness" (Rom. 4:9). The promise to Abraham that he would be heir to the world was not through the Law, but through the righteousness of faith" (Rom. 4:13). Abraham knew God was loving, just, mighty, and faithful, and would not deceive him. Abraham was faithful and would be obedient. The real faith of Abraham was in his will and Isaac's death was symbolic. Isaac became a type of resurrection. The teaching of receiving a righteousness from God by believing in the Lord in this passage is absolutely God. The righteousness of God is revealed through faith in Christ for all those who believe (Rom. 1:17, 3:21-22). Please listen to me. It is "through one transgression there resulted condemnation to all men." "It is through one act of righteousness there resulted justification of life to all men." "through the one man's disobedience the many were made sinners, even so through the obedience of the One the many will be made righteous" (Rom. 5:18-19). "The righteous man shall live by faith" (Hab. 3:3; Rom. 1:17). Amen.

The Bible makes abundantly clear that the study of types is a vital element, and link of God's plan for us to enjoy learning about Jesus. The above stories about Isaac and Jonah were real events in history, divinely ordained by God to be a prophetic picture to water our hearts for Jesus Christ. The Old Testament describes certain persons, events, and institutions which the Bible calls a "type" (Heb. 11:19) that are prophetic of the Person of

Jesus Christ. Jesus Christ is called the "antitype." The "death and resurrection" in the stories of Isaac and Jonah make them "types," in which they foreshadow the death and resurrection of Jesus Christ, the "antitype." The reality of the type in the Old Testament was designed by God to be fulfilled by Jesus Christ described in the New Testament. The types point to the superior spiritual, life-saving and heavenly treasure of our Lord and King, Jesus Christ. Let me cite you some examples. Though he was an imperfect shadow, Adam is a type of Christ (Rom. 5:14). Both entered the world in a unique and sinless way. "The first man, Adam became a living soul, the last Adam became a life-giving spirit" (1 Cor. 15:45). Adam was created from the earth a son of God (Luke 3:38), Jesus came from heaven as the only begotten Son of God (John 3:16). Adam's act of disobedience introduced sin and death into the world, while Jesus' act of obedience destroyed sin and death and brought eternal life (Rom. 5:15, 18; Cor. 15:52). All those born from Adam inherit the sinful nature, but those born again in Christ inherit a holy nature (1 Cor. 15:48-49, John 3:5).

Both Moses and Joseph share a lot of comparisons as a type of Messiah, and a lot of comparisons have been made between them and Jesus. For example, at the time of the birth of Moses and Jesus, children were ordered to be murdered (Ex. 1:22; Matt. 2:16). Both acted as intercessors (Ex. 32:30-33; Heb. 7:25). Moses led the people out of bondage in Egypt, while Jesus freed us from the bondage of sin and death (John 8:36; Rom. 8:2). Both spoke to God, performed miracles, made a covenant, and gave commandments (Ex. 33:11; John 13:34). Joseph, the favored son of Jacob, also was a type of Messiah and prefigures Christ in several aspects. Both Joseph and Jesus were loved by their father and rejected by their brethren (Gen. 37). Both were falsely accused and put into prison (Gen. 39-40). Both offered forgiveness and were saviors for their people (Gen. 50:15-21; Acts 7:9-16). Joseph and Jesus were both exalted after their suffering (Gen. 49:22-26). David was a type of Christ as a king (Ezek. 37:24; Jer. 23:5-6), and Melchizedek was a type of Christ as a priest (Heb. 7). Many folks in the Old Testament were not called "types," but the similarities to Jesus are unmistakable. Sometimes, the words like figure, shadow, pattern, and likeness can be thought of as a type (Heb. 8:5, 11:19, Col. 2:17, 1 Pet. 3:20-21). Bible study will reveal a great deal more in the way of blessings to your heart, mind, and thoughts than you expected.

Numerous Old Testament objects, places and situations can have significant meaning to us as a "type," when speaking about Jesus and the gospel, and of things to come. Let me cite some examples. The people of Egypt allowed Jacob and his family, because of Joseph, to move into the Land of Goshen during a famine. They lived in Egypt for about 400 years, and ended up as slaves in bondage. They multiplied as a people, and the Egyptians feared their potential to become an enemy and fight against them someday. The people would be delivered and come out with many possessions. This was told to Abraham in a prophecy when he was being promised a son to be his heir (Gen. 15). In this same passage, which is one of my favorites, are the words that Abraham "believed the Lord; and it was reckoned to him as righteousness (Gen. 15:6). Eventually, God called Moses into action, and after the plagues, they pass through the Red Sea and into the wilderness (Ex. 3-15). Egypt was a state of bondage. Prior to our conversion to follow Jesus, as a sinner, we lie in a state of bondage. Though we were slaves to sin, we are freed to become slaves of righteousness (Rom. 6:17-18). We were redeemed from being under the Law and receive adoption as sons (Gal. 4:5). The night before the last plague on Egypt, God instructed the Israelites to kill a lamb and apply the blood around their house. The blood was a sign for them. When the Lord saw the blood, He would pass over them, and no plague would befall them and destroy the first born of the people and the cattle as well (Ex. 11:5). The blood protected the Israelites from God's wrath (Ex. 12:23). The memorial of this redemption was called the Passover (Ex. 12:43). For the Christian, Jesus is the Lamb of God, and by His shed blood and dying for us, He takes away our sin (John 1:29). Jesus becomes our Passover Lamb (1 Cor. 5:7). It is His blood that covers us and protects us from God's judgment and wrath, and insures the forgiveness of our sin (Matt. 26:28). Amen.

The flood of Noah's day (Gen. 6-8), is a shadow of the sudden destruction the world will know at the time of the end, when the Son of Man comes again (Matt. 24:36-39). "For the coming of the Son of Man will be just like the days of Noah" (Matt. 24:37). The deliverance of Noah's family prefigures our salvation, through baptism, into the family of God. Once by faith, in baptism, we identify with Christ in death and life, Noah's ark becomes a type of Christ for us. We are united to Him in the likeness of His death and resurrection so we might walk in newness of life (Rom. 6:3-5). Water baptism is an illustration and an act of conformity to teach us what has happened to us when we believed in the Lord Jesus. Dipping our body into water is symbolic of death, burial, and resurrection. The operation of the Spirit puts us in Christ. We die to sin before we are baptized. Dying to sin and being resurrected is by Christ through faith. We have been justified by faith (Rom. 5:1). We are saved by the gift of faith, not works (Eph. 2:8). Noah became an heir of the righteousness which is according to faith (Heb. 11:7), and so have we. By faith, we trust in God's promises. Water, in Noah's day was the agent of God's judgment. God for us is the fountain of living water (Jer. 2:13), the source of sanctification and cleansing by the washing of water with the word (Eph. 5:26) for spiritual growth (Ps. 1:3). Water is emblematic of the Word of God in regeneration (John 5:3), the Holy Spirit (Ezek. 47:1-12), cleansing (Ezek. 36:25), and salvation (Isa. 55:1). "He who believes in Me, as the scripture said, from his innermost being shall flow rivers of living water" (John 7:38). The water from Jesus springs up to eternal life (John 4:14). The water "flows" forth for God to be a blessing to your family and others. God's word does not return to Him void (Isa. 55:11). Only those who were in the ark were saved; only those found in Jesus will be saved. Baptism is important; it is a calling upon God to take you into Christ, it is an appeal to God for a good conscience through the resurrection of Jesus Christ (1 Pet. 3:21). A good conscience is received by faith and not by works, it is a gift of God (Eph. 2:8-9). When we are born again from above (John 3:5), we receive a new heart and a good, and clear conscience, by the blood of Jesus (Heb. 9:14; Ezek.

36:26). We bear witness of Jesus, by the grace of God, through baptism and holy living.

The cross of Jesus means either the power of God unto salvation (1 Cor. 1:18) or the rock of stumbling (1 Pet. 2:8). We are saved by our judgment falling upon Christ. We gain confidence by looking more to Jesus as a result of our guilt having been removed. We gain confidence to enter the holy place by God's truth, that is, on the merits of His only begotten Son. It is called "a new and living way which He inaugurated for us through the veil, that is, His flesh" (Heb. 10:20). We look to Jesus for God's will. We look to Jesus in gratitude for what He has done for us. We look for Jesus in the Bible for understanding and grace. The Bible tells us that the Son of Man must be "lifted up" (John 3:14), and when He is "lifted up from the earth, He will draw all men to Himself" (John 12:32). Being "lifted up" refers to His crucifixion; which to us, points out His great sacrifice and love for us. His choice made it possible for us to be forgiven, and know a righteousness necessary to be reconciled to God. The cross proclaims God's goodness, grace, and power to save our souls. He draws all of God's elect to Christ. The overthrow of evil cost a great deal, and is the glory of God's grace. Satan's power over the world was broken at the cross, and he was cast out (John 12:31). "Our citizenship is in heaven, from which also we eagerly wait for a Savior, the Lord Jesus Christ" (Phil. 3:20). We do not look to our church attendance, repentance and good works, the resolutions we make or our baptism experience and various feelings. We look away from ourselves and look unto Jesus, "the author and perfector of faith" (Heb. 12:2).

Jesus said, "as Moses lifted up the serpent in the wilderness, even so must the Son of Man be lifted up; that whoever believes may in Him have eternal life" (John 3:14). Jesus likened Himself to the bronze serpent, indicating to us it was a type of Him. In the Old Testament, the people of Israel complained against God and Moses because there was no food and water in the wilderness (Num. 21:5). So, God sent fiery serpents among the people that bit them and many people died. The people repented and Moses prayed for them. God's answer to the people was for Moses to make a fiery bronze serpent, put it on a pole, and the people were to look at when bitten and they would be healed (Num. 21:6-9). The serpent was a curse and symbolized Jesus becoming a curse for us (Deut. 21:23; Gal. 3:13). When we look to Jesus and put our faith in Him, He saves us from the fiery sting of death (1 Cor. 15:55-57). The rock in the wilderness that supplied water for Israel to drink was a type of Christ (Ex. 17:6; Num. 20:2-8). Paul tells the Corinthians that all who passed through the wilderness were baptized in Moses. They all ate the same spiritual food and drank the same spiritual drink. They were drinking from a spiritual rock that was Christ (1 Cor. 10:4). The manna was a type of Christ crucified. The rock that the water came from was the confession of Christ upon which the church would be built (Matt. 16:16-18). The living water will bring satisfaction to the soul, springing up to eternal life (John 4:14). The living water will be from the Spirit of grace and be the joy in the heart of the Gospel of Christ. The living water we drink from Christ will quench our thirst forever.

The tabernacle was a type of Christ. When Moses was leading Israel in the wilderness, God had them make a portable tent called the tabernacle, where God would meet with His people (Ex. 25-27). The tabernacle consisted of a tent divided into a Holy Place and the Holy of Holies separated by a curtain or veil. The tent was surrounded by a courtyard with a high fence and one door. The courtyard contained a Bronze Altar and a Laver. The Bronze altar was on a raised mound and the place of animal sacrifice, and burning the sacrifice. This is a projection of the sacrifice of Jesus on the cross on a hill called Golgotha. The Law says that it is the shedding of blood that makes atonement (Lev.17:11), without which there is no forgiveness (Heb. 9:22). The blood would be sprinkled in front of the veil of the Holy Place. The Laver was a large bowl of water for the priests to cleanse themselves before serving in the Holy Place. The application for believers today is that we are washed daily in His word to cleanse ourselves (Eph. 5:25-27). The priest could now enter the first room called the Holy Place in the tent of the tabernacle. Inside this room was the Menorah, the Table of Showbread, and the golden altar of incense. The Menorah, also called the Golden Lampstand, was the only source of light in the Holy Place for the priests to fellowship with God and intercede for God's people. We are now "children of light" (Eph. 5:8), who draw our source of light from Jesus, the light of the world (John 8:12). "For with Thee is the fountain of life; in Thy light we see light" (Ps. 36:9). Our life is hidden with Christ in God. We do not see Jesus by the light of self, but we see ourselves in the light of Jesus. The Holy Spirit lights up our dark places. Faith is the gift from God that gives us light and life from God. The Table of Showbread was a small table with twelve loaves of bread on it representing the twelve tribes of Israel. Every week the priests would bake and place twelve fresh loaves of bread on the table and eat the loaves from the previous week in the Holy Place. God was willing to fellowship with man. Jesus was the bread of life, and he who comes to Him will never go hungry (John 6:35). The Golden Lampstand was also in the Holy Place. The priests were to continually burn incense as a symbol of the prayers and intercession going up to God as a sweet fragrance. "My house shall be called a house of prayer for all nations" (Isa. 56:7). The Golden Lampstand represents Jesus Christ interceding for us at the right hand of God (Rom. 8:34). The blood of the sacrifice was sprinkled on the horns of the Bronze Altar (Lev. 16:18) to represent the power of Christ's blood to forgive sins. The blood of the sacrifice was also sprinkled on the Golden Altar (Lev. 4:7) to signify the power of His blood in prayer, as we confess our sins and ask for His forgiveness (1 John 1:9). God knew the plans of grace He had for us (Jer. 29:11). Amen

The Holy Place is described as a type of the church (Acts 15:16-17; 1 Cor. 3:16; 1 Tim. 3:15), whereas the most holy place, the Holy of Holies of the Tabernacle, represented heaven (Heb. 6:19-20, 9:8, 24). Within the Holy of Holies was the Ark of the Covenant and the Atonement Cover or the Mercy Seat on top of it. Inside the Ark was a golden pot of manna, Aaron's Rod or Staff which budded and the two stone tablets of the Ten Commandments. The atonement cover was God's dwelling place flanked by two cherubim (Ex. 25:22). The presence of the Lord, sometimes called the Shekinah glory, appeared just above the atonement cover in inapproachable light (1 Tim. 6:16; Lev. 16:2). There are miracles associated with the presence of the Ark (Josh. 3:14-17; 1 Sam. 5). The pot of manna was the bread that God gave them in the wilderness to remind them that God fed them (Ex. 16:32). Aaron's staff that budded was included as a sign to the rebels to be careful about rejecting God's authority (Num. 17:10). The stone tablets of the ten commandments were a reminder that God had chosen them and they rejected His standard of living (Ex. 19:5-6,32). The people were helpless sinners, but when God looked down at the Ark, He saw the atonement cover.

Once a year, on the Jewish Day of Atonement, the high priest would take the blood of a slain goat into the most holy place and sprinkle it on the mercy seat. In fact, two goats were presented before the door of the Tabernacle. After lots were cast, one goat was sacrificed as a "sin-offering" and the other goat was sent into the wilderness as a "scapegoat" (Lev. 16:7-10). A scapegoat is defined as one that bears the blame for the others. Both goats constitute a type of Jesus Christ. One goat signified His death and the atoning work of His shed blood. The other goat (ex. Scapegoat) signified His resurrection and the removal of our sins. Jesus was the Lamb of God (John 1:29), that bore our griefs (Isa. 53:4). "He was delivered up because of our transgressions and was raised because of our justification" (Rom. 4:25). He died to make atonement, that is, peace with God. By His death, He paid our debt, and was raised to prove that God accepted His sacrifice. Jesus successfully laid the groundwork for our justification. The fact that Jesus was raised after He died, showed that God's justice had been satisfied and His honor restored by Jesus. It means that the righteousness of Christ can be credited to our account. It is "a great mercy to be born again to a living hope through the resurrection of Jesus Christ from the dead" (1 Pet. 1:3). The promises of God are all good. When God saw the blood, it appeased His wrath for their sins. The atonement cover on the Ark was God's throne for the Israelites.

Today, God the Father is on His throne in heaven with Jesus sitting at His right side as our High Priest. When we come to God, Christian, we are coming to a throne of grace. We are encouraged to draw near with confidence that we may receive mercy and grace to help us in time of need (Heb. 4:16). The Lord Jesus Christ appears as our High Priest bringing His own shed blood with Him for our forgiveness (Heb. 9:22). "He entered through the greater and more perfect tabernacle, not made with hands, that is to say, not of this creation" (Heb. 11:9). He entered the Holy Place once for all, having obtained eternal redemption" (Heb. 9:12). Christ is the substance of the Levitical shadows. The human nature of Christ excels the old tabernacle. The Jewish tabernacle was made by men's hands, the humanity of Christ was the product of God. Amen. Christ is the stone, cut out of the mountain without hands, that will crush the kingdoms of the world and set up a Divine kingdom that will endure forever (Dan. 2:44). God created a new and superior High Priest by His Divine power, and the blood of Jesus would obtain eternal redemption. He is the perfect mediator, without blemish, whose blood can cleanse our conscience (Heb. 9:14). Jesus is not manna, but He is the true bread that came down from heaven (John 6:32). He is the bread of life (John 6:48). Jesus submitted Himself to the Father's will, and came back to life, like Aaron's rod budding, as the first-fruits from the dead (1 Cor. 15:20). He is the resurrection and the life (John 11:25). Jesus obeyed God's Law and instituted a New Covenant based upon grace (1 Cor. 11:25). It is the righteousness of God, apart from the Law, that comes from God through the gift of faith in Jesus Christ (Rom. 3:20-22). To God be the glory for His love, mercy, and grace.

God made the world, all things in it, and man from one blood. He made every nation from mankind to live on the earth and determined their time and boundaries. He made man that He should seek God (Acts 17:24-27). He holds our souls and our time in His hand, and in Him we live, move, and exist (Acts 17:28). God created Adam and Eve, and Eve was the mother of all living (Gen. 1:26, 2:7, 22, 3:20). Sin entered the world; we had the flood and man spread out over the earth and nations were established. God had a plan to redeem humans from sin, and He chose the nation that descended from Abraham, the Jews (Gen. 12). God's plan involved bringing His Son into the world to redeem mankind. He chose the Jews to be His missionaries to bless the world spiritually. Despite unbelief and disobedience, a chosen believing remnant remains and follows the Messiah (Rom. 11:1-6). The devil wants to stop the gospel from going forward and the Messiah from coming again. Thus, the devil will try to persecute, kill, and promote anti-Semitism against the Jewish people. We see it going on today. Most importantly God's gracious choice and work to save souls is also still going on today. Amen.

The work of our redemption by Jesus is reflected or symbolized by the Jewish feasts. Once Christ came, the Jews purpose was completed and the door of salvation was opened to people of every ethnic group and nation (Gal. 3:28). The plan of salvation was set in motion before the foundation of the world (Eph. 4:1). The plan of salvation will be completed, in part, when Jesus comes again (Rev. 19). God provides a prophetic picture of His plan, fulfilled in Jesus, in the meanings of the annual Jewish feasts. The Jews had seven feasts spread over seven months at times appointed by God. The feasts of Passover, Unleavened Bread, First-fruits, and Weeks occur in the springtime and have been fulfilled by Christ in His first coming. The feasts of Trumpets, Day of Atonement and Tabernacles are yet to be fulfilled. Some folks think that they will be fulfilled at the second coming of Jesus. The sacrifice of the lamb for The Passover feast remembered and celebrated the release of the Hebrew people from Egyptian bondage and slavery (Ex. 12). The shed blood in the sacrifice of Jesus as our Lamb of God, marks our release from the bondage and the slavery of sin (Rom. 8:2). Some have noted that the imagery of spreading the Lamb's blood on the lintel and sides of the door are in the motion of a cross. The people were to observe the feast of Unleavened Bread on the very day they left Egypt (Ex. 12:17). In their haste to leave Egypt, there was not enough time to add leaven to the bread. Leaven is associated with sin in the Bible (Lev. 2:11, 6:17; Matt. 16:6-12). During this time, the Jews ate nothing leavened. The unleavened bread pointed to the Savior's sinless life, making Him a perfect sacrifice. Jesus is the bread of life (John 6:35). The feast of First-fruits was to honor God for all He provided (Lev. 3:10). It was celebrated the "third day," the 16th of Nisan, the very same day that Jesus was resurrected. The feast pointed to the Messiah's resurrection as the first-fruits of the righteous. In the order of the resurrection, Christ has been raised from the dead, the first-fruits of those who are asleep (1 Cor. 15:20, 23). He is the first in the great harvest of souls, including yours. The Feast of Weeks or Pentecost occurred fifty-five days after the Feast of Unleavened Bread. It was a celebration of the harvest. It pointed to the great harvest of souls, and the gift of the Holy Spirit for building the kingdom of God during the Church Age (Acts 2). The church was established on this very day when God poured out His Holy Spirit, and about three thousand souls were added to the church (Acts 2:41). God was faithful to the Lord Jesus and us, to bring about the testimony of His truth, when He lined up these events to witness Jesus Christ was the Messiah.

There are three feasts in the Fall that are yet to be fulfilled. In the Feast of Trumpets, the people are commanded to rest and present an offering by fire to the Lord. (Lev. 23:24). Some people believe that day points to the rapture of the Church, when Jesus appears in the heavens and comes for His bride. The rapture is associated with the blowing of a trumpet (1 Thess. 4:13-18; 1 Cor. 15:52). The observance of the Day of Atonement involved the High Priest entering the Holy of Holies to offer the blood sacrifice for the people's sins. It was a day of humility and repentance to God. Many believe that this prophetically points to the Second Coming of Jesus when He returns to the earth. The Jewish people will "look upon Him whom they have pierced" (Zech. 12:10), repent of their sins, and receive Him as their Messiah (Rom. 11:1-6, 25-36). "He Himself is the sacrifice that atones for our sins" (1 John 2:2). The Feast of Tabernacles or Booths follows the Day of Atonement (Lev. 23:34). The people live in temporary structures like they did in the wilderness for seven days. They celebrate God's provision and protection of the people for the forty years they wandered in the wilderness. This Feast points to the Lord's promise that when He returns, He will once again "tabernacle" with His people (Micah 4:1-7). This Feast is also to remind us that the earth is not our home, we are sojourners on the earth (1 Pet. 2:11). In the future, we will have a more permanent home (Heb. 11:13-16; 2 Cor. 5:1). Jerusalem or Zion typify the church and finally heaven (Heb. 12:22; Rev. 21:2), whereas Babylon is a picture of the apostate church (Rev. 14:8, 18:2). What we see in all these Feasts is the intentional and enduring love of God for His children in the Lord Jesus Christ. The Word of God has a great blessing inside it. It leads one to greater faith, understanding, and deep appreciation for Christs death and resurrection and the promise of His coming again. Faith to understand the Person of Christ as a shadow in the Feasts comes by reading the Word of God (Rom. 10:17).

Today, God is calling out a people for Himself that make up the Church. The people over all time that believed the Messiah was coming; and in Jesus that the Messiah had come and is coming again, will be the bride of Christ (2 Cor. 11:1-3; Eph. 5:23-33). In the Old Testament, God was often pictured as a bridegroom or husband and Israel was His bride (Isa. 54:5, 62:5; Hosea 2:16, 19). Jesus used this analogy for Himself in a discussion with the disciples of John about fasting (Matt. 9:15). In the New Testament, Jesus is mentioned as the husband and the believers as a pure virgin (2 Cor. 11:2). In the book of Revelation, the marriage of the Lamb has come and the bride or the redeemed of God, that is the church, has made herself ready (Rev. 19:7). In the last testimony of John, the Baptist makes it abundantly clear that Jesus is the bridegroom who has the bride, and is the One who has come from heaven (John 3:29, 31). "For He whom God has sent speaks the words of God; for He gives the Spirit without measure" (John 3:34). Christ fully had the mind of God, "For in Him all the fulness of Deity dwells in bodily form" (Col. 2:9). We are the bride of Christ, who is God. By the grace of God, we fall in love with Jesus and become faithful to Him in this life. Be patient, Christian, true love to Christ grows and matures because God is true and faithful. By faith in Jesus Christ, we come to know that God is a reality. The believer begins to live in "newness of Life," (Rom. 6:4), with a clear conscience, resting everything in his soul on Jesus. Jesus will become the husband of your heart. Amen. "He who believes in the Son has eternal life; but he who does not obey the Son shall not see life, but the wrath of God abides on him" (John 3:36).

In the Old Testament, the type of image the Jewish people had with God was as the bridegroom in a "marriage covenant" with the nation (Ezek. 16:8-14). In the Parable of the ten virgins in the New Testament, Jesus is presented as a bridegroom, and gives the encouragement to be ready when He comes again (Matt. 25:1-12). God "gave Him as head over all things to the church, which is His body, the fulness of Him who fills all in all" (Eph. 1:22-23). It is a mystical body, but it is His and He cares for it. The bride is "the wife of the Lamb" (Rev. 21:9), "made ready as a bride adorned for her husband" (Rev. 21:2). From His fulness we have received grace upon grace (John 1:16). In marriage, husbands are to love their wives, "just as Christ loved the church and gave Himself up for her" (Eph. 5:25). A man shall cleave to his wife and the two shall become one flesh (Eph. 5:31). "This mystery is great; but I am speaking with reference to Christ and the church" (Eph. 5:32). We become one with Christ, who made Himself one with His people. The marriage union between Adam and Eve was a natural type with a hidden mystical sense between Christ and His church. The plain sense is the husband is to love his wife, and the wife is to love and esteem her husband. In the natural relation, this is the will of God. We are to be controlled by the Holy Spirit. The brides love for Christ and husband is expressed in submission and obedience. The mystery means a truth not previously disclosed, but discovered by revelation. The bond between husband and wife should be close, and in this way, reflect the close bond between Christ and the church. We were created to have a human marriage on the pattern of Christ and the church. The true and powerful spiritual senses necessary for a great marriage are only found in a love and faith that originates and is nourished by God, in grace, and not from the self. The flaws of selfishness and fear are cast out by perfect love (1 John 4:18). As you grow in grace and knowledge in the love of God, Christian, the less fearful you become about what He could do to you. While you were yet a sinner Christ died for you. We have sinned enough to deserve death. God "is patient toward you, not wishing for any to perish, but for all to come to repentance" (2 Pet. 3:9). For a Christian, the judgment for sin is past because of what Jesus has done for us. We still will be judged as sons and give an account of ourselves to God (Rom. 14:10-12). We will appear before the judgment seat of Christ to be recompensed for what we have done, whether good or bad (2 Cor. 5:10). The Bible speaks of believers receiving crowns for different things (2 Tim. 2:5, 4:8; James 1:12; 1Pet. 5:4; Rev. 2:10). The Great White Throne Judgment of the wicked and unbelievers is last, prior to their being cast into the lake of fire (Rev. 20:11-15).

God always had everything under His control. It was grace that taught my heart to fear and grace my fears relieved (Amazing Grace, stanza 2, John Newton). God's eternal purpose for us is centered and carried out in Christ Jesus our Lord (Eph. 3:11). God's purpose was to reveal a mystery, hidden for ages, that the manifold wisdom of God might now be made known through the church to the rulers and authorities in the heavenly places (Eph. 3:9-11). In God's wisdom, He reveals a Savior to a fallen Adam. In God's wisdom, He typifies and represents the Savior to the Jewish people in sacred people, rites, and sacrifices. In God's wisdom and grace, He chose to have the Savior preached and revealed to the Jews and the Gentiles. In God's wisdom, He gives faith and humble boldness to accept this great Savior into our hearts and minds from His own love. God's purpose for us is to be born again, and learn God's love to be able to love others (1 John 4:8-21). The most important and precious truth we learn and live for, by the grace of God, is to know God's love. To God be the glory. Amen.

Questions for Reflection

Do you fear God in the way that it leads you to worship Him in truth?

Does knowing the dominion and the sovereignty of God make any difference in how you live your life?

Do you remember a time when God acted providentially in your life?

Is the glory of God the aim of your life?

Do you believe everything the world is telling you about God, or have you chosen to walk and live by faith in Jesus?

Do you think that nothing is impossible for God? Can God providentially step into your life to forgive you of sin and give you eternal life?

What do you mostly think about in your life? Are you walking and living like a natural man or like a person spiritually born again?

Have you learned to know the Lord from Bible study? Do you find yourself falling more deeply in love with Jesus?

Does the idea of the sovereignty of God make you nervous? Does your understanding of the nature of God fill you with fear and gratitude?

Do you think that the shedding of the blood of Jesus can forgive you of sin and save you? Has your life changed since you began to trust Jesus?

Do you believe the Bible was inspired by God and is profitable for training in righteousness? Does the Bible warm your heart when you read it?

Do you believe you are God's workmanship, created in Christ Jesus for good works, for His good will and pleasure?

Invitation to Receive Jesus

There is only one way to be saved from the penalty of your sins, and that is God's way. He created you for His glory, and will forgive you and save you for His eternal glory. He has His perfect plan. God's way for you to be saved is to receive His only begotten Son, the Lord Jesus Christ into your heart (John 14:6). The life and work of Jesus Christ will save you from the penalty of your sin, by His own sacrifice and shed blood on the cross (Heb. 9:26). We are saved by grace through faith, and not of our works; we are His workmanship (Eph. 2:8-10). He took our place. He paid the price. He will save you from the power of sin (1 John 2:1-2, Heb. 9:24) and the presence of sin (Heb. 9:28). With an open and sincere heart, please read and consider what is written below, that He may bring believing in Jesus into your heart and the salvation of your soul.

First, it is a fact that God loves you. "For God so loved the world that He gave His only begotten Son, that whosoever believes in Him should not perish, but have eternal life" (John 3:16). There must be a sense of gratitude to God, that even though you have sinned, He loves you and invites you to be forgiven of sin and saved by the mercy He shows you in Jesus.

Second, it is a fact that you are dead in sin. "For all have sinned and come short of the glory of God" (Rom. 3:23). For the wages of sin is death" (Rom. 6:23). There must be a sense that you are dead in sin and helpless to save yourself. You are lost and need help, and only God can help you.

Third, it is a fact that Jesus Christ died and shed His blood to save me by paying the penalty for my sin. "But God demonstrates

His own love toward us, in that while we were yet sinners, Christ died for us" (Rom. 5:8). There must be a sense of surrender to Jesus as the only way I can have peace and be saved. I must recognize that Jesus died for me, and through Him, I can experience God's love.

Fourth, it is a fact that you can be saved by a trusting faith in Jesus Christ. "What must I do to be saved? Believe in the Lord Jesus Christ and you shall be saved" (Acts 16:31). Say a prayer like the one shown below to receive Jesus into your heart. You can use your own words, but they must be from your heart.

Dear Jesus, I confess that I was wrong to have sinned against you. I did not keep my heart for you, but kept it for myself, because I wanted to sin. I am sorry and I need you to help me. Please forgive me and save me from my sin. Thank you for dying on the cross for me. I accept what you have done for me and receive you as my Savior and Lord. I turn from myself, and trust you to come into my heart. Thank you for forgiving me of my sins and giving me eternal life. Take control of my life and make me the kind of person you want me to be. In Jesus name, thank you. Amen.

If you prayed this prayer sincerely, then Jesus Christ has come into your heart as He promised. You are a child of God and your sins have been forgiven. You have eternal life. "For by grace you have been saved by faith; and that not of yourself, it is the gift of God.; not as a result of works that no one should boast" (Eph. 2:8-9). You have confessed with your mouth and believed in your heart for His righteousness to be saved (Rom. 10:9-10). God has given you a new heart and spirit and the Holy Spirit to help you grow in grace and knowledge. He will comfort you, and lead you into a holy and fruitful life for His good pleasure (Phil. 2:13). You are His workmanship (Eph. 2:10). Read your Bible a lot and pray. Find a local church to worship the Lord in, and get baptized. Establish friendships with fellow believers. God will prepare you for heaven by the obedience of faith with a holy life. God will bless and use you to humbly serve Him in this life. You are a letter of Christ, written with the Spirit of the living God in your heart (2 Cor. 3:3). "The righteous man shall live by faith" (Rom. 1:17).

Further Reading

Brooks, T. (1861). The works of Thomas Brooks (6 volumes). The Banner of Truth Trust (1980). Carlisle, PA.

Charnock, S. (1853). The Existence and Attributes of God (2 volumes). Baker Book House (1979). Grand Rapids, MI.

Henry, M. (1706). Matthew Henry's Commentary on the Whole Bible (6 Volumes). MacDonald Publishing Company (1983). Mclean, VI.

Pink, A. W. (1945). Exposition of the Gospel of John (Three Volumes in One). Zondervan Publishers (1975). Grand Rapids, MI.

Pink, A. W. (1954). Exposition of Hebrews. Baker Book House (1984). Grand Rapids, MI.

Pink, A. W. (1928). The Sovereignty of God. The Banner of Truth Trust (2004). Carlisle, PA.

Pink, A. W. (1969). Our Accountability to God. Moody Press (1999). Chicago, Il.

Spurgeon, C. H. (1885). The Treasury of David (3 Volumes). Macdonald Publishing Company (1990). Mclean, VI.

www. Preceptaustin.org (2017). Commentaries by verse.

Index

Printed in the United States
by Baker & Taylor Publisher Services